A Life on the Ocean Wave

Henry Russell, engraving by B. Hunt after E. Walker. *Source*: Author's collection.

A Life on the Ocean Wave

The Story of Henry Russell

ANDREW LAMB

REVISED EDITION ARRANGED
BY KURT GÄNZL

SUNY
PRESS

Cover portrait of Henry Russell, c. 1836. Source: Author's collection.

Published by State University of New York Press, Albany

Printed in the United States of America

EU GPSR Authorised Representative:
Logos Europe, 9 rue Nicolas Poussin, 17000, La Rochelle, France
contact@logoseurope.eu

For information, contact State University of New York Press, Albany, NY
www.sunypress.edu

Library of Congress Cataloging-in-Publication Data

Names: Lamb, Andrew, 1942– author. | Gänzl, Kurt editor.
Title: A life on the ocean wave : the story of Henry Russell / Andrew Lamb, Kurt Gänzl.
Description: Revised edition / arranged by Kurt Gänzl. | Albany : State University of New York Press, [2026]. | Includes bibliographical references and index.
Identifiers: ISBN 9798855805994 (hardcover : alk. paper) | ISBN 9798855807196 (epub) | ISBN 9798855806014 (PDF) | ISBN 9798855806007 (pbk. : alk. paper)
Subjects: LCSH: Russell, Henry, 1812–1900 | Composers—England—Biography | Singers—England—Biography | LCGFT: Biographies
Classification: LCC ML410.R963 L36 2026 | DDC 780.92 [B]—dc23/eng/20251126
LC record available at https://lccn.loc.gov/2025034738

Contents

Introduction and Acknowledgments to the First Edition

Henry Russell was not a seaman. He was an entertainer and song-writer—arguably the leading popular singer on both sides of the Atlantic in the 1840s. However, it is by his song "A Life on the Ocean Wave" that he is best remembered in his native Britain, and the important part the sea played in his life made it an apt title for this biography. He was born in a naval port, and his career took him across the Atlantic or the Irish Sea many times. He later commuted across the English Channel between homes in London and Boulogne-sur-Mer.

Until a few years back I knew of Russell only as composer of "A Life on the Ocean Wave" and as the father of conductor Landon Ronald. It was a commission in April 1996 to write Russell's entry for the *Oxford Dictionary of National Biography* that made me learn more, and I was fascinated by what I discovered. It was clear for a start that some of the most basic traditional information on him (even the date of his death) was wrong. It was fascinating also to discover that "Landon Ronald" was not an assumed name, as usually suggested, but the name under which the son grew up. Not least, though, I was fascinated by the career of a popular performer of an era much more primitive than today. Henry Russell may be seen as not only a musical counterpart of Charles Dickens—noted particularly for his treatment of social issues of his day—but also from a modern perspective as an Elton John of his day.

Thus hooked, I was inspired to discover still more, and to put the results together in this full-length biography. In bringing it to publication, I owe particular debts to four people. Bridget Duckenfield, biographer of Landon Ronald, and a descendant of Henry Russell's brother Samuel, shared family information. Kurt Gänzl from start to finish passed on obscure press references on Russell's activities. Gerald Bordman went out of his way to track down elusive material for me. Though I have had no contact with John Anthony Stephens, and have necessarily produced a very different version of Russell's career than in his 1975 University of Illinois dissertation, his groundbreaking research—especially his identification of Russell's musical self-borrowings—has been invaluable.

Perversely it was only in the final week of some ten years' work on the book that I discovered that Grahame Shrubsole (whose published writings I have cited in context) had for even longer been doing his own detailed research on Henry Russell. We immediately spoke on the telephone, but it was too late to have any effect on the content of this book. I wish him well with his ongoing study, and I hope that this book will contribute something to it.

Others whose varied assistance I do gratefully acknowledge are (in alphabetical order) Gordon Ashbury (a descendant of Henry Russell's son Jack), John Booker (Group Archivist, Lloyds TSB Group), Peter Dickinson, Pearl Foster, the late John H. Gibbs, Shirley Hinckly, Anthony P. Joseph, R. Allen Lott, Bridget Palmer (Royal Academy of Music), Howard Pollack, Lois Pratt (Sheerness Library), the late Eric Sams, Phyllis G. Sillence, Raymond J. Walker, Basil Walsh, and Susan Washington (Rochester Public Library).

Not least, of course, I acknowledge the support of my wife, Wendy, who has put up with Henry Russell for many more years than I ever suggested, or expected, would be necessary.

Andrew Lamb, Croydon, December 2006

Introduction to the Second, Revised Edition

Kurt Gänzl

Edit? Revise? A book by Andrew Lamb, the doyen of British musical-theatrical writers and . . . in my opinion, the best and most careful scholar of our era? Pretty presumptuous. And I wouldn't have undertaken such a task had not the man himself said "go for it." Well, if anyone were to dare to go there . . . it is I.

Andrew and I go back, as collaborators and best buddies, for something like half a century. Yes, we weren't always octogenarians. Long, long ago, when things like the Internet were way, way in the future, the two of us used to meet up at lunchtimes at Andrew's London city office and gallivant off to libraries, to Somerset House and other such repositories of fact (yes, we were and are devotees of "fact"), to delve and delve and delve some more . . . writing for *Grove, The Dictionary of National Biography.* However, in between times, we each nurtured a pet project on which, of course, we shared discoveries. They were, apart from their subjects, rather similar projects: take a well-known book of memoirs and remake it fundamentally, with facts to replace the frequent biographical fibs. My victim was the opéra-bouffe star, Emily Soldene. Andrew's was the great entertainer of the Victorian era, Henry Russell.

Both books finally appeared, years later, self-published. Why? Because neither of us would submit to the alterations, curtailments, etc., demanded by the new range of baby publishers which had largely replaced the friendly twentieth-century ones of our younger days. Then, there were family concerns . . .

We both finally got our books out in 2007. My *Emily Soldene: In Search of a Singer* in a limited edition of two vast volumes. Andrew's *A Life on the Ocean Wave* in more reasonable dimensions.

Well, Emily might have been the larger opus but, by and large, her original memoirs were fairly truthful, if "selective," leading me to only a couple of decades of elucidating. Andrew had had to cope with a deliberately falsifying "rememberer" and a lot of fanciful tales of the sort that take a bit of undoing. Undoing is famously harder than doing! Only rarely, in the last 20 years, have I come upon Emily info that has made me say, "Dammit, that should have been in the book(s)." I wish I could have a second edition, which I can't, because she's too big, and nobody publishes works that size in 2025.

Henry is another case. With the resources that have become available via the Internet and other communications, a bit more of the "light of truth" has been shone into some of his dark and dreamy corners and, although various folk have had a wee go at his history, no one has produced anything like Andrew's tome. I had hoped that Andrew would do the remake himself, but he is just a little more octo- than I, and suffering from a more recent "medical incident" than I, and well . . . he said "go for it." I didn't need to be told twice!

So, where Castor can't, Pollux will. Two-two-heads-heads-are-are-better-better . . .

PS I need to confess another interest. It appears that I am related—by an *invraisemblable* network of marriages, Jewish and other, to Henry's aunt: "Catherine Keila [Uri Feiss] Russell is your great uncle's brother's wife's sister's ex-husband's uncle's wife's brother's wife's second cousin's wife's first cousin's husband's grandmother." Fancy that!

1

Sheerness to Italy

Just off the northern coast of Kent, where the River Medway flows into the Thames estuary, lies the Isle of Sheppey—some forty to fifty miles east of London, by road. About nine miles long and five miles wide, it is only a short distance from the mainland, and thus has some of the advantages of both island and mainland. Its principal town is Sheerness, which owes much to its origins as a Royal Naval dockyard town. Samuel Pepys (1633–1703), secretary to the Admiralty and diarist, established the Royal Naval Dockyard at Sheerness, and it might have become one of the foremost naval bases in the country had it not been flooded during construction. Later, during the early nineteenth century, John Rennie (1761–1821) surveyed and designed a new dockyard for Sheerness. Work began in December 1813, and the dockyard was formally opened in September 1823. It served the British Royal Navy until 1960, since when Sheerness has become one of the largest and fastest-expanding commercial ports in the United Kingdom.

A significant Jewish congregation was established in Sheerness around the year 1790. The old Jewish cemetery—used during the early nineteenth century—still exists, just behind Sheerness's High Street. In 1811, there was a numerous attendance for the opening of a new synagogue in Sheerness, and among the Jewish community at that time were members of the Russell family. It was into that family that Henry Russell, future songwriter and entertainer, was born shortly afterwards. Precisely how long after, it appears impossible to resolve, more than two centuries later. We are consistently told that he was born on 24 December, and that we have no reason to doubt. As with so many performers, however—and, most particularly, those born before systematic record keeping—the quoted year of birth is subject to variation.

As with so much else of his life story, the traditional source of information has been his memoirs, which were published in 1895. There he is quite specific: "I, Henry Russell, was born in the year 1812, at Sheerness, in the County of Kent. This fact is not really a reminiscence at all. I must depend wholly on my dear Mother's memory and home records. None of us remember very clearly our first appearance on Life's great stage. Still I am assured that 1812 was the year, and Sheerness the place." That's all very well; but, by 1895, his mother had been dead for well over forty years, and his declarations to officialdom in the intervening years seem to have paid little attention to what she, supposedly, told him. Or the truth. In the 1871 British census, he gave his age as fifty-six, implying 1814 as his year of birth, and his wife's, seemingly correctly, as fifty-nine. (The fact that she was older than himself might have inclined him to *overstate*, rather than *understate*, his age!) In the census of 1891, by which time his first wife was dead, he gave his age as seventy-six, again implying that he was born in December 1814. That year is also implied in the US passenger immigration information for his entry into America in 1843. It is, moreover, the year specifically stated in an 1846 *Musical Treasury* biographical note and an 1849 feature based on it.

By contrast, in the 1881 census, he gave his age as sixty-seven, thus implying a year of birth of 1813. However, when the birth of his son was recorded in France, in June 1849, his brother-in-law gave his age as thirty-five—again implying that he was born in December 1813. That same year is also implied by two separate biographical features (*The New-York Mirror, Albany Evening Journal*) published in America in 1837, and also by the certificate of his second marriage. It is furthermore the year quoted in a *Strand Magazine* article of 1891 and, as late as 1921, in Frederic Boase's *Modern English Biography*. It was even the year that someone entered in the International Genealogical Index, the Mormon fund of not always very vital statistics. In the 1861 census, lodging at 104 Regent Street with his wife and younger daughters, his wife's age is given seemingly correctly as forty-nine, while his own appears optimistically as forty-four.

In fact, there seems to be nothing whatsoever from earlier than the 1890s to support 1812 as the year of his birth. Then, in the final decade of his life, not only his memoirs, but also newspaper references and family documents, such as those surviving in the collection of a great-grandson, Gordon Ashbury, finally began to state and imply that year. Maybe so. Yet it is difficult to avoid altogether a suspicion that, in his old age, Russell simply felt that 1812 had a suitably heroic ring to it. As we shall see in due course, other circumstantial evidence seems to support the idea that he was born later than the generally accepted 1812.

Such a "reimagining" would, certainly, be far from the only example of rewritten history in his memoirs. To what extent this economy with the truth was a deliberate aim to deceive, to what extent false or failing memory, and to what extent old-age acquiescence with what others wished to believe, is difficult to be sure. What is significant is that Russell's grandson, novelist Henry St. John Cooper, claimed for himself the authorship of Russell's memoirs in his own *Who's Who* entry. If the memoirs were, indeed, put together by his grandson (and it seems entirely credible), it would certainly explain why so much is demonstrably untrue or unreliable in dealing with events that took place long before Cooper was born. All too often, we get the impression that Cooper took down the memoirs piecemeal, got facts and spelling muddled, and then failed to get his aging grandfather to check the final written word. Wherever possible, therefore, we have to seek to verify the statements and stories in the "Memoirs" against documentary sources. Where we have no independent source, we must accept any such statements with a generous pinch of salt.

As for family background, it is said, in publications of the Society of Genealogists, that the Russells, in common with so many Jewish families, originally—a number of generations back—bore the name of "Levy." The same source, and what can be found of family documentation, names Henry Russell's father, Moses [or Moshe], as son of Michael Russell "of Sheerness." However, although the family spent many years in Sheerness, Moses Russell's 1841 and 1851 census entries show that he was born in Middlesex, the latter stating more specifically that he was born in Tower Hamlets. His brother, Phillip, assured they were from "Aldgate," and family records confirm it. The Sheerness period obviously came later.

Henry Russell's mother—apparently some years younger than her husband—is said to have been Sarah Levin alias Mordecai of Königsberg

Figure 1.1. Birth record for Michael Russell, 1894. *Source:* Author's collection.

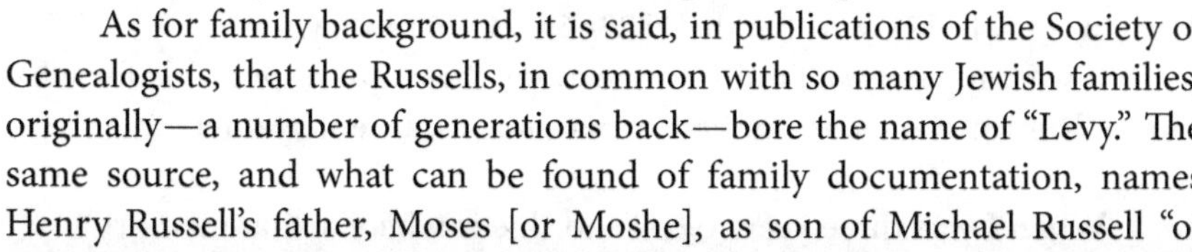

(now Kaliningrad), a great-granddaughter of Rabbi Zevi Hirsch Ashkenazi (1658–1718) and granddaughter of Zevi Hirsch Levin (1721–1800), Rabbi of the Great Synagogue in London. She would, thus, have been a niece of the latter's son, Solomon Hirschell (1762–1842), Chief Rabbi of Great Britain from 1802 to 1842 (*Forty Years a Chief Rabbi; The Life and Times of Solomon Hirschell*). The Russells were clearly well-connected in Jewish circles.

It's not even easy to pin down from surviving documentation precisely how many siblings Henry Russell had—let alone their sequence within the family. Official documentation was sparse in those days, and returns to census collectors often showed considerable invention. Lack of information is compounded by sundry claims for kinship with Henry Russell after he had attained fame. Some are veritable: a "vocal and ventriloquial entertainment" was given, in Christmas week 1858, by a certain Mr. W. M. Russell, "the brother of the far-famed Henry Russell." William Mark (1806–1901) was, indeed, one of Henry's elder brothers. One set of family historians posits that the children were the following: Israel (1794–1884), Samuel (1798–1857), John Jacob (1801–81), Mark (?; 1803), William Mark (1806–1901), Elizabeth Pessa (1808–48), Henry, George (1818–96), Anne Hannah (1821–47), and Sarah (1823–64). Others vary.

It was, apparently, family connections that were responsible for what Henry Russell claims as his first experience as an entertainer:

> When I was three years old—and this is where actual memory commences—Beverley, the actor, with a travelling company, paid a flying visit to our little town. Beverley was a friend of my father, and he asked my father, on the day of his arrival, to lend him his little boy for a few nights, as the play of *Pizarro* they were producing necessitated the appearance of a child on the stage. My father willingly acceded to Beverley's request, and thus, at the age of three, I made my first appearance on the boards. There was no application to a Police Magistrate for an order to permit a child to act in those days. Mr. Vincent Beverley could do pretty well what he liked with his own, and could borrow freely from enthusiastic neighbours.

Pizarro was a highly popular tragedy by Richard Brinsley Sheridan, first performed at Drury Lane Theatre in May 1799, and much revived and toured thereafter. It did, indeed, have a part for a boy, but one not usually played by one as young as three. Who, moreover, was Vincent Beverley?

"Beverley, the actor" would, at that period, immediately be identified as William Roxby Beverley (1765–1842), an actor-manager who was born William Roxby and added "Beverley" after his home town, the old capital of the former East Riding of Yorkshire. His wife, Mary, was also in the business, as were their four sons and daughter. The four sons were Henry (1796–1863), Samuel (c. 1808) Robert (c. 1809–66), and William (c. 1810–89), the last a celebrated scene painter. There was not a Vincent among them. As with so much else in Russell's memoirs, we must reserve judgement on the extent to which the story was true. Russell goes on to say that "Shortly after this little experience, my parents removed to London." One may note that the Napoleonic Wars had boosted the importance and prosperity of Sheerness, but that their conclusion, formalized by the Vienna Congress of 1815, sent it into corresponding decline. As a result, many Sheerness residents did indeed move elsewhere. By this time, of course, Moses Russell's eldest sons were already fully grown, and, when most of the family moved to London, Samuel remained behind in Sheerness. Henry Russell states that in London his father "held a position under Government, and lived upon his not too magnificent stipend." Though that reference to a government position relates specifically to London, we may surmise that the father's job in Sheerness had been, to some extent, linked with the Navy. It is recorded that Uncle Phillip Uri Feiss Russell was a "slopseller," a seller of cheap clothing, who had gone bankrupt in 1810. Apparently, Moses was in the same line of business, and it seems that the brothers supplied the navy yards and the garrison with work clothes.

As for Henry Russell's schooling, an interview with the Jewish violinist Barnett Isaacson (c. 1811–1901), printed in *The Jewish Chronicle* after Russell's death, refers to the two having known each other as boys at Westminster School. This, though, was clearly not the famous public school, but what was to become the Westminster Jews' Free School. Founded in 1820, for Jewish boys from poor families, the Western Society for Clothing and Educating Jewish Boys was an organization for which Henry Russell would, later in life, be active in fundraising.

For further details of his boyhood, we must once more fall back onto what Russell (or his grandson) provides in his 1895 memoirs. There he states that, two years after the move to London, his father "discovered in me an evident musical taste, if not talent." He continues:

> At six, I made considerable progress as a student of the pianoforte, and had those days been these, I might conceivably have become an infant prodigy. I thank my stars the dreadful fate

> never overtook me. I was never placed on a pianoforte stool, in a frilled collar, like a dog at a fair, patted by professors, or kissed by gushing ladies. As it was, my father decided that my musical bent should be encouraged, and for two years, I sat at the feet of Mr. M P King, then a deservedly celebrated musical instructor. I "possessed a fine contralto voice," my mentor told me, and, with this flattering unction to lay to my soul, I was taken to see Elliston—the great Drury Lane Robert William Elliston—who was, at that time, living in the Blackfriars Road—then a semi-fashionable district of private houses, quite near the site of the Surrey Theatre, of which he was destined to become the first lessee. Elliston had been ruined at Drury Lane, and retreated, as Planché says, *pour mieux sauter*, to the Royal Circus, re-christened the Surrey Theatre.

This meeting was said to have led to Russell's appearance in a juvenile opera company that Elliston promoted at the Surrey Theatre, and about which Russell says a great deal. Before continuing, however, we should note that the memoirs date these events as occurring "at the age of eight" and "seventy-four years ago," both references implying a date of 1821. Since we know that Matthew Peter King died at Chenies Street, Bedford Square, in January of 1823, if he introduced young Henry to Elliston, it was some five years after the said introduction that the boy was engaged for the Surrey.

For, in fact, we know perfectly well from a vast contemporary press coverage that Russell's appearances at the Surrey Theatre occurred not in 1821 but in 1828. The inescapable conclusion is that the whole childhood period—including, perhaps, the early acting experience and the move to London—has been compressed to accentuate the impression of Russell as a child prodigy. The same applies to his musical education, on which the 1837 Philadelphia biographical note referred to above expands as follows: "His first preceptor was Sir George Smart, an eminent musical director. Gavelli next had the charge of him, and afterwards M P King."

[Sir] George Smart (1776–1867), later Arthur Sullivan's mentor when the latter was attached to the Chapel Royal, was indeed a fashionable singing teacher, with whom Russell may well have had contact. Although Smart had the nasty habit of claiming (or pilfering) less fancy tutors' pupils as his own. But who in the world was Gavelli? As for Matthew Peter King (1773–1823), a prominent composer of instrumental, stage and other vocal music, as we have seen, he died when Russell was at most ten. The aforementioned 1846 biographical note tells us, more credibly: "His first musical instructor was Charles M King, son of the celebrated composer, M P King, under whose auspices, at the early age of twelve [sic!], he was introduced to the stage in the juvenile company collected for the performance of operas at the Surrey Theatre by the late Mr. Elliston." He was billed as being eleven. And, according to the chronicler Oxberry, at that stage, "of 18 Newcastle Street, Strand."

The Surrey Theatre lessee, Robert William Elliston (1774–1831), was one of the leading actor-managers of his time, noted as much for his portrayal of comic characters such as Shakespeare's Falstaff as for serious ones. In 1819, he achieved his ambition to manage the Theatre Royal,

Figure 1.2. Robert William Elliston engraved by Thomas Woolnoth from an original drawing by Thomas Charles Wageman, 1818. *Source:* Folger Imaging Department, Folger Shakespeare Library Digital Collection, https://digitalcollections.folger.edu/img21704.

Drury Lane, but in 1826, his alleged extravagances, ill health, and the importunities of others led him into bankruptcy. In November 1826, he was "sold up." By December, he was "of Leamington, bookseller." However, determined to continue as a theatrical manager, he responded by again taking his old house of 1810, the Surrey Theatre, south of Blackfriars, and he opened there on Whit Monday, 4 June 1827. He, himself, the "main attraction," appeared at the Surrey in a wide range of roles, but he put on a south-of-the-river variety of popular attractions, particularly successful among which were the appearances of the proven comic songster, Mr. Rayner, formerly of the York Theatre and of Drury Lane, and of the experienced ten-year-old Irish boy, Joseph Burke, a genuine prodigy who acted, sang, danced, played the violin, and, on occasion, conducted the orchestra. It was on the back of Master Burke's success that there appeared, on 4 March 1828, newspaper announcements that surely confirm the role of C. M. King as Henry Russell's teacher: "THIS EVENING . . . Master Russell (pupil of Mr C W [sic] King) will make his first appearance on this stage, and sing 'The Pilgrim of Love,' and the 'Horn of Chase.' " Master Burke was starred on that same bill, playing the title role in *Tom Thumb.*

Russell apparently made various other appearances at the Surrey before this announcement of its entertainment for 28 March: "During the evening, Master Burke will lead Two Overtures, sing Two Songs, with a Hornpipe, before the Battle of Navarino. Miss Fanny Woodham and Master Russell will also sing several popular songs." On 12 April he took part in a production entitled *The Talisman, or the Genii of the Elements,* with a song, and *The Age* reported, "He acted for the first time in the piece and really astonished the house with his song."

Elliston then had the idea of expanding his orchestra to thirty-two players and presenting a company of children in a short opera as part of an evening's varied entertainment. With juvenile performers such as Burke, Russell, and the delightful Miss Woodham on his books, it was a timely thought, if not exactly a novel one. In January 1805, a showman from Saxony named Friedrich Schirmer had come to London with a camera-obscura-with-mirrors exhibit christened the "Ergascopia" ("Schirmer and Scholl present . . ."). The support act to this display was a series of "musical and dramatical interludes" performed, in German, by a little troupe made up largely of members of his own family. They performed such Singspiele as *Die Drei Freier* ("music by Holst"), Schenk's *Der Dorfbarbiere*, Beneken's *Unschuld und Liebe, Die Eifersüchtigen, Adolf und Clara oder Die beidenen*

Gefangene (music: Dalayrac), *The Swiss* [sic], and something simply called *Das Singspiel oder Der komische Oper* et al., at Dibdin's former theatre in Leicester Square; were summoned before royalty; and accomplished a highly successful British season before heading home.

Come 1828, the press of the time reported that Elliston had been sent a German score for a similar little Singspiel. Weigl's *Die Nachtigall und der Rabe*, "ein Schäferspiel nach Lafontaine and Étienne, by Georg Friedrich Treischke," first presented ten years previously at Vienna's Kärntnertor Theater. He determined to present it during the summer featuring, allegedly, Braham, Miss Stephens, and Fanny Ayton, to whom, it was reported, he had offered "immense terms." They all turned it down. So, instead, he cast the four characters of the piece, translated into English by his utilitarian 'house dramatist," Charles A. Somerset, "author of *Shakespeare's Early Days*," and with the usual Continental interpolations from *La Dame Blanche* excised, with his junior players Master Burke, Master Russell, Miss Woodham, and Miss Coveney.

He began on 8 May 1828 with a performance reviewed thus in *The Times*:

> Considerable interest was excited at this theatre on Thursday evening by the production of an operetta called *Die Nachtigall und der Rabe, or Damon and Phillis*. It is a translation from a German operetta of that name, the music of which (by Weigl) has been much and deservedly admired on the Continent, where its chief part was frequently performed by Mademoiselle Sontag. One of its chief attractions on this occasion was that all its characters were performed by children who have been already much distinguished for their musical taste and acquirements. The talents and skill of Miss Fanny Woodham, and Messrs Burke and Russell, are well known to the public; and those of Miss Coveney, who on this night made her début in the character of *Phillis*, are likely to be soon as well known and equally popular. . . . The whole was got up in very good style, and went off with unmixed applause.

Sontag? Really?

Henry, himself, did not pull, initially, unanimously splendid notices for his appearance in the role of Miss Coveney's father, Lucas, "a poor peasant."

Although *The Weekly Dispatch* assured that "he sang and acted in a manner deserving of the warmest encomium," *Oxberry's Inquisitor* reported:

> The chief novelty is the introduction of several children in a piece called *Die Nachtigall und Der Rabe, or Damon and Phillis*, in which Miss Coveney and Miss F Woodham, execute some extremely difficult but delightful music in a most extraordinary style of excellence; and Master Burke acts the part of a burgomaster irresistibly. The worst actor among the little group is Master Russell, and on the evening we visited the theatre the young gentleman had omitted the ceremony of washing his face: his style of acting, too, he has evidently borrowed from a pantomimist, and his speaking tones are coarse and vulgar; he, however, sings well, and has more power than any boy we remember to have heard . . .

The Morning Advertiser granted him "modest and assuming merit" and decided "he has qualities which may make him an ornament on the stage," but *The Globe* sniffed, "Master Russell has a fine voice and great taste as a singer; but the poor boy, who is of a Jewish family, brings to the stage of the Surrey the corrupt accent of Whitechapel . . . the vys and verefores of young Russell [. . .] in a pastoral opera tend sadly to injure the piece." Henry was not alone. The same critic hatchetted little Burke's Irish accent . . .

But things would quickly get better. Come their third show, young Master Russell was being hailed as the best of the bunch!

What Russell, or his amanuensis grandson, writes about this season further typifies the unreliability of these memoirs, since they identify Miss Coveney as the later celebrated Harriet Coveney (1827–92). In fact, this Miss C was Catharine ka Kate Coveney, an elder sister of Harriet. Both (and their two successful actress sisters) were daughters of sometime actor, Henry Coveney, also sometime landlord of the King of Prussia, Wych Street—and his wife, Sophia Elizabeth née Dent (c. 1786–1854). Aged eleven, according to announcements of her appearance at the Vauxhall Gardens on 3 June 1828, the undoubtedly talented Kate Coveney would retire from the stage before her 1835 marriage, and apparently died in 1838.

Elliston's kiddie venture had been a clear success, and he followed it up promptly with another, rather earlier, Joseph Weigl piece, *Die Schweizerfamilie*, otherwise *The Swiss Family, or Home, Sweet Home* (text: I. F.

Castelli, 14 March 1809), which was first presented at a public rehearsal on 26 June. Henry played the role of Walter alongside his three compeers, with the Misses Matley and Clifford (Gertrude), and one Master George Taylor as Desmond, completing the cast of this most successful of Weigl's stage pieces.

The Times commented: "In order to obviate the grotesque effect of so many histrionic *Grildigs* [young performers], the stage decorations were all of a proportionate size, so that the whole spectacle was calculated to remind us of the whim of the Czar, who, to indulge his Imperial sense of the ridiculous, is recorded to have given an entertainment to all the dwarfs of his empire with suitable appointments." These performances *by* children proved a success particularly *with* children, and Elliston responded in late June with the following announcement: "The numerous patrons of this theatre are respectfully informed that during the Midsummer vacation, when the younger branches of their family are at home, the arrangements of the evening will be so formed as to introduce the Juvenile Opera Company in one piece, which will invariably terminate before half-past 10. Children under 12 years of age will be admitted to the boxes at half-price."

With children in the audience classified as being under twelve, Russell's later claim to have been born in 1812 is all the more striking. It implies that he was now approaching sixteen, with his voice not yet broken, and it makes a later birth year of 1813 or 1814 seem all the more likely. Moreover, one of his most rather transparent bits of "confusion" is created by a claim, in his memoirs, that the children's company made a trip to Brighton to perform before King George IV:

> One morning Elliston called his juvenile company together, and delighted us all with the information that the King—his Majesty, George the Fourth—had commanded that we should be taken down to Brighton to perform before him at the Pavilion.
>
> We should not have been children had we not been overjoyed at the prospect of visiting the king, and playing before Court. The journey to Brighton had to be performed by coach, for, of course, there were no railways seventy-four years ago [i.e., 1821!]. Our luggage and "properties" preceded us on the road in a large van.
>
> At Richmond—then a much lovelier spot than the Richmond of to-day—we broke our journey, in accordance with the

invitation of the great tragedian, Edmund Kean, who wished us to give a performance at his theatre on the old Green—very recently pulled down. Kean himself warmly welcomed us to his house, and sat us down to a hearty dinner.

But among the guests at this dinner table was one who caused us the greatest amount of uneasiness and alarm—this was nothing more nor less than a lion—a favourite pet and the constant companion of the great actor.

When we first entered the house, we had suddenly stumbled over the form of this king of beasts as he lay basking and blinking in the firelight. Needless to say, we were thoroughly frightened, and in spite of Kean's exhortations to us "not to be afraid," we gazed with eyes of apprehension at the brute, and more than one little heart beat more quietly when at last the noble animal stalked majestically out of the room.

In the evening, the theatre was crowded for our show, and the frequent rounds of applause testified the keen appreciation of the Richmond audience.

The next morning, Kean took me by the hand and gave me before parting a few words of advice. Advice by which, young though I was at the time it was given me, I profited much in after life.

"My dear boy," he said in his tragic way, "you will never become either a great actor or a great singer unless you learn to speak every word you utter distinctly and clearly. Unintelligibility and slovenliness in speech are the curse of the profession, though I admit with great pleasure that [John] Braham and [Charles] Incledon are bright exceptions to this rule." . . .

Kean then bade us all good-bye, and away our coach rattled in the direction of Brighton. What a difference between the Brighton of that day and "London on Sea" of this. What is now the Queen of Watering places was then a mere fishing village which could be easily lost in a London parish.

Rooms were engaged for the "Children's Opera Company," at the "Old Ship Hotel," and after a good night's rest, my companions and I sailed out to enjoy the sea, and beach. We could talk of nothing but the King and of the fine lords and ladies of the Court, before whom we were to perform.

> Many and fantastic were our childish conjectures as to what we should see and hear.
>
> At last the eventful night came. We gave our first success, *The Nightingale and the Raven*. The King declared himself pleased and gratified, congratulated us again and again, kissed us all round, and finally the Marchioness of Cunningham taking Miss Coveney and myself by the hand, led us into a splendid apartment, where a sumptuous supper was laid out. Oh! the boyish ecstasy I felt when the King congratulated me personally. I had certainly never been quite so proud or happy before.
>
> Supper over, his Majesty bade us all good-night, told us all to "be good," and expressed his opinion—which was not altogether unjustified by subsequent events—that there was a bright future before us.

The memoirs go on to state that, as a result of all this, he could "boast having been kissed and dandled upon the knee of the last of the Georges, at the Pavilion, Brighton." Kissed and dandled on the King's knee at the age of fifteen and a half? That, surely, must have been fantasy, designed to corroborate the pretense that the event occurred in 1821 rather than in 1828! How much of it, then, did actually happen? Well, the troupe actually did play for a week at Brighton . . . from 21 October 1828. Kean and the lion? . . . hmmmm. It might be added that the reference to "the Marchioness of Cunningham" is another typical example of oral reminiscences being carelessly written down, since the reference is clearly to George IV's mistress, Elizabeth Denison, by then the Marchioness of Conyngham (1768/69–1861).

But what we do know is that, when "Master Russell" was awarded a benefit performance of *Die Nachtigall und der Rabe* on 26 July 1828, the occasion was announced in *The Times* as "under the immediate Patronage of His Royal Highness the Duke of Sussex." The younger brother of King George IV.

Russell was certainly a stalwart of that 1828 Surrey Theatre season of juvenile performances; his major success coming in a third opera, Thomas Arne's venerable "serious recitative opera," *Artaxerxes*, produced on 16 September 1828. Kate Coveney was Mandane, a role that had introduced many a debutante to the major theatres; Miss Somervillle was Artaxerxes; and Henry was Artabanes, which role was being currently sung at Drury

Lane by Braham. Louisa Matley was Arbaces, Miss Clifford was Semira, and Rimenes was taken by Master Taylor. According to *The Times*, "Little Russell as *Artabanes* outdid any thing we ever heard him in." The *Theatrical Observer* noted, "Miss Somerville sang 'In infancy' with great feeling and was encored, as was Master Russell in his song 'Thy father away,'" predicting that "this young gentleman will one day be an ornament to his profession; he evidently understands *all* he undertakes."

Miss Coveney went right on to play the role of Mandane at the Theatres Royal, Dublin and Liverpool, in adult productions of *Artaxerxes*, so the competition was not light!

It's unclear whether the infrequent mention of the juvenile company in the theatre's advertisements thereafter meant that the company appeared equally infrequently, or whether its appearance in an evening's program was largely taken for granted. It has been suggested that they performed but thrice weekly. There are, however, periodic intermediate sightings of Russell in performance, as on 3 October, when the program promised: "A JUVENILE CONCERT, by Miss Coveney, Miss Matley, and Master Russell." On 3 November, he and the Misses Matley and Coveney appeared in a *stumer* entitled *The Young Queen on her Travels.* According to the *New Times*: "Master Russell sang a song 'Hail, sacred freedom" [by Blewitt] decently enough . . . the first time the young vocalist executed it, he sung it in a very clear treble voice, which, on repetition he managed to convert into a bass . . . He is a clever lad and [. . .] may make an excellent singer." The whole juvenile venture seems to have come to an end on 13 November, with "Master Burke's Farewell Benefit," the program of which included "a favourite song by Master Russell." Treble or bass?

We can't know for sure the full implications of the reference to "a favourite song by Master Russell." It probably signified "sung by." However, two items of printed music in the British Library do indicate that Master Russell already had pretensions as a composer. Both were deposited there many years later; but their 1820s origins are unmistakable. The first, a recitative and air entitled "The Tocsin of War," with words by J. M. F. Dodgson, is printed on paper watermark-dated 1825. Credited to "Master Russell," it was dedicated to "Mr. & Mrs. King," seemingly Henry Russell's music teacher and his wife, and published by "J Russell, Newcastle Street, Strand, London," Henry's home address and, undoubtedly, his eldest brother. Mr. Joseph Mathews Fraser Dodgson, sometime of Liverpool, was a Charlotte Street surgeon. Whence he came and whither he went is a puzzle; he is last seen (after an 1829 bankruptcy) heading for Barbados.

The second, entitled "My Father's to the Battle Gone," has words by G. Higham, whomsoever he may have been, and was published by the London Musical Repository, 176 Soho Square. It is specifically described as "sung by Master Russell at the Surrey Theatre." It can be seen on the bills there in September 1828. It was still for sale in 1831, when it was advertised in the *Morning Herald* and *Morning Advertiser* as being "sung by Master Russell with the greatest applause."

There may be yet another Russell song in the British Library that dates from this time, and certainly one that owes something to that Surrey Theatre season. This is "The Azure Eye," published by [J.] William Wybrow as a "prize ballad" and composed for Mrs. Waylett (1798–1851), a prominent singer of the time. Born Harriett Cooke, she had married an actor named Waylett in 1819, but in 1826 was married again to the composer [George] Alexander Lee. On 18 October 1828, during the juvenile company's period of residence at the Surrey Theatre, Mrs. Waylett had made her first appearance at the theatre as Susanna in *The Marriage of Figaro*. "Prize ballad"? This seems, if true, as if it may have been the annual prize of the Melodists' Society, which was won, in 1833, by Blewitt, conductor at the Surrey Theatre season. The song does not appear in Mrs. Waylett's considerable list of "new and popular songs" in December 1828.

If Master Russell promoted his own compositions during his months at the Surrey, he also gave a helping hand to the work of Charles King, most notably through his performance of the song "The Fisher Boy" (words: Fanny Eliza Lacy). Advertisements for this piece "sung by Master Russell" appear in the *Morning Herald* from May 1828 into 1829. It was King's crowning moment: He had a very modest career in music, emigrated to America (described on the immigration lists as "fiddler"), and can be still seen accompanying in minor concerts in the 1850s. In the 1850 New York census, he can be seen ("music teacher," aged forty-five) with mother, Mary P. King (sixty-one), brother William (thirty-four), and the wife of one of them, Frances (thirty) with child, William A. (two).

A piece entitled "The Merry Sea Boy" by Ball was also advertised by Messrs. George and Manby of Fleet Street in November 1830 as being "sung by Master Russell [and] Embellished with vignettes by eminent artists."

The juvenile company's season at the Surrey Theatre was recalled, over fifty years later, in the correspondence columns of *The Era*, when a children's version of Gilbert and Sullivan 's comic opera *HMS Pinafore* was proposed. George Taylor, who in *Artaxerxes* had played the part of Rimenes, and who, in the intervening years, had become chorus master

Figure 1.3. "The Fisher Boy" sheet music cover. *Source:* Author's collection.

at Her Majesty's Theatre, the Lyceum and the Surrey Theatre, recalled that he and Henry Russell were, by then, the only survivors from the company that had created such a sensation in 1828. He was, of course, wrong. Joseph Burke, who had reconverted, most successfully, to his first skill, the violin, was well and truly alive and fiddling, and he would live, a confirmed bachelor, in America, till January 1902 and his eighty-eighth year. But most of the team were, indeed, gone. Kate Coveney (Mrs. Henry Irwine) and Isabella Somerville distressingly young, Fanny Woodham (Mrs. Toulmin) in her thirties, and Louisa Matley, after a memorable career under her married name of Mrs. Caulfield, more recently.

The Surrey Theatre engagement was clearly a wonderful experience for a teenager, but Russell describes a correspondingly depressing one. His father, he says, sought the opinion of the great English Jewish tenor John Braham (1774–1856) on his son's voice. Russell claimed that Braham was most discouraging and that his verdict led to the lad being placed in a chemist's shop. Had it not been for his "natural energy and boyish elasticity," he asserted, he might have "lived his span unknown—save, of course, to those who patronized the chemist's shop wherein he worked." I suppose there is some truth in this? Could an East-End slopseller approach the reigning king of English opera thus? Well, there are other examples . . .

As it was, the Surrey Theatre experience was followed by a further major step in the teenager's life, in the form of a visit to Italy. For the details we are again reliant on Russell's 1895 memoirs:

> Italy, whither I went shortly afterwards to complete my musical studies, is associated in my mind with some of the pleasantest of my early recollections. After some time spent as an outdoor student of the Bologna Conservatoire, I went to Milan, and there made the acquaintance (which, rapidly, ripened into warmest friendship) of the great master, Rossini. During the four months I spent studying with him, Rossini introduced me to Donizetti, Bellini, and many another musical celebrity.
>
> Sarasi, the great banker, who was at that time staying in Milan, leased the Opera House—Teatro Carcono [*recte* Carcano]—and engaged a trio of Maestros to write three operas for successive production there. That was in the year of the carnival 1830. I played piccolo in the orchestra, and have a vivid recollection of the sensation caused by this great triple event in musical Milan. The first opera, *Il Marito Jealoso* by Majocc[h]i, fell very flat; but the second, *Anna Bolena*, evoked a great outburst of enthusiasm. *La Somnambula* [*recte Sonnambula*], the third opera, was also a great success.
>
> Sarasi, with whom I was then staying, was a man of much influence in musical circles. I shall never cease to be grateful

> for the interest he displayed in my behalf. He asked Bellini "to give his young friend, the *piccolo Inglesi*"—that was me—"some lessons in counterpoint, harmony and orchestration." This Bellini did gratuitously for some months, despite the fact that he was suffering from failing health.

Suggestions in various sources that Russell's time in Bologna was in the mid-1820s are undoubtedly consequent on the false dating of Russell's time at the Surrey Theatre. As he clearly states in the memoirs, his visit to Bologna followed the Surrey Theatre appearances, and we can date at least part of the trip from the references to the season at Milan's little Teatro Carcano. There were, indeed, three new operas composed for the theatre for its 1830–31 Carnival and Quaresima seasons, composed by the maestri to whom Russell refers. Two of them were to be resoundingly enduring hits. The first performances of Donizetti's *Anna Bolena* and Bellini's *La Sonnambula* at the Teatro Carcano took place on 26 December 1830 and 6 March 1831 (Quaresima) respectively. In between, on 11 February 1831, came the third, and not-liked, premiere, by the short-lived Luigi Majocchi (1809–36). The fact that this last-named opera was not his *Il Marito Jealoso* (or even *Il Marito Geloso*) but *Rosamonda* (lib: Pietro Cominazzi) does not alter the fact that Russell seems to have been speaking, here, from firsthand knowledge. Moreover, the fact that the title *Il Marito Geloso* crops up later in Russell's story provides further evidence that many errors in Russell's memoirs were simply a matter of his grandson getting his wires crossed. It seems that the putative piccolo player didn't get a mention in the orchestral listings.

Regarding the Rossini connection, there are, elsewhere, statements that Russell was "in Italy a pupil of Rossini for three years" or "studied at Milan with Rossini—occasionally sojourned in Paris." Since Rossini was resident in Paris, almost continuously, from 1824 until his death in 1868, all such claims, of any degree, seem highly questionable, though perhaps an incidental meeting could tally with Rossini's brief 1830 return to Bologna. There is also a link with both Bologna and with Rossini if, as seems highly likely, "Sarasi, the great banker" was the Marchese Francesco Giovanni Sampieri (1790–1861). "Maestro" Sampieri's influence in local musical circles, and specifically within the Accademia Filarmonica di Bologna, would also help explain Russell's otherwise obscure reference to being "an outdoor student of the Bologna Conservatoire." And, of course, the operas of "amico suo" Rossini (*Gazza ladra, Semiramide*) also featured

Figures 1.4a and 1.4b. No billing for the piccolo? Program for Rosamonda, Bologna, 1831. *Source*: Author's collection.

COMPAGNIA DI CANTO

DONNE

signore

Pasta Giuditta, Prima Cantatrice di Camera di S. M. I. R. A., ec.
Roser Lina
Ekerlin Fanny
Orlandi Elisa
Martinet Eugenia-Humberta
Laroche Enrichetta
Taccani Elisa
Hazon Marianna
Baillou-Hilaret Felicita
Ferretti Amalia
Piombanti Faustina
Lega Giuseppina

TENORI

signori

Rubini Gio. Battista, Cantante di Camera di S. M. I. R. A.
Valencia Leandro
Cervati Paolo
Musatti Gioachimo
Zambaiti Alessandro
Crippa Antonio

BASSI

signori

Galli Filippo
Frezzolini Giuseppe
Mariani Luciano
Schober Giovanni
Baroilhet Paolo
Biondi Lorenzo
Lodetti Francesco

POETA ADDETTO AL TEATRO
Signor Cominazzi Pietro

Maestro al Cembalo
Sig. Schira Francesco.
Primo Violino, Direttore d' Orchestra
Sig. Zamboni Petrini Nicola.
Altro primo Violino in sostituzione
Sig. Ferrara Bernardo.
Primo Violino pei Balli
Sig. Manzoni Camillo.
Primo Violino de' Secondi
Sig. Grossoni Luigi.
Prima Viola
Sig. Lavelli Alessandro.
Altra Prima Viola in sostituzione
Sig. Bussola Giovanni.
Primo Violoncello al Cembalo
Sig. Bussi Tommaso.
Altro primo Violoncello in sostituzione
Sig. Setti Giacomo.
Primo Contrabbasso al Cembalo
Sig. Ronchetti Fabiano.
Altro primo Contrabbasso in sostituzione
Sig. Bianchi Urbano.
Primo Corno da Caccia — Altro primo Corno
Sig. Bergonzi Benedetto — Sig. Gelmi Cipriano.
Primi Clarinetti a perfetta vicenda
Sig. Cavallini Pompeo — Taveggia Alessandro.
Primi Flauti a perfetta vicenda
Sig. Pizzi Francesco — Pagani Luigi.
Primi Oboe a perfetta vicenda
Sig. Daelli Paolo Emilio — Pighi Carlo.
Primi Fagotti a perfetta vicenda
Sig. Cantù Antonio — Spotti Cesare.
Prime Trombe a perfetta vicenda
Sig. Viganò Giuseppe — Siccarz Giovanni.
Primo Trombone — Altro primo Trombone
Sig. Bernardi Luigi — Sig. Goldini Giovanni.
Suonatrice d' Arpa
Signora Vergani Teresa.

on the Carcano's 1830–31 program, as sung by Pasta and Rubini. Odd that Henry doesn't mention them.

The identification of "Sarasi" would also provide the link with a young Irish musician, who had also been staying at the Villa Sampieri in Bologna. The memoir continues:

> During this period, I was invited to dine with Lady Goldsmid at the Hotel d'Italia. I had a very agreeable evening, meeting many men of genius and reputation, among whom were Romani, the poet, and author of the libretto of *La Somnambula* [*sic*], and my fellow-countryman, Balfe, then a young man—very little older, indeed, than myself. The acquaintance thus formed ripened soon into warm and staunch friendship; we speedily became inseparable, and lived and travelled together. Balfe was the possessor of a very sweet baritone voice, and he, being a

good musician, of course made the most of it. An engagement was offered to us by the proprietors of the Opera House at Varesi [*recte* Varese], a little town about thirty miles from Milan. We accepted the engagement readily enough, on the principle that half a loaf is better than no bread, the terms offered to us being far from liberal. Balfe was engaged to undertake the part of Henry VIII, the opera to be performed being *Anna Bolena*, and I was engaged as *Maestro de* [sic] *piano* and *Maestro de* [sic] *Cori*.

In a pecuniary sense, as I before said, our engagement was not enticing. The reader, bearing in mind the enormous salaries that are paid to the leading artistes in this day, will laugh when I tell them that Balfe's weekly salary amounted to eighteen scudi, and mine fourteen scudi. But notwithstanding our small salaries, we were enabled to save, at least, half our income, although we lived, I might say, almost luxuriously. Living in Italy sixty-five years ago was a very different matter to living in the Italy of to-day—then a five centissimi piece, about equal in value to our English halfpenny, would procure for you a light and wholesome breakfast. A dinner of many courses, including wines, was purchasable for something under a shilling, English money, and all other necessaries of life were cheap in a proportionate degree.

The town of Varesi itself we found to be anything but a pleasant abiding place; the streets were beyond all description filthy, disgusting, and the mobs of dirty, unkempt Italians that thronged them were even more repulsive than the streets themselves. The town itself was a hotbed of disease and superstition, and the population was composed principally of rogues and ruffians.

Judge then of our surprise and pleasure when we found that the little Opera House was most tastefully decorated, and worthy in fact of a much larger and more prosperous town than Varesi.

Dirty, superstitious, idle, and vicious as were the Italian population of this little town, yet their love for music knew no bounds. Night after night they filled the Opera House to its utmost capacity—an unprepossessing, but certainly an appreciative, audience.

The operas that were here produced were of the highest order. Think of a small town like Varesi, its population consisting of about five or six thousand, producing *Anna Bolena*, *Gazza Ladra*, *Donna del Lago*, Bellini's *Pirata*, and Rossini's *Cenerentola*. We numbered some fine voices in our little company, Grisi accepting an engagement as Seconda Donna. Our tenor, whose beautiful voice won the admiration of all hearers, sang in sacred selections given in the old church of Saint Vittore. His rendering of Mozart's "Domine Deus," and Haydn's "Gratias agimus tibi," created a great sensation among the music-loving Italians.

Though the town of Varesi itself left much to be desired in the way of beauty and cleanliness, the environs and outlying districts were very lovely, and we frequently made excursions into the country, when we had the time at our command.

Once, when visiting the Madonna del Monte, a resort of the faithful, our little party was particularly struck with the view of the monastery on the mountain, but as Bollo (our tenor) observed, "The view is magnificent, but what a splendid place for rheumatism and catching on the mountain a lasting cold!"

The period of our engagement at Varesi over, we departed thence to Milan, from Milan on to Spezzia, Lugano, Genoa, Bologna, from which latter place we passed on to Parma. Here we remained for a few weeks, and when opera was produced, Balfe and I had lucrative engagements offered to us, which we gladly accepted.

Even if we have no specific independent corroboration of Russell's involvement with Balfe in these months of operatic travels around Italy—and no record at all of a tenor named Bollo—his account accords sufficiently well with what can be uncovered of Balfe's movements to leave little doubt of their essential veracity. Balfe, already established as both singer and composer, had spent much time in Bologna from December 1829 onward, he can be seen playing Il Conte di Culagna in Filippo Celli's *La Secchia Rapita* at Varese (so Balfe was already known in Varese!) in Autumn 1830, and it was during Milan's operatic season of 1831 that he met and fell in love with a leading member of the Teatro Carcano company, Lina Roser (1806–88), whom he married in Lugano, over the Swiss border, during the Carnevale season in Bergamo in 1831. What is known of Balfe's subsequent operatic appearances around Italy again accords pretty well, for a while, with Russell's story. Balfe and his wife were in Varese in October 1831, and the Ducal Theatre at Parma, where Mme. Balfe was prima donna and sang for the birthday of the local Herzogin, was also on their itinerary. Although Russell's name is never mentioned, this appears to have been the touring company, headed by Pasta and Elisa Taccani, playing *Il Falegname di Livonia* (Balfe is specifically mentioned in Varese), *I Capuleti ed i Montecchi*, *Chiara di Rosemburg*, *Norma*, *Elisa e Claudio*, et al., with Balfe in the casts, through Brescia, Varese, Bergamo, Turin, Parma . . . and, so it seems, Signor Russell on piccolo and as rehearsal pianist.

It was his time in Parma that, supposedly, also gave Russell a meeting with one of the many men of history about whom colorful tales litter his memoirs:

> Among the many people we met at Parma was a Major Nolan, a gentleman, who showed us many kindnesses, and who one evening invited us to dinner to meet a few friends, and a very pleasant evening we had. The following morning, the Major, accompanied by his young son, a lad of about 15 years of age, called upon us, and together we went out to take our mid-day meal. During lunch, young Nolan leaned across the table and asked me if I could fence.
>
> "No," I replied, "I cannot fence, but I can use my fists pretty well."
>
> "Very well," he said abruptly, "Then I challenge you."
>
> The challenge was no sooner offered than it was accepted, and leaving our lunch we repaired to the small garden at the back of the Hotel, and had a round or two at fisticuffs. The many years that have passed since that memorable day have tended to make my memory rather hazy as to the issue of the combat. I think, however, that the bout was an extremely innocent and harmless one, and that perfect good humour, and good temper, prevailed upon both sides.
>
> My readers will no doubt be interested to know that the pugnacious youth, who thus early in life displayed such devotion to manly sports and the noble art of self-defence was none other than the famous Captain Nolan, the account of whose heroic end at the memorable Charge of Balaclava has been so often sung in song and told in story.

The Charge of Balaclava is, of course, better known, through Lord Tennyson's poem, as the Charge of the Light Brigade, and it took place on 25 October 1854, at the battle of Balaclava during the Crimean War. It was the culpable Captain Lewis Edward Nolan (1818–54) who delivered to Lord Lucan the written order from Lord Raglan, which, thanks to his high-handed style of transmitting it ("There is your enemy!"), led to the infamous charge. Nolan was struck by a fragment of shell and killed instantly, becoming one of the first of the episode's victims. That Russell met him in Italy is perfectly credible, since Nolan's father, Londonderry-man John Babington Nolan (c. 1782–1850) was British vice-consul in Milan.

Russell goes on to report that, soon after this, he bade good-bye to what seems to have been an enjoyable, if not hugely productive, time in Italy and proceeded "by means of a jolting and comfortless diligence" to Paris. There, he reports, he met many eminent musical people, including Giacomo Meyerbeer and the singers Laure Cinti-Damoreau, Adolphe Nourrit, and Nicolas Prosper Levasseur, creators of leading roles in the hit of the era, *Robert le Diable*. Produced at the Paris Opéra on 21 November 1831, it was the opera that first gave Meyerbeer his great fame. Presumably, Henry is not suggesting he was there at the first night: There were to be many, many more. So, lacking the Dover customs' papers, his brief stopover in Paris can only be approximately dated.

Russell then "proceeded to Calais, and thence across to Dover in a small crazy cockleshell, which for courtesy's sake, was styled a boat." He adds a comment that applies as much today: "Present-day Channel trippers, who can cross the Straits in comparative comfort in less than two hours, would hardly envy me my four hours' tumbling and tossing in a diminutive steamer." Nor was this the end of the rigors of a journey in the early 1830s:

> On landing at Dover, we were subjected to a rigorous examination by the Customs officers. I secured, with some little difficulty, my seat on the stage coach, and the following morning we started on our journey Londonwards. Along the old Dover Road, through Kent, justly named the "Garden of England," the freshness and tranquillity of the beautiful English landscape was inexpressibly soothing and homelike after the more rugged grandeur of the Italian lake and mountain scenery. Whilst charmed with the scenery, I found, however, much to be desired in the way of companionship from my fellow-passengers. The weather being cold, they were arrayed, for the most part, in

> huge caped coats, with large plaid shawls twisted around their necks, hiding most of their features, with the exception of here and there a frost-bitten red nose poking out over the top of its owner's shawl, looking much like the figures of fun which [John] Leech and [George] Cruickshank used to portray in the earlier numbers of *Punch*. So, it was with some feeling of relief when, after a journey that lasted ten hours, we at last sighted the outskirts of the great city—London.

And the next chapter in young Mr. Russell's life.

2
London in the 1830s

Russell's account of his time in Italy suggests that he was away from London for much of the years 1830 and 1831. On his return, he says: "For three or four months after my arrival in London, I did comparatively nothing, till I fell in with Mr. Lumley, who was then managing the box office of His Majesty's Theatre, under the La Porte management. La Porte failed, and Lumley assumed command. Benjamin Lumley had known me from boyhood, and when we met in London he offered me an engagement as chorus master at His Majesty's Theatre." Again, this presents us with some difficulty in unravelling the precise dating and chronology. Benjamin Lumley (1811–75), originally also called Levy, was a young Jewish lawyer scarcely older than Russell himself. He did, indeed, become very much involved with what at that time was still named the King's Theatre—it became Her Majesty's Theatre at Queen Victoria's accession in 1837. However, it was only from 1835 that he was concerned with sorting out the bankruptcy of the Italian opera's longtime manager Pierre-François Laporte (1799–1841). Lumley ("solicitor of 6 Parliament Street") may, of course, already have been a legal advisor to Laporte earlier in the 1830s, and there is some evidence of Russell's involvement with both Lumley and the King's Theatre before, if not the disaster of 1832, the contractual hassles and monetary finagling of 1835.

As for the duration of Russell's involvement as chorus master at the King's Theatre, the 1846 *Musical Treasury* memoir says that it was "two years." This, though, seems less likely than the few weeks to which Russell refers in his book. Neither, however, says when this is supposed to have occurred, or why it was of such short duration. However long the engagement was, and when it occurred, there is no reason to doubt Russell's claim that the connection gave him the good fortune to meet many celebrated men and women of the day. These, allegedly, included the violinist Niccolò Paganini (1782–1840), who performed in London between 1831 and 1834, and the mezzo-soprano Maria Malibran (1808–36), who sang at the King's Theatre between 1825 and 1832 and, thereafter, at Drury Lane Theatre. Other celebrities he cites are the violinist Charles-Auguste de Bériot (1802–70), who travelled with Malibran during the 1830s and married her shortly before her death, and Nicolas Mori (1796–1839), who led the King's Theatre orchestra during the 1830s.

Russell claims that at the end of his engagement he found himself very hard up and dispirited:

> Then it was that generous Malibran, De Bériot, Mori, and others came forward, and proved that they were friends indeed. They organised, under the conductorship of Tom Welch [*recte* Welsh], for my especial benefit, a concert at the Argyle [*recte* Argyll] Rooms, then situated at the top of Regent Street, on the east side—near the Oxford Circus. The concert, owing to the power of the artistes' world-famous names, was a great success, and it put fresh hope into my heart, as well as money into my well-nigh empty pocket.

Tom Welsh (1779–1848) was a bass singer, former musical director of the English Opera House, and a distinguished singing teacher, who had formerly directed the Royal Harmonic Institution at the Argyll Rooms, 246 Regent Street, of which he was, by now, the proprietor. He advertised his school as: "Mr. T Welsh's Vocal Academy, Wednesdays and Saturdays . . . terms 4 Guineas for eight lessons."

Fortunately, we are able to date this event and, through it, confirm Russell's involvement with the King's Theatre as being in the early summer of 1833. The concert was heralded by a letter in *The Times* of 4 July 1833 from someone signing himself (in Greek characters) "Philomosos"—presumably intended to be "Philomousos" or "friend of the Muses":

> . . . I think it but right that you should be informed . . . that Mesdames Malibran, de Méric, &c., and Signori de Begnis, Begrez, Donzelli, Galli, Puzzi, Tamburini, de Beriot, &c., and last, though not least, our own countryman, H Phillips, have

> gratuitously offered their services in behalf of Mr. H Russell, a young man of great talent, and attached to the King's Theatre, but without many friends, whose concert takes place at the Argyll Rooms on Monday evening, the 8th of July . . .

So, he's "attached" in July 1833? *The Morning Chronicle* further foreshadowed the concert with the following note: "Mr. H Russell, a very promising vocalist, and an excellent young man, pupil of Signor Tamburini, takes a Benefit Concert this evening at the Argyll Rooms. Russell is so much esteemed in the musical world that Madame Malibran, Madame De Méric, Madame Sala, and Miss Bellchambers, Donzelli, Arigotti, Begrez, Tamburini, H Phillips, and Monsieur De Bériot, lend their gratuitous and powerful assistance. We wish the youth every success." Russell was a "pupil of Tamburini"?

The concert itself was briefly noticed in *The Times*; otherwise proof that it happened is hard to find: "On Monday night Mr. H Russell gave a very elegant concert at the Argyll Rooms, in which Madame Malibran displayed her great powers, to the delight of a numerous and fashionable audience; and the instrumental performance of M De Bériot was scarcely less attractive. The whole entertainment was highly creditable to the different artists." Concerts of the day were advertised largely through the distribution of concert bills and paid press announcements, and such newspaper plugs and free publicity were not common. This was not a one-off involvement for Russell with the Argyll Rooms, as is confirmed by newspaper announcements of a previous concert there on 27 May. Its promoter was William A. King (1816–67), another son of M. P. King and, thus, brother to Russell's teacher, C. M. King. Besides Russell himself, those mentioned as performing included Josephine de Méric ("Di piacer"), Juliet Bellchambers, and Susan Bruce ("Lo, here the gentle lark") on the female side, and J. W. Hobbs, Handel Gear, Theodore Victor Giubilei, and George Stretton on the male side. Henry sang "The Fine Old English Gentleman" and was praised for "a voice of remarkable richness, and his style of singing is marked with style and judgment." This seems as if it may be the earliest date at which the mature Henry Russell—aged, nevertheless, no more than twenty—sang publicly in London.

From another source, we hear that Russell was also promoting concerts around this time, since his former schoolmate, Jewish violinist Barnett Isaacson (c. 1811–1901), recalled in his memoirs (*A Veteran Musician*, Jewish Chronicle) making his first appearance at a concert given by Henry Russell at the Surrey Theatre in 1833: "Russell sang and I played the violin, giving a performance on one string à la Paganini." No record of said concert seems to survive. Russell's activities would doubtless also, of course, have taken him into the provinces. Years later, for instance, he recalled hearing John Braham (1777–1856) singing in Händel's *Messiah* in York.

We also know that Russell was continuing to have songs published, though few seem actually to have been deposited, at the time, in what is today the British Library. One Russell song that is reasonably specifically dateable is "When the Wild Wind Blows (A Song of the Waves)," since it is described as being sung by Madame Laure Cinti-Damoreau (1801–63); this was the distinguished French soprano whom Russell claims to have met in Paris. Her only appearances in London as Mme. Cinti-Damoreau (i.e., after her marriage) were in 1832 and 1833, when she sang at the King's Theatre. The song was advertised briefly in 1835.

Yet more songs we can date from those music publishers' newspaper advertisements that appeared regularly in the press. As early as November 1832, for instance, G. Walker and Son of 17 Soho Square was advertising Russell's setting of Lord Byron's "When I Rov'd a Young Highlander." Russell gave the well-known words a Scottish Highland dance setting, with, as John Anthony Stephens (in his *Henry Russell in America*) declares, "a particularly fine melody." The printed music's title page describes it as sung at the Theatre Royal, Covent Garden by the Scottish soprano Eliza Inverarity (1813–46). Miss Inverarity had made her London début at Covent Garden in 1830 in the title role of Rophino Lacy's "adaptation" of Rossini's *La Cenerentola*, and she remained a leading soprano there through the early 1830s. The song was well enough liked to be selected, more than a decade later, to be featured in Mr. T. H. Tomlinson's lecture on Russell, alongside the—by that time—many more obvious hits.

Another song advertised at the same time had apparently achieved sufficient popularity to be described by its publishers as "Russell's celebrated Bandit's Song." A rousing call to arms, it has uncredited words and was apparently known more specifically by its opening lines, "Let Others Rejoice in the Merry Moonlight." It appears to have been particularly liked in Australia, but stayed around for many years. Then, in a further advert of February 1833, publisher George Walker added to his list of Russell songs "Come, Maidens, Come," described on the title page as sung by Alsatian soprano Margarethe Stockhausen (1803–77). It, too, was sung freely on both sides of the Atlantic.

Figure 2.1. “When I Rov’d a Young Highlander” sheet music cover. *Source:* Author’s collection.

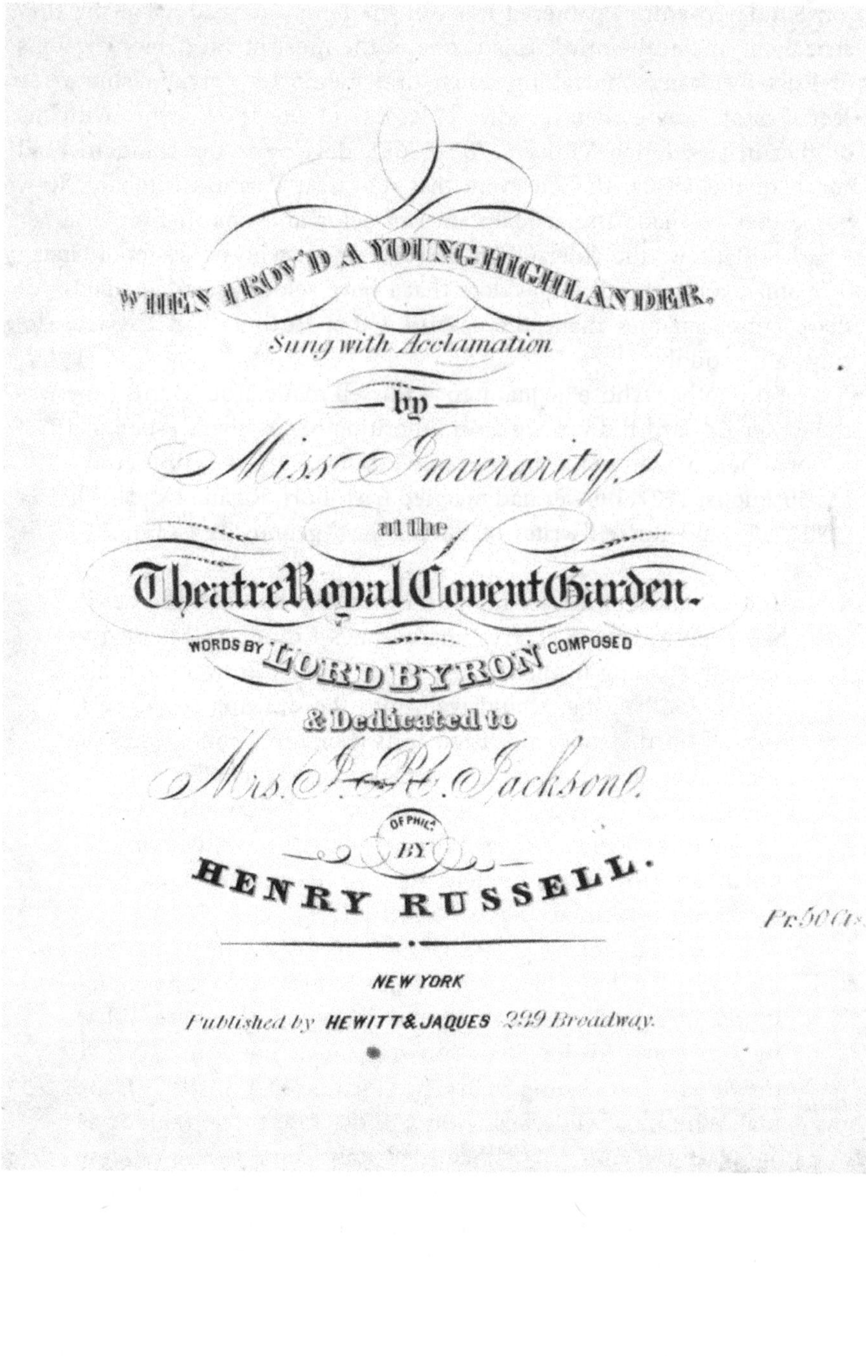

Russell credits Benjamin Lumley for his introduction to a Mr. Parrot, a government contractor for mail coaches, at whose house at Millbank "on Sunday evenings gathered most of the light and leading of the theatrical and musical world." This is one of the most literal demonstrations of Russell's grandson's taking down oral memories parrot fashion, for "Mr. Parrot" was evidently Edward Parratt (1796–1867), who, with his brother-in-law, Finch Vidler (1787–1868), developed the standard mail coach of the 1830s. Russell avers that it was at Parratt's Millbank Row home that he made the acquaintance of actor and one-man entertainer Charles Mathews the elder (1776–1835), "a man who possessed a charm of manner and a fund of anecdote that I have seldom seen equalled." All these famous names make the assertion that Russell "had few friends" ring rather oddly.

Yet another whose acquaintance Russell made around this time was the writer Edward Bulwer, who, on inheriting his mother's estate in 1838, adopted her maiden name and became Edward Bulwer-Lytton (1803–73). On 30 August 1827, Bulwer had married Irish-born Rosina Doyle Wheeler (1802–82), and Russell writes of the Bulwers' generosity to him:

> In their house in Mayfair, I was as much at home as though it had been my own. . . . Yes, many times I dined and passed a pleasant evening in their house. After dinner, Bulwer, with his aristocratic bearing, would walk into the drawing-room, seat himself on the sofa, and listen to two or three songs which I might sing, accompanying myself on the piano. Presently he would leave the room, beckoning me to follow him. When we got to his study he generally sat himself near the window and filled a big pipe, politely offering me a cigar. One such occasion I remember very distinctly.
>
> We had not long taken our seats, when he remarked, "Perhaps you have heard that Mrs. Bulwer and I are going almost directly to Naples to spend a few months there. What are you going to do? Shall you stay on in London?" "No," I answered, "I am going to try my fortune in Canada." "Canada! Why it's a wilderness; you will do little there. London is the place for you." "Yet, since I left Italy, some twelve months ago," I replied, "I have done very little here. Perhaps a new country might encourage any little musical talent I possess." After a brief silence, he said, "Did you not tell me you were

in Italy some considerable time?—if so, you must be able to speak the language well?" I replied that I did. "Then what do you say to joining Mrs. Bulwer and me, and coming with us to Naples—of course, as our guest?" Need I add that I jumped at such an agreeable proposition, and, in fact, I scarcely slept that night with the excitement his kind offer had engendered. For a wonder, the anticipation did not exceed the realisation. At last we started. I knew every step of the road. But with a very different heart I now traversed it. Formerly, I had had to count every franc, now I was travelling *en prince*. After a pleasant, yet fatiguing, journey, we arrived at Naples, and put up at the "Hotel de la Grande Brittania [sic]." I remained with the Bulwers six weeks, and during that time I was introduced to many of the best families. Bulwer was much engaged writing his "Last Days of Pompeii!" Naturally, Mr. and Mrs. Bulwer frequently visited Pompeii, and on several occasions I accompanied them. . . .

On the conclusion of my visit I returned to England by sea, as Sir George Talbot had offered me a berth on his yacht, which I gratefully accepted. After a delightful voyage, I landed at Cowes and eventually arrived in London . . .

Sir George Talbot was, in all likelihood, the wealthy Belfast baronet of that name who died in 1850. As for dating this journey, Bulwer's visit to Naples took place in 1833, the year before publication of his novel *The Last Days of Pompeii*. Talbot gave up his home in Naples that same year. There is, moreover, supporting evidence that Russell was in Naples at this time. "During this second visit," according to the 1846 *Musical Treasury* biography, Russell "contended for the prize given at the Conservatorio at Naples for the best musical composition. He won it—a gold medal; and in November of the year 1833, it was presented to him by the hand of the King of Naples—a distinction which entitles him to the title of Chevalier in that country." According to another source, he won this "gold medal of Prince Charles (Naples) for his composition of the operatic farce *Il Marito Jeloso*—the first time it was ever gained by an Englishman." It will be noted that this is the context for the title correctly written as *Il Matrimonio Geloso*, rather than as in Russell's memoir. The subject of a jealous husband was, of course, a staple of operatic farces, Domenico Cimarosa (1749–1801) having composed a piece of the same name for

Naples in 1785 (seen in Bologna in 1788), another by Giovanni Bertati in 1781. Whether Russell borrowed the text for one of these as the basis for his putative piece is unknown, as the prize . . . medal or not . . . doesn't seem to have included publication or staging of the winning work. Pinch of salt? American journals would later accuse Russell of having had the medal which he displayed struck himself, to support his "fiction."

What Russell does not say is that the Italian trip followed a breakdown in Bulwer's health, and that it took place in the year that Bulwer first separated from his wife. Not until 1836 were the couple finally estranged, and Russell evidently continued his association with them when they were temporarily reunited, after the journey to Naples. He describes, particularly, his friendship with the Bulwers' infant son Edward Robert, the future statesman Lord Lytton (1831–91) and an author of poetry under the name of "Owen Meredith." Since he was born on 8 November 1831, the child must have been at most a toddler by the time of this Russell memory:

> Their little boy (the late Lord Lytton) greatly interested me, and I flatter myself he was much attached to me. Many an afternoon would the little fellow sit on my knee, chatting away with delight, as I taught him to make a little carriage out of white paste board. When the wheels were fixed, and the yellow paint (gamboge) was laid on, the boy's delight knew no bounds. "Mamma," "Papa!" he used to shout, "Look how beautiful it is, see how well it runs!" It was very touching to note how Mrs. Bulwer was charmed with her boy's delight.

The ultimate breakdown of the Bulwers' "unusual" marriage resulted from the accentuation of Rosina's natural eccentricities through her friendships firstly with Lady Caroline Lamb (1785–1828), and later with the poetess Letitia Elizabeth Landon (1802–38). The latter was known as "L. E. L.," and the Bulwers actually appear as characters in her novel *Romance and Reality* (1831). Russell makes no mention of "L. E. L." in his memoirs but, late in 1834, his settings of her verses "The Orphan Ballad Singers," "Ivy Bridge," and "Cottage Courtship" were published in *Fisher's Drawing Room Scrapbook for 1835*, the first-named carrying a dedication to Mrs. Edward Lytton Bulwer.

Earlier in 1834, Russell had been busy with the composition of an opera. *The Court Journal* gossiped in its pages:

> A new opera, founded on a German legend, to be entitled, as we understand, *The Bride's Band*, and in which Mrs. Wood is expected to perform the principal female character, is now completed, and, we believe, in rehearsal, (except so far as regards the latter vocalist), and will be produced by Arnold, at his new Theatre, on the 28th of July next. H[enry] Phillips has the leading part assigned him, with which he is understood to be perfectly satisfied. The music, of which report speaks favourably, is composed by Mr. H Russell, already known to the public by various original compositions of much merit and by his own talents as a bass-singer. There is also an opera in preparation, founded on *La Sylphide*, for which 168 new dresses have been ordered.

We have already encountered Henry Phillips (1801–76), the outstanding British bass singer of his time, as a participant in Russell's concert in July 1833. Mrs. Wood (1802–64) was the former Mary Anne Paton, the celebrated soprano who in 1826 had created the role of Reiza (with its huge aria "Ocean, Thou Mighty Monster") in Weber's *Oberon* at Covent Garden. She was, in June 1834, sailing back from triumphs in America, with her tenor husband, and agents of theatrical managers were reportedly stationed at Portsmouth to propose terms of engagement for her on arrival. In the event, she chose not to accept the proposals of Samuel James Arnold (1774–1852), who had for a quarter of a century been promoting opera in English at the Lyceum Theatre, which was named the English Opera House for his summer seasons.

The Lyceum had burned down in 1830, forcing Arnold to move to other venues, but, in July 1834, the rebuilt English Opera House, Royal Lyceum, opened its doors. John Barnett's *The Mountain Sylph*—the opera based on *La Sylphide*—produced there on 25 August 1834—was to become a landmark in English opera. But Russell's opera was never seen: "Owing," he said later, "to my leaving England about this time, Mr. William B. Bernard, the author of the opera of the 'Bride's Band,' withdrew it." William Bayle Bernard (1807–75), an Englishman born in Boston, Massachusetts, and recently the supplier of the operatic farce *The Mummy* to the Adelphi, was to be a prolific author of material of all kinds for the British stage. In 1839, he would score a major success with the farce, *His Last Legs*. But he doesn't seem to have recycled his contribution to *The Bride's Band*. We can only guess what lay behind the reference to Russell "leaving England about this time." About what time?

Meanwhile, on 23 June 1834, Russell promoted a concert at the Argyll Rooms that was, reported *The Court Journal*, "numerously and fashionably attended." The female singers included Matilde Cascelli Kyntherland, Henrietta Sala, Mlle. Laborde, and the Misses Smith, sisters Kitty and Julia, inevitably billed as "the fair nieces of Miss Stephens" (the celebrated soprano Catherine Stephens (1794–1882), who would, in 1838, marry the aged fifth Earl of Essex.) The gentlemen included the two English-born Signori Giubilei—Theodore Victor (1801–48) and Augusto (d. 1851)—the top tenor, Alberico Curioni, buffo della Torre, and the Lombardy tenor, Gaetano Arigotti of the King's Theatre. Russell himself, "whose deep rich voice was heard to the greatest advantage in the *Old English Gentleman*, contributed much, both by his Italian and English songs, to the gratification of the evening." "The beneficiaire was in excellent voice, and sang 'Largo al factotum [della litu]' [sic] and 'Stand to your guns [my hearts of oak]' exquisitely" (*Satirist*). Among the instrumentalists, *The Morning Herald* reported, "Master Viotti Collins and his brother [George Lindley Collins], of the ages of seven and five years, charmed the audience with their performance on the violin and violoncello." Joseph Viotti Collins (1822–99), later a prominent London orchestral leader, was actually about twelve at the time, and his brother (1828–69) six!

In October 1834, newspapers carried advertisements for two further Russell songs, "When the Tempests Fly o'er the Cloudy Sky" and "On the Brave Who Have Fallen No Tear We Bestow" (otherwise "The Patriot's Welcome"), both published by Balls and Son of 408 Oxford Street, London. The good old *Morning Herald* proclaimed: 'This beautiful and much-admired production does its young and talented composer great credit . . . it is far superior to nine-tenths of the musical publications of the day." The second of the pair had words credited to Jane Porter (1776–1850), the well-known, voluminous authoress of historical novels (*Thaddeus of Warsaw*, *The Scottish Chiefs*, *The Pastor's Fireside*).

More importantly, the first represented a confirmation of Russell's involvement with Charles Mackay (1814–89), with whom he had created a set of sacred songs the previous year, and who would be his major lyricist over many years to come. Born in Scotland, the son of a naval lieutenant, Mackay was brought up by foster parents after his mother died early. At sixteen he became private secretary to William Cockerill, an iron-master based in Belgium, but, increasingly, he devoted himself to writing. He returned to Britain from Brussels, with his father, in 1832, met and first collaborated with Henry Russell soon after, before, in 1835, he achieved his first permanent post in journalism when he was appointed as assistant to George Hogarth, sub-editor of the *Morning Chronicle*, where he worked alongside Charles Dickens.

Meanwhile, Mackay had made important contacts in Britain, as he writes in his 1887 memoirs, *Through the Long Day*:

> Among the earliest acquaintances which I made in London, through the medium of Messrs. Stewart and Barron, of 26, Parliament Street—who had acted for my father for many years, during his residence in Brussels, as his agents for the receipt and the transmission of his military half-pay—was that of Mr. William Brewer Roberts, connected with the then well-known publishing firm of Fisher, Son and Jackson of Newgate Street, the proprietors of *Fisher's Drawing-room Scrap-Book*. This favourite annual was edited by the popular poetess, Miss Letitia Elizabeth Landon, better known as L.E.L. Mr. Roberts had a large connection among water-colour artists, and acted as an intermediary between them and the booksellers for the sake of their copyrights, for engraving in the annuals and other illustrated periodicals.
>
> . . . By this gentleman I was introduced to Mr. Benjamin Lumley, a young solicitor, residing in Quality Court, Chancery Lane, acting at that time as legal advisor to Monsieur Laporte, the lessee of the Royal Italian Opera. Mr. Lumley, a few years afterwards, on the bankruptcy of Monsieur Laporte, became the successor of that gentleman, and carried on, with great personal credit and more or less pecuniary success, the affairs of that establishment. I read Italian with Mr. Lumley, and grounded him in the grammar of that language, which I had studied both at Brussels and Aix-la-Chapelle, and in which I had become so proficient as to be able to converse with facility.
>
> I also made the acquaintance, about the same time, of a young man named Henry Russell, a friend of Mr. Lumley, and, like him, of Hebrew parentage, though not of faith. Mr. Russell had been known in his boyhood for his musical accomplishments, and especially for his brilliant playing on the pianoforte. He had also made a successful début as a vocalist

at the transpontine theatres, and was considered by his family and friends as a musical prodigy. He was my senior by three or four years (sic!), and had made himself a growing reputation in the musical profession by the composition and publication of some songs and ballads, of which he found the poetry in the works of Lord Byron, and older authors. He aspired to write an oratorio, or an English opera, if he could but procure a libretto. He learned by some means or other that I had written a few ballads, and applied to me, in the hope that the much-needed libretto might be forthcoming from my pen. In this hope he was disappointed; but I fell in with his desires so far that I showed him some of the songs I had written, which he took away with him.

Two days afterwards, he asked me to accompany him to Walker's music warehouse, in Soho Square, where he played over and sang to me two of my songs to which he had composed the melodies. After I had expressed my pleasure at hearing them, he asked my permission to publish them. This I gave him, nothing loth, but highly flattered, and never thought of asking for payment. One of them, a very inferior composition, entitled, "Some love to roam o'er the dark sea-foam," happened to tickle the taste of the town, and became extremely popular. It was to be heard for many months on all the barrel-organs, that then, as now, infested the streets of the metropolis. The other—which, as a poem, was infinitely superior, in my estimation—attracted no notice, and, in fact, fell still-born. The publisher ultimately cleared about two hundred pounds by "Some love to roam." Mr. Russell, I believe, received a guinea for the music, and I received nothing, but a barren "Thank you" from the composer, though not even as much as that from the publisher—unless a couple of copies of the song might have been considered an equivalent for the thanks which he did not render. I allowed Mr. Russell to compose music to, and the publisher to publish, two or three other songs, on the same unremunerative terms; but none of them achieved the popularity of the first, though, in my opinion, and in that of everybody among my friends who had either taste or judgment, they were all infinitely more worthy of it.

> Mr. Russell also composed the music to a set of six sacred melodies that I wrote, which were published at the expense of my friend, Mr. Roberts, by the bookselling firm of Fisher, Son & Co. The speculation was not successful, excepting as far as it made me favourably known to a publishing house with which in after years I became profitably connected. Mr. Russell, however, found the partnership of his music with my verse to answer his purpose, inasmuch as he was not only a composer but a vocalist by profession, and was extremely popular as a singer.

In discussing their collaboration, Russell was the first to stress that Mackay had received a disproportionately small amount of the praise for the

Figure 2.2. Charles Mackay in later life (*The Illustrated London News*, 14 May 1892). *Source*: Author's collection.

songs' success. "What fame there is to be obtained through song writing," Russell wrote, "generally falls to the lot of the composer of the melody. Surely the author of the poem has as much right to public recognition as the musician who sets his words to music; but no, it is not so. All the honour and glory of a successful song is awarded to the composer, and the poet must be content with the monetary recompense alone, provided he be lucky enough to get even that."

He went on to give his own version of their first collaboration, which is, predictably, more fanciful, as well as less convincing, on how far back their relationship went. He also disagreed on the distribution of the spoils:

> Charles Mackay and I had been friends from our earliest boyhood, and our friendship had grown up with us. In privation and prosperity, we had ever been the best of comrades. . . . I remember well the time in the far-away days of our youth, when Mackay and I—unlike that little hero of nursery lore, "Little Dan Tupper, Who Sang for his supper"—wrote, composed, and sold a song for a breakfast. It happened thus:
>
> One morning as I sat disconsolately pondering over that problem, which has never yet been satisfactorily solved—how to exist on an income of nothing at all—Mackay entered my rooms.
>
> "I am very hungry," quoth he.
>
> "And I also," I responded, gloomily.
>
> "Have you no money?" he enquired.
>
> "None," this in a still more gloomy tone of voice.
>
> "Well, I daresay they will let us have a breakfast at the usual place."
>
> We could but try, and so we sallied forth, but our hopes were rudely shattered when we arrived at the little coffee-house which we usually patronised in common with some of the rising men of the day.
>
> "Two cups of coffee, two rolls and butter," I demanded of the coffee-house proprietor, on our arrival.
>
> The man looked at us vacantly.
>
> "See 'ere, Mr. Russell," he said, pointing over his shoulder, "'ave you read that notice, "No Trust?' I've suffered so much from the customers you and Mr. Mackay have recommended here that I've made up my mind, and it's all up now, I ain't a

going to trust no more. If you ain't got the money, why you can't 'ave the heatables."

This perfectly staggered us both; we left the shop in indignation and in hunger, and returned to my room.

What was to be done?

Suddenly, I said, "Can you write the verses of a song, and I will at once put them to music?"

Mackay said, "Yes," he thought he could, and sat down and wrote the first verse of the song, commencing:

"Some love to roam o'er the dark sea foam,
Where the shrill winds whistle free."

As Mackay finished each verse, I composed the melody to it, and a little after noon the song was completed. Without losing a moment, we started for the shop of a music publisher, of the name of Walker, in Soho Square. I went in, assuming that air of humility which best befits a man who has not breakfasted.

"Good morning, sir," said I.

Mr. Walker never condescended to reply, which was discouraging.

"I have a song here," I continued, "which has just been composed."

"Well," he growled; "sit down, and let me hear it."

I sat down to the piano, and played and sang it over, but, in my state of hunger and excitement, I am sure I did not do the song justice.

"What do you want for it?" he asked.

My heart beat violently. I thought of my empty interior, and of the hungry versifier outside.

"Oh! anything you like, sir."

"Well," said Walker, "I'll give you a guinea for it."

I took it. He brought out a paper for me to sign. My heart was so gladdened that I never even read it. It might have been a promissory note for all I knew.

I rushed down with Mackay to the coffee-shop, and demanded two large cups of chocolate, two bacon and eggs, and two rolls and butter, etc., etc., and throwing down a sovereign said, very pompously:

"Take the money, sir, and bring the eatables at once," which he did. I received 17s. 3d. change. Added to the 1s., this

> made 18s. 3d. I handed my dear friend 9s. 1½d. as his share, and placed the balance in my pocket to meet the demands of a tyrannical landlady.
>
> Never before, or since, have I enjoyed a meal as I enjoyed that breakfast that Mackay and I partook of late in the afternoon of a certain day many, many years ago."

The song "Some Love to Roam" was, indeed, one of the most performed among Henry Russell's early songs, on both sides of the Atlantic. In the Britain of the 1830s, it was probably his most successful, going into numerous editions for the publishing firm of George Walker & Son of 17 Soho Square. Its sheet music credits it as sung at the Theatre Royal, Covent Garden, by basso Henry Phillips. Its stirring outdoor atmosphere typifies the Mackay lyrics that Russell set, and it incidentally contains an early instance of the repeated "Ho! Ho! Ho! Ho!" that was to become a feature of Russell's songs to indicate good humor and enjoyment. Dating, precisely, its publication, and thus the Mackay-Russell collaboration, their stories, and the connection with Walker has been a tad tricky, but both *The Age* and the *Morning Herald* advertise "Some Love to Roam," "The Bandit's Song," and "The Rhine Glee" ("the celebrated prize glee") by Russell as early as May 1833. "Some Love" was advertised as "sung by Phillips" before the end of 1833. Incidentally, George Walker Sr. was not, as he suggests, unknown to Mr. Russell. It was his "Piano Repository" that, in Surrey Theatre days, had published C. M. King's "Windmill Rondo" and the songs of Kate Coveney. "Tempests Fly" was still being performed by Russell in 1843 (3 April) when he opened his concert at Niblo's Gardens with the old song, and it can be seen in British concert programs as late as 1867 (Margate) and in Wales (1897).

On the evening of 7 April 1835, Russell and a "competent" pianist named Thomas Haydon gave a "concert of vocal and instrumental music" at the modest Music Hall on Store Street. *The Literary Gazette* published a detailed review, written by someone who was obviously a Russell admirer. He declared the evening a triumph for Russell and his musicians, who, besides Haydon, included soprano Clara Novello (1818–1908), violinist Henry Blagrove (1811–72), and singers Handel Gear (1805–84) and Henry Horncastle (1801–69), supported by "a full band of some forty or fifty instruments." The reviewer of *The Literary Gazette* continued: "And we feel peculiar pleasure in this, having, from his *début*, anticipated but one result from Mr. Russell's talents, not only as a singer, but as an accomplished musician; and, as it appears on this occasion, an able composer and very successful teacher. His pupil, Miss Steele, sang charmingly with him the duet "Bella Imago" [from Rossini's *Semiramide*]; and, also, a song, "I love to dwell," composed for her by Mr. Russell, and encored by the audience."

The soprano Mary Sarah Steele (1818–81)—here making her first public appearance—would remain associated with Russell over many years. "The Lay of Hope" or "I Love to Dwell in the Bosom's Cell" had words by [Christian Frederick Weiles] Leigh Cliffe (1801–63), dramatist and author of *Tales of Legitimacy*; the publisher George Luff ran featured advertisements for it, through the next few weeks, in *The Morning Post*, and it was still in his lists in the 1840s. Luff was also responsible for the issue of another work that was a much more ambitious indication of Russell's pretensions in a different direction—as a teacher. Russell's memoirs state that the publication was dedicated to the future Queen Victoria when she "was a child of eleven years of age," i.e., in 1830 or 1831; but this is typical Russell nonsense. In fact, *L'Amico dei Cantanti*, subtitled "The Singers' Friend," bearing a dedication to "Her Royal Highness The Princess Victoria With the Most Profound Respect," likewise dates from 1835. Russell describes having sold the copyright to George Luff for £50 plus £20 for every 2,000 copies sold, and having received the permission of dedication in a letter from Sir John Conroy, Secretary to the Duchess of Kent.

This sixty-page work was credited to "Henry Russell, Pupil of Rossini," and was described as "A treatise, on the art of singing, containing . . . rules for the management of the voice . . . to which is added a variety of exercises on the solfeggio, from original manuscripts by Rossini, Reghini [*recte* Righini], Mozart Junr., Zingarelli, Meyerbeer, and other masters, etc." The publication includes an introduction, a section on "The Elements of Music," and then "Rules which every Singer must strictly attend to" [sic]. The flowery first paragraph of Russell's introduction indicates the basis of his approach:

> Singing is truly the soul of Harmony as the warbling of the feathered choir is the music of Nature. But, in the human race, the voice requires the aid of Science to bring its natural powers to perfection. The power and compass of the voice are like a hidden treasure; they must be sought for, and when found, cultivated with as great a care and attention as the most skilful botanist would bestow on the most rare and valuable flower.

More interesting from a biographical standpoint is the passage in which Russell sets out his qualifications for writing the manual:

> Far be it from me to arrogate to myself a superiority of knowledge over all my brethren in the Profession, but I conceive that a practice of seven years passed in studying without intermission, both in Italy and England, with the advantage of having been a pupil of Rossini for three years, and in the course of the four subsequent ones having benefitted by the lessons given me by Generali, Reghini [*recte* Righini], Mozart Jun., Maijoci [sic], Meyerbeer, Zirelli, Zingarelli, and others, I may be allowed to have had opportunities of forming a correct taste; and having studied the styles, and reflected on the abilities evinced by Pasta, Grisi, Rosa, Tamburini, Galli, Lablache, Rubini, Donzelli, and those of many pupils dilletanti [sic], I may, I trust, have the privilege of delivering my opinions, and giving my advice, which, if followed judiciously, I hope will enable the pupil to attain an eminence in the Vocal art; this cannot be attained without perseverance.

This, evidently, was the view of his life and work to date that Russell believed he could purvey, and it was evidently the basis of various subsequent statements on his training. Yet, however we look at it, there are problems, lots of problems. We have already questioned (to put it mildly) the veracity of the three years—or was it four months?—study with Rossini. As for the various masters from whom he supposedly benefited subsequently, they seem to comprise musicians with whom he may well have had passing contact, but scarcely more. Among the most readily identifiable are Pietro Generali (1782–1832), choirmaster in Novara Cathedral; Wolfgang Amadeus Mozart junior (1791–1844); the Luigi Majocchi whose opera *Rosamonda* had been produced in Milan in early 1831; Giacomo Meyerbeer (1791–1864); and Nicola Antonio Zingarelli (1752–1837) of Naples. "Zirelli" is a puzzle. Righini is presumably the Bolognese Vincenzo Righini . . . who died in 1812.

We shall return to the clutch of claims later. Meanwhile, in July 1835, the work—according to its compiler—received a favorable enough review in a publication that Russell, subsequently, identified as *The Harmonicon*. He must have been mistaken, though, since that publication ceased in 1833:

> Here are some honest, well put home truths told in this volume, of a nature to disappoint the vulgar taste of those who are everlastingly attempting when they do attempt to sing things far above their capacity, and not suitable to it. . . . The circulation of Mr. Russell's book will produce its fruit in due season. The didactic part of it is much too short. His observations are made with great judgment and show an acute mind and highly cultivated taste; but they are too limited in their details for the elucidation of all the proper points in a singer's education. The lessons also which follow are limited in their extent, though all of them are without exception excellent, but the author doubtless intends this as only laying a firm foundation, whereon the pupil may build his future structure. And the edifice, we have no hesitation in saying if Mr. Russell's precepts are obeyed, will not only be solid and substantial, but will bear the polish of judicious and appropriate ornament.

Others would have much less complimentary things to say, and this scissors-and-paste publication would almost cause the shipwreck of his career.

Other song publications during 1835 include "Dear Janet," which George Walker advertised in the *Morning Herald* in March 1835, and which sheet music editions associate with soprano Jane Shirreff (1811–83), another leading light at Covent Garden, and one advertisement with Eliza Vestris. Its lyricist, Frederick West, who seems to have been the Hon. Frederick [Richard] West MP (1776–1852), son of the Earl de la Warr and husband to the poetess Theresa Cornwallis West, dedicated it to William Mansfield King (1815–90), who was later to become Assistant Surveyor of the General Post Office. Yet another song from around this time, with the same lyricist, bore a dedication to Benjamin Lumley. This was the "bacchanalian song," "Pledge Me in Ruby Wine" (otherwise "Drink! Drink! Drink!"). The edition deposited in the British Library dates from 1858, but—from the style of the title page, as from its dedication to Lumley and the description as sung by Henry Phillips—it may have been originally an edition from the early 1830s.

Yet another song was to have a particular personal significance for Russell. The ballad "Believe Not the Tales They Have Told Thee of Me" bears a dedication to one Emma Lloyd. This was evidently not the Miss Lloyd "pupil of M Harris" (anyway, pre-named Catherine and soon

Mrs. Edward Lewis Johnson), who was educated at the Royal Academy of Music, and who sang at some good London concerts up to her 1835 marriage. Rather, it was the elder sister of the Isabella Lloyd whom Henry Russell would himself marry during 1835. The two girls were members of a Quaker banking family and the granddaughters of Charles Lloyd (1748–1828), founder of Lloyd's Bank.

Some sources have described Isabella as a daughter of banker Charles Lloyd's eldest son, the poet Charles Lloyd (1775–1839); however, press announcements of Isabella's death in 1887 described her as "daughter of the late Plumpstead [sic] Lloyd, Esq., Banker." Both the International Genealogical Index, and the certificate of Emma Lloyd's marriage, in November 1837, to Thomas Holmes Forrest (1803–75), son of a lime merchant of Blackfriars, City of London, confirm Plumstead as their father.

Plumstead Lloyd (1780–1836) was the fifth son of the banker Charles Lloyd, and a history of the Lloyd family describes him as "a colourful person." It continues that he "was apprenticed to a brewer at Ipswich and lived his life in brewing and related avocations, and from Ipswich in 1804 came his [first] wife, Fanny Bet[t]enson, not from a Quaker family. Cheerful, talkative and impetuous, Plumsted [sic], for a Lloyd, had bred quite different from the rest of his generation." Emma and Isabella were the second and third of Plumstead's daughters, both being somewhat older than Henry Russell, with Isabella being born—if official returns and death announcements are correct—sometime in later 1811. There were at least three other daughters—Frances Bet[t]enson, Mary Elizabeth, and Jane.

So, was Plumstead (by whichever spelling) Lloyd a banker, as in the first reference above, or a brewer as per the second? The matter is resolved firmly by *Times* coverage of an 1828 court case involving a debt incurred by maltsters and brewers named Cowell. It refers to testimony by "Mr. Plumpstead [sic] Lloyd, a malt factor." When he was adjudged bankrupt in 1813 he was "maltster, of Birmingham" and, again, in 1824 "malt factor. Blackfriars Road." On his son's baptism registration he is again "brewer," and spelled 'Plumsted."

So, it seems that Plumstead was involved rather less with his family's banking connections than with his brewing affairs. But poetry and literature also ran in the Lloyd family. In addition to Plumstead's brother Charles's poetic calling, sister Priscilla (1781–1815) "of Bingley Hall, Birmingham" married (in 1804) Christopher Wordsworth, brother of poet William Wordsworth, and fathered a Bishop of Lincoln. Charles Lamb was also a close friend of the Lloyd brothers—the two Charleses had published a joint book of blank verse in 1798—and, in 1801, he described Plumstead as "the benevolent, loud-talking, Shakespeare-loving brewer."

The marriage between Henry Russell and Isabella Lloyd took place, at St. Pancras Old Church, on 20 April 1835, thirteen days after Henry Russell's London concert with Thomas Haydon. Haydon and his wife, Caroline, were the witnesses. Since the couple's first child—a daughter named Isabella, after her mother—was apparently born in America later that same year (precise date and place unknown, but christened in Rochester, 30 October 1836), it seems that Henry Russell may have married because, according to the conventions of the time, he felt obliged to. It just may also—just "may"—have been the acquisition of a pregnant wife and the attendant financial pressures that finally persuaded him to try his luck in the Americas.

3

Toronto, Rochester, and New York

In his memoirs, Henry Russell recalls the prospect of his first voyage to America: "In casting about for some way in which to employ myself I listened favourably to the suggestion of a Mr. Darcy Bolton that I should visit Toronto. The prospect of a trip to Canada, and thence, perchance, to the United States, fascinated me, and I needed little persuasion. Mr. Bolton gave me a letter to Sir John Cockburn, the Governor of Upper Canada, which I kept for some time, as it was uncertain when I should leave." "A" Mr. Darcy Bolton Jr., Esq. (b. 1814) was Master in Chancery for Upper Canada. His father was a Puisne Judge and author of an 1805 book on Canada. James Cockburn, Canada's "Father of Federation," was not yet active at this time, and his father, who was a merchant, had died in 1832. John Colborne, 1st Baron Seaton (1776–1863), was Lieutenant Governor of Upper Canada from 1828.

Henry describes his ultimate crossing to Canada:

> I left for Canada in the good old ship, *Great Britain*. That respectable vessel could hardly be called an ocean greyhound; it took nine weeks to make the journey, which is now commonly accomplished in six days.
>
> When I landed at Montreal, my purse was by no means a heavy one, and if the truth must be confessed, I was not without trepidation as to my chances of replenishing it.
>
> Sir Peter McGill, with whom I quickly struck up an acquaintance wanted me to remain at Montreal, but I declined. Toronto was my destination, and thither I meant to go. And

> thither I went. The journey (performed in a public van, the only available vehicle), I do not care to dwell on; the mere recollection, even at this late date, is too painful.
>
> Arrived at Toronto, my first feeling was one of disappointment. In place of the stately city I had pictured in my mind's eye, I found a small township—a "one-horse town," your up-to-date Yankee would call it. I mentally assessed the population of the place at from seven to eight thousand, and I don't think I was far wrong. Young [*recte* Yonge] Street (now one of the handsomest thoroughfares to be found in the length and breadth of Canada) was then simply a rough forest road, with scarcely a house or living creature to be seen. However, this was Toronto, and the mere fact that I had arrived was pleasing, after a four days' jolt in a rough van. The people, I quickly found, were as primitive in their habits as their taste in architecture was crude.
>
> I wanted a hall in which to perform, but all they could give was a large room in the market place. This, though large for Toronto, was in reality such a small place for entertainment purposes that when I had with great difficulty placed my pianoforte in position there were [sic] scarcely any room left for the audience. However, I managed by eking out the space to accommodate just a hundred. They were very appreciative, I must say. The applause was most pronounced, and many of the folks stayed behind to compliment me in person. But fine words buttered no parsnips. The account of this, my first concert on the other side of the Atlantic, showed an adverse balance of eighteen dollars.
>
> Toronto was a glorious failure, the sooner I made my escape from it, the better for me; but anxious as I was to try new fields, I must acknowledge, with gratitude, the hospitality I received from some of the few good families who personally called on me at the "Ontario Hotel"—Mr. Robinson, who became the distinguished Chief Justice of Upper Canada, and Bishop Strachan, who was noted for his hospitality.

Scottish-born Peter McGill (1789–1860; he seems not to have been knighted) would be a member of the Legislative Council of Lower Canada and Mayor of Montreal from 1840 to 1842. Of those mentioned in

Toronto, John Beverley Robinson (1791–1863) was Chief Justice of Upper Canada from 1829 to 1862, and Bishop John Strachan (1778–1867) was the first Anglican Bishop of Toronto.

Russell also refers to a dinner invitation from the lawyer who became Judge William Henry Draper (1801–77) of the Supreme Court of Canada, and he describes a curious incident that arose when he sought to take up this "quiet family dinner" invitation:

> Now, in order to reach the house from my hotel, I had to cross several uncultivated fields, until I reached a long avenue surrounded by trees and underbrush. Near by a large cluster of trees stood a little shanty. Above the door was a signboard, and upon it were these words: "GINGER BEAR SOLD HEAR ALSO GOODE STUMBLING FOR ORSES AND GOODE BEDS." As I stopped to read it, I felt that the schoolmaster was abroad here. In due time I reached my friend's house, and a right merry evening we spent. When the time for departure arrived, I thanked my host for his hospitality, slipped into my sheepskin coat, and off I started. Hardly had I left the shelter of the house, when a violent, blinding snow-storm came on, and soon I was drifting about, not knowing which way to go. My footsteps were no sooner made, than all traces of them were obliterated by the heavily-falling snow. I wandered and wandered about, without the slightest hope of discovering my whereabouts, without a house or a light to guide me, nothing but a white sea of snow before, behind, and around me. Soon utter despair took possession of me. I did not know what to do, my feet were paralysed by the intense cold, and soon that worst enemy of snow-bound travellers began to assail me; an intense drowsiness began to steal over me. By extraordinary efforts I sought to shake it off; had I succumbed to it, the morning would have found me cold and stiff, frozen to death. Slowly I made my way on, on, the snow still falling thickly, and covering everything as with a mantle of pure white; there did not seem the slightest chance of the steady downfall abating, the unearthly stillness that surrounded me was horrible, awful—the very silence could be heard. In utter despair I walked to and fro, when, lifting up my eyes, with a prayer for deliverance on my lips, I beheld the signboard, "GINGER BEAR SOLD

> HEAR." I dragged myself up to the door of the little hut, and knocked as loud as my strength would allow me. The barking of a dog inside the house speedily awakened the inmates, who soon came and opened the door, and were completely staggered by my unexpected and melancholy appearance. A glass of brandy was given to me, my boots and socks were removed, and animation was speedily restored by rubbing my feet with handsful of snow. A wood fire was still burning, the little room was warm. To me, at least, it was Heaven. I explained to them how I had lost my way, and according to their time I had been at least six hours wandering about in the snow. So to "GINGER BEAR SOLD HEAR" I owe my life.
>
> To those who have never experienced a Canadian snow storm, it is hardly realisable. The snow in large flakes begins to fall gently and quietly at first, and then with ever-increasing power, the wind in its course, more powerful than a hurricane, levels trees, forcing in windows and doors, burying log cabins, crushing whatever happens to be in its way, leaping about like a huge mass of dense white vapour, till it starts with a bound, rushing headlong across miles of forest, and blinding every living creature in its path, roaring like thunder, tons of falling snow obliterating every track. Such, as far as language can describe, was a Canadian snowstorm of sixty years ago.

The Russell biography that was published in *The Musical Treasury*, in 1846, gives 1834 as the date for his departure for Canada, whence he migrated to the United States. However, this raises complications. Either the date is incorrect, or Russell returned to Britain before his concert and marriage in April 1835 and then crossed the Atlantic again. In support of the latter could be Russell's statement that the projected production of *The Bride's Band* in 1834 was scrapped when he left the country. However, that is scarcely enough evidence that it was at that time that he left to go to Canada. In fact, quite the opposite is indicated.

There is also a statement in Frederic Boase's *Modern English Biography* that Russell appeared in America in 1834 at the Olympic Theatre, New York (as the Savage in *The Savage and the Maiden*), and then on 17 October 1834 in *The Shipwreck of Medusa* at the Arch Street Theatre, Philadelphia. However, that is provoked by a total misunderstanding of information in Allston Brown's *History of the American Stage. The Savage and the Maiden* was not produced at Mitchell's Olympic Theatre until January 1840, being adapted from Dickens's *Nicholas Nickleby*, which was not written until 1838. Moreover, we know from other sources that the Russell associated with the Arch Street Theatre was a different person altogether.

The belief that Russell went to America only after his marriage in 1835 is encouraged by the statement in the 1837 *New-York Mirror* biographical notice that "he married the accomplished daughter of an opulent and distinguished merchant [sic], and soon after came to Canada" (see James F. Otis, "Henry Russell," *New-York Mirror and Ladies' Literary Gazette* [29 April 1837]). But what may be the strongest evidence of all seems to lie in the original entry of Burke's *Landed Gentry*. Its entry on Plumstead Lloyd, apparently compiled between daughter Isabella Russell's marriage in April 1835 and Plumstead Lloyd's sudden death on 13 February 1836, describes Isabella as having married "Henry Russell, Esq., of Toronto, Canada," seemingly linking the Russells' time in Toronto to the autumn of 1835.

Whichever winter it was that Russell was in Montreal and Toronto, his main problem was seemingly to have chosen the wrong time of year to be there. He goes on:

> Toronto, after this, seemed more uninteresting than ever. I did not stay long. A Mr. Norbury, whom I shall always remember as one of my best and earliest friends on the "other side," induced me to visit Rochester, in the State of New York. The difficult question was one of transit, and, in the end, I had to perform this journey also by cart. At Rochester I commenced my acquaintance with the American people—an acquaintance which warmed and ripened until, at this moment, I doubt whether I am not a little more than half American in thought and sentiment.

The 1846 biography of Russell in *The Musical Treasury* adds an important further slant to the decision to move to Rochester that is absent from the memoirs: "At Toronto, he was heard by some gentlemen of Rochester, N.Y., and by them urged to settle in their city. He accepted their invitation, and was appointed professor of music in an academy devoted to the cultivation of that science, in the year 1835." It seems to have been in October 1835 that the Rochester Academy of Sacred Music was first organized, and it was to that organization that Henry Russell was appointed as a teacher of piano and singing.

Rochester at that time was a rapidly growing town, and had been granted city status in 1834. It was supposedly the fastest growing community in the nation, exceeded in size by only three towns in upstate New York and three in New England. The first house in Rochester had been built only in 1814, the town growing up around the Genesee Falls, which supplied power for the riverside mills that manufactured flour for export. Completion of the Erie Canal, in 1825, linked the town with New York and Buffalo and thus with valuable trade. It was very much a young person's town, and relatively few of the arrivals in the town stayed long. Russell gave this account of his early days in Rochester:

> Rochester received me well. I made many friends—they are soon made in America—and before long I became quite well known throughout the city. But I was by no means amassing a fortune, and when the deacons of the Rochester Presbyterian Church offered me the post of organist and choir master, I thought fit to accept, though the pay (300 dollars a year) could not be called magnificent. With the aid of several good voices I succeeded in forming a really capital choir.

By the 1830s, Rochester boasted a First, Second and Third Presbyterian Church, and it was evidently the First Presbyterian Church to which Russell was appointed organist. An impressive stone building to the south of the Rochester courthouse, it was the oldest church in Rochester, dating from 1815. From his work at the First Presbyterian Church, Russell recalls one amusing occurrence:

> I always laugh when I think of an incident that occurred when I was organist at the Presbyterian Church. Among other items, as a voluntary, was the "Halleluiah Chorus," at that time comparatively unknown to the good folks of Rochester. I thought it would please them, certainly, I never dreamed for a moment that it would give offence. But it did. After the performance one of the elders came to me and accosted me thus:
>
> "You will excuse me, sir, we are all pleased with your smartness on the noble organ. Your playing 'Old Hundred' was grand, but that last piece of music of yours is too theatrical, and I guess you'd better not play it again."

> "You astonish me!" I exclaimed. "Why, Deacon, it is one of the finest choruses ever composed. The Handel and Haydn Society of Boston are always presenting it as one of their stock pieces."
>
> "The Handel and Haydn Society, did you say?"
>
> "Yes."
>
> "Wall [sic], I've heard of the house before, and I believe them to be a most respectable firm—so I calculate you may play it when you like."
>
> Thus encouraged, I introduced several of the exquisite works of Handel, Haydn, and other classic composers into my repertoire with the tacit sanction of my critical friend, the Elder. I have no doubt to this day that whenever he caught sight of a "Handel" or a "Haydn" on my concert programme, he thought of that most "respectable firm," the Handel and Haydn of Boston. Had I talked to him of the two great masters whose works I performed, he would have been more difficult to convince; but he firmly believed that "Handel and Haydn, of Boston," could do no wrong, and it was the easier course to leave it at that: in other words, to grin and bear it.

Another story of his days as organist in Rochester relates to the provision of song material for his future career as entertainer:

> One hot summer afternoon, when I was playing the organ at the Presbyterian Church, Rochester, I made a discovery. It was that sacred music played quickly makes the best kind of secular music. It was quite by accident, that playing the "Old Hundredth" very fast, I produced the air of "Get out o' de way, Ole Dan Tucker," this was the first of a good many minstrel songs that I composed or rather adapted, from hymn tunes played quickly. Among them are "Lucy Long," "Ober de Mountain," and "Buffalo Girls." I here give the sacred song contrasted with the secular:
>
> "Hark! the Vesper Hymn is Stealing" → "Lubly Rosa! Sambo come!"
>
> "My good ship! Come home! Come home!" → "Buffalo Girls! Come out to-night."
>
> The "Old Hundredth." (Christmas Carol in the days of Henry VIII) → "Going over the Mountain."

> Afterwards, when giving my entertainments about the country, I would occasionally illustrate this principle to my audiences by playing slowly and pathetically the "Vesper Hymn," and then repeat it, gradually quickening the time till it became a humorous plantation song, "Oh! Take your time, Miss Lucy," or "Coal Black Rose."

Here, it seems, we have Russell (or his grandson) up to his tricks again. As J. A. Stephens has rightly commented, Russell is here "[laying] claim to almost all the well-known minstrel songs of his day." Russell would certainly go on to introduce versions of minstrel songs to his British audiences and have them published in association with his name, but there is not a shred of evidence to support the notion that he was their creator. Stephens aptly dismisses the line about converting "The Old Hundredth" to "Old Dan Tucker" as "nothing more than a competitively glamorous whitewash."

Meanwhile, it seems that by early 1836 Russell had already given the concert that he described as "a brilliant success, indeed, my first real success in America." It was presumably the concert announced, as follows, for 7 January 1836:

> CONCERT.
>
> THE *Rochester Academy of Sacred Music* will give a Concert on *THURSDAY EVENING*, January 7th, at the First Presbyterian Church, consisting of Anthems, Choruses, Solos, Duetts, Trios, &c., under the direction of Mr. *H. RUSSELL.*
>
> Tickets may be had at Messrs. C. & M. Morse, Hoyt & Porter, William Alling & Co., L. B. Swan, and of M. Brown, jr, Treasurer of the Society.
>
> Doors open at half past six, to commence at seven precisely.

Russell was evidently also busy, in Rochester, on more ambitious, if ultimately less successful, creative work. This was the composition of an oratorio, *The Sceptic* (or, to the Americans, *The Skeptic*). News of it soon traveled beyond Rochester, even if not altogether to its (or Russell's) advantage. The July 1836 edition of the *Musical Magazine* of choirmaster and hymn writer Thomas Hastings (1784–1872) contains this high-handed comment on an impending performance, which may perhaps have been at a concert that Russell gave in aid of the Rochester Musical Academy on 14 June 1836. This *Musical Magazine* response would be far from the only example of prejudice that Russell would encounter over *The Sceptic*:

> A bill sent us shows that an orotorio [sic] "The Skeptic" is to be given in the First Presbyterian Church under the direction of Professor H Russel [sic]; it was composed expressly for the Academy by the Professor. Of the merits of the music we know nothing, the subject is sufficiently solemn if we may judge by the words. One of the solos of "The Skeptic" however, embraces more than forty long lines of poetry; yet the subjects of the choruses are very short, while the piece appears not to have a single recitative! Can such a production be properly called an Orotorio? . . . It is well for Academies to be modest and call things by their right names."

The *Boston Musical Gazette* suggested that the text of *The Sceptic* was "adapted from works by Dr. Young and Shelly." "Dr Young" would be Edward Young (1683–1765), poet, essayist, and divine, and author of *The Complaint: or Night Thoughts on Life, Death, and Immortality* (1747). The skepticism of poet Percy Bysshe Shelley (1792–1822), expressed in his writings, is said to have been one influence behind the poem *The Sceptic* (1820) by Felicia Hemans (1793–1835), and her recent death might be thought to have spurred Russell's interest in the subject.

However, Russell's most immediate inspiration was clearly a further poem, *The Sceptic,* written by the lyricist of Argyll Rooms days, the prolific Leigh Cliffe. This appeared in London in 1835 as a subscription publication from Simpkin and Marshall. "H Russell, Esq." and "Mrs. Russell" (!) were among the subscribers, as indeed were his sometime publisher George Luff and lyricist Frederick West, who subscribed for five copies and to whom the second canto was inscribed. Russell's oratorio does not seem to be a direct setting of Cliffe's words, except for the most frequently performed excerpt from *The Sceptic*, "The Sceptic's Dying Lament." Its first line, "'Twas one night, one bitter cold night" may perhaps derive from page 62 of Cliffe's published poem.

At this same time, Russell was taking steps that would lead to his becoming a popular public performer in America. The following is his memoirs' account—however truthful—of the background:

> About this time, Henry Clay, the great Kentucky orator, paid a visit to Rochester. I went to hear him speak at the Court House, the only place of public meeting, besides the church, Rochester could boast of in those days.
>
> Such oratory I had never heard before; nor have I met anything to equal it since. His voice had the peculiarly musical tone, at once sweet and sonorous, which proved so effective in the large assembly room in which we gathered to hear him. That speech of Henry Clay affected me to a singular extent. It may sound a strange statement, but I don't think I should be talking extravagantly, if I declare that the orator Clay was the direct cause of my taking to the composition of descriptive songs. Certainly, it was his speech on that memorable occasion in Rochester that first put the idea into my head. While reading in my room, at the "Eagle" Hotel that night, I asked myself: "Why, if Henry Clay could create such an impression by his distinct enunciation of every word, should it not be possible for me to make music the vehicle of grand thoughts and noble sentiments, to speak to the world through the power of song?" The idea gained upon me. I became more and more fascinated with the thought not only of trying my fortune as a vocalist but also of composing my own songs. With me at that time to devise was to act. I commenced there and then to set to music Mackay's beautiful poem, "Wind of the Winter Night, Whence Comest Thou?" All the night through I paced up and down my room arranging the music for the poem, and I remember that the notion uppermost in my mind was to infuse into my music, as it were, the subtle charm of the voice of Henry Clay. It was a quaint idea, but it took entire hold of my mind, and I hope my readers will not laugh at me for saying that I believe it inspired me. A few days later I had my musical rendering of Mackay's fine verses all ready, and I took the opportunity of playing it over to some friends. They applauded it, and their praise was emphatic enough to be sincere. This success decided me. From that day, song composing became the serious object of my life.

Typically, this 1895 account is an embellished version of the one supposedly contained in a letter that he wrote in the United States and provided for his brief 1846 biography. According to this, his acquaintance with Clay occurred when he was one evening a guest at a party graced by Clay's presence. The letter then goes on:

> The first tone of his voice attracted my attention, and I listened to him, whenever I could without an appearance of intrusiveness, until the breaking up of the party. His discourse was most eloquent music, and his voice sonorous, majestic, and full of melody. I went to my home, and retired to rest. It was a stormy night, in the winter time, and the sound of the keen north wind came to my ear mingled with the recollection of the rich tones of the great orator. I could not sleep—I could not rest; and recollecting that I had in my possession a beautiful poem, by my friend Charles Mackay, descriptive of such a warfare of the elements as was then raging, I arose and endeavoured to wed it to a melody which should be true to nature, and admit of that clearness and distinctness which had been suggested to me as so necessary to successful musical execution, by the conversation of Mr. Clay. Before the dawn of day, I had completed the music to "The Wind of the Winter Night," which was the basis of my American reputation.

Of all the events that determined Russell's future career, this was seemingly one of the most important. However, in verifying and dating it, alas, we run again across major contradictions. According to the chronology so far sort-of-established, Clay's visit to Rochester would probably have occurred as part of the 1836 presidential election campaign. Yet the indices of Rochester newspapers record no visit by Clay to the city during that year. In any case, Russell could not possibly have composed "Wind of the Winter Night" there in 1836, since, following the words' publication, in April 1833, in *The Welshman* newspaper, the song had already been advertised on editions of "Believe Not the Tales They Have Told Thee of Me" and "I Love to Dwell in the Bosom's Cell" (shelf marks H.1320.2 and H.1320.3), deposited by publisher Luff in May 1835. The latter edition had already been advertised in *The Morning Post* of 9 April 1835, eleven days before Russell's marriage. Prentiss of Boston advertised it as being by Rossini.

If he really did compose the number on a winter night in Rochester, it could only have been on a putative preliminary visit to America in the winter of 1834–35, before returning briefly to London for his marriage in

April 1835. As we have seen, the evidence is against such a trip, which would, moreover, have been before the Rochester Academy of Sacred Music came into being. Even if there had been such an earlier trip, how would Russell have had Mackay's verses so conveniently to hand in Rochester? Was the story of Clay, Rochester, and "Wind of the Winter Night" another complete fabrication? It seems so.

That the contradictions defy resolution is all the more regrettable in view of the significance of the work itself. Far from being a straightforward strophic ballad, it was the prototype of the dramatic *scenas* with which Russell was soon to be winning over audiences, comprising an instrumental introduction followed by recitative, arioso, and lyrical passages. The virtuoso piano introduction is itself reminiscent of a Beethoven piano sonata, after which tremolo chords represent the winter night's wind, leading in turn to contrasted calm and tempestuous passages and finally a morendo ending. Though Russell's memoirs misled J. A. Stephens into dubbing the work as "his first musical composition," his description of it as "the most complex among all of Russell's published works," with a "totally uncharacteristic" sequence of harmonies and, in the introduction, "contrapuntal writing, which is simply not to be found in later [or earlier] works" is completely apt. One feels that only some sort of Pauline conversion induced by determination to translate Henry Clay's oratory into song in order to capture the minds of the American people could indeed have inspired such a work. If it did.

Living in Rochester, with his wife and infant daughter (named Isabella, after her mother), Henry Russell had evidently entered fully into local affairs and ingratiated himself with the townspeople. He would go on doing so for some months more, but his reputation, very soon, began to spread well beyond the city, aided, no doubt, by his Rochester concert in June 1836 and by private performances there and elsewhere. Wider recognition was furthered upon the publication of some of his songs by Firth & Hall of New York City. These received notably favorable mention in the weekly *New-York Mirror*, founded in 1823 and edited by journalist and poet George Pope Morris (1802–64), widely known as "Colonel" Morris.

In its issue of 1 October 1836, *The New-York Mirror* welcomed "three pretty songs," all with words by Charles Mackay and music by Russell. The first was the sacred melody "Resignation" from the *Scripture Melodies*, and the second "Wind of the Winter Night," whose American edition bears a dedication to the Rochester Sacred Music Academy and the legend "sung with much applause by Mr. Brough." This was the bass William F. Brough

(1798–1867), one of the many British singers who found the pickings in America richer than in Britain, and who had crossed the Atlantic in 1833, in support of tenor Joseph Wood (1801–90) and his celebrated wife, née Mary Anne Paton.

The New-York Mirror liked "Some Love to Roam" "better than either" of the other songs. Its words, declared the journal, "are in a fine, jocund, buoyant, and exulting strain," and the paper printed them as evidence of approval. As for the composer, it described him as "the musical preceptor of the Princess Victoria," providing a fine example of manufactured truth becoming exaggerated. He was now, it went on, "very successful as a teacher of musick in Rochester." The edition carried a dedication to Mrs. Gardiner of Rochester, aka Mary Selkrig Gardiner (1806–69), wife of Judge Addison Gardiner. This homage to Rochester would be evidenced further when, in 1837, James L. Hewitt published Russell's arrangement of Edward Loder's "The Brave Old Oak" (words by Henry F. Chorley) with a dedication to Dr. [Alexander] Kelsey of Rochester, New York (1810–67).

Russell's first public appearance in New York City seems to have taken place on Thursday, 6 October 1836. The occasion was an oratorio concert of the New York Sacred Musick Society for the opening of the "new and powerful Organ, recently built by Mr. Henry Erbern of this city, for the Society." The proceeds were designated to go toward the cost of the organ, and Henry Russell was just one of the artists who gathered together for the occasion. At the head of the list was the very consequent Mrs. Gibbs (late Miss Graddon) "from Drury Lane Theatre and Italian Opera Concerts, London, making her first appearance in New York." Margaret Graddon had been prima donna at the Surrey Theatre in Henry's juvenile days. Then there was one John Jones, making "his first appearance at the Oratorios, since his return from Europe" (he had "returned" on 5 September), together with slide trumpeter John Thompson Norton, "professor from the Royal Academy, London." The Sacred Musick Society itself contributed a "Band . . . of the first Professors and the Chorus numerous and complete; the whole consisting of upwards of one hundred and fifty performers." One of the organists on the occasion was William A. King, brother to Henry's early teacher, at whose Argyll Rooms concert Henry Russell had sung, in London, over three years previously, and who was now successfully established in America.

It was not stated what Russell's contributions to the concert were; but it is clear that he was a great success. The concert as a whole was sufficient of a triumph for a repeat to be organized for the following

Tuesday, 11 October. Mrs. Gibbs was no longer available, whereas "Mr. Russell, who was received with such approbation at the last oratorio, has been induced to defer his departure." Mrs. Gibbs's replacement was Miss Horton: "positively, for the last time in publick, previous to her departure for the South." This was mezzo soprano and singing teacher Mary Anne Horton (1811–87), who on 17 March 1838 would marry the composer, singer, and actor Charles Edward Horn (1786–1849). She was the elder sister of the memorable contralto and actress Priscilla Horton (1818–95), also sometime a juvenile of the Surrey, who later married composer and entertainer Thomas German Reed (1817–88).

The New-York Mirror printed an enthusiastic review of both concerts, and specifically the latter. Of Russell it commented that

> the greatest possible excitement has prevailed in the musical world respecting him, since his first appearance . . . at these concerts, owing, probably, to the very unusual circumstance of such brilliant talents, and so much vocal excellence, being so unexpectedly and *so unostentatiously* introduced. For our own part, we feel no hesitation in saying that, for chasteness of style, purity of intonation, and brilliancy of execution, he stands unrivalled in this country. We witnessed abundance of tears trickling down the fair cheeks of the ladies during his beautiful and impressive song of the Sceptick. . . .

A later description of this piece in the same publication perhaps gives the best indication of the dramatic—perhaps, one should say "melodramatic"—presentation with which Russell, thus, first took New York City by storm:

> It commences with a description, in very simple language, of the death-bed scene of a father, surrounded by his weeping children. His end is peaceful and happy, and such as to give sure hope of ever-during bliss beyond the grave. This hope diffuses a placid resignation among the silent group around his pillow, and all breathes of happiness and heaven. A deep sigh is heard from the recesses of the apartment as the last breath quivers upon the lip of the dying man. This sigh is raised from the over-burdened spirit of a *stranger*, who proceeds to explain the nature of that mysterious impulse, which

> habitually urges him to seek such scenes as that now passing before him. He describes his early destitution of parental teachings—his doubts—his attempts to disbelieve in the existence of a God—his stiflings of conscience amid the indurating influences of worldly excitement—and his fears, amid his doubts! Thus agitated by contending emotions, he sleeps, and lo! a vision of terrour [sic] rises before his troubled mind! An awful form presents itself—an indescribable, incomprehensible form—the first glance of whose terrible eye renders him sightless—though he yet feels its searching, withering power. He hears the shrill, piercing, deafening blast of a trumpet, as if blown by an archangel, having power to pervade all space, and then a voice, proclaiming judgment. He doubts no longer. All is awful reality; and now, all is fear—deep, despairing, trembling, overshadowing fear! He shrieks and calls for mercy: it is too late. Shrinking from the terrible anger of the Judge, of whose promised coming he had been skeptical, he sinks prostrate, and then—he goes to meet the doom of the doubter.
>
> Throughout the whole of this song, there is a perfect adaptation of sound to sense. The words are simple; no flights of poetical expression are attempted. The musick is left to tell the whole story; and from the commencement to the close, the audience, though a thronging multitude, are, as it were, entranced by the spell with which the subject enthrals them. They, too, hear the trumpet: they also feel the intense gaze of the shadowed Judge of the universe. They start at the announcement, in the deep-resounding bass of the singer, of the Judgment day. They sympathize with the fear so forcibly depicted by the troubled skeptick. They look in upon the deep, dark despair of that ineffable torture into which he sinks at the close.

Russell's other engagements in New York in October 1836 included the Benefit of Italian double-bassist Cesare Casolani (1807–52) at the Concert Hall, 406 Broadway, on 15 October and, more significantly, a further concert at the City Hotel on Monday, 31 October. The promoter was old friend W. A. King, and the guest performers, this time, included his faded brother Charles M. King. The enthusiasm exhibited for Russell on this latter occasion is indicated by a review in the *New Era* newspaper that ends:

> All deficiencies, however, were redeemed when Mr. Russell made his appearance, and when he began, we were fully conscious that true music was melody and sweetness, and not difficulty, and bawling and noise. Unassuming, quiet, and chaste, the audience were so delighted with his execution, that his songs were encored, till Mr. King stepped forward, and stated that Mr. Russell was too fatigued to repeat them. The glorious song of the "Old English Gentleman" was strikingly effective, and we saw tears rolling down several cheeks, that did not appear much used to such visitants.

> To this the *Albany Evening Journal* added:

> When Mr. RUSSELL finished his last song, the whole audience rose spontaneously and left the Room, leaving half of the Songs in the 2d part of the entertainment to be sung on some future occasion, if ever! This, though truly mortifying to the persons whose Songs were left unsung, was the highest compliment that could be paid to the superiority of Mr. RUSSELL.

> What, one wonders, does a performer have to do to achieve notices such as these? One can certainly sense the astonishment that Russell, as much as his audiences, must have felt as—after years of struggle in London and elsewhere—his very personal style of performance of his own compositions met with such resounding acclaim.

If it is from this New York visit that Henry Russell's significant success in the US can be dated, it is clear that it was not due simply to public performances. That private performances were at least as influential is clear from a long and glowing feature in the November 1836 issue of the New York monthly publication *The Knickerbocker*. It provides the clearest indication of the impression that the young Henry Russell made on the American people:

> MUSIC—MR. RUSSELL.—Perhaps there is no one thing, at the present day, in which there is more affectation and humbug, than what is termed "music," by common courtesy. Oratorio and opera-goers will sit for hours listening to, and pretending to admire, *strains*, to execute which requires so much exertion,

that if the hearers were as honest as Dr. JOHNSON, they would wish were not only "difficult" but "impossible"; for all the while their hearts are not touched with a single emotion, such as genuine melody is capable of producing. Foreign music-masters and professors, with their shakes, trills, and whiskers—"difficult passages" and moustaches—diamond rings, self conceit, and quavers,—have succeeded in imposing upon the Atlantic cities a "fashionable taste," in relation to music, which the good citizens have received with due deference to the opinions of crowned heads and petty dignitaries, before whom the operators—as they say—have sung, and by whom they have been applauded. Now and then, however, we have a gratifying evidence that this taste has a very loose hold upon the regards, and none upon the affections, of our people. One touch of nature—one exhibition of the simple melodies, by a competent master, who knows what he professes, and professes no more than he knows, takes the public ear captive—and the heart, its trammels of fashion thrown off, really feels without prompting, and enjoys without dictation.

These thoughts have been suggested by hearing Mr. RUSSELL, of Rochester, who recently made a casual visit to this city, execute a few of his favorite airs at an oratorio, and in private society, before a select circle of friends. This young gentleman has eschewed all attempts of taking the public by storm, on his first arrival in this country. Although his musical education has been of the best description, and his powers are of the very first order of excellence, he makes no special parade of either. He takes up his abode in a flourishing and public-spirited western town, and by natural superiority, unaided by "flourish," he soon stands at the very head of his profession. Such is the career, in this country, of one whose equal as a melodist we have never seen in America. His voice is round, full, and rich—capable of high elevation and deep depression, without losing either its sweetness or its softness. His execution is chaste, simple, and faultless, beyond the reach of the disciples of the "difficult" school. We thought we saw, in the countenances which glowed with emotion as the notes of "The Old English Gentleman," "Wind of the Winter Night," etc,—both composed by Mr. RUSSELL—fell on delighted

> ears, sufficient proof that it needs only a proper direction to the public taste, to place it above and beyond the influence of the elaborate Italian school, which has already begun to decline abroad.
>
> We cannot hope to convey to the reader an idea of the descriptive power which characterizes Mr. Russell's execution of the closing stanzas of the following spirited and beautiful song, which now appears for the first time in print. So distinct was the singer's enunciation, and so perfectly adapted his voice and manner to the event which he was portraying, that we remarked an involuntary shudder—a general "holding of the breath for a time"—in the hushed listeners around him. The shipwreck was before the eyes of every hearer; the grating keel—the crash of the fallen mast—the flapping of the storm-rent sail—all, were present. . . .

There followed the complete five-verse lyric of "Wind of the Winter Night, Whence Comest Thou?" and also that of "A Fine Old Englishman." The latter was, of course, not an original Russell composition. It allegedly included a chunk of Cimarosa, and had been (allegedly) arranged by one named Dewar to words by Murray, and popularized by Farren and Phillips. In other words, it had been around and much "arranged." Russell had re-rearranged it for his own purposes, and had, in fact, sung at his London concert in June 1834. The words, too, were "adapted, arranged and partly written," and attributed to Charles H[enry] Purday (1799–1885) of the music-publishing family, by that gentleman. The "adaptation to a well-known air" by Dewar was aired in court, and the melody's greater antiquity was confirmed, as Henry Phillips relates, in two court cases at the Court of King's Bench, Westminster, which were reported in the *Times* in June 1834. Along with his other adaptation, "The Brave Old Oak," it would be a staple constituent of Russell's concerts for some years.

Already, "A Fine Old English Gentleman" had created sufficient interest in America for the *New York Mirror* to publish both words and music in its issue of 12 November. It appeared with a further eulogy: "We wish all the subscribers of the *Mirror* could hear Russell sing it, as, by universal acknowledgement of all who have had that gratification, he is unrivalled for purity, strength, and sweetness of tone, and exercises quite a thrilling effect upon the feelings of his audience." The following week, the same publication went on to publish the ballad "We Have Been

Figure 3.1. "A Fine Old English Gentleman" sheet music cover. *Source:* Author's collection.

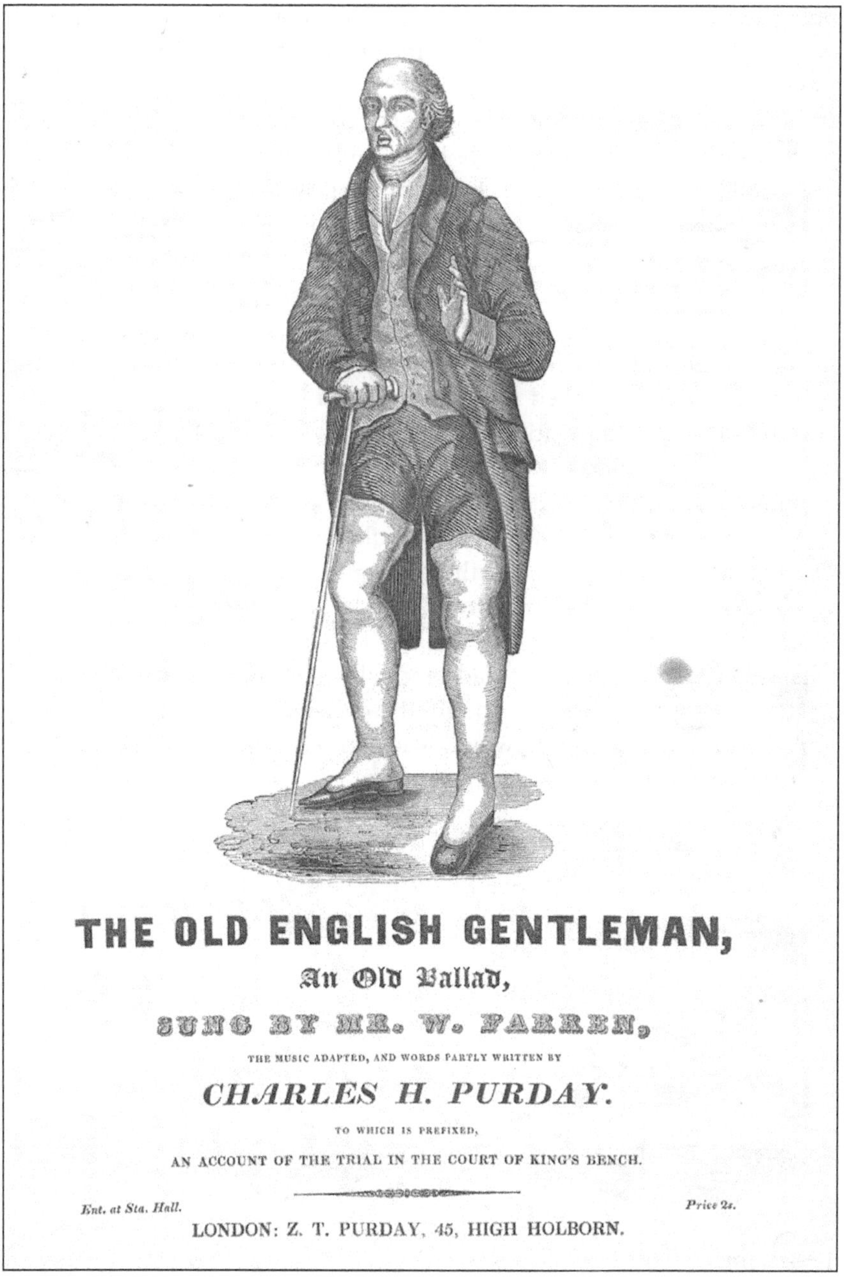

Friends Together," "written expressly for *The New-York Mirror*." A setting of a poem by Mrs. Caroline Norton (1808–77), which had been first published in London in 1830, it is a ballad more ambitious than many of his later efforts, with shifts, from major to minor, to indicate the jump from childhood to the present.

Russell himself wrote of his New York debut that "My Rochester friends gave me a warm welcome home, and I remember how it gratified me to find that my New York fame, so to speak, had reached them." We cannot doubt that it increased the demand for his services in Rochester. In November 1836, for instance, the *Rochester Gem & Ladies' Amulet* published Russell's arrangement of a song "Sleeping Maggie," stating, "The melody of this old Scotch ballad was presented to Mr. Russell by a gentleman of this city, and we are assured by those who are acquainted with it, that it stands unrivalled for simplicity and beauty among the choicest ancient ballads of that nation."

Three days later, a Rochester press advertisement announced "that in compliance with the wishes of numerous gentlemen interested in the cultivation of the voice, Mr. Russell will instruct a class of gentlemen in singing, commencing from the solfeggio, during the coming winter." Applications from gentlemen were solicited for lessons of an hour and a half each, two evenings a week, at a fee of $6 per quarter. However, whatever Russell's intentions had originally been for a continuing career in Rochester, they were very soon to be overtaken by a rapidly widening acclaim and ambitions that would lead him elsewhere.

4

Albany, Philadelphia, and Boston

"While I stayed at Rochester, several lucrative offers came to me from New York, Brooklyn, and Boston," Russell recalled. Immediately after New York, though, came Albany and Philadelphia, of which the former was especially welcoming. Even before the second of the New York oratorio concerts, in early October 1836, the *Albany Evening Journal* had announced Russell's debut in the capital of New York State: "Mr. H Russell, Professor of Music, of Rochester, has been prevailed upon by his friends here, to give a Concert in this City on his return from New York, being recently engaged in the Oratorio given by the New York S M Society, where his performance was received with enthusiastic approbation."

Relaying Russell's account of his very first visit to Albany, an interviewer many years later wrote:

> . . . strolling on the steamboat wharf (long before the days of the Hudson River Railroad) he saw a raw but aristocratic young Englishman, cumbered with a portmanteau, and greatly enjoyed the joke when the Britisher evidently took him for a professional porter. The stranger went to the hotel at which Russell was staying, and at the door handed him half a dollar, which was accepted and pocketed. At dinner that night Russell sat opposite the stranger and another Englishman, and heard one remark to the other, "Aw! Beastly democratic country, where the fellow who carries your bag from the pier sits opposite to you at dinner."

Russell soon became closely associated with Albany, and Albany in turn was happy to consider him one of its own. His first concert there was on the evening of 20 October 1836 in the Chapel of the Young Ladies' Academy. The advertised program is worth quoting in full as typical of the concerts with which he first enraptured the American public at large:

PART I.

Overture to *Semiramide*—Piano Forte, Rossini.

Song—Some love to roam, Russell.

Song—Wind of the winter night, whence comest thou? Russell.

Song—The brave old oak, arranged by H. Russell.

The sceptic's lament, from Mr. Russell's Oratorio of the Sceptic—'Twas one night, one bitter cold night

PART II.

Marseilles Hymn, with variations.

Song—The old English gentleman.

Song—Stand to your guns, Crouch [sic].

Song—Come brothers arouse, from Mr. Russell's Opera of the *Bride's Band*.

Largo Factotum [sic], Italian song, Rossini.

Some other pieces may be expected.

It will be seen that the concert was designed to exhibit Russell's skills as both pianist and singer, as well as to highlight his putative attachment to Rossini and his ambitions as a composer of not just songs but also opera and oratorio. His original compositions were restricted to "Some

Love to Roam," "Wind of the Winter Night, Whence Comest Thou?," the number from the oratorio *The Sceptic*, and one from the opera *The Bride's Band*. This last set new words to his 1832 success "The Bandits' Song" ("Let Others Rejoice in the Merry Moonlight"). One may wonder particularly what his performance of the Marseillaise with variations sounded like. At all events, it's clear that, whatever allowances one makes for the dearth of culture in American cities at that time, his reception in Albany was as remarkable as in New York City. "More than four hundred of our most refined and discriminating citizens were in attendance," reported the *Albany Evening Journal*. "On no similar occasion has there ever been such a general turn-out. Mr. RUSSELL fully realized the high expectations which had been excited."

A return concert in Albany was arranged for 4 November 1836. This time, instead of Rossini's overture to *Semiramide*, Russell introduced that to his own opera *The Bride's Band*, and instead of the *Marseillaise* variations an unspecified "Air with variations." Of the replacement songs, "Where [*recte* When] the tempests fly" (in place of Rossini's "Largo al factotum") was one of Russell's that had been published in England. "My Heart's in the Highlands," with its fine uplifting melody, was not an original Russell composition but another arrangement. Its words were by Robert Burns, and the composer was the great Covent Garden baritone Henry Phillips. The song had been published as being by Phillips in London, in 1835, and was announced as such at Russell's Albany concert. However, the credit for Phillips as composer would disappear from Russell's concert bills over time, and when the piece was published in New York and Boston in 1837 the only musical credit was "The Symphonies, Accompaniments, & Part of the Melody, Composed by Henry Russell." Had Russell perhaps arranged it from memory, with his own instrumental introduction and accompaniment?

The *Albany Evening Journal* demonstrated renewed enthusiasm: "The remarkable peculiarity of Mr. Russell's singing is its extreme simplicity. It is simple, even to plainness, yet graceful above all our previous conceptions of gracefulness, and ornamental in the highest degree by its own peculiar attribute of simplicity." It seems that Russell was achieving just the sort of popular impact that he had set out to, using Henry Clay as his model. In the *Albany Evening Journal*, there was talk of the city hearing the whole of his oratorio, *The Sceptic*, during the winter; but this seems not to have happened. Perhaps Russell was too busy with his commitments in Rochester, or with the invitations that came in from other cities, such as Boston and Buffalo. For the residents of this last city, his first concert in January 1837 "only served to sharpen their appetite for a second," and "the room, on both occasions, was overflowing." Henry gave the Buffalonians the whole hog: three pieces of *The Bride's Band*, the Sceptic's "Dying Lament," "My Heart's in the Highlands" (Phillips), "The Brave Old Oak" (Loder), "Stand to your guns" (Carter), "Blow High, Blow Low" (Dibdin), "When the Tempests Fly," "Wind of the Winter Night," "The Old English Gentlemen," "Some Love to Roam," plus "Largo al factotum" and . . . a chunk of *La Muette de Portici.* Local British music teacher W. R. Coppock (1805–63) and his pupils topped up the program.

Meanwhile, three weeks after his first New York appearance, and a week after that in Albany, Russell made his Philadelphia debut at the Musical Fund Society's Hall on Thursday, 27 October 1836. The concert featured his fellow artists from his New York début: J. T. Norton (the concert promoter), Mrs. Gibbs (late Graddon), and John Jones. At Niblo's Pleasure Garden, New York, on 22 August 1834, British-born, Royal Academy of Music–trained slide trumpeter John Thompson Norton had been involved in a celebrated contest with well-known Italian valve trumpeter Alessandro Gambati. Of the latter, we shall hear much more later. For the present, it is relevant that Norton included, at this October 1836 Philadelphia concert, the pieces that he had played on that occasion at Niblo's. In the first half of the concert, Russell ("a vocalist who will appear on the occasion before a Philadelphia audience for the first time") gave "Some Love to Roam" and "Wind of the Winter Night." He then joined Margaret Gibbs and fellow soloists Miss Pool (a pupil of Norton) and John Jones (who sang Sidney Nelson's "The Hunter of Tyrol") in John Braham's quartet "Mild as the Moonbeams" from the opera *Artaxerxes.* In the second part Russell gave "The Sceptic's Lament" and "Stand to Your Guns." This last was another patchwork, with words allegedly by Dibdin, and on this occasion music credited to Henry Bishop although normally to Carter, Crouch, and, eventually . . . yes, to Russell.

It sounds to have been a grand concert program and, as elsewhere, Russell's contribution was received—for better or worse—as recognizably out of the ordinary:

> Mr. Russell, the bass singer, made quite a sensation. All his songs were warmly encored. His voice, though weak in the higher notes and of no remarkable compass, is of an admirable quality, and he uses it in a way to give the fullest effect to his peculiar style. We do not, however, particularly relish his

> compositions. They are monotonous beyond mere mannerism, and have a good deal more show than substance. At first, they may "take," but they must soon become wearisome. "The wind of the winter's night," and "The sceptic's dream" have more than a family resemblance; they are twins so much alike that it is difficult to tell them apart. The words, by the way, of the latter, are in very bad taste. . . .

On Tuesday, 8 November, Russell was back in the same hall in Philadelphia—again with Norton and Mrs. Gibbs—for the first concert of the third season of the Philharmonic Society.

With reference to Russell's activities in Albany, it's worth reiterating that he was not the only performing Russell around at the time. Already, in its issue of 25 November 1836, the *Albany Evening Journal* had pointed out that a second gentleman of the same name was appearing in the city. Then, in February 1837, when advertising thrice-weekly concerts by a Mr. Russell at the Albany Museum, the paper reiterated that "there are two Vocalists in this city of the name of RUSSELL. One of these gentlemen, a Professor of Sacred Music, is connected with the Female Academy, in

Figure 4.1a. Portrait of Henry Russell, c. 1836. *Source:* Author's collection.

Figure 4.1b. “Wind of the Winter Night” sheet music cover. *Source:* Author’s collection.

the Chapel of which, we are happy to learn, he is to give a CONCERT to-morrow evening. The other Mr. RUSSELL is connected with the Theatre, and has given Concerts, occasionally, at the Museum." As if there were not confusion enough, press announcements the following month listed Henry Russell among the managers of the Fireman's Ball. However, the idea that—like a later musician, Arthur Fiedler—Henry Russell was combining music with an interest in fire engines should be resisted. In June, the press announced that fireman Henry Russell had been transferred from Hook and Ladder Co. No. 2 to Engine Co. No. 1. Clearly this was yet another Henry Russell!

All this time, our Mr. Russell was strengthening his links with Albany. In an announcement in the *Albany Evening Journal* on 23 February 1837, Elihu Russell—seemingly another unrelated Russell, and Chairman of the Trustees of the Female Academy—announced that Henry Russell had been appointed Professor of Music of the Academy. Through this appointment, Elihu Russell declared, Henry Russell would "infuse the spirit of minstrelsy into our Church Choirs." He announced that a meeting of the Board of Managers of the Albany Sacred Music Fund Society, on 22 February, had decided that a Sacred Music Academy should be established in the city, under the care and instruction of Henry Russell. The Board expressed "its high gratification at the prospect of Mr. Russell being established as a resident of this city." An appeal was made for all persons wishing to become members of the Sacred Music Academy to meet Henry Russell in the Chapel of the Female Academy on the evening of 27 February.

Albany's enterprise in securing Russell's services was sufficient to attract envy in New York: "There is to be a MUSICAL INSTITUTION at Albany. The Albanians are before us in their love of sweet sound. We are half inclined to be envious of our neighbours, and heartily ashamed of our city for its neglect of a science which every man and woman ought to love. . . . Mr. HENRY RUSSELL, the distinguished composer and vocalist, will make Albany his home, and take charge of the Institution." From this time on, for a while, Albany rather than Rochester was to be his base.

Among the musical numbers to which he introduced the Albanians at a concert on 28 February was a descriptive poem "The Wreck of the Mexico." This commemorated a disaster on 2 January 1837, when the *Mexico*, "a substantial eastern-built vessel of 280 tons" carrying Irish immigrants to America ("the unfortunate passengers were of a very superior class"), ran aground on Hempstead Beach, Long Island, with the loss of 108 lives. Minute details of the ice-bound wreck were printed in the press in the following days, and in its February 1837 issue, *The Knickerbocker* published a poem on the subject, taken up by other journals, possibly the same one as printed in *Republican Herald* of 28 January, and it may have been this that Russell set. The "poetry" was, however, credited to one H. Harrington "of Boston," who would seem to have been H. Hannington, the promotor, with his brother, of a number of Brooklyn concerts with a goodly Russell content, around this time, and the sometime owner of a "Bird Museum" and a "Dancing Automata" show in Charleston. Hannington had a moving diorama of the wreck on show at Broadway's City Saloon "next door to the American Museum" before the month was out. Russell included the song in his programs for some time; it was a precursor of other topical descriptive pieces that would feature effectively on his programs. ("For descriptive music nothing that we ever heard was equal to 'Wind of the Winter Night' and the 'Wreck of the Mexico'—*Alexandria Gazette*). Since these were less readily suited to drawing room performance, they were always slower to reach publication than his strophic compositions. *The New-York Mirror* perhaps provided an explanation of why this one, seemingly, did not make the transition at all: ". . . though containing much that is beautiful and powerful, [it] compares with the other sea piece, 'The Winter Wind' [i.e., 'Wind of the Winter Night']," so feebly, as to merit, in our eyes, no other award [than as a failure]. The subject, indeed, is too vast, and its actual occurrence took place so near us, and its incidents are so real to our apprehensions, that we cannot but own how far short of the terrible reality is the artist's description." On Thursday, 9 March, Russell made his first appearance in Boston, at the Masonic Temple. Among other things he accompanied local German music teacher William Isenbeck in some flute variations. Because of a storm, the house was not full, but those who turned up were typically impressed. The *Boston Galaxy* declared that "he actually chilled our blood in 'Wind of the Winter Night,'" and that his "Largo al factotum" "was the best ever heard in the city." The newspaper appended the view of a correspondent that "He has none of the fol rol lol of music which is so much in vogue, but appears to rely upon giving expression to sentiment, by nice discrimination, tasteful judgment, and a powerful and rich toned voice."

Of this widening field of activity, Russell recalled:

> At Boston, the "hub of the Universe," as they are fond of calling it, I met with great encouragement. From this time onwards, I became a confirmed wanderer. Montreal, Toronto, Louistown

> [Louisville?] I visited successfully, then made my way back to Rochester, through the State of New York, stopping at such towns as Geneva, Syracuse, and the little village of Rome. I was much amused, by the way, while at Rome, N Y, to find a bootmaker's shop appropriately kept by a Mr. Romulus. . . .
>
> In these smaller towns, I found a great love for the old English songs. The inhabitants were kind and hospitable, and their goodness to me—a stranger within their gates—will always linger in my memory as exemplifying one of the best characteristics of the American people. Every acquaintance I made welcomed me to his home, and made me just as comfortable as if I were a member of his own family. That is the American way.

Russell's progress was noted with pride back in Rochester: "Russell, the distinguished vocalist, everywhere meets with enthusiastic applause—in Boston, New York, Albany, &c. as formerly in Rochester. Not only are his conceptions exquisite," says a city paper, "but his singing affects you as a work of the soul and mind quite as much as of the voice. He can never sing in public without doing a great service to good taste and the higher branches of musical art." "It would be difficult to speak of his powers in terms of too high praise," exclaims another journal:

> and if there is any one who has felt the pressure of the times; any one wearied with disappointment, or severe study, or laborious occupation; let him listen to Mr. Russell, and one of those thrilling old ballads will put him in good humor with himself and all around him. As Mr. Russell's musical career in America commenced among us in Rochester, the citizens and the Society by whom his talents were first appreciated will doubtless be generally highly gratified at his extraordinary success in the prominent cities of the Atlantic.

In April 1837, Russell's travels took him back to New York City, where, even in his absence, his fame had continued to expand. This was most particularly through the advocacy of *The New-York Mirror*, to whose editor, George Pope Morris, Russell had dedicated the published edition of "Come, Brothers, Arouse" from *The Bride's Band*. In its issue of 7 January 1837, *The New-York Mirror* published the words of Morris's "The Oak,"

Figure 4.2a. “Woodman, Spare That Tree!,” sheet music cover, New York publication, 1837. *Source:* Courtesy of the Lester Levy Sheet Music Collection, The Sheridan Libraries, Johns Hopkins University.

Figure 4.2b. "Woodman, Spare That Tree!," sheet music cover, London edition, 1841. *Source:* Author's collection.

Figure 4.2c. "Woodman, Spare That Tree!," sheet music cover, London edition. *Source:* Author's collection.

with music already credited to Henry Russell. Within days, publications all around the land had picked up the combination that would become celebrated as the ballad "Woodman, Spare That Tree!," the epitome of the sentimental songs with which Russell would attract the ordinary citizen.

In his memoirs Russell gave his version of the song's origins:

> It happened one day that I was driving, in the vicinity of New York, with George Morris, the American poet. We turned into Bloomfield Road, then a woodland lane of great beauty, to view at Morris's request, a stately old tree, which had been planted by the poet's grandfather. I well remember the ring of genuine pathos in Morris's voice as he told me, on our way towards the tree, of the tender recollections associated with the old homestead to which it was contiguous. His happy boyhood in the old home, surrounded by father, mother, and sisters, all came back to him at the mention of that old tree. Little did we dream of the drama that was to follow.
>
> As we neared the homely cottage which had once housed the Morris family, my friend noticed an old man with his coat off, sharpening an axe.
>
> "What are you going to do?" asked the poet, with a tremor of apprehension in his tone. "You surely do not intend to cut down that tree?"
>
> "Yes, sirree," was the blunt reply of the old man, who was evidently the occupant of one of the cottages.
>
> Morris and I descended from our trap to hold a parley with the old fellow. In conversation it transpired that the old man did not fancy having the tree so near his house. Besides, he wanted it for firewood. We asked him how much the wood would be worth, and he replied, "About ten dollars." So, a bargain was speedily made; the money was paid to him, and the daughter of the woodman pledged her word that the tree should stand as long as she lived.
>
> Now this incident made a deep impression upon me, and I suggested it to Morris as a fine subject for poetic treatment. He took the hint and wrote the well-known poem, "Oh, Woodman Spare that Tree"—

"Oh, woodman, spare that tree,
Touch not a single bough!
In youth it sheltered me,
And I'll protect it now."
which I immediately set to music.

Well, that was the story that, fifty-eight years later, Russell was happy to go out to his British readers, and in due course to posterity. Note particularly the claim that "I suggested it to Morris as a fine subject for poetic treatment." This serves merely to underline the "unreliability" of Russell's memoirs. Early editions of the song include a quite different account of the origins, which Russell himself clearly authorized. It took the form of a letter from Morris, which Russell apparently read out to his

Figure 4.3. George P. Morris (Ballou's Pictorial Drawing-Room Companion, 1855). *Source:* Author's collection.

audiences as a preface to his performance. Its authenticity is confirmed by the fact that Morris, too, published it with his collected poetry. It clearly shows that, far from having suggested the subject to Morris based on a personal experience, neither Russell nor Morris's grandfather was in any way involved with the origin of the verses.

Here is Morris's preface, followed by the letter:

> This ballad was written for Mr. Henry Russell, to whose exquisite musick it is indebted for all its popularity. The following letter enclosed the verses, and was intended exclusively for private perusal; but as it has seemed good to the composer, to read it several times before crowded assemblies, and to publish it in the newspapers, and as there is certainly no great harm in it, perhaps the reader will not object to its insertion here. (George P. Morris, *The Deserted Bride; and Other Poems* [New York, 1838], 76–78)
>
> New York Mirror Office, 1 February 1837.
>
> My Dear Sir,
>
> You did me the honor to request some lines of mine for music; and at the moment, being delighted with your fine voice and exquisite taste in singing, I said I would write you a song. Now I think with our friend Knowles, that a promise given, when it can be kept, admits not of release, "save by consent or forfeiture of those who hold it," and so I have been as good as my word, as you will perceive by the enclosure of "The Oak." I hope it will answer your purpose. Let me tell you how I came to choose an old tree for my subject. Riding out of town a few days since, in company with a friend, who was once the expectant heir of the largest estate in America, but over whose worldly prospects a blight has recently come, he invited me to turn down a little romantic woodland pass not far from Bloomingdale. "Your object?" inquired I. "Merely to look once more at an old tree planted by my grandfather, near a cottage that was once my father's." "The place is yours then" said I. "No, my poor mother sold it"; and I observed a slight quiver of the lip, at the recollection of that circumstance.

"Dear mother!" resumed my companion, "we passed many happy, happy days, in that old cottage; but it is nothing to me now—father, mother, sisters, cottage—all, all gone;" and a paleness overspread his fine countenance, and a moisture came to his eyes as he spoke. But after a moment's pause, he said: "Don't think me foolish. I don't know how it is, I never ride out but I turn down this lane to look at that old tree. I have a thousand recollections about it, and I always greet it as a familiar and well-remembered friend. In the by-gone summer-time it was a friend indeed. I often listened to the good counsels of my parents there, and I have had such gambols with my sisters! Its leaves are all off now, so you won't see it to half its advantage, for it is a glorious old fellow in summer; but I like it full as well in very winter time." These words were scarcely uttered, when my companion cried out, "There it is!" and he sprang from his saddle and ran toward it. I soon overtook him, wondering at his haste; but what met my sight, made it no wonder. Near the tree stood an old man, with his coat off, sharpening an axe. He was the occupant of the cottage. "What are you going to do with that axe?" "What's that to you?" was the reply. "A little matter, but not much—you're not going to cut that tree down, surely?" Yes, but I am though," said the Woodman. "What for?" inquired my companion, almost choked with emotion. "What for? Why, because I think proper to do so. What for? I like that! Well, I'll tell you what for; this tree makes my dwelling unhealthy; it stands too near the house; prevents the moisture from exhaling, and renders us liable to fever-and-ague." "Who told you that?" "Why, Dr Smith." "Have you any other reason for wishing to cut it down?" "Yes, I am getting old, the woods are a great way off, and this tree is of some value to me to burn." He was soon convinced, however, that the story about the fever-and-ague was a mere fiction, for there never had been a case of that disease in its neighbourhood; and then was asked what the tree was worth for firewood. "Why, when it is down about ten dollars." "Suppose I should give you that sum, would you let it stand?" "Yes." "You're sure of that?" "Positive." "Then draw me a bond to that effect." I drew it up, it was witnessed by his daughter, the money was

> paid, and we left the place, with an assurance from the young girl, who looked as smiling and beautiful as a Hebe, that the tree should stand as long as she lived. We returned to the turnpike, and pursued our ride. These circumstances made a strong impression upon my mind, and furnished me with the materials for the song I send you. I hope you will like it, and pardon me for this long and hurried letter.
>
> With sentiments of respect, I remain yours very cordially,
>
> Henry Russell, Esq. Geo P Morris.

Morris was elsewhere quoted (or burlesqued) in much longer versions of the epistle (*Morning Herald*, 20 October 1837), but the $10 remained the same, and papers such as the *Schenectady Reflector* and *The Herald of the Times* imaginatively extended versions of the birth of Morris's poem. Russell didn't come into them.

The lyric or poem was, in any case, not exactly original. It owed very largely to Thomas Campbell's popular "The Beech Tree's Petition" of 1800:

> O leave this barren spot to me!
> Spare, woodman, spare the beechen tree

According to an anecdote that Russell later told, in England, the sentiment behind the song was not to the taste of everyone in America:

> Mr. Russell sang it to a party in the backwoods of the west country; and when he came to the line, "Oh, let that old oak stand," one of the company said to him, "Stranger, are you a friend to the government of the United States?" "I calculate that I am," said Russell—"why do you ask?" "Because no friend to the government of the United States ought to sing that song. We have been for years trying to clear away the trees; but if you go about singing that song, why they'll none be cleared away at all."

It was, though, with this song that Henry Russell consolidated his reputation in America, as he stated in his memoirs:

> "Oh, Woodman, Spare that Tree" caught on with startling rapidity. No matter where I sang, for weeks after its publication I was never permitted to conclude my entertainment without Morris's affecting lines. The story of the song's origin somehow leaked out and this tended to heighten the interest therein. A very dear friend of mine, now well-known as a public man, and a bit of a poet, has often told me that he dates the birth of his sentimental nature to the fact that an old nurse used to sing "Woodman, Spare that Tree" at his bedside, and that scores of times he cried himself to sleep over the simple song.

Russell may, almost sixty years later, have let pass the statement that "the story of the song's origins somehow leaked out," but, as we have seen, it did so through Russell quoting it as a preface to his performance. This was not to everyone's taste, and one might wonder whether reservations by George P[ope] Morris himself lay behind this admonishment from the New York monthly *The Knickerbocker*:

> [We] would counsel our friend, as he journeys eastward, to omit the perusal of the long letter, before singing the pretty song of "Woodman, Spare that Tree!" by our contemporary, Col[onel] MORRIS. We but speak the sentiments of a large majority present at the concert, when we say, that the perusal referred to is in exceeding bad taste, and altogether unnecessary, since the lines need no explanation. Any person can understand them, who understands any thing; and a long preface to that old and noble song, "The Brave Old Oak," which has quite the same general features, would be equally appropriate.

The song's appeal, though, was enormous—most particularly, of course, for the sentiment of its verses. Yet the music plays its part. Charles Hamm has commented, on the sleeve of a modern recording of Russell songs, that its instrumental prelude "could almost serve as an introduction to a cavatina or aria in an opera of *Norma* vintage," and the gently rippling piano accompaniment heightens the appeal. Allied to that is a simple melody, described by Johannes Riedel, in an essay on *Henry Russell's American Experience*, as "Rossini-inspired," which touches the listener's heart. Composer John Hill Hewitt (1801–90) selected the song to illustrate the nature of Russell's appeal over his audiences:

> Russell's voice was a baritone of limited register; the few notes he possessed he turned to advantage. . . . In person he was rather stout, but not tall. His face was quite prepossessing, of the Hebrew cast, dark and heavy whiskers and curly hair. He was an expert at wheedling audiences out of applause, and adding to the effect of his songs by a brilliant pianoforte accompaniment. With such self-laudation he used often to describe the wonderful influence of his descriptive songs over audiences. On one occasion he related an incident connected with "Woodman, Spare that Tree." He had finished the last verse of the beautiful words, written by his highly esteemed friend Gen[eral] George P. Morris. The audience were spell-bound for a moment, and then poured out a volume of applause that shook the building to its foundation. In the midst of this tremendous evidence of their boundless gratification, a snowy-haired gentleman, with great anxiety depicted in his venerable features, arose and demanded silence. He asked, with a tremulous voice: "Mr. Russell, in the name of Heaven, tell me, was the tree spared?" "It was, sir," replied the vocalist. "Thank God! thank God! I breathe again!" and then he sat down, perfectly overcome by his emotions. This miserable bombast did not always prove a clap-trap; in many instances it drew hisses.

According to the original Firth & Hall sheet music, it was Mrs. Bailey (née Charlotte Watson), rather than Russell himself, who introduced "Woodman, Spare That Tree." It is difficult to believe, though, that Russell didn't sing it during his time in New York City, even if it is not listed in surviving published programs, at the sort of entertainments in which he was still just part of the evening's attractions. There was a pair of concerts at City Hall—on 12 April, at least, Russell sang "Woodman"—a Grand Musical Soirée given by the flautist J. L. Downe at the City Hotel on 17 April, where his fellow performers included W. A. King, Boston soprano Mrs. Franklin, and Scottish-born singer-composer William Richardson Dempster (c. 1808–71), later to be famous as the composer of the "Lament of the Irish Emigrant" (1843). Mrs. Franklin and Dempster appeared at the Brooklyn Institute (20 April) and the City Hotel (24 April), where the lady gave "Come, Maidens, Come" and the gentleman "Some love to roam" (tickets: 50 cents each). On 20 April, meanwhile, Russell and King were also among the featured musicians at a sacred music concert in the Chatham Street Hall of the Sacred Music Society. Then, on 24 and 25 April, Russell gave two concerts of his own at the Brooklyn Lyceum, with Mrs. Franklin again among the supporting artists at the second. The lady sang "Come, maidens," Henry gave "Wind of the Winter Night," "The Wreck of the Mexico," "Come, brothers, arouse," his one-man version of "Ecco mi a voi," "The Fine Old English Gentleman," and . . . "Woodman, spare that tree."

Thomas Hastings, who the previous year had commented so loftily on *The Sceptic* in his *Musical Magazine*, could not avoid a hint of sarcasm: "The impression lately made on our citizens by Mr. Russel [sic], as a vocalist, was of a favourable kind. We regret that we had not the happiness of hearing him. His manner is stated as having been remarkable at once for chaste simplicity and vivid expression,—things not often combined."

This last was clearly a dig at *The New-York Mirror*, whose support continued unabated. In its issue of 4 February, it had already reprinted the introduction to Russell's singing tutor *L'Amico dei Cantanti*, and on 15 April it likewise printed "A Little Cock Sparrow Sat Up in a Tree," "an original comic glee—composed by Henry Russell for the "Rochester Gem." More particularly, on 29 April it printed a detailed biographical and analytical note on Russell that has already here been much quoted. Then, on 20 May 1837, it published a further new Russell song, "I Love the Night," with words by Morris.

Meanwhile, Russell had been back in Philadelphia, performing on 11 May at the Masonic Hall, Chestnut Street. Then, to mark Independence Day, he gave a concert at his usual Albany venue of the Chapel of the Female Academy, assisted by a thirteen-year-old young lady flautist. Besides a scene from *The Sceptic*, his own contributions were noteworthy for two items new to Albany. One was "Woodman, Spare That Tree," the second, a descriptive song, "Washington's Tomb," the words written "specially for him" by the Hartford, Connecticut, poetess Mrs. Lydia Howard Sigourney (1791–1865). Russell dedicated the composition to the Whig politician Daniel Webster (1782–1852), champion of American nationalism.

Following that Independence Day concert, the *Albany Evening Journal* reported, "Russell's intention is to give a concert at Troy, previous to his departure for Utica, Rochester, and the far west." In those days, the far west was Detroit, Cincinnati, and St. Louis. The same paper reported him, later in July, in Syracuse, and in August in Cleveland, Ohio. On 28 August there was a farewell concert in Rochester "previous to his departure for Boston." By early September, however, he was back in Albany, where a concert at the Female Academy on 8 September was "previous to his departure, on a long Professional tour." Clearly Russell was finding himself in demand, to the extent that the Trustees of the Albany Female Academy announced that "a wider field having opened to Mr. R., the Trustees felt bound to release him" from his post of professor. By way of recompense for the expense "incurred in preparing and furnishing the Musical Department of the Academy," Russell agreed to give his services free at a further Albany concert.

Announced for 11 September, this concert was postponed because of unfavorable weather until the following evening, when it was held in the hall of the Albany Academy "in consequence of severe illness in the vicinity of the Female Academy." Russell was assisted by flautist John Underner and by violinist J. C. Andrews from neighboring Troy. New to Russell's Albany audiences at these two concerts was his version of William Reeve's "I Am a Friar of Orders Grey," another traditional British song that, remade, would prove a staple constituent of his concerts.

The fact that Russell gave his services free at the second concert did not prevent the *Albany Evening Journal* from launching a somewhat pompous protest at the comic songs that Russell customarily served up as encores:

> Mr. R, in our judgment, is acquiring one injurious habit. His comic songs are in bad taste. He destroys the effect and mars the beauty of his great phrases, by descending from the touching sweetness of "*The Old English Gentleman*," the rich, rolling melody of "*The Brave Old Oak*," the thrilling interest of the "*Wind of the Winter Night*," and above all, the sublimity of the "*Sceptic's Lament*," down to the light, vapid, senseless nothings which he too frequently introduces. These idle comic songs are unworthy of Mr. R.'s voice and powers. And besides, we can hear them better sung at the Theatres, the Circus and the Museum. . . . *His* admirers are from the intellectual classes, and cannot be interested with trifles and frivolity. They want the gold without the dross.

Then, as now, a musical performer's ability to speak to the public at large—the very attribute for which Russell was aiming—was dismissed by the soi-disant culturally superior!

From Albany, Russell once more traveled, in September 1837, down the Hudson River to New York. On 19 September he gave a concert at the City Hotel, supported by vocalists Charlotte Watson (later Mrs. Bailey),

Miss Lewis (her first appearance), William F. Brough, and the recently arrived English tenor Mr. William Edwin, once primo tenore of the London Haymarket and Surrey Theatres; Edwin had portrayed Tom Tug, Osbaldistone, and Count Belino at William Dinneford's Bowery Theatre in January, Don Giovanni et al. at the Franklin in February, and sung with Russell at the New York Sacred Music Society on the previous 20 April. Valve trumpeter Alessandro Gambati was also on the bill. Then, on 21 September, at a benefit performance for Edwin, Russell was at Niblo's Garden, the popular entertainment centre at 537 Broadway. The other, theatrical Mr. Russell had performed there as recently as 16 September. Now, for his Niblo's debut, sacred music's Mr. Henry Russell announced just four items—"Come, Brothers, Arouse" from his opera *The Bride's Band*, "Wind of the Winter Night," "The Old English Gentleman," and "The Brave Old Oak."

Russell would appear at Niblo's many times more, and it was a venue he particularly enjoyed. Writing in 1895, he had this to say:

> Niblo's Gardens were then situated some miles out of the city, and were the favourite evening resort for the good people of New York, much the same as the Vauxhall Gardens were to the citizens of London in the earlier days of the century. The spot where Niblo's stood is now, of course, built over, and is a thickly populated neighbourhood. The gardens are nothing more than a memory. My efforts at Niblo's were immediately crowned with signal success. My songs were of the kind that reached the hearts of my audiences, my melodies were taking, and the poems to which they were wedded were of a high order, filled with a manly, sterling sentiment which interested and excited the sympathy of the people.

Still in New York, Russell gave a concert at the City Hotel on 26 September with William F[rancis] Brough, and on 28 September he appeared there again at a concert given by trumpeter Gambati. Russell was just one among a long list of participants, the major attraction of the occasion being the American debut of Josefa Ruiz-Garcia. She was an older half-sister of Maria Malibran, the celebrated mezzo-soprano whose death in Manchester the previous year at the age of twenty-eight, from a riding accident while pregnant, had shocked the musical world.

Russell had also crossed the water to the Lyceum in Brooklyn, on 22 September, when an incident occurred that had wide press coverage at the time, and which he also recalled in his autobiography:

> I was singing "The Gambler's Wife," and just at the most effective passage of this dramatic song, there flew in, through the open window of the hall, a large white bird, which, circling round and round, descended upon my head as I concluded the last verse of the song. The audience cheered and applauded uproariously. One lady, after the performance, asked me quite seriously whether the bird was a part and parcel of the entertainment. The papers made much of the incident, and chaffed me unmercifully about the bird. The *New York Herald*, then edited by my friend the late James Gordon Bennett, said: It reminded them of the old proverb about "Birds of a feather," for the large white bird was a gull.

Something of the sort did probably occur, though Russell's memoirs again distort the details. It seems that the beautiful white pigeon merely alighted on the edge of the gallery immediately above the vocalist, rather than actually on his head. More particularly, he did not introduce "The Gambler's Wife" into his repertory until 1841. Further, the supposed reference in the *New York Herald* has proved elusive, and, as we shall soon see, the venal James Gordon Bennett (1795–1872) does not exactly seem to have been a friend of Russell at this particular time.

From New York, Russell went on to Boston, giving concerts at the Masonic Temple on 13, 21, and 27 October. As everywhere else, the response surpassed expectations. *The Boston Morning Post* reported after the second concert that "A large number of tickets, sold for his last Concert, are still out, the purchasers being deprived of admission by the crowded state of the hall. These will be 'good as new' for the next." It seems to have been at this third concert that Russell first introduced, in "The Ivy Green," another of what were to remain his most popular songs. Extolling the delights of the ivy creeper, the song was a setting of a poem from *The Pickwick Papers*. Published in London only the previous year, as the work of "Boz," the nom de plume of Charles Dickens (1812–70), the work was currently being serialized with great success in American newspapers.

Meanwhile, back in Albany, on 22 October, Russell's wife, Isabella, gave birth to their first son, whose name of Henry Lloyd Russell marked both sides of his parentage. Russell's next concert in Albany was for the benefit of local music teacher and music seller Isaac P. Cole, who had done much to assist Russell's initial acceptance in the city. Given in Albany's Second Presbyterian Church, on Thanksgiving evening, 30 November, it was a concert of sacred music, its first half including music from Haydn's *The Creation* and *Judah*, Rossini's *Moses in Egypt*, and Handel's *Messiah*. Then, in the second half, the audience finally heard substantial extracts from Russell's much vaunted oratorio *The Sceptic*, from which no more substantial piece than "The Sceptic's Dying Lament" had hitherto been aired. The items now announced included several choruses, a solo, and an organ selection. Russell himself sang the solo, and the *Albany Evening Journal* pronounced it "a rich banquet."

5

Charlatan, Plagiarist, Pirate, Quack

"My first experiences of New York were not altogether pleasant," recalled Russell:

> My advent evoked great jealousy among other musicians there, and after a time, I was made the victim of an organised opposition. Each concert-giver who wanted to engage me to assist him in his programme was boycotted by all the other artists to whom he looked for support. Thus, by sheer force of circumstances, I was driven to give entertainments on my own account. "'Tis an ill-wind that blows nobody any good"; and the ill-wind of professional jealousy blew me the best of fortune.

Signs of Russell being forced to give solo entertainments are not immediately obvious. Rather, one gets the impression that he had sufficient allies to continue New York appearances jointly with the many performers—particularly of British origin—who were doing the rounds of American cities and joining in ad hoc performing alliances whenever their paths crossed. If he was soon developing predominantly solo concerts outside the major cities, it was simply because such crossing of paths was less common, and because it was more profitable.

Yet the success he had so readily gained in New York, as well as resentment among other performers at the lavish praise his appearances received in the press, must inevitably have invoked jealousy in some quarters. The New York monthly *The Knickerbocker* had become increasingly over-effusive, ever since its original notice in November 1836. Following Russell's visit to New York "and several eastern towns" in April 1837, the journal offered a self-congratulatory notice reasserting "that this distinguished vocalist deserves the full measure of praise which was awarded him in these pages, previous to his first public appearance before a New-York audience." Its editors asserted that "People thronged to hear Mr. Russell sing, not because he had studied under the best English masters, and had been an accomplished pupil of Rossini; nor yet because he had received, as a meed of professional excellence, a golden medal from the King of Naples." The reason, the notice declared, was that:

> Mr. Russell's style, though chaste and refined, is powerful, yet mellow, in all its tones, as the soft notes of an organ; and it has always a strong rich effect. His enunciation is as distinct as if he were only speaking; and his *musical expression*, if we may use the term, is wholly unsurpassed by that of any vocalist we have ever heard. He depicts scenes with the palpable truth of a painter; and he so clothes his subjects with life, that we are not quite sure that he would not "sing the ten commandments, and give an appropriate character to each prohibition."

The paper praised Russell's performances of "Wind of the Winter's Night," "The Old English Gentleman," "Come, Brothers, Arouse," as well as Loder's "The Brave Old Oak." Nowhere, though, was there any indication that this last song was anything but Russell's own composition. Moreover, it was rather rubbing salt in that potential wound to comment that "The music of most of his songs is either entirely his own, or made essentially so, by adaptation and improvement." The piece ended with an entreaty: "May he [. . .] in the Albany Musical Academy, of which he is the capable President, train up in the way they should go a long band of pupils who will do honor to his instructions, and effect a happy reform in the fashionable 'systems' of the day."

Russell's further visit to New York, in September 1837, brought from *The Knickerbocker* another burst of enthusiasm. Beginning with a reference to "his soul-stirring music," it went on: "His late concert at the City Hotel was crowded with the élite of the city; and he gave many of his old, and one or two new productions, with surpassing effect. Indeed, his superior has never been among us." If the editors then modified their rapture with the exhortation that Russell should omit reading the letter from George P. Morris before singing "Woodman, Spare That Tree," jealousy and resentment can only have been stoked by the following summary treatment of his fellow artists at his concert on 19 September:

"We must not omit saying a word for Mr. Brough, Mr. Edwin, and Mrs. Watson. They sang with their accustomed skill and feeling; and a Miss Lewis acquitted herself with great credit."

What seemingly brought such jealousy and resentment out into the open was a further long encomium that appeared in the same journal the very next month, November 1837—this time accompanied by an engraved portrait of Russell: "Would that every reader upon whom the portrait of Russell, in the present number, may smile, could hear the 'voice of melody' roll from those lips which has gone to the hearts of so many in our Atlantic cities!" the editorial began. "Simplicity, tenderness, strength, and mellowness, are the agents by which Mr. Russell produces his effects; and the result is always the same," it continued. The editors then virtually invited reaction by declaring:

> His style, so simple yet so effective, which "catches a grace beyond the reach of art," is lightly regarded, we believe, by certain of those who consider themselves as "great *shakes*" in the musical world, simply because they can shake, and trill, and quaver, in that "difficult" manner which it was *once* so much the mode to admire, but which, thanks to Russell, and one or two other distinguished melodists, has had its little day. These demurring professors may find some countenance in their attempts to foist upon the public an unnatural taste for a species of music wholly unsuited to the genius of our people, but it will proceed from such as care more for the music of fashion than of the heart, and who have travelled abroad to import new ideas of the art, with not a little conceit, arrogance, and foppery. But the crowds who attend the concerts of Mr. Russell, carry away with them "remembered harmonies" which will not die, nor fade with the changes of time. Success to simple melody! Success to that music which can awaken human sympathies, and enliven and enlarge the affections!

There followed a paragraph of biography. Beginning with the statement that Russell had "but recently completed his twenty-fourth year," it continued with the usual information that he had been "for three years a pupil of Rossini." Later came the claim that he had "studied under Generale [sic], Mayerbeer [sic], and other masters, and received a gold medal from the hand of royalty, for the best composition at the conservatorio at Naples." Just to rub things in, the editors stuck out their chests in declaring: "It is a source of personal gratification to the editors of this Magazine, that they were the first, in this community and that of Philadelphia, to call public attention to the rare musical endowments of one who was himself too modest and retiring to present his claims to general patronage and regard, beyond the precincts of the public-spirited town where he had been generously taken by the hand, and his gifts properly appreciated."

"Modest" and "retiring" are perhaps not the first adjectives that come to mind in describing Russell. Altogether, as red rags to bulls go, this one was bright scarlet. A response came in a long letter, over the signature "Honestus," that was addressed to the editors of not only *The Knickerbocker*, but also the Philadelphia daily newspaper *The National Gazette and Literary Register*. The latter published it, complete, in its issue of 17 November 1837 under the heading "The New York Knickerbocker and the Science of Musical Composition." After some introductory words, referring to the editor of *The Knickerbocker* being "led astray by his good nature and his ignorance of music," "Honestus" wades straight in:

> I assert that if Mr. Russell . . . was, as it says, "a pupil of Rossini for three years," and "studied under Generali, Meyerbeer, and other masters," then those composers teach a style of practical and scientific music which their works and fame belie. And I assert, too, that if the same individual . . . "received a gold medal from the hand of royalty for the best composition at the Conservatorio at Naples," then the professors of that venerable and renowned institution have so degenerated as to be ignorant of the primary rules of the science of composition which they profess to teach.

He goes on to comment on the extravagant name-dropping on the title page of Russell's *L'Amico dei Cantante*, recently published in the United States:

> Now in this finery and flourish of the title-page, there is no mention of one Rodolph, now dead and gone, though five-sixths of the work are taken note for note, from Rodolph's work on Singing, without the shadow of an acknowledgement. But the plagiarist and ignoramus generally go together. He who filches ideas can mutilate them too. So with Mr. Russell the laureate of the Naples school. He has made a number of abortive attempts to supply trebles to Rodolph's basses, and vice versa, and a precious botching it is. . . .

This "Rodolph" was, one must assume, Jean-Joseph Rodolphe (1730–1812), an Alsatian horn player, violinist, and composer, who wrote a *Solfège ou Nouvelle méthode de musique* (1784, revised 1790).

Warming to his theme, "Honestus" goes on to comment on specific songs associated with Russell:

> The editor may also analyze note for note the song of "Woodman spare that tree," and tell how many mistakes there are on the first page. There is also a song "Some love to roam," with another name than the real author's to it; this will be found pretty correct. There is, too, "The brave old Oak," transposed without acknowledgement from Loder's arrangement in D, except where it is altered much for the worst. There is, too, an abortive attempt to make an accompaniment to the "Fine old English Gentleman."

"Honestus" continues, "The editor of the *Philadelphia Gazette* has set the seal of just condemnation on such pieces as the 'Sceptic's Lament,' from the oratorio (*?*) of the Sceptic." This was substantiated when, the following day, the *Philadelphia Gazette* entered the fray, stating that "the piece, with few exceptions, . . . meets our approbation." It continued that "We confess that until lately we have never heard of Mr. RUSSELL, *as a composer*." On "The Sceptic's Lament," however, it confirmed that "we have ever deemed it a precious bundle of discord, and bad poetry. The wailings of the agitated sceptic when the weather was 'awfully terrific and he shook with awe,' were always, to us, the concentration of unpleasant sounds. The scope of both words and music, is like the filing of a saw." It added that the charges of "Honestus" "should be either admitted or disproved."

This encouraged "Honestus" to expand upon his theme, and *The National Gazette* dutifully (and perhaps gleefully) published the resultant second missive on 21 November. Now "Honestus" declared:

> As for Mr. Russell himself, I heard him once, and agree precisely with the *Gazette*. The piece was mainly, as I remember, an exhibition of a chromatic scale; the idea taken partly from the incantation scene in *Der Freischutz* [sic], and also from the method of tuning on a piano forte, to which operation it bore a striking or precise resemblance; and by the aid of a grating sound "like the filing of a saw," as the *Gazette* very appropriately describes it, he completed the "electrifying effect."

"Honestus" sought to correct the comment of the *Philadelphia Gazette* editor on never having heard of Russell until recently *as composer* by declaring:

> On the contrary, Mr. Editor, the heaven-born merits of Mr. Russell have been based chiefly on his genius in composition; they have been trumped through the land, and oft embalmed in the Knickerbocker. He, himself, lays signal stress on his powers in that way, and being destitute of all musical science and originality, and having an utter and truly *British* contempt for the acumen of the American public, he appropriates other people's brains and toils to himself by the wholesale—tinkers up old English ditties with accompaniments, filched from London arrangements, and with the ruthless hand of blundering ignorance attempts to alter the originals.

For the benefit of his readers, "Honestus" went on to quote verbatim the original *Knickerbocker* eulogy to which he had taken exception. He then offered this jibe: "Mr. Russell, rightly appreciating his humble powers, settled in Rochester, but discovering there, as he thought, that the Americans could not distinguish between a Hand-organist and a Handel, he determined to try their gullibility." As with his original letter, "Honestus" sent this follow-up not only to *The National Gazette* but also to *The Knickerbocker*, which however received it only after having typeset a response to the original. Clearly embarrassed, its editors restricted themselves largely to summarizing the claims of "Honestus," seeking to duck responsibility by denying that they had written the biographical paragraph. Rather, they pointed out (as if reproduction without acknowledgment of source was a virtue), that it was "quoted from an article in the " 'New-York Mirror,' far more laudatory and elaborate than the one which embodied it, as an extract. The *onus*, therefore, in so far as these statements and the remarks which they elicited are concerned, rests not with this Magazine." They pointed out, moreover, "that there are *two sides* to this matter, and that Mr. Russell is extant, to reply for himself to these anonymous accusations."

Russell had meanwhile been seeking to do just that, and on 29 November *The National Gazette* printed his response (written from Albany on 25 November) to the first "Honestus" piece. With respect to "Some Love to Roam," he declared that, "If I am not the author of the music of this song—who is?" As regards *L'Amico dei Cantanti*, he evidently felt that vindication lay in citing the authority for dedication and details of the work's acquisition by publisher George Luff, together with a reproduction of an 1835 review that he attributed to the *Harmonicon* (which, however, had ceased publication in 1833). As for the rebuttal of the claims for his musical education, he declared:

> To the first charge I reply—without an "if"—that for three years I was a pupil of Rossini, that I afterwards studied under the above-named professors, and I demand of him that he disprove these assertions. To the second, I reply that the Gold Medal which I received from the hand of Royalty at the Conservatorio of Naples, is now in my possession, and that I am at all times ready to show it to any *gentleman* who may desire to verify the truth of my assertion. . . . Whatever fame I earn I shall try to gain by an honest ascent, not by dragging down others who may have risen to a higher eminence.

After receiving the second volley of "Honestus," Russell sent off a second response: "In regard to the manner in which my own songs, or arrangements of other songs, are got up by their publishers, I may be allowed to say, that I give myself no trouble, the style of the title page they arrange as may best suit themselves; it is for the facts contained on them, and for these only, that I hold myself responsible." In then seeking to demonstrate his credentials as a composer, he regretted "that, at present, I have not access to the *Musical World*, but the kindness of a friend, has supplied me with a series of numbers of the *Court Journal*." In fact, *The Musical World*, established only in 1836, seems not to have mentioned Russell up to that point. As for *The Court Journal*, the first of the two references he quoted was no more than the publisher's advertisement for "On the Brave Who Have Fallen," which contained a complimentary quotation attributed to *The Morning Herald*. The second, more importantly, was that from June 1834, already quoted, announcing rehearsals of *The Bride's Band*. Russell declared: "From the above extract it appears that I am known in London as the composer of an Opera, (according to Honestus, I cannot write four bars of a symphony) that Mr. Henry Phillips (whose fastidiousness on such subjects is proverbial) was satisfied with the part assigned to him, and that I was 'already known by various original compositions of *great merit*.' "

Russell also returned to his treatise on singing:

> From the manner in which that work is spoken of by Honestus, he evidently intends his readers to infer that it made its first appearance in this country, that it never was published in England, and that I would not have dared to produce such an impudent plagiarism there, where detection would have been so easy.—He speaks of a re-publication of a work of Rodolph's in Philadelphia, from the original of which I have stolen five-sixths of my little volume. Now, with respect to this work of Rodolph's, I have never seen it, and cannot, as I am at present located, have access to it . . .

Stuck in Albany, thousands of miles from home, the embattled Russell was at a disadvantage in producing evidence to support such credentials as he had. He evidently recognized the need to strengthen his case, for on 2 December *The Albany Evening Journal* published this intriguing small advertisement:

> MR. H. RUSSELL will feel much obliged to any person who possesses the London *Literary Gazette*, from April 1835 to May 1835, for a sight of them, it being of the utmost importance that he should have them as early as possible, in consequence of a long critique upon his last London Concert, given the 7th April, 1835, which he is anxious to bring forward on a particular occasion. Direct to this office.

Whether or not the advertisement brought any success was anyway scarcely relevant. "Honestus" now had responses from both *The Knickerbocker* and Russell himself, and he evidently felt confident enough to come in for the kill, with a detailed analysis of Russell's supposed transgressions. Since it ran to around six broadsheet columns, *The National Gazette* was obliged to split it into two parts, the first of which appeared on 13 December 1837. In it "Honestus" declared:

> Mr. Russell has hazarded two replies to my former communications. I deem them of course unworthy of notice myself, and were all your readers skilled in the law of evidence, or would they compare exactly the charge and replies, I would let the latter go as the strongest proof of the essential accusations I made against him; as his self-condemnation. Mr. Russell carefully avoids responding to the proposition of having

> a page of his book submitted to twelve of the best professors he might name, who should in turn give an opinion on it, and on his pretensions as a harmonist. This, Mr. Russell will not do. I now make another, which no man who had taken a first prize in a Conservatory for high musical composition, would refuse. Let him, in the presence of Messrs Meignen, Hupfeld, Huttner, Homann, Jr., Darley, and De Conninck, write figures to a given bass and place the harmonies to it; correct certain false musical syntax; and also arrange a page of music written for four parts with a false bass, for a full orchestra, correcting the bass. Each piece to be one single page. . . .

The musicians named were among what passed for the hidebound musical elite of Philadelphia at that time.

After admitting error in attributing *The Knickerbocker*'s biographical paragraph to the editors of the journal, rather than the *New-York Mirror*, "Honestus" stressed that he had no quarrel with Russell's voice or his popularity as a singer, purely with his pretense to great genius as an original composer. He gave a detailed dissection of Russell's responses—not least his recourse to what was no more than an advertisement from *The Court Journal*: "I must say that Macassar Oil is noticed editorially in the London papers, but it is understood as advertised." It was Macassar oil, used in the nineteenth century as a hairdressing, that created the need for the antimacassar cloth on the back of a chair.

"Honestus" now turned to the technical merit and originality of works published in Russell's name. Responding to the claim that he was responsible for only the factual content, rather than the presentation, of the title pages of the arrangements with which he was associated, "Honestus" began with "The Brave Old Oak":

> Will Mr. Russell pretend that he did not supply this title and the dedication and stick his own name down three times to another man's work, besides his autograph, and then botch it? This is the real title of the song:—"The brave old Oak, written by H F Chorley, Esq., the music by Edward Loder."—Would any man of true professional pride come so near to an indecent piracy as Mr. Russell does by sinking altogether the name of the real composer, and putting his own name in place, with a shelter, in case of detection, under the word "*arranged*." But what is worse, all that Mr. Russell has arranged he has made

> worse by the arrangement. Where did Mr. Russell learn to make consecutive fifths and resolve the seventh of the dominant by ascension?

The very next paragraph might then have been designed expressly to make Russell regret his description of Henry Phillips as someone "whose fastidiousness . . . is proverbial":

> " 'My Heart's in the Highlands,' a favorite song sung at the principal concerts by Mr. H RUSSELL. The poetry by ROBERT BURNS. The symphonies, accompaniments & part of the melody composed & most respectfully dedicated to Mrs. Lewis Gaylord Clark, by HENRY RUSSELL. . . . Entered according to act of Congress, in the year 1837, by Henry Russell, etc.!" And over the first page of notation, "My Heart's in the Highlands, H. Russell." How dare he to pirate *Henry Phillips*'s song, and get a copy right for it and his musical fooleries in it? Does he think because an ocean rolls between the United States and Europe, that he is to play the brigand on the composers of that country, and when I call him to account he is to bully me and to bully the public? To test the morality of this conduct we need only imagine a similar use to be made of a poem; the author's name being omitted, the arrangement of his subject mutilated and his sentences rendered ungrammatical, etc., and the whole served up with a new name. . . .
>
> As for "Some Love to Roam," I really deemed it too good to be from an unpractised hand, even though on simple chords; and besides it is current among some musical men that Mr. Russell is not the author, and he has been told so. These circumstances induced me to mention it *en passant* along with other suspicious property, as it happened to meet my eye. I thought as a matter of course, for I am so accustomed to see this second-hand work, that the London edition could be found here along with others, but it seems it cannot. . . .

On "Some Love to Roam," at least, "Honestus" seems to have been on shaky ground, basing his accusation on rumor and the fact that no London edition could be found. In fact, we know full well that such an edition did exist.

Figure 5.1. "Some Love to Roam" sheet music cover. *Source*: Author's collection.

Before finishing the first part of his grand denunciation, "Honestus" touched briefly on the ambitious Russell work that was then in the pipeline: "I have seen on the authority of the *New-York Mirror* and others, that an oratorio, *The Sceptic*, is to be produced. I am a sceptic as to its existence." The second part of "Honestus"'s critique was published by *The National Gazette* on the following day, 14 December 1837; this constituted a microscopically detailed analysis of *L'Amico dei Cantanti*. It began with such comments as "Up to page 6 inclusive . . . I find nothing but a few truisms." Then came comments such as "Pages 16, 17, 18 and 19 are taken from Rodolph," and "Pages 21, 22, 23, 24 and 25, are from Rodolph with the impossible second." The denunciation came to the boil with comments on Russell's claim to have based some of his examples on original manuscripts of various classical masters:

> Pages 52, 53, 54, 55, 56, 57, 58, 59, 60, 61 and 62 contain, respectively, original MSS., compositions presented to Mr. Russell by Rossini, Mozart, Jun., Reghini, Zingarelli, Zerelli, and Meyerbeer. What is the reader to infer from Mr. Russell's statement that these are original compositions presented to him by these composers? He can infer nothing else, along with Mr. Russell's other statements than that he is a man of genius and science, and a favorite pupil of all of them. For no one supposes that such men as Rossini, Zingarelli, and Meyerbeer, would present to a musical ignoramus their original MSS. compositions as tokens of their personal regard for him. . . .
>
> With regard to the original manuscripts of [sic] Zerelli, Mozart, Jr., and Reghini, I would ask Mr. Russell, who are these composers? I never heard their names. . . . With regard to the *original* compositions presented to Mr. Russell by his teachers, Reghini and Zingarelli, and found on pages 56, 57, 58 and 59 of his book, I make this discovery. They are taken consecutively note for note (the clef only of one of them altered) from the work of an old composer named Righini, who flourished during the French Revolution, and was chapel master to the King of Prussia. . . .

As a final flourish, "Honestus" provided full publication details of this work by Vincenzo Righini (1756–1812): *Exercices pour se perfectionner dans l'art de chant, composés par Vincent Righini.*

Russell seems to have made no further published response. There was probably little he could say that would carry much weight. It was game, set, and match to "Honestus." Yet "Honestus" had made the occasional iffy claim along the way, and a summary of the dispute published in the *New York Evening Star* made it clear that Russell had, at least, won the odd game:

> MR RUSSELL, THE VOCALIST.—A writer in the *National Gazette*, evidently a professional singer, has made several violent attacks on Russell, charging him with being a charlatan—no composer—ignorant of Italian—not a pupil of Rossini, &c &c. Russell, in reply, exhibits his gold medal from the King of Naples—makes various extracts from English papers and periodicals relative to his musical compositions, and proves himself to have had a much higher standing in the musical world than was supposed on this side of the Atlantic.

Of course, he had "proven" nothing of the sort.

Who "Honestus" was seems to have remained a mystery. As we have seen, the *New York Evening Star* suggested that he was a professional singer, probably one trained in the exact old tenets of composition. Certainly, as *The Knickerbocker* commented in a footnote to its reply to the first "Honestus" piece, there was "something of personal feeling and private pique" in his attack. Beyond that we can say only that it seems to have been someone of some standing in America. If so, why did he feel it needful to attack a simple songwriter? Or was it, perhaps, that he feared for his own employment if he revealed his identity? Indeed, his failure to do so took a certain edge off his criticisms.

The immediate consequence of the dispute must have been to make not only Russell, but also those who wrote extravagantly about him, take greater care than before. Certainly, *The Knickerbocker* seems to have left him well alone thereafter. But the American musical establishment was never going to forget what "Honestus" had unearthed, and the matter was inevitably going to be brought up whenever Russell seemed to be getting a little above himself, or when a journal wanted a bit of "scandal."

As far as the general public was concerned, however, the whole episode appears to have made little impact. That was readily demonstrated by the fact that Russell happened to be in Philadelphia at the very time the final crushing analysis of "Honestus" was published. The program announced for his concert at the Masonic Hall on Saturday, 9 December conspicuously attributed "The Brave Old Oak" to Loder, "Some Love to Roam" to Russell, and "The Friar of Olden Time" to Reeve, though it also attributed "Largo al Factotum" to Russell himself! One other item on the program presents us with an unresolved puzzle. This was the song "On Old Long Island's Sea Girt Shore" (aka "Rockaway"), described as "the words by J Sharpe, Esq., MSS." What is curious is that the song, which had been heard in the composer's repertoire since September, seemingly, after this, did not appear again on a Russell program for well over two years, after which it became something of a favorite. Why was it put in cold storage for all that time? Was Sharpe temporarily reluctant to be associated with the discredited Russell?

At all events, the *Philadelphia Gazette* declared the concert "a simple but delightful musical treat—no strained efforts, no unnatural distortion, but music alone, such as it exists with true musicians—no daubings to cover defects, and no affectation of *shakes* and trills to hide deficiencies of science." In other words, melody instead of ornament. Once again, Russell's ability to win over his audiences is clearly demonstrated, and he was able to announce that, "in consequence of several families being unable to attend his last Concert, he has been solicited to give another." This duly took place—again at the Masonic Hall—the following Saturday, 16 December, with the Groningen violinist Wilhelm Keyzer acting as support. The *Philadelphia Gazette* reported: "On Saturday evening, Mr. Russell's concert was attended by the fullest assemblage that was ever convened in the Masonic Hall. There was not 'a nook or coin of vantage,' in the whole Saloon, which was not filled to repletion. The performance went off with great *éclat*, and Mr. Russell has abundant reason to be flattered with his reception." As far as the popular press and general public were concerned, it was business as before. Yet one wonders what tactics Russell might have been able to employ to achieve even this impression. One is led to do so, rather, by a piece from a New Yorkish journal, *The Musical Review,* of 27 October 1838, which was reproduced across the Atlantic in London's *Musical World* in June 1839—a full eighteen months after the "Honestus" affair. Nowhere did it dare mention Russell by name. Yet the American musical cognoscenti, at least, would have had no difficulty recognizing to whom it referred, and they could have sniggered into their coffee over a piece that, in equal proportions, mocks Russell's sharp practices and the American public's gullibility. Here it is—just slightly abridged—from London's *Musical World*, where it was headed THE WAY TO GIVE CONCERTS IN AMERICA:

> Embark from your native country with the well-fixed impression that the Americans have a superabundance of curiosity, credulity, and gullibility; this is important that you may lay your plan well. Think that they are eager to see and to hear any thing that is new; and that if it be unlike what they ever heard

before (no matter how absurd—it must deviate from all *rule of right* or it can't be *new*) it will surely take. The Americans are an enterprising people, totally absorbed in the thoughts of *experiments, improvements*, and *new inventions*. They think that the *world*—i.e. this country—is making prodigious strides in knowledge, and that the *march of mind* actually goes by *steam*. Innovation and improvement are words now used as synonymous; and the same changes are expected to be made in the *fine arts* as have been made in the mode of picking, spinning, and weaving cotton, or in the propelling of land or water carriages; and such is the avidity with which every thing of a *labour-saving* nature is seized upon, that if you can show the principle to be applied to music, by giving them that which cost no *labour* of mind to compose—no *labour* of practice to perform—and which requires no musical taste to hear, then your fortune is sure. It must not show any marks of possessing method, or be such as can be set down to any distinct school; this would be considered as being behind the times—absolutely vulgar. . . . The candidate here, must *improve* so rapidly that, even if he come over by steam, or a balloon, his style when he arrives here will bear no resemblance to that which he possessed when he left his native shore.

Being thus impressed, set out your expedition of quackery. Proclaim yourself the "pupil of Rossini." If you have ever been a *chorus singer* in the Opera at Paris, you can do this with the greatest propriety; for Rossini, while he was bringing out his operas, must have given you such *drillings* as your stupidity made necessary. Publish a book and dedicate it to the Queen, to bring along with you—let it purport to be a Treatise on the Art of Singing; give it an Italian title by all means. In doing this, you will of course copy it all from other books; and if you take *fifty* pages direct from "Rodolph's Solfegge," and twelve pages from the published works of various other authors, say nothing in your title or preface about Rodolph—let that part of the book be taken as your own; and for the other selections, announce them as "Exercises on the Solfeggio, from *original manuscripts*, by Rossini, Reghini, Mozart, jun., Zingarelli, Meyerbeer, and other masters." This will give you a distinguished reputation; and although "Rodolph's Solfeggio" may have been published entire in this country, and the published methods of Rossini, Reghini, &c., from which you take your "original manuscripts" may be in many a musician's library, it will not affect you. That class of the community which you must depend upon to crowd your concerts, and the editors whom you will get to puff you into notice, know not of the existence of such works. And if in attempting to improve Rodolph by writing out the harmony where he has given only a figured bass, you should commit the grossest errors, and show to the profession that you are ignorant of the first principles of composition—no matter. What do those who will support you know about harmony? And if a musician expresses his opinion, you can easily make your friends believe that it "springs from envy." Keep up your reputation as an author by accrediting the songs which you sing, as taken from an opera of your own composition. No matter if there be no such opera in existence—it may be considered as unpublished; and even if the very songs are stolen from other authors, note for note—shrink at nothing; a good amount of impudence is sufficient to surmount all difficulties. Announce likewise an Oratorio as being forthcoming—hypocritically work yourself into the good esteem of religious persons, by representing (not as perfectly as might be) the death of a "sceptic"; this will be a decided hit. The oratorio (or *thing* which may pass under the name) you can complete—there is material enough in the world to make any sort of composition; and although three-fourths of it be taken in "whole cloth" from other authors, and the remaining part made up of patch-work, who will know it? You can easily find ignorant persons enough to help you bring it out—fools enough to pay their money to hear it—and knaves enough to puff it, if you pay them. Then your name will be recorded on the same page with Handel, Haydn and Spohr, as an oratorio composer! Let not any part of your *thing* be published, lest the critics get hold of it and think proper, as it is called an *oratorio*, to give it a reviewing; this would be carrying your humbugging a step too far. As for such *small fry* as songs, you may publish them. If it be a song not very well known, and the author of it be dead, call it your own composition at once. If it be a popular song by a living composer—Loder, Phillips, or any other—put in the author's name in *small letter*, and contrive to insert your own name in *glaring capitals* three or four times—once in the fac-simile of your own hand-writing. This you will do as the *arranger* of the song—(put "*arranged*" in small letters)—you can easily arrange the song; no matter how injudiciously it may be done, only introduce a few *tiddle-tumtees*, and after hearing you sing and play it at your concerts, the public will say that the original accompaniments are "mere senseless and unmeaning thrummings," in comparison with yours.

When you announce your concerts, send at least one hundred and fifty tickets to the press—dine with the editors—call upon all lovers of music who don't know you—talk about the superior advantages of being *educated* in Italy—(*if you was ever a music copyist there, that is sufficient*)—having a medal made for the purpose, show it as being awarded at Naples for writing the best opera—[ha! ha!]—(don't laugh—it will all go down)—say that you can speak six foreign languages as well as you can your own—(this may be all true, especially if you murder the King's English when you write it, and give it the Yorkshire caterwaul, "*yeeaouoo*," when you speak or sing it)—tell every thing that you did not do in Paris; but don't say that you was a chorus singer in the opera. In regard to London, where your reputation must have arrived at its climax, represent yourself as the "teacher of Her Majesty." If the enquiry be made why you left such an elevated position to take up your residence in Montreal and Rochester, say that the extravagances in living—such as the support of livery, giving parties, &c., &c., consequent upon being the preceptor of so royal a personage—were not congenial with your retiring disposition; and therefore you sought relief in the quietude of the country. Don't mention that you ever *played* in a Theatre or Circus, lest the editor of some Journal of Commerce should fancy that the "atmosphere" you had breathed was such that you "cannot feel at home" in sacred music. Pretend that you can write for the orchestra; and promise to arrange one of your songs for Mr. Jones to sing at the Park. Put him off with promises until he finds you out and cuts your acquaintance.

Was the comment about "Mr. Jones" based on an actual incident? It may be recalled that Russell had sung with John Jones "of the Park Theater, New York City," on the occasion of his Philadelphia debut. Could the only mildly successful Jones perhaps have been the mysterious "Honestus"?

The piece continued:

> While you are introducing yourself among the people to secure a good attendance at your concerts, give to a friend who has a wife and daughters *one* ticket, and he will be under the necessity of buying several more; be sure to give away enough to fill the concert-room if you feel doubtful of your hold upon the public favour. This will create a jam, and give you an opportunity to repeat your concert, and to announce that "those who purchased tickets for your first concert, and were unable to get admission, will be admitted with the same at the second"; this will be all *hum* of course. Never sing with the *orchestra*, or with another to *accompany* you; for if you do, your *deficiency* as a musician will be discovered, and the cat let out of the bag. When you are encored in a song by your friends employed for the purpose, introduce some comic song—"The cork leg," "Why don't the men propose?" "The lion and the jackass"—(the latter will be excellently chosen, for you can personify both characters at once)—and other such *morceaux* with which you entertain the *men of taste* that you are in the habit of associating with.
>
> If you go into a city or small town, where they want a teacher to reside with them, tell them that you will be the man; make a contract to conduct the music in one of the churches, and to teach in some seminary of young ladies. This will bring you into the favourable notice of the people who take an interest in these arrangements, and you can thus get the church for your concerts free. Carry this imposition as far as it will bear, and then make a sudden exit without paying your bills.
>
> Get some credulous and generous publisher to *puff* you into notice by publishing your "Treatise on the Art of Singing," and your songs which you give him in manuscript, with the copyright. If one song should happen to be popular and sell well, go and sell the copyright to another publisher, and then say that the same had been previously published in England. When one publisher finds you out to be a dishonest man, go

> to another—if he sees any prospect of gain, he will bite at your bait. . . .
>
> Finally, practice every sort of trickery and deceit that you can think of, and so long as your *brass* holds out, you will succeed in gaining full houses; be considered as the "only man who can give a concert alone"—a "model for all to listen to who undertake to sing in churches"—[ha! ha!]—(don't laugh)—by which they would "learn to lose [forget] themselves in the elevation of their themes"—and then you can return to Europe with a handsome fortune.
>
> Now you *may laugh*—at the gullibility of the Americans—the easy practicability of making *charlatanism* succeed where genuine talent is neglected—and enjoy, for the rest of your life, the fruit of your daring impudence and imposition . . .

In a few years, the British were to prove that they were just as, if not more, "gullible" than the Americans, as Henry Russell's songs sold by the thousands and his concerts sold out all round the United Kingdom.

6

Oratorio in Boston, Song in New York

Back in Albany, from Philadelphia, in December 1837, Russell ostensibly carried on as before. He offered the choruses from *The Sceptic* on the evening of Christmas Day, when the Sacred Music Fund Society held a concert in the Second Presbyterian Church in Chapel Street, under the direction of Isaac P. Cole. This year, it was made clear that, whereas the Society had traditionally distributed the proceeds of its oratorio performances to local charities, on this occasion they were to go toward reducing the Society's debts. Following the abortive attempt to set up an Academy of Music, under Russell, whose success had now expanded his horizons far beyond the New York state capital, their finances needed shoring up!

New Year of 1838 saw Russell back in New York City—staying, if its nomination as a source of tickets for his concerts is a guide, at the Astor House Hotel. Opened in 1836 on the site of the home of fur tycoon John Jacob Astor (1763–1848), it had 309 rooms and was New York's first mammoth luxury hotel, and the first to offer bath and toilet facilities—the water being pumped by steam. On 4 January, Russell gave a concert at the City Hotel—again with violinist Keyzer—followed on 10 January by another that was "literally crowded from top to bottom." On the 25th he gave a solo concert; nine of the items performed were his own works, with only "The old English Gentleman," "Largo al factotum," and "Eccomi a voi" from Donizetti's *L'esule di Roma* making up the one-man program.

Then he went on a little tour. We see him down Washington way in late January with his big successes ("for descriptive music, nothing we ever heard was equal to "Wind of the Winter Night") and, of course, "Washington's Tomb."

When he finally arrived back in Albany, in late March, the *Evening Journal* reported that he "has been passing the winter at the South. He was on board the *Neptune*, in the late tremendous gale, which, from the description he gives us, must have been terrible and appalling." The steamship *Neptune* had set out for New York from Norfolk, Virginia, on Friday, 16 March 1838, but the following day encountered a severe gale. For a time, those on land feared her lost, before she put back into Norfolk on the following Monday, minus one smoke-pipe. "From noon on Saturday to twelve at night, scarcely any hope of life remained," reported the *Norfolk Beacon*:

> Death seemed inevitable. The sea was running mountains high, and the boat was sometimes lifted to an angle of forty-five degrees. . . . She was off the capes of the Delaware during the severity of the gale. When the front smoke-pipe was blown off, and the thick iron fastenings, which bound it to the boat, and to its fellow in the rear, were rent asunder like pack thread, hope seemed to have departed to return no more. But the other pipe still remained firm. . . . We visited the *Neptune* yesterday, and walked over the decks and through those cabins which beheld the dreadful exhibition of Saturday. The wide folding-doors of the dining-cabin—an apartment constructed and equipped in a style of princely splendor—was [sic] torn off by the wind. Here and there some detached piece was seen, and the absence of the smoke-pipe made a sad hiatus in the appearance of the upper deck.

Anticipating Russell's concert at the Albany Female Academy, on 30 March, the *Evening Journal* excitedly referred to "a witchery in his voice which holds his admirers in a species of musical bondage." Assisted by a Mr. Glynn, Russell began the concert with a two-piano arrangement of the overture to *Zampa*. His songs began with "The Brave Old Oak," "Wind of the Winter Night," "The Ivy Green," and "My Heart's in the Highlands"—the last still attributed to Russell alone. "It is by particular request that Mr. Russell repeats the two first songs," declared the press announcement. He then traveled once more to New York, where on 6 April he appeared again at the City Hall—this time with the soprano Mrs. Emily Sutton, victim of the spiteful journalism of Walt Whitman. The concert was, reported *The Herald*, "very numerously attended, considering the counter attraction of

Madame Caradori . . . There is a richness and volume about Mr. Russell's voice which is peculiarly his own. . . ."

A subsequent reference indicates that it was during this New York visit that Gotham audiences first heard what would become one of Russell's most famous compositions: "The Maniac." Probably inspired by Charles

Figure 6.1. "The Maniac" sheet music cover. *Source:* Author's collection.

Horn's current success with Purcell's "Mad Tom of Bedlam," subtitled "The Maniac's Song" (unless it were the other way round!), it was perhaps the most ambitious and striking example of the type of composition upon which Russell had entered with "Wind of the Winter Night"—the descriptive *scene*, with music progressing from instrumental prelude, through recitative, arioso passages and piano interludes, and sometimes extreme vocal effects.

Using a text said to be partly taken from Mathew Lewis (1775–1818), author of the novel *The Monk*, "The Maniac" might also be considered Russell's most outrageous composition. After an introduction that reveals his familiarity with Schubert's "Erlkönig" (then only twenty-three years old), the voice enters above pianissimo octave chords: "Hush! 'tis the night-watch! He guards my lonely cell." Later comes the madman's cry, "No! by heaven, no, by heav'n I am not mad! Oh! release me!" With the words "I lov'd her sincerely. I lov'd her too dearly. I lov'd her in sorrow, in joy, and in pain," we learn of the source of the man's problems. To a snatch of a dance melody we gather how this affair has affected his mind, as he repeatedly intones the words "I see her dancing in the hall." Then, in recitative, we suffer his deranged ranting: "For lo you, while I speak, mark how you demon's eyeballs glare! He sees me now; with dreadful shriek he whirls, he whirls me in the air! Horror! The reptile strikes his tooth deep in my heart, so crush'd and sad!"

With good reason does J. A. Stephens declare that "The Maniac' is Russell at his best; . . . a great piece of Victorian musical drama." It was also one of Russell's most successful attempts to address social issues. "[It] was written," the composer said, "with the intention of exposing that great social evil—the private lunatic asylum, and, with all humility, let me say I think the song went far in achieving its object." His later concert announcements proclaimed the supposedly factual incident on which the number was based:

> Some years since, a gentleman of a large fortune was taken to a Mad House, and there confined seven feet under ground. The persons that accompanied him took oath, to those entrusted with the care of the establishment, to the fact of his being a maniac. The more the poor fellow implored for his release, the more forcibly were the keepers convinced of his madness.
>
> The treatment he received while thus confined affected his reason, and he became frantic and shortly died from the effect. The strangers that carried him to the mad house were

supposed to have been hired by some of his brutal relatives, who, at his death, were to come into possession of his property.

That "The Maniac" was apparently not published until 1840—almost two years after its first performance—is perhaps an indication of the work's individuality. After all, this was not the sort of number that amateurs would perform in their drawing rooms in the way they would Russell's more conventional ballads.

According to his memoirs, Russell was still in New York later in April 1838 when an event of great historical significance occurred: the arrival of the first steamships to cross the Atlantic:

> I was somewhat elated at receiving an invitation from one of the leading citizens of New York to be one of the deputation to welcome the captain and the officers of the first steamship that crossed the Atlantic from England to America—the *Sirius*. We gave them a right hearty welcome. The week following, a reception and a magnificent dinner was attended by upwards of five hundred of the merchant princes of New York. The second steamship was the *Great Western*.

This time there can be no two ways about it. Russell's claims are quite simply untrue, since he was, without doubt, in Boston at that time. The *Sirius* arrived in New York on 22 April 1838, after a crossing of eighteen days; the *Great Western*, only a few hours later after a crossing of fifteen days. However, in Boston on that same 22 April, Russell's oratorio *The Sceptic* was finally heard, complete with full chorus and orchestra. Russell naturally took the leading part in the performance, for which the press announcements hedged bets on the spelling of the work's title:

> RUSSELL'S ORATORIO OF THE SKEPTIC.
>
> BOSTON MUSICAL INSTITUTE.
>
> THE public are respectfully informed that the Oratorio of the SCEPTIC will be given by the Boston Musical Institute on SUNDAY EVENING NEXT, April 22d, at the Masonic Temple.
>
> The part of the SKEPTIC will be sustained by MR RUSSELL.

> Vocal Performers—Mrs. Baker, Mrs. Phipps, and Mr. T
>
> Comer.
>
> Choruses by the ladies and gentlemen of the Institute.
>
> Conductor Mr. T Comer
>
> Mr. Russell will preside at the Piano Forte.
>
> Tickets $1 each, to be had, at Parker & Ditson's, and Ashton & Prentiss's Music stores, also, at the Temple on the evening of performance.
>
> Performances commence at 7 o'clock.
>
> Programmes of the order of performance will be ready for delivery at the door of the Temple.

The press reception was enthusiastic, the *Boston Transcript* reporting:

> The Oratorio of the Skeptic was performed last evening to the entire gratification of a large and discriminating audience. Although [it is] contrary to the canons of Boston propriety to applaud at Oratorios or Concerts given on Sunday evenings, it was almost impossible to repress the delight, even until the conclusion of the performance, when it burst forth in one spontaneous and uncontrollable expression. Mr. Russell's reputation as a composer as well as a vocalist, will be much enhanced by this fine production. The solos executed by himself were given with thrilling power and effect. The choruses were admirably sung—particularly "Oh, thou eternal Being," "Oh, thou Skeptic," and "Hush, she comes."

Mr. Honestus must have squirmed.

The following Saturday, 28 April, Russell introduced "The Maniac" to Boston at a concert, at the same venue; the concert was promoted by local singer Mrs. G. H. Andrews, whose own contribution to the evening included the ballad "We Have Been Friends Together."

Figure 6.2. Review of "Mrs. Andrews's Concert" from the Musical Gazette. *Source:* Author's collection.

[For the Musical Gazette.]

MRS. ANDREWS'S CONCERT.

The friends of Mrs. Andrews, and we believe she has many in the city, will expect to see some notice of her "Farewell Concert." Mr. H. Russell added to the interest of the Concert by singing several of his most popular songs. Mrs. Kellogg and Mr. Andrews assisted as vocalists, and Mr. Card presided at the piano-forte. It will be impossible here to give anything more than a brief notice of the items of the bill.

1. "*Here in cool grot.*" Cleverly done. Mrs. Andrews did not, however, sing with her usual spirit. This was observable during the whole evening.

2. "*My heart's in the highlands.*" Sung by Mr. Russell, in his usual style. The song was encored, and he sung "Come, brothers, arouse."

3. "*Sweet bird.*" Sung by Mrs. Andrews with flute obligato. The word *sweet*, very often repeated, was sung with a sharp, pinched note. This double E is not of easy execution, to be done gracefully.

4. "*Home, fare thee well.*" Mrs. Kellogg and Mrs. Andrews. It was probably a rarity to hear the second voice sing partly soprano and partly contralto. It was a fair performance, but would have been more agreeable by two even sopranos.

5. "*A song for the oak.*" Mr. Russell. This was encored, and Mr. Russell gave, "Why dont the men propose?"

6. Tyrolean air, "*My own sweet native vale.*" Mrs. Andrews. Generally, very well sung, but some of the notes too attenuated and refined. It was encored, and the "Hunter Boy" was given.

7. "*The Loadstars.*" By Mrs. Andrews, Mrs. Kellogg and Mr. Andrews. The voices were not well balanced, and the Glee did not make much impression.

Part II. 8. "*Peaceful slumbering.*" Mrs. Andrews, Mrs. Kellogg, Mr. Russell and Mr. Andrews. This did not go off well. We have often heard this better sung—seldom so indifferently. The alto was sung by a contralto voice, and the tenor by a bass.

9. "*The Maniac.*" Mr. Russell. A specimen of musical eloquence; and parts of it sung with great effect. The passage, "No, by Heaven, I am not mad," was particularly forcible; and the passage, "I see them dancing in the hall," was attractive by its descriptive appropriateness, and its light measure.

10. "*Arrayed for the bridal.*" Mrs. Andrews. Too tame. The running passages were well executed.

11. "*Largo al factotum.*" Mr. Russell. This was encored, and he sung, "Some love to roam."

12. "*Going out a fishing.*" Mr. Andrews. Little can be said of this either for its composition, or its presentment.

13. "*We have been friends together.*" Mrs. Andrews. She took breath so audibly, and so frequently, that it sounded like the sobbings of grief. She was, probably, really affected.

14. "*The Chough and Crow.*" Mrs. Andrews, Mrs. Kellogg and Mr. Andrews. Well done. The opening solo was particularly good.

The concert, generally, went off very well, and the audience testified their gratification.

P *

The following evening (Sunday, 29 April) brought a second performance of *The Sceptic*. Even after its long gestation period, the oratorio was evidently still being developed, since it was now performed for the first time with an overture. A third and final performance followed on Sunday, 6 May. Along the way *The Sceptic* gained further strong praise, as from *The Boston Morning Post*:

> There are few modern productions of the same kind, within our knowledge, calculated to afford so much gratification as this. The style is entirely new—and, while the choruses combine harmonies that abundantly show the great science and research of the composer, the *recitatives* and *airs* display a power and expression that will be felt and appreciated by every one. . . . This *Oratorio* promises to become a standard work, and we may, perhaps, hear it after Mr. R's departure. . . .

Inevitably, following the "Honestus" revelations, there were also dissenting voices, including a response from another "shy" individual, identified only as "S.I.," who wrote: "*The Skeptic* was performed three times, and the papers good-naturedly said 'with success.' This "success' simply means that it was played before respectable, though not numerous audiences, with applause." "S.I." insisted that approval came only from "a few zealous but mis-judging friends, and young gentlemen, with 'lovelocks' and large canes, arranging themselves judiciously, and determined to support. . . ." In other words, that there was some sort of a claque. Henry had a claque of lovelocked lads?

More particularly, the word "plagiarism" was once more bandied around, though Russell was not short of supporters. *The Boston Morning Post*, having praised his vocal powers, went on, "As a composer, Mr. Russell stands very high in our estimation, and we think the charge of plagiarism a most unjust one, for his compositions have been thoroughly examined and we know of no composer who has more originality." One "H," perhaps Russell's friend Houghton, publisher of the *Boston Transcript*, summed things up:

> There was no little speculation and controversy relative to this Oratorio. . . . The Hounds were all out ready to seize upon the victim, the moment it was known to be abroad. They attacked it from Capo to Coda, with their merciless fangs, determined on its annihilation; but it still lives in health and soundness. There

> are some who, having been delighted with the compositions of Handel, Haydn, Mozart, Beethoven, King, Neukomm, and other great Masters, can give no credit to such daring adventurers as Russell. . . . It is agreed that the *Skeptic* has faults; but it also has its beauties. It has some strange harmony. . . .

It is, of course, the age-old story of popular music. No more then, than now, could Henry Russell satisfy popular taste, musical academics, and traditionalists at one and the same time.

Russell's influence on the *Boston Transcript* defense is suggested by the inclusion of (presumably) Matthew Peter King—composer of the oratorio *The Intercession*, after Milton's *Paradise Lost*—among the masters cited.

All things considered, Russell probably got off lightly in Boston in April and May 1838, and he certainly left most people well satisfied—not just by his performances but also by various compositions he dedicated to local residents. Besides the dedication of "The Ivy Green" to "Lynne M. Walter of Boston," who just happened to be the editor of the *Boston Transcript* (1799–1842), there was a four-part male chorus, "The Corsair Glee," dedicated to the gentlemen of the Corsair Boat Club. This was a club composed entirely of members of the Boston Light Infantry. According to a letter to the editor of *The Boston Morning Post*, in April 1838 they were celebrating the launch of a new boat. The author of the letter was one "Ione," presumably the young Boston writer Mary Ann Hewitt (1818–94), who also turned up as the lyricist to Russell's ballad "We Met in Other Years," which was dedicated to Mr. Claudius Edward Habicht, a Boston Swedish-born insurance man, to whose wife, née Emmeline Hunt, "The Maniac" had been, in turn, dedicated.

All of this local activity helped to cement Russell's relations with the residents of Boston, and it was perhaps with good reason that, in his memoirs, he was effusive about his reception there:

> Boston, I think, went a little mad about me and my songs. . . . "D'ye know who that is?" I heard once a street urchin say to one of his fellows—"That's 'Enry Russell, the song man." And the little beggar struck up my latest song in excellent tune, and voice, to the great delight of a knot of other boys, and—I confess it—to my own keen satisfaction. All the applause and encores of the entertainment I gave in the evening of that same day did not gratify me more than the evident admiration of that little street corner connoisseur.

Figure 6.3. “The Corsair Glee” sheet music cover. *Source:* Courtesy the Lester Levy Sheet Music Collection, The Sheridan Libraries, Johns Hopkins University.

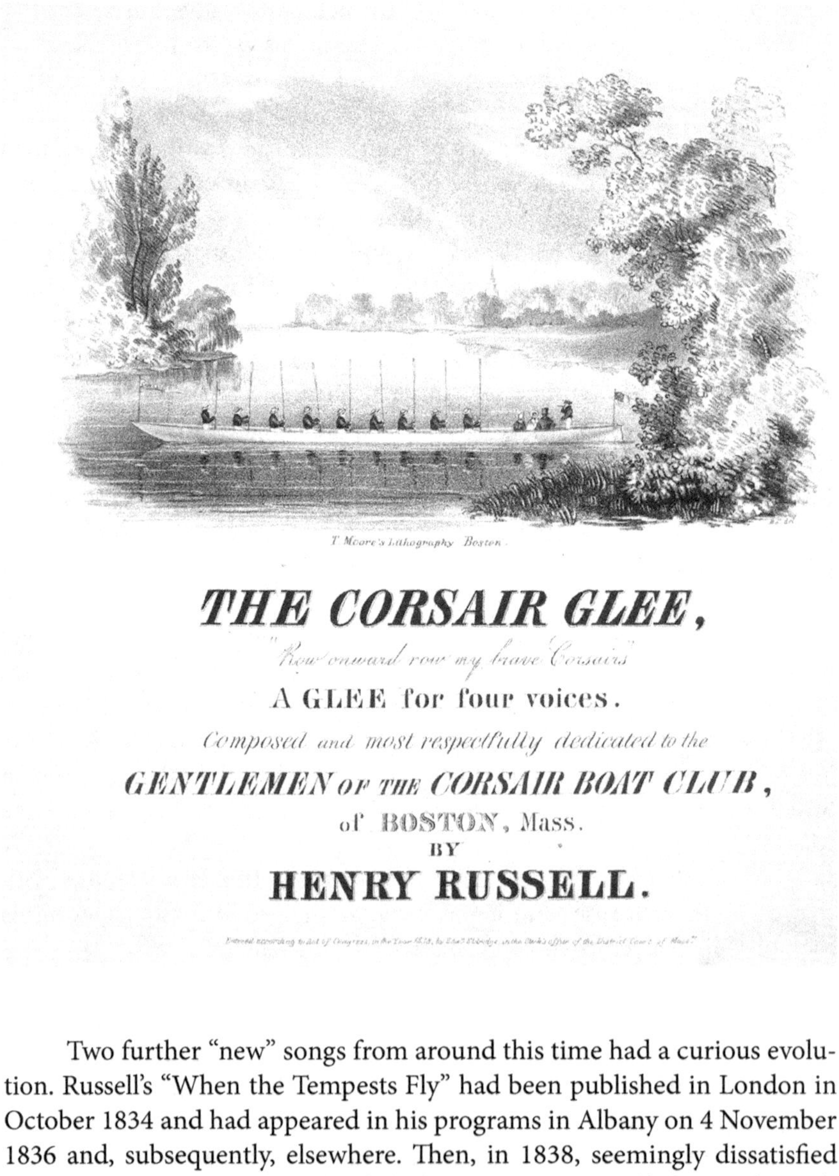

Two further “new” songs from around this time had a curious evolution. Russell’s “When the Tempests Fly” had been published in London in October 1834 and had appeared in his programs in Albany on 4 November 1836 and, subsequently, elsewhere. Then, in 1838, seemingly dissatisfied with his setting—which, indeed, lacks potency—Russell divorced words and music. He had more fitting words added to the original music, as “The Minstrel of the Tyrol,” and provided new music for the original lyric, with the addition (much repeated) of words that became the new title: "Our Way Across the Mountains, Ho!" This reuse of melodies would be a major feature of Russell's career as his catalogue grew larger; but it was not really, as J. A. Stephens suggests, "an essentially English phenomenon." Ponts-neufs had been a wholly accepted part of continental music making for centuries.

"Our Way Across the Mountains, Ho!" was on the program on 12 June for a concert in the Chapel of the Young Ladies' Academy, Albany, that also introduced "The Maniac" to the city. Coincidentally a Mr. Lewis—clearly not "Monk" Lewis, part author of "The Maniac"—performed variations on "Home, Sweet Home" and "My Heart and Lute" on the valve trumpet. In addition, the previously mentioned Mr. Glynn joined Russell in a two-piano rendition of Rossini's overture to *La Cenerentola,* as well as playing Henri Herz's *Variations on a Swiss Air*. Russell's return to Albany had begun with a meeting of chorus and orchestra in the Music Hall on 6 June for a proposed performance of *The Sceptic* (as it was still spelled there). However, a full performance seems not to have ensued.

Where Russell went thereafter is unclear, but it was around this time that he composed one of his most lastingly successful creations: "A Life on the Ocean Wave," a simple strophic song and chorus that is a rousing tribute to the joys of the open sea:

> A life on the ocean wave!
> A home on the rolling deep!
> Where the scatter'd waters rave,
> And the winds their revels keep!

We get the most informative version of the song's creation by combining Russell's own account with that in the song memoirs of "poet, story writer, musician and teacher" John Hill Hewitt (1801–90) of Baltimore. According to the latter, "Russell asked Mr. Epes Sargent to write songs for him, leaving the subject to the author's selection. In a walk on the Battery, New York, the sight of the vessels in the harbor, dashing through the sparkling waters in the morning sunshine, suggested the 'Life on the Ocean Wave.' " "His walk and my song were completed together," continues Russell, "and Sargent went to the office of our mutual friend, George P. Morris, and wrote the words. 'This is not a song at all,' said Morris after reading it. 'It will not do for music.' Sargent, somewhat disheartened, put the verses into his pocket . . ."

Hewitt concludes:

> A few days afterward he met Mr. Russell in the music store of J. L. Hewitt & Co., and showed him the lines, informing him at the same time that they would not do, but that he would try again. "Let us go into the piano-room, and try it on the instrument," said Russell. They went. Russell sat down before the piano, placed the words before him, studied them attentively for a few minutes, humming a measure as he read, then threw his fingers over the keys; tried once, twice, thrice, and finally exultingly struck out the present melody to which "Life on the Ocean Wave" is set. He certainly was not more than about ten minutes about it, though he gave a day afterwards to scoring and writing out the music. The song became immensely popular *on* land, and many thousands were sold before the year was out.

This is perhaps one Russell number where, for all its poetic nautical appeal, the verbal content is secondary to the melody. The words do not always fit comfortably, as with "But with a stout vessel and crew" in the third verse. Yet its bright, uninhibited melody was the catchiest he ever composed. The song was an immediate success in America, and it remains to this day the one Russell composition at all familiar in Britain.

Russell was by this time fully engaged with concert tours around the United States. It would be fascinating to re-create his full itinerary, but it is unrealistic to hope to do so. There are so many possible directions in which he may have turned at any stage, and newspaper files of the time are far from complete. Worst of all, the accounts in his memoirs give false leads and at times are demonstrably incorrect. It is nonetheless to those accounts that we are forced to turn for personal aspects of his tours. A reference to "A Life on the Ocean Wave" suggests that it is to 1838 that one such account refers:

> I proceeded up the North River to Albany, and thence to Owego [*recte* Oswego], by way of Schenectady, the seat of the Knickerbockers. Fenimore Cooper, whose home was at O[s]wego, invited me to stay with him, and for a week I enjoyed the cordial hospitality of the distinguished novelist. Many famous men were among my fellow guests, including

Figure 6.4. “A Life on the Ocean Wave” sheet music cover. *Source:* Author’s collection.

> Longfellow (then quite a young man), Cullen Bryant, the poet, General George Morris, and Epps [*recte* Epes] Sargent.
>
> This was not very long after the publication of "A Life on the Ocean Wave," the popular song written by Epps Sargent, in conjunction with myself. So delighted were both Sargent and I with the generous hospitality and the charm of manner of our host that we begged him to allow us to dedicate our song to him as a small mark of our personal esteem and admiration for his genius.

Alas, the suggestion that "A Life on the Ocean Wave" was dedicated to Fenimore Cooper is not borne out by the published edition of the song, which instead bears a dedication to Joseph B. Green of [Muscogee] Columbus, Georgia—perhaps an indication of where Russell resided during the summer of 1838. Fenimore Cooper (1789–1851) was, of course, celebrated as author of *The Last of the Mohicans* (1826). Of the other guests mentioned, the poet Henry Wadsworth Longfellow (1807–82) was to become famous for *The Song of Hiawatha* (1855), while William Cullen Bryant (1794–1878) was said, by some, to be the first American verse writer to achieve international acclaim. General (or was it Colonel?) George Morris and Epes Sargent have already featured as lyricists of Russell's songs "Woodman, Spare That Tree" and "A Life on the Ocean Wave," respectively.

Russell continues his account of his travels around the US as follows:

> Leaving Cooper's place, I paid my second visit to Syracuse, and pushed my way further North, halted successively at Rochester, Buffalo, Cleveland, and Detroit, giving my entertainment at each town—or, to call a spade a spade—each village, as it really was in those primitive days.
>
> At Detroit, which was my ultimate destination, I was met by a deputation of three prominent citizens, who earnestly requested me to give a concert at a little village, eight miles out, in aid of a destitute family. I agreed, but on arriving at—(I forget the name of the village) there was great difficulty in procuring a pianoforte. At last I obtained one, but, dear me, what an instrument it was. It was an antique piano of the curious old square spinet pattern, and of equally curious tone. The next difficulty was to get it to the hall, or rather to the Presbyterian meeting-house, where my entertainment was to be given.

The half-dozen negroes, whose services I enlisted to haul the poor piano along, were six of the most ignorant and superstitious fellows I ever met. I truly believe they had never seen such a thing as a square piano before. As they lifted the instrument on their shoulders, their whispering, and the glances they exchanged, caused me some uneasiness. One brawny negro exclaimed:

"Jose, ye tink anybody inside yere?"

"Now look yeah," said the nigger, addressed as Joe, "if you'se going to get frighted, say de word."

"I'se not frighted, but I tink it's a corpse," said a third man, while a fourth sang out, "hold on, I'se got my foot in a rut."

That rut spoilt all, for, by a sudden jerk, one of the strings inside the piano snapped in twain. The look of alarm on the faces of the niggers was wonderfully droll, and would have made me laugh had not more serious considerations occupied my mind.

Down went the piano with a bang, and away ran the affrighted darkies, as if the Evil One was at their heels.

"De corpse is inside," shouted the nigger who at first aired his misgivings: "I tole you so. Run, boys, run for de life of yo—he's inside, he's a-comin'!"

As their voices died away, I stood mournfully gazing at the harmful but necessary piano, which lay—luckily uninjured—in the road. Several people, attracted to the spot by the noise, recommended that the meeting-house bell should be rung—and this we accordingly did. The bell brought the whole village out of doors, and at last I had the satisfaction of seeing the piano placed in its proper position in the improvised "Concert Hall."

. . . At seven o'clock, the time fixed for the entertainment, very few people had arrived, although several tickets had been sold. With a view to bringing more people, one of the elders of the meeting-house recommended that the bell should be tolled again. This was done, and it brought more people, but, to the surprise and chagrin of the gentlemen who had invited me to give the concert, nearly all the new arrivals objected to pay, on the score that they had paid an annual fee for their seats in the meeting-house, and claimed the right to occupy

> them now. Thus, although the little meeting house was filled to its utmost capacity, only seven dollars was taken at the door.
>
> When the performance was over, a tall, knowing-looking villager sidled up to me, and said, in a stage whisper, "Next time you sing, boss, don't have the bell rung."

Russell tells us that, from Detroit, he journeyed on to Cleveland and then to Cincinnati. His further reference to what were known as "shin plasters" (promissory notes of dubious value) seems to date this story to the recession of 1837–38:

> Just at this time, by the way, there was the greatest difficulty in obtaining coin, and one had to put up with a paper currency, and very curious "paper" at that. One had to take pay in what were colloquially termed "shin plasters"—bits of paper entitling the holder to articles or accommodation up to a specified value. For instance, on paying your hotel bill you would tender, say, a ten dollar note. The change would consist of a shin-plaster, inscribed "good for board," with the amount and name of the host at the bottom. Meeting a friend, and inviting him to lunch or a drink with you, you would pay by means of your goods for board, and the change, if any, would be in the form of small tickets, each bearing the words, "good for a drink." This was the currency used for a considerable time, gold being at a fabulous price, or rather, notes being at a ruinous discount.

Perhaps the most intriguing of all Russell's travel stories is of a supposed journey with George Catlin (1796–1872), so-called "medicine painter," in order to satisfy Russell's wish to "visit the Redskins on their native prairies with a view to studying original melody." Russell recalls:

> To Catlin, therefore, I wrote, asking him to be so kind as to allow me to accompany him on his next trip to the far West. The reply was a cordial acquiescence. It was arranged that I should meet Catlin at Troy, N.Y., and we were to travel thence to the hunting ground of the Redskins. With as little delay as possible this was done, and I found myself in the company of the "Great Medicine Man," en route for the prairies.

> From Troy to Cincinnati, we went through the loveliest country imaginable, and over, I think, the wretchedest roads ever devised by the art of man. The weather, when we left Troy, was delightful, and the journey stands out in my memory as one of the pleasantest of my American experiences. At almost every stopping place we met friends—Catlin's friends mostly. That man's capacity for making friends and keeping them was something wonderful to behold. He had an indescribable charm of manner, a personal magnetism which earned him unlimited popularity. . . .

Russell tells how, on the boat across Lake Erie, he "was accosted by a bright and essentially canny Scot of the name of McLaren, who made himself my friend inside five minutes." In a broad Scottish accent, McLaren kept Russell occupied throughout the voyage with his warnings of the perils of venturing among the Indians, recommending bagpipes as the most effective means of keeping danger at bay. McLaren left at Cleveland, after which Russell continues:

> From Cleveland, after a good night's rest, Catlin, myself and other travellers, set out in the stoutest waggons obtainable for Cincinnati. But alas! "the best laid plans," etc. Ohio, I must tell you, was at that time almost all forest. We found an apology for a road, but the further we advanced the worse it got, and denser grew the forest on either side. At last, completely worn out, and with each man's stomach a yawning vacuum, we hit upon a little tumble-down cabin, which happily proved to be inhabited. Never was oasis more welcome to the traveller of the desert than that log cabin to Catlin and myself. It was hopeless to think of proceeding further that night. So, after eating the best that the keeper of the log cabin could lay before us, we made up our minds to sleep as best we could, curled up in blankets on the ground. Bad as this was, it was certainly preferable to the interior of the ridiculously diminutive cabin.
>
> Cincinnati reached—and oh! how glad were we to get there. We pulled up at the "Memphis," and were soon discussing an excellent table d'hôte. The sight of a well-spread table warmed our hearts, and our privations in the forest soon became mere

matters of memory. Our stay at Cincinnati extended only to five days, during which Catlin made active preparations for our march upon the Indians. He engaged five negroes to carry our boxes and cooking utensils. On the eve of our departure I was in high glee at the prospect of meeting the Redskins. Alas! my confident hopes of hearing some charming specimens of original melody were soon to be dashed to the ground.

In writing or recalling my reminiscences, I am most anxious to impress upon my readers that the United States was comparatively in its infancy at the time I first visited the country and they must not suppose that I exaggerate in any of the anecdotes I relate. Seventy years is a long experience. For in those days, Arkansas, Michigan, Florida, Texas, Iowa, Wisconsin, California, Oregon, Minnesota, Nevada, etc., were territories, now no longer territories (*i.e.* Wildernesses), but States differing widely from one another in climate, in manners, in resources, in taste, and in character. Music in these territories was at a very low ebb—in fact, out of the meeting-houses and churches it did not exist. . . .

On an ideal morning our little expedition party consisting of Catlin, myself and niggers, set forth, availing ourselves of the broad track leading through the dense Missourian forest. Here and there from rising ground we caught glimpses of the distant prairie. Prairie and woodland alike were the varied colours of early spring. The grassy roads were in the pink of condition, soft as velvet, and delightful to walk upon. Tracks of all kinds of animals we frequently struck, and one thing that amused and interested me greatly was the danger signal of the rattlesnake, a creature I had not previously seen.

And so we marched on, never dull, because there was so much to claim our attention; never depressed, for our niggers kept us in the best of spirits with their jokes and songs. The lightheartedness and downright Mark Tapley temperament of the American negro has been dealt with by pens more competent than mine; so I will not enlarge upon the subject, suffice to say that our negroes were no exception to the rule. So long as they ate well, drank well, and had a blanket in which to wrap themselves at night they were always a little happier than the day was long.

For several nights we plodded on like this, sleeping at night round a furze fire, beneath some gigantic tree. A loaded Colt's revolver was each man's bedfellow. Invariably one of us remained awake to keep watch and ward over his comrades. On, I think, the sixth day of our march, when the denser part of the forest had been traversed, we came suddenly upon the Indians, or, perhaps, it would be more correct to say that the Indians came suddenly upon us. Before any one of us could say "Jack Robinson," twenty or thirty Missourian Redskins were glowering at us from all sides. . . .

Catlin quickly made himself known, and the Indians at once assuming a pacific attitude, invited us to join them. My feelings at that moment were mixed. I did not altogether relish the idea of rubbing shoulders with these fellows now that I was in their midst. Catlin seemed quite at home with them, however, and that gave me confidence. It was evident that any friend of Catlin was as welcome as himself, for the chief of the band, advancing towards me, placed his hands (the horniest I ever saw or felt) in mine, and said "Wo wah wo schah ka to ya," or something of that sort. Probably the worthy chief meant that he was "awfully pleased to meet me."

Said Catlin, in an undertone when the greeting of the chief was over:

"These fellows are a curious lot, but you're safe where I am. We shall see them to-morrow in the wigwams with some eighty or ninety others of the tribe."

That night we slept as usual upon the underbrush with our faithful Colts ready for any emergency. Shortly after our not too luxurious breakfast in the morning, we were waited upon by a number of the "head" men of the Indian tribe, who squatted down with us and handed round the pipe of welcome. Each man was supposed to take a whiff and pass the pipe on to his neighbour. To refuse would have been to risk one's scalp; but it was about the dirtiest, most unsanitary process a man could possibly undergo. When the pipe was handed to the chief, I thought I should have exploded as a result of my efforts to restrain my laughter. The picture of the painted chieftain swelling with dignity, and puffed up with a sense of his own importance, was ludicrous in the extreme. Most of

> the Indians, by the way, were tall, athletic fellows. Their arms were bare and tattooed with fantastic designs of animals and reptiles. Some wore armlets of brass, leggings and moccasins, and several were equipped with tomahawks and scalping knives.
>
> With the exception of the chief, they took but little notice of us, but sat motionless as Sphinxes, stolidly smoking their pipes, the fumes from which reminded one strongly of the vapour from the funnel of a steam boat.
>
> "The noble red man that one reads of in my friend Fenimore Cooper's books is fast becoming a thing of the past, and soon will be but a mere memory and a name," Russell added, continuing:
>
> In his stead, there still lives the degenerated, half-civilised Indian, whose days, like those of his erstwhile companion of the prairies, the buffalo, are still numbered. At the time, however, of which I am writing, the degeneration of the Indian race had hardly commenced; indeed, it was not perceptible—they were still the hardy children of the forest, possessing some ideas on the subject of honour and of gratitude. Catlin, in the past, had worked what appeared in their eyes marvellous cures. They looked up to him as a great medicine man; consequently, he was always a welcome guest.

Russell's avowed intent in traveling with Catlin was to hear some original Indian melody. However, the result was not quite what he had expected:

> After a short parley with the chief, in which Catlin made known to him my wish to hear some original Indian melody, the chief made a sudden signal, and, like lightning, the surrounding braves started to their feet, and burst out with what I suppose they called song. I was intensely disappointed, nay, I was more than disappointed, I was disgusted. The chief, however, seemed delighted with the uproar they made. Their yelling was truly fearful. Imagine one man commenced: "Woo-oot! Wo-oot! a, ah, a aaah!" A second instantly added, "Whaar—wha—aar—ya a h!" A third man cried, "Eear! Eear! Ear!!" "We—eewe! Weeee!" howled a fourth one. Considering the distance I had travelled in search of melody, there can be little wonder that I did not exactly enjoy these hideous noises.

Sensible now of the folly I had perpetrated in coming there to hear such sounds, I tried to persuade Catlin to turn his thoughts towards home. "My dear fellow," said he, "I am here to sketch the Indians, and, though I am sorry for your disappointment, I could have told you that none of the tribes have any idea of music, or have any melody." "Perfectly true," said I; "I do not blame you, as my own judgement ought to have told me that there was no melody to be met with in such primitive people."

For many days after this, Catlin was engaged in sketching each chief, and, during that time, I amused myself wandering about, always taking care that a couple of negroes should accompany me. Returning from one of these trips, I found Catlin taking the likeness of two or three of the chiefs. Their dress was splendidly adorned with eagle feathers, beads, etc., instead of the tufts of hair and shaven crowns usually worn by the Pawnees and other Indians. Each expressed infinite surprise and gratification when he beheld his own likeness. . . .

At last I was able to prevail upon Catlin to think of the homeward journey, and we at once made preparations for our departure. The negroes were as delighted as myself at the prospect of leaving, and began to smear themselves with a villainous-smelling compound of oil, fat, and marrow. The next morning we were off, but our march to St. Louis appeared interminable, and several times I almost gave up the hope of getting back to civilisation, for which my soul yearned. Our line of march lay across huge stretches of prairie land. The little Indian ponies which we bestrode could make but little headway each day, owing to the tall, rank grass, which grew to the height of nine or ten feet, and—like a great yellow sea—stretched before and behind us, as far as the eye could reach. Here and there, but, for the most part, many miles apart, arose out of the sea of grass small eminences, crowned with trees and verdure, which afforded us grateful rest and shade, after toiling under the scorching prairie sun. . . .

At last, after about three months' incessant journeying we came across a little log hut inhabited by a white family. In Gulliver's Travels, Dean Swift makes his hero recoil with loathing and disgust from his fellow creatures, on his return from the land of the Houyhnhnms. With me the case was entirely

> different, it was with a positive feeling of rapture that I gazed upon the white faces of the inhabitants of the hut, theirs was the first I had seen for many and many a month, of course, with the exception of Catlin's—and his, as I said before, could hardly be termed white, after the days and nights of exposure that we had been subjected to. A few days later we arrived at St. Louis, and my experience of life among the Indians in the Far West was a thing of the past.
>
> Before closing this chapter, I must do my friend Catlin the justice to say that throughout the trip he had been most thoughtful and kind, and had borne petty troubles and caprices on my part with unfailing geniality and good humour. I bade farewell to Catlin at St Louis, and made my way back to New York, where on my arrival I returned to my old life, and proceeded to give my musical entertainments at the now extinct Niblo's Gardens.

It is altogether a colorful account of his journey west with Catlin. But when did it occur? Did it occur at all? It's noteworthy that, in 1900, Russell gave a quite different account of how his involvement arose, stating that "I was in Chicago. . . . Catlin was there, just starting on a journey West. I was in search of melodies, and as he was going amongst a primitive people there was sure to be prospect of primitive melodies, so I begged to be included in the party." Catlin's movements are pretty well documented, and it seems that during the 1830s he traveled west five times to portray the Plains Indians and their way of life, becoming the first artist to record them in their own territories. However, he completed those trips to Indian territory in 1836. Seemingly it is only on that final trip, in August 1836, that Russell could have accompanied him.

In fact, we know that, in August 1836, Catlin traveled westward with an Englishman named Robert Serrill Wood. Of travels with an Englishman named Henry Russell there is no sign. After that, following a trial run in Buffalo, Catlin opened his Indian Gallery of Indian artefacts in Albany in the summer of 1837. In September 1837 he was at the Clinton Hall in New York, subsequently touring the US before taking his exhibition across the Atlantic to England, in November 1839. Catlin and Russell must have known each other from their time in Albany in the summer of 1837. However, it is difficult to see when they fitted in a journey such as that Russell described. Once more we must take his account with a particularly large pinch of salt.

7

A Trumpeter's Lip

"A Life on the Ocean Wave" was soon a regular feature of Russell's concert programs. He sang it, for instance, at the City Hotel, New York, on Monday, 8 October 1838, when he shared the platform with a pianist, Miss Jackson, described as a pupil of Paris-based, Austrian-born virtuoso Henri Herz (1803–88). As usual, the large room was crowded. A repeat concert with Miss Jackson on 15 October was the occasion for the introduction of another new song, "I Care Not for Spring on Its Fickle Wing," the Christmas carol from Charles Dickens's *The Pickwick Papers*, alongside the still popular "Wreck of the Mexico," 'The Maniac," 'The Ivy Green," "The Skeptic's Dying Lament," "Some Love to Roam," "Let Us Be Gay," and the newly revamped "Our Way Across the Mountain, Ho!"

As in Boston, though, Russell's appealing to popular taste met with disdain in loftier musical circles. Of the earlier of those two concerts New York's *Musical Review* commented:

> Miss Jackson in the performance of two pieces on the Piano Forte acquitted herself creditably. Of the other performances, which were all by Mr. Russell himself—music . . . composed by himself, sung by himself, and accompanied by himself, Mr. Russell also usually attends the door himself—what shall we say? What ought we to say, when witnessing a large company of ladies and gentlemen, thrown apparently into extacies [sic] of delight, from hearing "stuff" . . . ?

"Stuff," as J. A. Stephens comments, "should not be mistaken for a compliment."

In fact, this was just part of a campaign by that journal against Russell's success, built upon the accusations of "Honestus" the previous year. In December 1838, it published an extended critique of *L'Amico dei Cantanti*, seizing upon the slightest opportunity to diminish Russell's standing. Of its assault on the volume's introductory paragraph, J. A. Stephens reports that "Russell certainly does not say much, but neither does the critique. Russell wrote a flowery little introduction, and the critic approached it with the magnifying glass of a semanticist."

But such negativity didn't stop Russell. And there were plenty of newspaper writers to take the opposite line. At Boston's Temple, on 15 December he took part in a two-bass concert. The other bass was the famous Giuseppe de Begnis (1795–1847), and their program was a stunning one. Russell got to sing three bass-bass duets with the great man, alongside his own songs, and a scena on a Bear Hunt. And with an orchestra! "That eccentric fellow, Russell . . . to many of us who had never heard him, the effect was electric."

Following his October concerts in New York, Russell had returned to Albany, giving his services, free, at the Female Academy on 1 November for a concert that introduced Miss Jackson to the Albany public. He was said to be anticipating a return to Boston for a repeat performance of *The Sceptic*, and he was also planning a concert for the widow of his recently deceased local supporter, music teacher, and music seller Isaac P. Cole. The latter event finally took place on 3 January 1839, Russell having "thought the concert would be more successful by waiting until the sitting of the legislature." Alas, tongues were again wagging. When next he gave a concert in Albany, in March 1839, Mrs. Cole felt compelled to take space in the *Albany Evening Journal*:

> **A CARD.**—Mrs. I P COLE regrets extremely that circumstances of a nature very painful to her feelings, have again induced her to appear before the public. . . . It has been currently reported that the proceeds of the concert given to her by Mr. H Russell, the 3d of January last, were appropriated by him for his benefit—and that the one hundred dollars which he promised to give her exclusive of the concert, have likewise not been paid. In answer to this uncalled for and slanderous report, Mrs. Cole can only assure the public that such is not the case, and that Mr. Russell has acted up to all the promises he ever gave, and furthermore had it not been for the generous

Figure 7.1. Program for Signor de Bentis and Henry Russell's concert, 15 December 1838. *Source:* Author's collection.

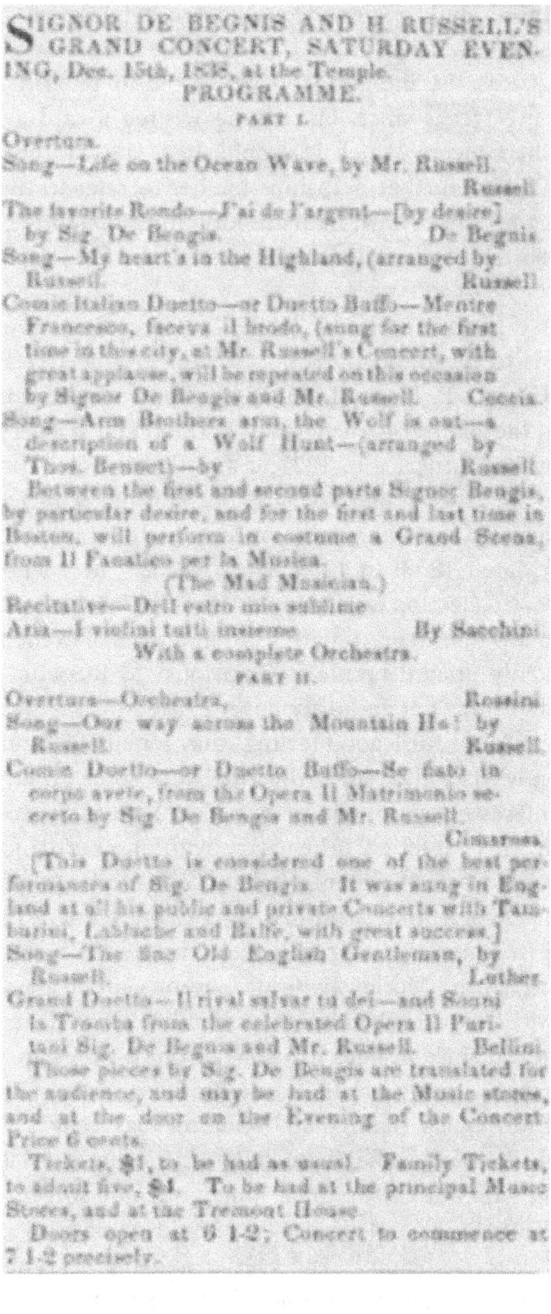

SIGNOR DE BEGNIS AND H. RUSSELL'S GRAND CONCERT, SATURDAY EVENING, Dec. 15th, 1838, at the Temple.

PROGRAMME.

PART I.

Overture.

Song—Life on the Ocean Wave, by Mr. Russell. Russell.

The favorite Rondo—*J'ai de l'argent*—[by desire] by Sig. De Bengis. De Begnis.

Song—My heart's in the Highland, (arranged by Russell. Russell.

Comic Italian Duetto—or Duetto Buffo—Mastro Francesco, faceva il brodo, (sung for the first time in this city, at Mr. Russell's Concert, with great applause, will be repeated on this occasion by Signor De Bengis and Mr. Russell. Cocchia.

Song—Arm Brothers arm, the Wolf is out—a description of a Wolf Hunt—(arranged by Thos. Bennet)—by Russell.

Between the first and second parts Signor Bengis, by particular desire, and for the first and last time in Boston, will perform in costume a Grand Scena, from Il Fanatico per la Musica.

(The Mad Musician.)

Recitative—Dell estro mio sublime

Aria—I violini tutti insieme By Sacchini.

With a complete Orchestra.

PART II.

Overture—Orchestra, Rossini.

Song—Our way across the Mountain Ho! by Russell. Russell.

Comic Duetto—or Duetto Buffo—Se fiato in corpo avete, from the Opera Il Matrimonio secreto by Sig. De Bengis and Mr. Russell. Cimarosa.

[This Duetto is considered one of the best performances of Sig. De Bengis. It was sung in England at all his public and private Concerts with Tamburini, Lablache and Balfe, with great success.]

Song—The fine Old English Gentleman, by Russell. Luther.

Grand Duetto—Il rival salvar tu dei—and Suoni la Tromba from the celebrated Opera Il Puritani Sig. De Begnis and Mr. Russell. Bellini.

Those pieces by Sig. De Bengis are translated for the audience, and may be had at the Music stores, and at the door on the Evening of the Concert. Price 6 cents.

Tickets, $1, to be had as usual. Family Tickets, to admit five, $4. To be had at the principal Music Stores, and at the Tremont House.

Doors open at 6 1-2; Concert to commence at 7 1-2 precisely.

> conduct of Mr. Russell, and the sum she received through his kindness, she would have experienced such difficulties, which only those could experience, who are helpless and need the assistance of a friend.
>
> It was the intention of Mrs. Cole to publish this card some five weeks since, but having written a card a few days after the concert, which was published, she had hoped there would be no further occasions for her to refer to the subject, but having since heard many reports injurious to Mr. Russell's interests, she feels called upon to state the facts as they are.

What seems like a plea of "guilty" to spreading adverse remarks of some kind is to be found in a note to Russell, dated 7 February 1839, written by Charles E. Horn (1786–1849). Tenor singer, and composer of such as "On the Banks of Allen Water" (1812) and "Cherry Ripe" (1826), Horn first visited America in 1827 and settled in New York in 1832. His second wife was the former Mary Anne Horton, who had participated in one of Russell's first New York concerts in 1836, and whom Horn had married in March 1838. In 1839, Horn writes—in a letter now held in the Houghton Collection at Harvard (MS Thr 476), and addressed to "my dear Sir"—a few lines regretting that "in moments of excitement" [he] may have mistakenly uttered opinions "injurious" to Russell's "interests" and "believing that sufficient authority never existed for the statements made." He hopes that "our future good feelings may remain without interruption."

Evidently, they did, since the two were soon performing together during an interesting set of concerts in New York in February 1839. They began at the City Hotel on 8 February with another concert that found Russell in support of the iconic Italian *buffo* de Begnis (1795–1849), a leading Rossini interpreter who had sung many years in Britain and who had arrived in America the previous autumn. Also on the program were soprano Mrs. [Ann] Morley (wife of Covent Garden bass John Morley) and a pianist Edward L. Walker "from London." Russell's support was the most significant, since besides five songs from his repertory ("Woodman, Spare that Tree," Tom Cooke's "Arm, Brothers, Arm" (The Bear Hunt), "The Fine Old English Gentleman," "Charter Oak," and "The Ivy Green"), he joined de Begnis in the three *buffo* duets that the latter had, more usually, sung with one of two great Italian operatic singers: the bass Luigi Lablache (1794–1858) and baritone Antonio Tamburini (1800–76). The three duets were, as before, "The Master and the Servant" (in which de Begnis reputedly sang 600 words and 300 bars of music in four minutes),

"Se fiato in corpo avete" from Cimarosa's *Il Matrimonio Segreto* (the piece from which "Fine Old English Gentleman had allegedly been filched), and "Suoni la tromba" from Bellini's *I Puritani*. The showpiece "J'ai de l'argent" (by Castelli) was, more correctly, 600 bars and 300 words long.

The song "Charter Oak" was another for which Russell's faithful supporter Mrs. L. H. Sigourney had supplied the words. It came with a message from her from Hartford, dated 21 December 1838: "I send you a few stanzas upon our 'Charter Oak,' which, you know, we Hartford people regard as one of the dearest relics of our country, and with somewhat of that veneration which the ancient barons of England exhibited for the Magna Charta, extorted from King John, at Runimede." Russell repeated the song when he was again at the City Hotel with Ann Morley and Walker on 13 February 1839. He also sang another number new to New York, "The Old Year's Gone and the New Year's Come," with words by his young Boston contact "Ione."

A further concert, at the Stuyvesant Institute on 18 February 1839, found Russell performing with Mr. and Mrs. C. E. Horn and flautist W. J. Davies. Horn and Russell opened with the overture to Hérold's *Zampa* for four hands, and later sang the Act 1 Almaviva/Figaro duet from Rossini's *Il Barbiere di Siviglia*. Horn also sang Beethoven's "Rosalie" (otherwise "Adelaide"), with Mrs. Horn giving three of her husband's songs, and Russell one of Horn's in addition to several of his own. Versatility was very much the order of the day, and it was roundly appreciated.

"The concert," declared *The Morning Herald*, "was an admirable one, and gave great delight; over 1,000 persons were there, and hundreds were unable to obtain admittance. Russell must assuredly repeat it." However, the paper also offered some advice:

> He must *actually* limit the number of tickets, and not *profess* to do so; on Monday night, ladies had to stand for three hours, and brutes, in the form of men, sat quietly and saw them suffer without rising to relieve them. He must get better door-keepers—men that are civil; one behaved like a ruffian, and another looked the character of *Jerry Sneak* to the life—and both kept walking about in the lobby, making a noise and not minding their business.

Russell appeared again soon enough: at the City Hotel on 21 February and in a Sacred Music Society bill on 25 February. On 1 March he was at the Apollo Saloon, 410 Broadway, and on 4 March at the Lyceum,

Brooklyn. On the latter occasions he appeared with one or more of the Horns (in Brooklyn, also with Charles Horn Jr., 1811–87) and with British organist/vocalist/composer Joseph P. Knight (1812–87), making his first New York appearances. Knight and the Horns were again in attendance on Russell on 5 March, at Chatham Street Chapel, for the benefit of three charities: the Respectable Aged and Indigent Female Assistance Society, the Widows' Society, and the Female Assistance Society. At this concert, postponed from 28 February because of the weather, Russell introduced a new song, "I Love the Man with a Generous Heart," which apparently remained unpublished.

Back in Albany, Russell's concert at the Female Seminary on Tuesday, 12 March 1839, had all the trappings of a farewell to the city that had been his base for the previous couple of years. That this was rather more than the customary "farewell concert," at the end of any visit to a city, is evidenced by the footnote to the concert announcement in the *Albany Evening Journal*: "The Piano used for this occasion is manufactured by Messrs Nunns, Clark & Co., New York—it was made expressly for Mr. Russell's private use, and has already undergone the ordeal of three concerts without once being tuned. After the concert the piano will be for sale."

In the event, "at the earnest solicitation of several families," Russell did give a second concert in Albany, at the Female Academy on Tuesday, 19 March. Having presumably already sold "his" classy piano, he was provided with one by the local manufacturers, the Messrs. Meachams, who were thereby able to advertise Russell's endorsement of their product. Russell also advertised the concert as "positively his last public appearance in this city" and announced "that he will on this occasion sing several of the favorite songs which he introduced when he first had the pleasure of appearing before the Albany public." The atmosphere of a farewell to the city that had been home to himself and his family is all-pervasive.

During this time back in Albany, Russell also gave a concert at Troy House in neighboring Troy. Then he went west, and in August he renewed his links with the fast-growing city of Rochester. The second half of his farewell concert there, on 9 August, opened with a newly composed march (or quickstep), *The Rochester Union Greys*. The Rochester Union Greys had been organized as an independent military company on 19 November 1838, and, on 28 June 1839, they marched to the city's Court House yard to receive their colors. Russell evidently composed the piece in commemoration. Following it on the program, reproduced in the *Rochester Daily*

Democrat on 9 August, were two new songs, "The Old Bell" and "My Old Wife" (var. "The Auld Wife"), the second of which, when published the following year, would bear a dedication to "Mrs. Frederick F[anning] Backus of Rochester." Her husband (1794–1858) was a local physician; Mrs. was née Rebecca Ann Fitzhugh (1791–1869).

"Old" would become something of a staple in the titles of Russell's songs. As Mr. Stephens has remarked, the passage of time and the contrasts between the past and present were "the simplest and most common of Russell's sentimental themes." Russell himself asked the question, "What is more beautiful than the association of the present and the past?" Hence these two new songs:

> For full five hundred years I've swung
> In my old grey turret high,
> And many a different theme I've sung
> As the time went stealing by!
> ("The Old Bell," words "W")

> Time has dimm'd the lustre of her eyes that brightly shone,
> And her voice has lost the sweetness of its girlhood's silv'ry tone;
> But her heart is still as cheerful as in early days of life,
> And as fondly as I priz'd my bride, I love my dear old wife.
> ("My Old Wife," words Jonas B. Phillips)

Inevitably Russell's overuse of the word "old" made him a target for satire. This was apparent most notably, perhaps, in the 1841 publication of "The Old Night-Cap," described on its title page as "a descriptive ballad, sung by Principal Comic Singers in the United States, poetry by William By Esq., Music by The Composer [sic], and dedicated to the Admirers of Henry Russell." Its text includes this passage:

> This grogram old gown, and an old flowered vest;
> Put an old English gent, in an old oak chest:
> Old time, and old Care, of old things get perplex'd on,
> For the grogram old gown, got on an old Sexton;
> And when on his old back, it fitted him well.
> He kept an old house, they call'd the old Bell!
> The old Bell, the old Bell!

New York City heard "The Old Bell" and "My Old Wife" during further Russell appearances in October 1839. At the first, at a concert scheduled originally for the City Hotel on Thursday, 10 October, but seemingly deferred until the following Monday, he appeared alone. However, at the City Hotel again on 18 October, he appeared in support of Joseph Knight, along with an old London acquaintance, the soprano Ann Seguin, née Childe (1811–88). She was the daughter of a singer at the Covent Garden of the 1810s and of James Wearin (or Waring) Childe (c. 1778–1862), a London portrait painter; more immediately, she was the acclaimed soprano wife of the bass [Arthur] Edward [Sheldon] Seguin (1809–52), with whom she had sung at the King's Theatre, Covent Garden and Drury Lane. Edward and Ann Seguin had gone to America with their three children in 1838, and they later formed their own opera company there, which toured the US and Canada extensively during the 1840s.

Then, on 24 October 1839, Russell was reunited with Mr. and Mrs. Horn, J. P. Knight, and W. A. King at the Stuyvesant Institute. Horn, Russell, and Knight opened with the glee "Winds Whistle Cold," and Knight introduced his subsequently celebrated new song "Rocked in the Cradle of the Deep." Besides the usual Russell offerings, Knight and Russell duetted in Rossini's "*All'idea di quel metallo*" from Il Barbiere di Siviglia, Horn sang Beethoven's "Rosalie' (alias "Adelaide"), and Horn and Knight offered Henry Bishop's "Tell Me, Where Is Fancy Bred," while William King played a fantasia at the piano. A week later, at the City Hotel, Knight and Russell appeared in support of King, with George Loder (1816–68), cousin of composer Edward Loder (1813–65), as conductor. Knight and Russell sang the famous duet "Suoni la tromba" from Bellini's *I Puritani*—which would not have been quite the same as the Russell/de Begnis rendition! Finally, after further concerts at the Lyceum, Brooklyn on 1 November, and the Apollo Saloon, Broadway, on 4 November, Russell departed for Philadelphia.

Preceded in Philadelphia by the Seguins, who gave a two-week opera season at the American Theatre in Walnut Street, Russell gave four concerts at the Philadelphia Museum on 11, 13, 15, and 20 November. Announced with him were J. P. Knight, George Loder, a soprano Miss Hardwick, and the ubiquitous valve trumpeter Gambati. The concerts were ostensibly as successful as ever, but Russell's association with Signor Gambati and "Miss" Hardwick would soon come back to haunt him. While Gambati continued his music making in Philadelphia, Russell returned to New York, where on 9 and 18 December he and the Seguins were at Niblo's Saloon with Knight, George Loder, and Gambati. Russell joined in a glee and a catch ("A House on fire") with his operatic confrères. According to Odell's *Annals of the New York Stage*, he was again with the Seguins and Loder at the City Hotel on Christmas Day, and at the Lyceum, Brooklyn, on 27 December. Then, for the evening of 28 December, Russell was announced with Knight, the Horns, and a quartet of Hungarian vocalists at the City Hotel, New York, for the benefit of Mr. Dinneford, former lessee of the Bowery Theatre. Also on the bill, by contrast with the "Miss" Hardwick who had sung in Philadelphia, was now "Mrs." Hardwick. She'd been "Mrs." at the National Theatre, where her husband was "principal machinist," with Seguin and Mrs. Bailey in June. And "Mrs." at Brooklyn's Military Gardens and New Saloon. Typo or fakery?

However, an item in that day's *Morning Herald* may have entertained the public rather more than any musical performance. Perhaps short of real news, between Christmas and the New Year, *The Morning Herald* had decided to treat its readers to some seasonal fun. Once more, controversy had followed Russell around, and for once it brought his wife, Isabella, out of the shadows:

> The musical and fashionable world, has lately been convulsed with an affair that has reached the eye of the public first through the medium of a police report. But reporters generally only look at the surface of a story, and seldom dive deep into the rich soil that it contains. The present case is an instance of that kind, for it is richer in music, morals, matrimonial philosophy, pistols, courage, cowhides, discord, harmony, gallantry and fashion, than any thing we have heard of for a long time.
>
> The parties concerned are Signor Gambati, the celebrated valve trumpet player, and Mr. Henry Russell, the celebrated *baratone* singer. These are the principal actors in this serio-comico-tragico-operatico drama. The performances consist of a grand concert and a melodrama, in which a pistol and a cowhide took prominent parts; there was also a beautiful little underplot, in which a lady took part, as is generally the case in all important dramas in real life, and the whole wound up with an interesting farce. The particulars, as they have been stated to us, are as follows: and, as they have reached us from the most unquestionable sources, none other than Signor Gambati and Mr. Russell himself, of course they are most authentic.

It appears that a short time since, (so says Gambati) Mr. Russell engaged him to play his trumpet at twelve concerts at Niblo's. There being some leisure time between these concerts, or before they took place, Russell engaged Gambati to blow his trumpet also at one or two concerts in Philadelphia, and for that purpose took him to Philadelphia. Gambati put up at the Marshall House, and Russell at the Washington Hotel. Finally, Gambati, at Russell's persuasion, removed to the Washington Hotel, and Russell introduced him to his wife and family as his dear, particular, and bosom friend; and he was at once installed into the best seat at the table, the arm chair by the fire place, and had the entrée of Mr. Russell's rooms, as it were, at all times.

Matters moved on smoothly, and in harmony, as time rolled on. Mr. Russell gave a concert, and Gambati played his trumpet at it; his "lip" being considered most excellent, it being an indispensable matter that a trumpeter should have what is called "a good lip." At the concert, therefore, Signor Gambati's lip worked well. Mr. Russell gave a dinner and here again Signor Gambati's "lip" worked well. Mr. Russell gave a grand soirée, and here again the Signor's "good lip," worked well; and as will be seen by the sequel to this story, this was not the last occasion upon which Signor Gambati's "good lip" worked well.

Time passed on, and Mr. Russell went to New York, leaving his amiable and excellent wife, his interesting children, and his dear friend, Signor Gambati, all at the Washington Hotel at Philadelphia, whilst he was in New York arranging for a series of concerts to be given at Niblo's. "I was very happy," said the Signor, "whilst I remain dere, for dey was all so kind; I spend some several hours in de day wiz Madame Russell, a very fine ladie, and I blew ma trumpet and play for her two, tree, several hours in her room several day, and I spend ma time vera mooch pleasant, *bien* what you call delight, and she seem vera happy to have me wiz her, and to play on the valve trumpet to please her, as I shall play on the valve trumpet to please every lady who wish me. I stay dere; I do all I sink shall be right, I respect Madame Russell as my sister; I esteem her, what you call love, platonic. By and by her husband send for me to play

> my trumpet, in New York; I say to Madame Russell, "addio, bon jour, Madame, I shall see you, good by; sometime shall pass before I shall have de pleasure to see your face again!" She sorry to part from me; I take her hand, so, comme ça; I put my lip to hers, so, comme ça; I kiss her as my sister, toute la même chose. So, I shall leave her and come to New York to play on de valve trumpet before de ladies at New York."

Here the signor's "good lip" was brought in play, and at this point in his narrative, the Signor was not a little affected, and paused for breath, but soon resumed.

> Some day shall come soon that we had nothing to do, and Mr. Russell say he shall give some concert again at Philadelphia, and take me on again to play my valve trumpet again. I go; I see Madame Russell; she say, "how do you do, Mr. Gambati? I am glad to see you!" So she did not seem angry dat I kiss her, wiz de fashion of my country, when I leave her before. I say to her, "Madame, I am glad I have some pleasure to see your face once more." So I stay dere—play on de valve trumpet once more. I come to New York; I take my leave of Madame Russell again; I take her hand once more, comme ça; I kiss her once more comme ça, as de fashion of my country, toute la même *chose*, and I come to New York, and I sink no more for de kiss, or for any ding but to play on de valve trumpet, as de custom of my country is to kiss de ladies so, comme ça.

This, according to the Signor's statement, is the "very head and front of his offending." He has done no more to Mr. Russell's amiable lady than he would do to any other lady whom he esteemed as a sister; he played his trumpet at the public places of amusement, and in his friend's private apartments—he chastely saluted his friend's wife twice on leaving her, in accordance with the injunction of St Paul, who said, "Greet ye one another with a holy kiss," and he played on his trumpet in New York, and as he says, he took Mr. Russell's note in exchange for his notes; this he expected shortly to exchange for good bank notes, and that he thought would end the whole affair amicably.

This is the Signor's statement; and now, not to be beforehand with our story, we must give Mr. Russell's statement. He admits all about the concert, and the playing on the valve trumpet, and his introduction of Gambati to his excellent lady, but he says that the Signor (who has some reputation for gallantry, as well as a "good lip," and who is said to be no Joseph) took advantage of his (Russell's) absence, to seize his wife by the waist with rather more force than a friend would do, kissed her in any but a platonic way, threw her on the floor in any but an harmonious way, when she screamed in a most unmelodious way, and the Signor ran off in any but a concerted manner.

Such is the discord between the two statements. That they do not harmonize is not our fault; we tell the tales as they are told to us by Gambati and Russell themselves. Whether they were concerted beforehand or not, we have no means of knowing. One fact appears clear, that Gambati kissed Mrs. Russell; the motive or manner of doing this does not appear quite so clear; neither can we ascertain how the éclaircissement took place at last between the lady and her husband. How she came to mention the second kissing and not the first, if two there were, and how the husband came to take offense at a chaste salute, from a friend with a "good lip," done in a platonic way, after the fashion of his country, *comme ça*, are matters entirely beyond our comprehension; we are impartial historians, and confess our ignorance rather than surmise errors.

Gambati says that Russell found his wife in tears, because some scandal monger had made remarks about Gambati spending so many hours with her; Russell questioned her, and she unburthened her bosom by telling him that Gambati had kissed her. On this, Russell brings his wife on to New York—takes rooms at the American Hotel, and sends for Gambati to call on him. A great deal of maneuvering appears to have taken place at this stage of the proceedings, and the result appears to be that Gambati was apprised that Russell had some dreadful design toward him, which might, probably, spoil his "good lips," or put an end to his playing upon the valve trumpet, or saluting any ladies, *comme ça*, again. He therefore borrowed a pistol, loaded without a cap (so he says); entered Russell's room, the door of which was instantly locked by Russell, and the key taken by a Mr. Sharp, who was also there with Mrs. Russell. But we will give the dialogue in Gambati's own words:-

> *Gambati*—Madame Russell, *bon jour*; Mons. Russell, how you do; you sent for me, to give me some money, eh?
> *Russell*—(looking daggers and broad swords)—I sent for you to give you a

d—d good flogging. Look there, sir, (pointing to Mrs. R.) what have you done to that lady?

Gambati—Done to her? Nozing!

Russell—Did you not kiss her? rudely kiss her?

Gambati—Me! ne-vare!

Russell—'Tis false, Sir.

Mrs. Russell—It's no use to conceal it, Mr. Gambati; I have told Mr. Russell all that you did!

Gambati—*Mon Dieu*! what shall I have done. I kiss her, as my country custom, *comme ça*.

Russell—You are a scoundrel, and I shall chastise you.

Gambati—Now I know why you send for me. I was warned—to take care of you; now you take care of me. If you shall hit me, I shall break your head clean through—(at the same time suiting the action to the word, by pulling out his pistol without a cap).

Russell—Lay down your arms. I want to speak to you.

Gambati—You can speak; my pistol shall not prevent your lips from de speak.

Russell—But I'll prevent your lips from moving as they have done. Lay down your arms.

Gambati—Open the door.

Russell—Lay down your arms.

Gambati—Open the door.

And in this way, the war of words was continued for nearly two hours, until at last the Signor made his escape from the room, leaving his hat and cloak behind him. Russell kicked and knocked his castor into a cocked hat, leaving about forty watch house kinks in it. Finally, they "met i' the hall," and there Russell demanded satisfaction with the fists, like "A fine old English gentleman,—one of the olden time."

Gambati replied—"You are English; your education is English; the first part of your education is to learn to fight wiz de box and de fists, and then you learn your gramma. I do not know the English language, and so I cannot fight wiz de box. But I have hurt your honor by de kiss to your good lady, I will give you de satisfaction by blowing at you wiz de pistol or de small sword."

Mr. Russell's version differs somewhat from this. He says, "the scoundrel came into my room armed with a pistol, which he fired at my head, the ball grazing my hair." Which is right, and which is wrong, as we said before, we have no means of knowing, and we prefer giving the version of each of the principal actors in this tragico-farcico-operatico-domestic drama, *comme ça*, to making erroneous surmises. The result was that no fight took place, and Russell meeting Gambati soon after, spat upon his beard, for which he has been held to bail.

This event has created an immense sensation in the fashionable world. These two distinguished musical men, for whom we have severally the highest opinion, will now become more distinguished than ever. Fortunately, there was no harm done to any one, and there is even a discordant diversity of opinion as to whether the pistol was or was not fired. Hats, cloaks, kisses, cowhides, pistols, and all sorts of curious and inflammatory matters seem mixed up together, but neither the Signor's "good lip" nor the vocalist's "good hair" have been injured. The part that Mrs. R has performed in this drama has been involuntary. She has not been in the least to blame; she is a most amiable and worthy lady, and was the mere creature of circumstances over which she had no control. When Signor Gambati pressed her hand and kissed her, comme ça, she believed what he told her, that it was out of esteem, and platonic regard, and according to the custom of his country. When her worthy husband told her that it was wrong, she of course believed him, and cried for regret at what she could not remedy; and as a matter of course despised Sig Gambati for what he had done. There is still a *hiatus* to be filled up which the trial will doubtless develope [sic]. Meantime these two leaders in the musical world will be more sought after than ever. If Russell gives a concert he will have crowds to hear him; and if Gambati should give a concert he will have greater crowds than Russell; there will be no end to the numbers who will attend; for nothing gives so much *eclat* to a man in the eyes of the fashionable world as to have a "good lip," and to get into a scrape about a pretty woman.

The "Mr. Sharp" involved in the Christmas Day encounter was Henry John Sharpe, a friend of Russell's who has already appeared—and would again—among his lyricists. Sharpe felt the need to supply his own version of events, which the paper duly published on 31 December. If rather less entertaining, at least it added worthwhile additional information:

> I then told Sig. Gambati (as I had previously done) that if he would put aside his pistol, that he might depend upon my honor, not to interfere in any way, let what would occur during my presence. He remonstrated, that his antagonist was strong,

> but if he was allowed to send up for a friend who was below, that he would comply. Upon inquiring who this friend was, he replied, *the master of the house*, Mr. Russell stepped out to bring up Mr. Coggens, and observing that Sig Gambati had his eye attracted to the door, I took hold of the key, thinking I had turned the bolt and put it into my pocket.
>
> Turning round to Mrs. Russell, who was in deep distress, Gambati, aware of the mistake, instantly made for the door, sprung out of the room, leaving his cloak and hat behind him, ran down the back stairs, and halting for a moment, on the first landing, presented his pistol at me, and exclaimed "what you want?" Mr. Russell immediately ran down the other stairs, and interrupted Sig Gambati in the hall, where he inflicted an indignity upon him and retired to his apartment. Presuming the affair to be settled, I left the hotel, and was not present at the subsequent assault in the street, but I was afterwards told by an eye witness, that Sig Gambati, with a companion, both exhibited pistols in the affray, and that the former afterwards repaired to the Police, and affirmed that he considered his life in danger, although Mr. Russell, the whole time was without any weapon of defence, save the manly courage, which a sense of injury inspired.

Who do you believe?

As if all this was not enough, Russell was, simultaneously, in a scrape with the other major associate at his Philadelphia concerts in November—"Miss" (as she had been billed) Hardwick. Philadelphia's *Public Ledger and Daily Transcript* gave this summary of the matter:

> Mr. James Hardwick, husband of Mrs. Hardwick, formerly an actress in the National Theatre, N Y, on Thursday last [26 December] preferred a complaint before a magistrate of that city, against Mr. Russell the vocalist, for an assault and battery, which the latter had committed upon him with a cowskin. It appears that Mr. Russell has determined to flog every body into a belief that he is a gentleman.

The cowskin again! And it was "Mrs. Hardwick," as billed for the City Hall, New York, on Saturday, 28 December, and not "Miss Hardwick," as billed in Philadelphia. That was the crux of this further problem, as *The Morning Herald* took great delight in explaining, a few days later, in a piece that incidentally adorned the Hardwick name with an extra "e":

> It will be recollected that some morning paper gave a report of a *rencontre* between Mr. R and a Mr. Hardwicke, a clerk in Horne's music store, Broadway. The causes and consequences are these:
>
> When Russell and Seguin gave concerts in Philadelphia, the former engaged Mrs. Hardwicke, the wife of Mr. H. to sing for him. She had been engaged as a *secondo* [sic] *donna* at the National, before it "went up to heaven in glory." In announcing his concerts at Philadelphia, Mr. R put Mrs. H into the bill thus:-
>
> "Love has eyes, or any other song, by Miss Hardwicke"
>
> This very naturally made the exquisites of Philadelphia examine the young lady through their eye-glasses, there being more interest for youth and beauty than for a married lady. It was soon discovered, however, that Miss Hardwicke had a fine-looking boy, who trudged along the streets with her, a fact which by no means corresponded with the bill of the play. This annoyed Mrs. H., who had no idea of sailing under false colors. She wrote to her husband, and her husband wrote to Mr. Russell, demanding an alteration in the next concert. This, by some means or other, Mr. R neglected to do—probably he was engaged in doing the amiable to Gambati. He received another letter from Hardwicke, in no very gentle terms, and at last the vocalist was made aware of the impropriety of passing off a very respectable married lady, with a fine plump boy, for a young and sentimental maiden of nineteen. He excused himself, gave Mrs. Hardwicke a party, was polite and attentive, and introduced her into fashionable society—that is, the society of composers and *primas donnas* [sic].
>
> These doings were pari passu with the interesting movements of Gambati; but unlike him, Mr. Russell kissed no pretty woman, comme ça, "after de fashion of his counterie."

Thus matters stood in Philadelphia, but the storm still raged in New York. Mr. Hardwicke was indignant. Under such feelings, he met, one day, Mr. Russell, in company with Seguin, in Broadway, and said—"there goes a d—d rascal," or some such imputation. Russell was on the verge of taking satisfaction of him on the spot, for he is a capital *savan* [sic] in the science. "No," said the amiable, gentlemanly, and peaceable Seguin, his *moustaches* curling up in very contempt—"he's only a shop boy—don't trouble him." Russell passed on; but in a few days got another letter from Hardwicke, more piquant than ever. Russell, like a man of metal, as he is of music, went down to Horne's store, where Hardwicke is employed with a bright pair of shears, three feet long, in cutting music. Russell made his appearance, and demanded an apology on the spot or he would take satisfaction. Hardwicke looked up in astonishment, and immediately drew his long shears—"if you approach me a step nearer, I will run you through." At this instant, Horne entered, and the combatants separated.

> On Saturday evening last, Hardwicke employed an officer, who went to Russell's lodgings, about the hour he was proceeding to the Concert at the City Hotel. Russell was dressed, and ready to start. "Is your name Russell?" asked the officer. "Yes." "Then you're wanted," said he, quietly tapping him on the shoulder, and exhibiting his warrant. This spoiled the music for that night. Russell got bail, and remained at home; but no concert was given.
>
> We understand and hope that all these interesting passages will soon be set to music. General Morris will supply the words, Gambati the trumpet score, Mrs. Hardwicke the soprano, and Hardwicke will cut it up with his long shears, three feet long.

All this coverage, it will be noted, was printed in the *Herald*, the New York newspaper edited by the James Gordon Bennett who had been involved in the pay-for-puff and poison scandal over the singer Emily Sutton, and whom Russell describes in his memoirs as his "friend." Not yet he wasn't!

Quite how the two contretemps were resolved is unclear. Seemingly they blew over. Mrs. Hardwick was singing at Niblo's, still, in 1845. Signor Alessandro Gambati lost "all his teeth but five," which ended his trumpeting until he got some "artificial teeth on a gold plate," and he hurried off to teach music in Charleston, SC. However, these scandals demonstrate yet again Russell's ability to attract controversy and newspaper paragraphs, and they leave little doubt that he caused jealousy and resentment among fellow artists.

Of course, nothing at all of this finds its way into Russell's memoirs, where everything is sweetness and light. What does appear in his account of this phase of his career is perhaps the most bizarre of all the distortions of truth to be found there. He writes:

> I . . . made my way to New York, where it was my good fortune to meet a trio of old friends: Edward Seguin and Mrs. Seguin, his charming wife, whom I had previously known as Miss Child [*recte* Childe], of the Royal Academy of Music; and last, but by no means least, Vincent Wallace, the composer. . . . When we four met together in New York City, it was proposed that we should unite forces, and give jointly six concerts at New York, Brooklyn, Jersey City, and several other towns in the United States. These concerts, which were under the conductorship of Vincent Wallace, proved an enormous success, both financially and artistically. Our tour finished, we returned once more to New York, where we bade farewell to the Seguins, who departed Philadelphia-wards, in which place they had to fulfil an engagement, Wallace and I returning meanwhile to our old quarters, the "Astor" Hotel.

As we have seen, it was in late 1839 that Russell met and teamed up with the Seguins, and, as we shall see later, Russell and the Seguins did, indeed, move on from New York to appear elsewhere. But what of Vincent Wallace (1812–65), who, with his *Maritana* (1845), was to share with William Balfe the distinction of composing one of the most successful British operas of the nineteenth century? Nowhere, in press of that time, is there any sign of him. Indeed, Wallace is well attested not to have appeared in New York before June 1843. Even though he did, then, appear in New York around the same time as Russell, the two seem not to have appeared at the same concerts.

Yet this story, in Russell's memoirs, is merely the lead-in to even more bizarre claims. Russell gives a lengthy account of a night when he and Wallace were strolling on Broadway and came across a mob crying, "Down with him!"; "Lynch him!"; "We'll have no more of him!"; "Down with the Britisher!" They discovered that the object of the mob's wrath was the British actor William Charles Macready (1793–1873). In order to drive Macready from the country, the American actor Edwin Forrest

(1806–72) had hired ruffians, who "had attacked the Opera House where Macready was performing, and the great actor had barely escaped with life." Russell continues:

> Burning with indignation at the unjust and cruel treatment to which Macready had been subjected, Wallace and I repaired to the Carlton Hotel, where Macready was then staying. We were speedily ushered into the actor's presence, and found him in a very depressed and despondent frame of mind, which was, indeed, but natural under the circumstances. Nevertheless, he extended to us a cordial welcome, and, after complimenting Wallace upon his able compositions, he turned to me and gracefully expressed the great pleasure he had experienced in attending my entertainments in the large room at the "City" Hotel. The interview was very short, but in shaking hands with us, he told us that he intended to leave for England in a very few days, and begged that we would again visit him before he left. Needless to say, we greedily accepted his invitation, and a more pleasant evening than we had it would be difficult to imagine. Macready made himself most agreeable and communicative, though it was not until Wallace and I had played and sung to him that he quite recovered his natural animation and good spirits.

Russell goes on at much greater length about the subsequent conversation between himself and Macready. But what can we make of this story? Is it not an account of the Astor Place riot, in which a crowd of 15,000 gathered outside the Astor Place Opera House, ostensibly to protest against Macready appearing there, resulting in twenty-three deaths and over one hundred wounded? History records that Macready left the theatre in disguise, hid at the home of a friend, and, in the early hours of the morning, escaped in an enclosed carriage to New Rochelle, from where he traveled to Boston. History also records that the feud between Forrest and Macready began only in 1845, that the Astor Place Opera House was not built until 1847, and that the Astor Place riot took place neither in 1839–40 nor 1843, but on 10 May 1849. By then both Russell and Wallace had been back in Europe for several years. Clearly the whole episode must be filed, along with being dandled on King George IV's knee, and much more, on the Henry Russell fiction shelves.

However, there just may be a basis for the bones of this fictional tale, as there are for many such. When Henry arrived first in New York, it seems that he sang his "Fine Old English Gentleman" at the Park Theatre, during the stay there of Mr. and Mrs. Wood. And toward the end of that season, a demonstration was arranged against the "blawsted Englishman." Has Henry mixed a reminiscence of the Wood episode with his non-reminiscence of the Macready one? Clearly, possible. And purposely. Fiction is made up of many memories.

Yet, even now, Russell was not finished with his demonstrably false claims of a partnership with Vincent Wallace. He concludes:

> We remained in New York for some little time after this, until the travelling mania seized upon Wallace, and he made up his mind to visit Mexico. He was greatly anxious that I should accompany him thither. Though at a loss to understand the object of visiting a country where my entertainments could not be understood but by a limited few, I was reluctant to part from my friend, and, therefore, according to his earnest entreaties, I joined him, and we started on our long and tedious journey to Mexico, by the way of New Orleans. On our arrival at Vera Cruz, it did not take me long to find out that I was landed in a most uncongenial country. The few people whom I met were offensive in manner, and gave me a very unfavourable impression of the place and its society. In fact, such an unfavourable opinion did I conceive of the whole country that I promptly made up my mind to shake the dust of Mexico from off my feet at the very earliest opportunity, and, therefore, much to our mutual regret, I bade farewell to Vincent Wallace at Vera Cruz, and we parted with many expressions of affection and good-will—he to pursue his journey onwards to the City of Mexico, and I to make the best of my way back to New Orleans and civilization.

We know that Wallace was in Vera Cruz and Mexico City in 1840–42 and New Orleans in 1842 and, indeed, that he composed a mass for the cathedral of the latter city. However, he arrived there from the West Indies rather than New York and, as we have seen, only later visited New York. We also know that Wallace was not around when Russell made his own visit to New Orleans, in January 1844. There seems absolutely no way that these stories about Wallace can have a grain of truth. Quite why it mattered to Russell to claim dealings with Wallace is a mystery, but it can only add further doubt—if doubt were needed—on other supposed relationships. If we are to believe Russell, no musical or theatrical artist of repute could resist the appeal of his company, whereas history seems, all too often, to have had other ideas on the matter.

8

Old Tippecanoe

At the same time that he was building up a very visible set of concert appearances in New York, Russell's regular visits to Boston likewise continued to attract audiences. George F. Root (1820–95), later a successful writer of ballads and Civil War songs, was one who heard him in 1839 and commented, in his book *George F. Root: The Story of a Musical Life* (Cincinnati, 1891), on his influence: "He had a beautiful baritone voice and great command of the keyboard. . . . I was so taken with Russell's songs, that I worked harder than ever before to be able to play and sing them as he did. When the accompaniments were too much for me, or the pitch too high, I modified and simplified and transposed . . ."

Russell and the Seguins made their way to Boston from New York in January 1840. They gave their first concert together there at the Melodeon on Saturday, 18 January, attracting the usual large audience. Edward Seguin and Russell ended the first part with the duet "Se fiato in corpo avete" from Cimarosa's *Il Matrimonio Segreto*, and were joined by Ann Seguin for the finale of the second part, the oft-sung laughing trio "Vadasi via di qua" by Martini. Their second concert, at the Melodeon on Wednesday, 22 January, was notable for Edward Seguin introducing "The Free, the Free" (alias "I Love, I Love the Free"), which Russell had composed "especially for him." At their next concert on 25 January, Ann Seguin likewise sang a Russell song, composed "especially for her," "The Fisher Boy Merrily Lives."

At this third concert, Russell, too, had a new song, and one that was to prove among the most popular he ever composed. Like the aforementioned songs for the Seguins, "The Old Arm Chair" had a lyric by the young English poetess Eliza Cook (1818–89). It was one of a bundle of sentimental numbers that appeared around the time, about the chair in which the singer's mother had sat and, eventually, died:

> I love it, I love it, and who shall dare
> To chide me for loving that old arm chair?
> I've treasured it long as a sainted prize;
> I've bedewed it with tears, and embalmed it with sighs.
> 'Tis bound by a thousand bands to my heart;
> Not a tie will break, not a link will start.
> Would ye learn the spell? A Mother sat there;
> And a sacred thing is that old arm chair.

The song composer and publisher John Hill Hewitt, demonstrating how Russell turned the few good notes of his voice to advantage, pointed out that the song "has but five notes in its melodic construction."

Now the Seguins departed for the South, leaving Russell pitched against Joseph Knight in Boston. Knight had made his Boston debut at the Masonic Temple on 4 January, when *The Boston Morning Post* described him as "a charming vocalist" but reported that the concert was "not numerously attended." "Charming" is not, of course, an adjective that was commonly applied to Russell, whose forceful command over his audiences contrasted vividly with Knight's softer approach, which—for all his accomplishments—failed to attract quite such an enthusiastic response. Russell gave concerts with the four "Euterpian Vocalists" at the Masonic Temple on 1 and 4 February, and, on Saturday, 8 February, he and Knight took part with others in a grand concert promoted by the actor Edward Bertie Ranger at the Melodeon. Besides "The Old Arm Chair" ("by particular request"), Russell sang Knight's "The New Year's Come," and Knight reciprocated with Russell's "The Fisher Boy," which had been dedicated to Ranger in its published edition.

The Boston Morning Post reported that the concert of 8 February "was crowded to excess" and that, "from our own observation, we should judge there were nearly as many went away disappointed at not being able to obtain admittance, as were fortunate enough to get in." *The Musical Magazine* confirmed that "Mr. Russell's organ of voice is better than Mr. Knight's. It has more vigor and flexibility." It added, though, that Knight was a more sensitive musician. Moreover, it repeated the old criticism of Russell for having given a comic song (by Jonathan Blewitt, 1782–1853)

Figure 8.1. "The Old Arm Chair" sheet music cover. *Source:* Courtesy the Lester Levy Sheet Music Collection, The Sheridan Libraries, Johns Hopkins University.

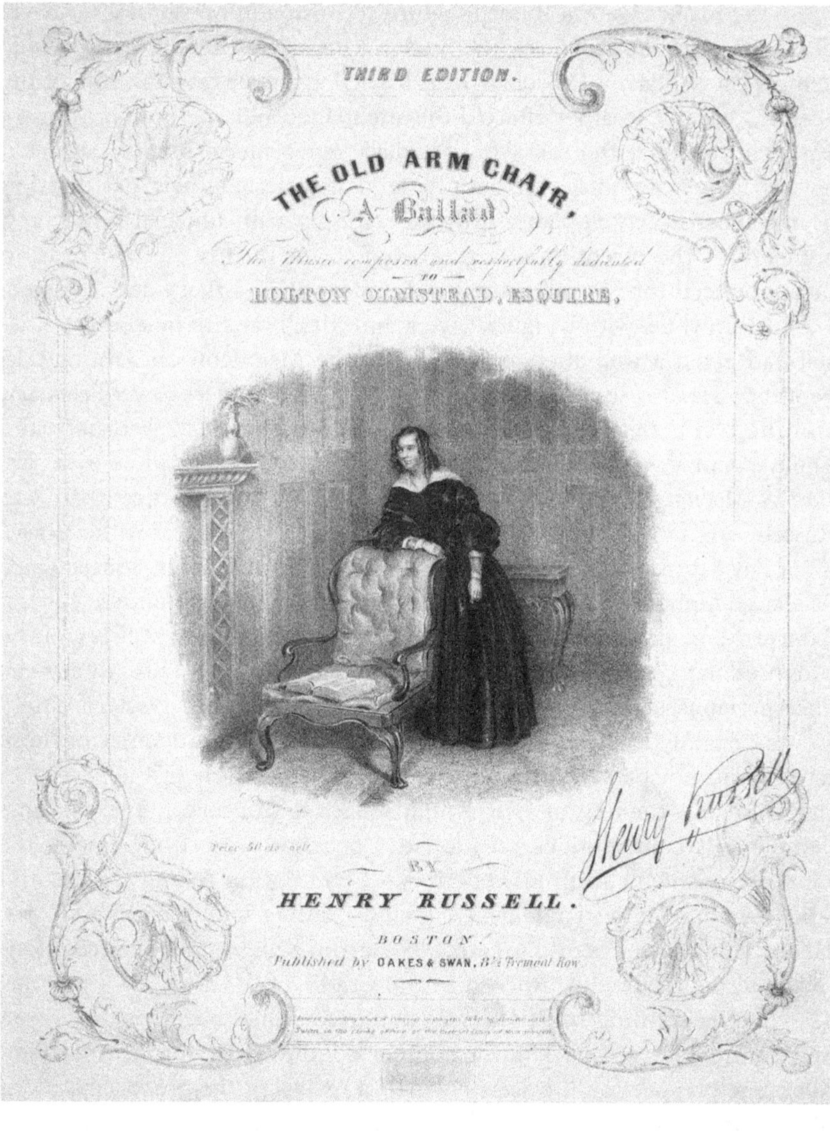

as encore for a tender one. "The Fisher Boy" and "The Old Arm Chair" are both very pleasing. The simple touching melody of the latter pleased the audience so that they called for a repetition; Mr. Russell came and sang "Why Don't the Men Propose?" This certainly shows a great want of judgment, or respect, for the public."

The major event of Russell's return to Boston, however, was a revival of his oratorio *The Sceptic* by the Boston Musical Institute at the Masonic Temple on Sunday, 9 February, with Russell again singing the role of the Sceptic. Adverse weather affected the attendance, but *The Boston Morning Post* reported that the following Sunday's repeat performance "attracted a very large assemblage of people, who manifested their gratification by the most hearty applause. Mr. Russell sang with unusual power and animation." The reception was good enough for further performances to be announced for the following two Sundays, 23 February and 1 March.

Meanwhile, with Knight, Hayter, and Mrs. Franklin in support, Russell had given a well-attended concert at the Melodeon on Saturday, 15 February. He also supported Knight at the latter's concert on 19 February, and the two appeared together at Ranger's concert on 22 February and Thomas Comer's on 26 February. At this last, well attended as ever, *The Boston Morning Post* (28 February) took delight in reporting that "Mr. Russell sung so well that even his pantaloons split themselves with ecstasy."

For Saturday, 29 February, Russell announced that "in consequence of a large number of persons not being able to gain admittance at his last Concert, and having purchased their tickets, which they still retain, he proposes giving a FAREWELL CONCERT, being positively his last appearance previous to his departure for Cincinnati and other Western cities." It was certainly the last of his own concerts; but, in the manner of those days, it did not prevent him making another "positively last appearance" the following evening at J. P. Knight's Sacred Concert at the Masonic Temple. His contributions on the latter occasion were from among the more serious items from his repertory—"Wind of the Winter Night" and "The Sceptic's Dying Lament"—as well as joining with Knight and Mrs. Henry Wallack in oratorio excerpts by Haydn. Knight's solo contributions included his celebrated "Rocked in the Cradle of the Deep."

Not everything in Russell's Boston garden had been rosy, however, and controversy of one kind or another continued to dog his footsteps. The mere prospect of *The Sceptic* stirred a revival of the press accusations of plagiarism that had surfaced over two years earlier. The specific suggestion now was that *The Sceptic* was more than somewhat the work of the aforementioned British-born Boston organist, musical director, and composer Thomas Comer (1790–1862), who had conducted all its Boston performances. Russell issued a writ, claiming damages of $10,000. He also compiled a long letter of defense, written from the Tremont House Hotel (the first Boston hotel with indoor plumbing) and dated 8 February 1840—the day of his appearance at Ranger's first concert, and the day before the first revival performance of *The Sceptic*. Here is just part:

> Sir,—I regret very much that necessity which impels me to enter the arena of newspaper controversy. . . . I am called upon, however, and I lament that it is so, to vindicate myself from the malignant aspersions of professional jealousy. . . . Now, I wish to distinctly state that my Oratorio of the *Skeptic* was a production of myself alone; Mr. Comer having aided me only in "instrumenting" it for the band. I composed it, got up the choruses, and attended to its rehearsal, all in the brief space of three weeks. . . .

Russell challenged his critics to back up their charges, and then switched to the subject of his singing: "The great peculiarity of my singing, it will be conceded, is its distinctiveness, and for this style and peculiarity, if I may term it, I am solely indebted to the great Kentuckian [i.e., Henry Clay]. My professional brethren have undertaken to sing my compositions—the same that have drawn thousands nightly to my concerts—without success. I may be in error, but it seems to me that a "humbug" could not so command the public sympathy. . . ." He concluded: "To my professional brethren I say, "I dare do all that may become a man" in my defense. I can meet your opposition or your anger, in the same undisturbed manner that I would confront any ordinary inclemency of the weather. . . . I can appeal to the last umpire and authority, THE PUBLIC."

The Musical Magazine reproduced the letter in the issue of 28 March 1840 (long after Russell had moved on from Boston) with this prefatory note:

> Before the excitement, which the late sojourn of Mr. Henry Russell in our city has caused, has been entirely forgotten, we beg to call the attention of our readers to it. They will recollect, that, while he had in his concerts [. . .] full houses and brilliant audiences, he was in other quarters denounced as a musical charlatan, as a humbug [. . .] having been the principal mover in the late direction which it has given to the course of the art for this winter. The direction is a false one, and it would

> have put the popular taste for music back, if it had not happily been counteracted by . . . the Boston Amateur and Social Glee Clubs; by Mr. Knight's classical concert, which has opened the way to the enjoyment of a higher class of songs, than we have hitherto been used to hear. . . .

In other words, Henry Russell's sin was to appeal to the man in the street rather than pursuing what was perceived as a loftier art. Joseph Knight's farewell classical concert on 14 March had included such items as Beethoven's "Adelaïde," Schubert's "*Erlkönig*," and items by Haydn and Mozart. It was not typical of Knight's programs, but it suited the editor of *The Musical Magazine* to hail it. He insisted that he made no accusation of plagiarism, simply that Russell's compositions "show a want of originality in their conception and a want of theoretical knowledge of the art in their execution." He curiously termed Russell's compositions "Reminiscences" and pointed out examples of consecutive octaves and fifths. As for Russell's singing, he acknowledged that it was indeed distinctive:

> The hearers do not lose a single word and their imagination has a thread by which to wind through the inextricable labyrinth of mere music. His singing is a medium between speaking and singing, or rather between the recitative and cantabile. . . . There are no stubborn tones, which break forth into life, before the singer has mentally subjected them to his conceptions.
>
> The editor then returned to the effect on public tastes, concluding that "Mr. Russell's style of singing misleads to a false taste . . . his effects are not genuine effects of art . . . [but] bribe the untutored ear." He conceded that the fault lay not with Russell but with the public for its poor taste. Altogether the coverage confirms the power of Russell's singing, whilst leaving him victim of a combination of his own dubious conduct and the musical snobbery that disapproves of appealing to the public at large. The proof of the pudding, of course, was in the eating, and for all that Joseph Knight won friends and admirers it did him little good financially. On 20 August 1840 *The Boston Morning Post* reported that "Mr. Knight—the bird of song—has flown, and left some sad remembrances behind him. The packet ship *Sheffield* bore him from New York, but left his unreceipted bills behind him."

The *Musical Magazine* feature also dwelt on a further way in which Russell had not helped his cause. This was his performance of political songs in support of the Whig party, which the editor considered cheapened the idea of liberty. In the wake of the Great Depression, which had begun in 1837, the Whig party was enjoying a great upsurge in popularity. For the 1840 presidential election, the Whigs chose to bypass strong but controversial politicians such as Henry Clay and Daniel Webster and, in February 1840, ratified the nomination of William H. Harrison (1773–1841) and John Tyler (1790–1862) as presidential and vice-presidential candidates.

Harrison was a man without strong views but with the virtue of being a national hero—an aging general who was known as "Old Tippecanoe" for defeating the Indians at the Battle of Tippecanoe, Indiana, in 1811. Russell himself writes in his memoirs: "Martin van Buren was a man of culture and one who knew his country better than any statesman, except, perhaps, Henry Clay and Webster. General Harrison was more of a soldier than a statesman, and so party feeling ran very high, as party feeling will at such a time, and resulted in the estrangement and separation of many good old friends." The 1840 election seemingly prompted more political songs than any other American election before or since. They included a vast repertory of Whig songs, centered particularly on presenting Harrison as a man with a modest background, and with his home at North Bend, Ohio, represented as a log cabin with a barrel of hard cider outside. The songs usually took the form of popular airs with new words added, as witness an example whose musical setting is readily apparent even today:

> Oh, where, tell me where, was your Buckeye "Cabin" made?
> Oh, where, tell me where, was your Buckeye "Cabin" made?
> 'Twas built among the merry boys that wield the plough and spade
> Where the "Log Cabins" stand in the bonnie Buckeye shade!

Henry Russell's compositions provided obvious material for this pastime, as witness one adaptor's transformation of "Some Love to Roam" into "The Soldier of Tippecanoe." Likewise, "The Brave Old Oak," which Russell had helped make so popular, appeared, in June 1840, in the Harrison songster *The Log Cabin* transformed into "The Brave Old Chief." Adaptation was dearer to nobody's heart than to Russell's own, of course, and he entered into it wholeheartedly—relishing the publicity, controversy, and, of course, additional income it brought him. He may even have started the whole process, as it was, indeed, claimed in a newspaper feature that may have had Russell's hand behind it:

> In the latter end of the month of December, 1839, about three weeks after the nomination of General Harrison, Russell was one of a private party at the Tremont House, Boston, (one of the best hotels in the United States.) He sung several songs, in his peculiar style. "I wonder, Russell," said one of the company, "if you can read as distinctly as you sing." "I'll try," said Russell. He accordingly selected a passage from a speech of an English orator, in which he said—"gentlemen, you may make the laws—but let me make the ballads of a nation." On reading this passage, Russell paused—struck his forehead—"Gentlemen, I have an idea—a grand idea." "What is it?" asked one, laughing. I can elect General Harrison." "Bah!" cried another. "By all the gods of Greece and Rome, I can elect Harrison." Accordingly, a Mr. Hayden wrote a "national whig song," which Russell sung to thousands in Boston, to the tune of the "Old English Gentleman." This was the origin of the famous Tippecanoe minstrelsy, which revolutionised the country—thus confirming the great maxim, that songs have greater effect on a sensitive people than laws.

Whether it was December 1839 or, more credibly, February 1840, Russell indeed began with his "National Whig Song," an adaptation with revised words by William Hayden of "The Fine Old English Gentleman." The adaptation culminated in this final verse:

> Let every sound, true-hearted whig now raise his voice on high,
> And, for the triumph of the cause, join Freedom's loudest cry;
> Come to the fight; we'll win the field—away with doubts and fears;
> The people's man is Harrison; let's give him three good cheers,
> For he's a fine, true-hearted gentleman,
> All of the olden time!

The impact of the song was such that the Democrats soon attempted to counter with a parody of their own. Published in the Boston Bay *State Democrat* of 15 February 1840, it dwelt on Harrison's advanced age:

Figure 8.2. "The National Whig Song" sheet music cover, showing President William Henry Harrison. *Source:* Author's collection.

I'll sing you a good old song, made by a whiggy great,
Of a weak old *Western Gentleman* who wished to serve the state
And keep up the *white mansion* at a bountiful old rate,
With a good whig household to receive of spoils a heavy weight,
Like a weak old Western Gentleman all of the olden time.

If anything was weak, it was perhaps this parody of a parody, and it can only have encouraged Russell. He prominently announced his "National Whig Song" for a concert at the Melodeon on Saturday, 15 February 1840. *The Boston Morning Post* was not alone in being apprehensive about the outcome:

> *Mr. Russell's Concert*, this evening, at the Melodeon, we hope will pass off quietly. Mr. R. is a clever fellow, and if he has fallen in with indiscreet advisers we are sorry for him. The story started by the whigs, that a plan has been organised by a party of democrats, to break up the Concert, is false, and propagated, probably, for the purpose of freeing those from pecuniary responsibility who promised him that a thousand tickets should be sold if he would sing Mr. Hayden's parody of the "Old English Gentleman." No one has a right to attend the Concert for the purpose of interrupting the performances; for the bill is advertised in full, and those who are not satisfied with the pieces should stay away.
>
> We understand that the means of egress from the Melodeon are simple; therefore no apprehension need be entertained on that ground by those who may be present.

Fortunately, the fears proved unfounded, and Russell would go on singing the Whigs' praises throughout the 1840 election campaign, though he seems to have changed his prime vehicle for doing so along the way. The aforementioned references are to a song with the melody of "A Fine Old English Gentleman," in which form it was published by Parker & Ditson of Boston, with an aristocratic-looking General Harrison on its title page. However, later references are to Russell's "Grand National Whig Song" using the tune of the Marseillaise. Did he perhaps feel the need to make his song a little more rousing? The change was seemingly initiated at Russell's farewell Boston concert on Saturday, 29 February, for which he announced "a National Song to the tune of the Marseilles Hymn, by William Hayden."

The Boston Morning Post again expressed its disapproval of his singing of partisan songs, but commented positively on his stay in Boston as a whole:

> *Mr. Russell* will give his last Concert, at the Temple, on Saturday, and we regret to see that he has resorted to the electioneering trick of singing a partisan song to ensure a large audience. His room will be filled, we have no doubt—but, Russell, my boy, did it ever occur to your mind, that what may be meat to you here, may be poison "elsewhere?"
>
> We think that Mr. R deserves severe reprobation for the course he has pursued, and we are confident that he will regret it before he dies. We will do him the justice to say, however, that he has gained in some things by visiting Boston this winter. For a long time there had been vague rumors afloat disreputable to his professional and private character. He has met them boldly, and in the most public manner, challenged his assailants to the proof of their assertions—but not one has substantiated any thing against him. A penny paper made some definite allegations, but recanted them all, and Mr. Russell has passed the ordeal unharmed.

Yet the paper was still not inclined to let Russell get away too easily. Having reported that his farewell concert "was attended by as many as could get into the room," the paper went on: "The Whigs are doing the business up in good style for Russell, that's a fact; and the way he is pocketing their loose change, isn't slow. By the way, we would intimate to the Democrat Tammany Hall [New York Democrat headquarters] Committee in New York, to assess Russell twice as much this year as they did last, for electioneering expenses; he can afford to pay the increased amount, after lowering the Whig Fund so essentially here." With questions raised about his probity and artistry, but with pockets well lined, Russell left Boston at the beginning of March 1840. Seemingly the foreshadowed visit to Cincinnati and the West did not materialize for, within days, he was back in New York. The "National Whig Song" was given at Niblo's on 12 March. *The Boston Morning Post* had already stated that song had preceded him there, and on 13 March it further reported that he had been singing Whig songs in Brooklyn. Cynically highlighting the money-spinning potential, it predicted, "If he is cunning he can made [sic] $20,000 out of the whigs before November, and he says he intends to do so."

Russell's return to New York prompted a final chuckle from *The Morning Herald*. "Where is Gambati?" the paper asked. "He must blow his horn now." Poor, toothless Gambati was in Carolina, hors de combat.

Russell had announced for Niblo's Saloon on 12 March a "Grand Vocal Concert" at which he would introduce "The Grand National Whig Song." He did not get through without audience disapproval, and a similar concert announced for Niblo's on Wednesday, 18 March was canceled at a late stage. Russell took newspaper space to announce the postponement "in consequence of Mr. Niblo having peremptorily refused to allow the 'Grand National Whig Song' to be sung." He added that, having announced the concert in the press the previous Thursday, he was not notified of the objection until Monday afternoon, "after the bills had been posted, the programme issued, and the widest notice given of the Concert." Niblo responded by denying reports in several papers that he had been influenced by the advice of Democrat lawyer and poet William Cullen Bryant, and by a fear that his Saloon would be torn down. He had, he said, acted solely from regard to the reputation of his establishment. He stated that, in his letter to Russell, he had expressed the fear of a repetition of what occurred at the previous concert, "which must be anything but desirable where there is a numerous company of respectable ladies."

The episode served to stir up further controversy, with *The Morning Herald* once more in the forefront:

> Niblo says it was for fear of giving annoyance to the ladies, that he refused to give Russell the use of his saloon to sing Whig songs. Capital!—"Them's my sentiments." Take care of the delicious petticoats, Niblo, and you are a greater man than Napoleon. Russell has been in many scrapes of late, with trumpeters, editors, and we know not what else; so that we suppose he feels like a fish out of water until he can get into a new row here. Let him get Tammany Hall, to sing his Whig songs in,—that is used to riots, and no harm can be done to its iron walls. If the locofocos [Democrats] dont [sic] like these stirring verses, why Russell is a capital pugilist, as well as a singer, and will knock them down if they prefer that to vocalization. . . .

Finding a replacement venue, Russell eventually announced a concert at the Masonic Hall for 31 March. Its program is notable for including the songs "The Old Sexton," with words by Park Benjamin, and "Rockaway—On Long Island's Sea-Girt Shore." The latter, with words by Russell's supporter in the Gambati affair, Henry John Sharpe, was ostensibly the same song sung in the "provinces" by Russell over the last two years. Regarding the "Whig Song," *The Morning Herald* reported ahead of the concert that "many anticipate a row, and have requested the ladies not to go." It was evidently performed, but to no great effect:

> . . . strange to say, there was only $100 in the house. Amongst the company there were 100 ladies. There was no row and no locofocos there. This was a most unexampled result; but it shows that both parties are determined not to encourage this introduction of politics into our otherwise pleasant and social amusements. Russell should take the hint and abandon politics; stick to his profession as an artist, drop the political mantle, and he will succeed much better. Neither party will pay him money either to create a disturbance or to give him the means of laughing at their folly.

Russell, though, was not one to give in to mere hints—particularly when there was money to be made. Rather, he determined to continue his efforts on behalf of the Whig cause outside New York City. On 6 April he was at Knickerbocker Hall in Albany, hailed as ever by the *Evening Journal* as "our favorite Vocalist." "If his 'National Whig Song' *should* be called for," the paper added, "we hope there will be no objection to his singing it, as he will as cheerfully sing a Van Buren song also, if called for." In the event, when part of the audience objected to requests for the song, he asked to be excused, evidently unwilling to create trouble in what was, currently, his hometown. Ahead of a second Albany concert two days later, the *Evening Journal* hinted that "after the Concert is over, those who desire it can have the 'National Whig Song,' sung in the exciting, glorious music of the Marseilles Hymn." Two days later the paper published words for yet another "Grand National Whig Song," written for Russell by Henry John Sharpe.

When Russell then gave a concert in nearby Troy, he met with renewed opposition. The press reported that "at the call of the Whig portion of the assembly, he came forward with his music sheet to sing a 'hard cider' ditty, but the attempt was promptly resisted and put down by the democrats." Things were evidently smoother the following month in

Rochester. He opened a concert at the National Hotel on 8 May with the overture to Weber's *Oberon*, and for a further concert the following week he was "requested by several Clergymen and Families, to adopt the course of introducing in his Concerts, Sacred Classical Music." He obliged with music from Haydn's *Creation* and Mendelssohn's *St. Paul*, plus the inevitable "Sceptic's Dying Lament" and also Joseph Knight's "Rocked in the Cradle of the deep" ("sung at Philadelphia for the benefit of 'distressed Seamen and their Families.'"). In addition, there was a new Russell composition, "Our Native Song," which introduced the melody of "Yankee Doodle."

Russell remained in Rochester long enough to add another concert at the Court House on 15 May for the benefit of the Rochester Orphan Asylum. Then, at the Eagle Hotel on 9 June, he not only performed a work honoring General Harrison's triumph in the siege of Fort Meigs, Ohio, in 1813, but seemingly subjected the residents of Rochester to the risk of civil unrest:

> Notwithstanding the varied rumors of "mobs, bludgeons and pistols," which produced such a beautiful excitement, the Concert on Tuesday evening was attended by a crowded and enthusiastic audience. The seats were all occupied, and a large number were compelled to maintain a standing position during the whole evening. Mr. Russell's favorite songs were greeted with prolonged cheering, and bursts of applause, the most enthusiastic we ever heard.
>
> The delightful ballad, "*On auld Long Island's sea-girt shore*," will be found in our columns this morning. "*The Hero of Fort Meigs*," which we also publish, made a decided *hit* and was "*encored*" by acclamation. The "*Grand National Whig Song*," with which the Concert concluded, was received with long and deafening applause.
>
> The enterprising Loco Focos who have been gloriously engaged for a few days past in getting up incendiary hand-bills so full of "*awful warning*," threatening mobs, riots, &c., must, we think, feel somewhat unpleasant about the perfectly triumphant result of the Concert. Rows, single and double combats, daggers, blunderbusses were distinctly seen in "fancy's eye." But after all this variegated display of "*chivalry*" they were as "calm as a summer's evening," and "Gentle Peace" was victorious. No lives were lost. The desperate opposition of the

> "*British Tories*" was unavailing. And we only echo the testimony of every one present, when we say that the *Whig Concert* was a *complete* triumph. The elegant Assembly room of the Eagle was brilliantly lighted, for the occasion, and ornamented—by a beautiful log cabin transparency.

Another story in Russell's memoirs must be associated with visits to Rochester in this election year, though the details of a journey from New York via Albany do not seem to fit any specific occasion:

> Wishing to return to Rochester shortly afterwards, I took the boat up the North River to Albany. Few trips have given me greater enjoyment than that cruise up the North River, a noble stream abounding in beautiful scenery; from Albany I had to push on to Rochester by canal boat. This was not so interesting, but there were plenty of instances to enliven the trip. Political feeling in the States ran very high just then, for it was the time of the memorable fight for the Presidency between Harrison and Martin Van Buren. There happened to be an enthusiastic Van Burenite on board our canal boat. . . . Raising his voice to its utmost extent, he shouted "All those for Martin Van Buren, bow down!" A moment afterwards there was a cry of "Bridge!" and every one, whether Harrisonite or Van Burenite, had either to stoop down or get his head knocked off by the bridge. The laugh, of course, was on the side of the Van Buren faction, and they did not forget to take advantage of it. This was only one of many quaint incidents which occurred during a trip that lasted two days and a night.

One way and another it must have been a thoroughly eventful summer for Russell, touring the country while the electioneering became ever fiercer. He evidently sang many Whig songs, not least in Nashville, during the southern Whig convention in August. By the time of a concert at the Rochester House on 10 October, however, it was announced that he "has abandoned the practice of singing political songs at his concerts" and "has given assurance that he will not, under any consideration, sing any thing of a political bearing."

Of all the Whig songs that flourished during the election campaign of 1840, one especially caught on for its lilting, alliterative reference to

"Tippecanoe and Tyler Too." It is the one that, once again, Russell singled out for mention in his memoirs:

> I was one day sitting in the office of the *Boston Transcript*, and to beguile the time while waiting for my friend, Houghton, the editor and proprietor, I sat idly turning over the pages of some of the numerous exchange journals with which the office was littered, when my attention was attracted by a poem on the subject of the forthcoming elections. The name of the paper in which it appeared has escaped my memory, but the poem was called "Tippecanoe," after the famous battle fought and won by General Harrison.
>
> I only now remember the chorus, which ran as follows:
>
> "For Tippecanoe and Tyler, too,
> For Tippecanoe and Tyler, too—
> With them we'll beat little van,
> Van! van! van!!! A used up man,
> With them we'll beat little van."
>
> I had a singular remembrance of an old Irish song, known by the poetic title of "Three little pigs lay on very good straw," the chorus of which ran thus:
>
> Lila bolara, lila borara, Lila bolara
> Och Hone,
> For my dad is a bonny wee man, man, man!!!
> My dad is a bonny wee man.
>
> Almost unconsciously, I put the words of the poem before me to the melody of the old Irish song, and when Houghton came in I sang them over to him. He appeared delighted, and at his suggestion I sang the song from the window of the *Boston Transcript*, to an enormous crowd which had assembled in the street below. The song was hailed with enthusiasm by the Harrison party, and it spread like wild fire through the States, where it is sometimes sung even to this day.
>
> Such is the true origin of this at one time popular election song. There has been much discussion about it from time to

> time in the American Press, and while I do not claim to have written either the words or the music, I do claim to having adapted the one to the other—wedded them together, as it were—and giving the song its start in life by singing it from the window of the *Boston Transcript*.

So what do we make of this? Firstly, the words "Lila bolara, lila bolara" sound curiously reminiscent of the seventeenth-century "Lilliburlero." But was Russell really the originator of this 1840 "Tippecanoe" song? Printed editions of the time variously describe it as "respectfully dedicated to the Tippecanoe Associations" or "respectfully dedicated to the Louisiana Whig Delegation to the Bunker Hill Convention [in September 1840]." They also describe it as arranged "by a Member of the Fifth Ward Club," and it is hard to believe that Russell would hide his identity thus.

There has, in fact, been much debate over the years about the song's origins, and American sources have long attributed it firmly to Alexander Coffman Ross (1812–73), from Zanesville, Ohio—a jeweler and a pioneer in the daguerreotype photographic printing process, as well as a songwriter. A 1905 article on Ross documented in some detail his authorship of the words and his setting of them to what is, there, called "Little Pigs." The article suggests that Ross wrote the piece around August 1840 and sang it more widely in September 1840, when the Bunker Hill Convention was held. The article refers specifically to Russell's claim and says that he "seems in his later years to have developed a penchant for claiming pretty much everything that has been written in his line." It also expresses interest in how "an enormous crowd" had suddenly appeared below the window of the *Boston Transcript* to hear Russell sing the song.

Russell repeated his claim a couple of years before his death, when he was visited by a granddaughter of Thurlow Weed (1797–1882), editor of the *Albany Evening Journal* during Russell's time there. Yet it is obvious nonsense. There was no question of lyrics needing anyone to wed them to a tune. The various Whig lyrics were published not as verses awaiting a musical setting but precisely because they were satirical verses *already* attached to familiar tunes. The New York *Morning Herald* began publishing them in March 1840, clearly stating the tune to which they were sung. It was as late as 22 September 1840 that it published the words of this particular song, giving its tune as that of "Little Pig's Tail."

That same *New York Herald* publication also refers to "Joseph Hoxie & Co., singing [it], in great glee, at all the log cabins around the country."

Appleton's Encyclopedia, in its article on Joseph Hoxie (1795–1870), concurs: ". . . as a campaign vocalist he was unequalled, and he appeared as such in most of our large cities during the 'Harrison log-cabin and hard-cider campaign.' His small band of singers held the attention of thousands, who readily joined in the refrain of 'Tippecanoe and Tyler too,' and 'Van, Van, Van's a used-up man.' These immense vocal gatherings won over to the Whig side hosts of voters, who sang themselves into convictions that were beyond the reach of political argument." There is no mention of Russell anywhere.

Yet, for all Russell's patently false claims for the song "Tip and Ty," his story, as so often, does have elements of truth. What's more, as is often the case, the truth is hardly less interesting than the fiction. As already stated, there is ample evidence that it was Henry Russell's singing of his "National Whig Song," in February 1840, that launched the most extensive bout of minstrelsy of any US presidential election ever. What's more, Russell really did sing Whig songs from a Boston newspaper proprietor's window.

This occurrence took place after he had returned to Boston and given a concert in the Masonic Temple on Saturday, 31 October. By the time of his second concert, on Thursday, 5 November, the polls had closed and news of Harrison's success was drifting in. On Saturday, 7 November, *The Boston Morning Post* reported: "Mr. Russell, the English vocalist, amused the crowd around the *Atlas* office on Friday night, by singing Harrison's songs from one of the Major's windows. The audience was somewhat lessened by the watchmen, but quite a large number remained to hear him through. The whigs should do the handsome thing for Russell, and get him up another Concert."

And get him up another concert the Whigs did! Or, at least, Russell presented it on behalf of the Whigs. In celebration of Harrison's victory, he announced a Grand Whig Concert for Wednesday, 11 November. The first half began with a set of Variations on "Rosin the Bow" and concluded with "Come all you young men of Ohio," to the tune of "Old Rosin the Bow"—"sung by Mr. Russell at the great Nashville Convention, with a chorus of nearly 10,000 whigs." The second half then began with the "National Whig Song," to the tune of the Marseilles Hymn, written by William Hayden, Esq.—"the first Harrison song written, and originally sung by Mr. Russell." The concert, as reported by the *Boston Morning Post,* included "Tippecanoe and Tyler too," but, significantly, without any attribution of authorship to Russell. The concert's conclusion was a Grand Triumphal Whig Song. Truly were Russell's colors nailed to the Harrison mast!

9

Dreaming of Home

Following his "Grand Whig Concert" of November 1840, Russell's programs seem to have reverted to their previous format. Apart from a solo appearance in Roxbury Town Hall on 17 November, his Boston farewell, for that particular visit, took place on 14 November 1840. He gave it in conjunction with three further old acquaintances from Britain, who had already appeared with him in concert on 5 November. They were the baritone Charles T[homas] Martyn (1803–71), his once starry but now somewhat struggling soprano wife, Eliza, née Inverarity (mentioned in connection with Russell's early song "When I Rov'd a Young Highlander"), and her sister, Barbara Inverarity (1815–45). The program included several of the Scottish songs with which the three were closely linked.

For Russell, the most significant item on the 14 November program was another of the "grand scenas" or "descriptive ballads," depicting social ills of the time. After the pattern of "The Maniac," and running in its published form to fifteen pages of music, it had words expressly written for Russell by Philadelphia Quaker Dr. Reynell Coates (1802–86). It was listed on this occasion as "The Gambler" but would become immensely popular as "The Gambler's Wife": the story of a wife and child left at home without food and warmth by a husband squandering everything on gambling. The clock ticks relentlessly on, and the child eventually dies of starvation:

Dark is the Night! How Dark! No Light! No Fire!
Cold on the hearth the last faint sparks expire;
Shivering she watches by the cradle side,

For him who pledged her *love! Last year a Bride!*
Hark! 'tis his footstep! No! 'tis past, 'tis gone!
Tic! tic! how wearily the time rolls on!
Why should he leave me thus? He once was kind!
And I believed 'twould last. Oh! how mad, how blind!
Rest thee, my babe! Rest on! 'Tis hunger's cry!
Sleep! For there's no food! The fount is dry!
Famine and cold their wearying work have done!
My heart must break! And thou! My child, Hush!

One can very well imagine its impact. Was there a dry eye in the house? By leaving Boston in mid-November 1840, Russell just missed the appearance there of a British singer whose great reputation went back many years. The English tenor John Braham (1774–1856) was by then well into his sixties, but financial circumstances had forced him to continue performing when he was well past his prime and nowadays more comfortable in the baritone register. Braham began his 1840 visit to Boston with performances with the Handel and Haydn Society on 20 and 22 November.

Though he and Russell were to miss each other on that occasion, their paths did cross briefly in Boston the following February. Russell's memoirs give this version of events:

> One of my first experiences in Boston recalled early and painful associations. John Braham, the great English tenor, was engaged to appear at the Handel and Haydn Society's concerts. He also announced three miscellaneous concerts on his own account. The first was a success, but the second was poorly attended, while the third was a failure. . . . Just after the second of them, I received this letter:
>
> "DEAR MR. RUSSELL,—At what time would it be convenient for you to see me?
>
> "Yours truly, JOHN BRAHAM."
>
> To which I replied:
>
> "Tremont House."
>
> "DEAR MR. BRAHAM,—I shall be happy to see you the time most convenient to yourself.
>
> "Yours truly,

Figure 9.1a. Broadside lyric sheet for "The Gambler's Wife." *Source:* Author's collection.

THE

GAMBLER'S

WIFE.

Poetry by Dr. Crofts.—Music by Henry Russell.

Dark is the night! how dark! no light—no fire!
Cold, on the earth, the last faint sparks expire:
Shiv'ring, she watches by the cradle side,
For him who pledged his love—last year a bride!

Hark! 'tis his footstep!—No: 'tis past—'tis gone!
Tic! tic!—how wearily the time rolls on.
Why should he leave me thus? he once was kind,
And I believ'd 'twould last,—oh! how mad, how blind.

Rest thee, my babe, rest on,—'tis hunger's cry!
Sleep: for there is no food: the fount is dry!
Famine and cold their wearing work have done;
My heart must break—and thou, my child!—
Hush! the clock strikes one!

Hush! 'tis the dice-box,—yes! he's there—he's there!
For this he leaves me to despair;
Leaves love—leaves truth—his wife—his child—for what?
The gambler's fancied bliss—the gambler's horrid lot!

Yet I'll not curse him,—no: 'tis all in vain;
'Tis long to wait, but sure he'll come again;
And I could starve and bless him, but, my child, for you,—
Oh, fiend! oh, fiend!—Hush! the clock strikes two!

Hark, how the sign-board creaks,—the blast howls by;
Moan, moan, ye winds, through the cloudy sky.
Ha! 'tis his knock! he comes, he comes once more;
No, 'tis but the lattice-flaps—my hope, my hope is o'er!

Can he desert us thus? he knows I stay,
Night after night, in loneliness to pray,
For his return, and yet he sees no tear;
No, no, it cannot be,—oh! he will be here;

Nestle more closely, dear one, to my heart;
Thou art cold—thou art freezing!—but we will not part!
Husband! I die!—Father! it is not he,
Oh, God, protect my child!—Hush! the clock strikes three!

They're gone,—the glimmering spark hath fled!
The wife and child are number'd with the dead,
On the cold earth, outstretch'd in solemn rest,
The babe lies frozen on its mother's breast,
The gambler comes at last, but all is o'er,—
Dread silence reigns around,—the clock strikes four!

Andrews, Printer, 38 Chatham St. N. Y., Dealer in Songs, Games Toy Books, Motto Verses, &c., Wholesale and Retail.

Figure 9.1b. "The Gambler's Wife" sheet music cover. *Source:* Courtesy the Lester Levy Sheet Music Collection, The Sheridan Libraries, Johns Hopkins University.

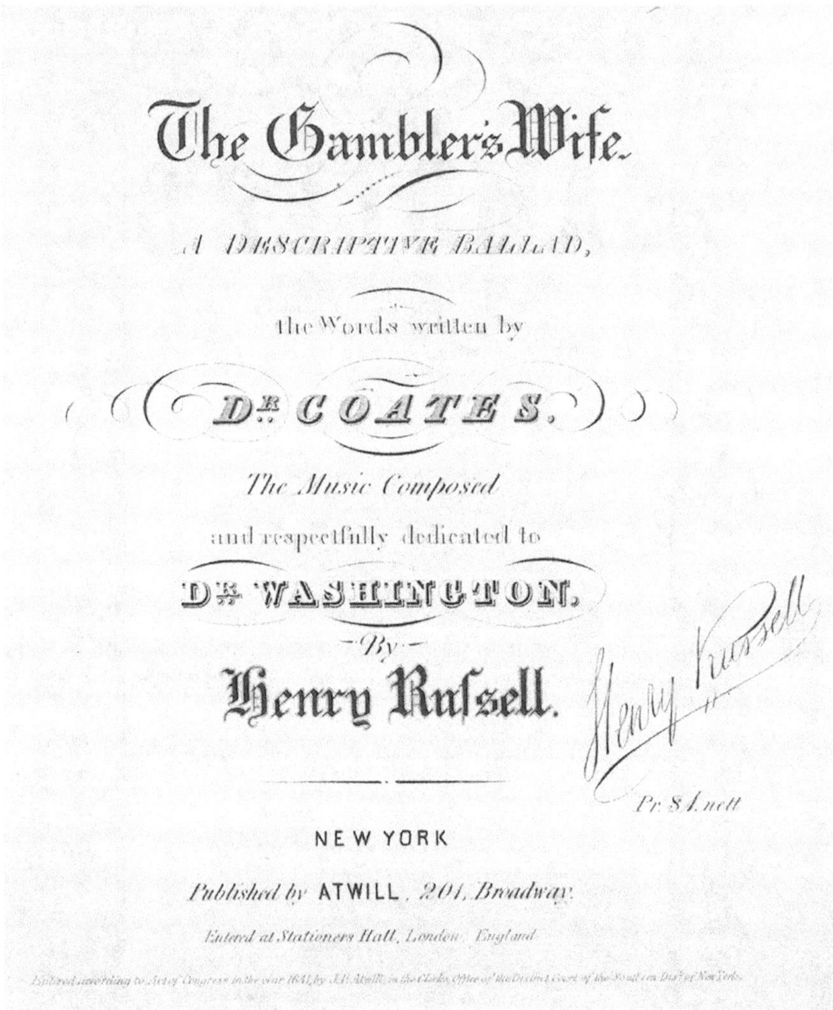

"HENRY RUSSELL."

Shortly after the despatch of my answer, a messenger called at my hotel, the "Tremont House," and said that Mr. Braham would be with me in half-an-hour. Punctually to the moment, the famous tenor was ushered into my room at the hotel. We shook hands with every appearance of cordiality, and I begged Mr. Braham to be seated.

"I want to know," he began, "whether you would be willing to sing at my third concert, and, if so, what your terms would be for two songs?"

I had guessed his errand and my answer was ready:

"Mr. Braham," said I, "my terms to you,"—I placed particular emphasis on the "you"—"would be five hundred dollars per song."

Mr. Braham started, which was only natural. Then he rose, looking much flustered, and very indignant.

"Your terms, Mr. Russell, are simply preposterous. Why ask me—a well-known professional man—such an exorbitant fee?"

"Well, the terms are high, almost prohibitive," I admitted. "But, sit down again, Mr. Braham, and I will explain. Allow me to recall to your memory a little incident that happened many years ago. You will probably recollect a gentleman bringing to you—by appointment—his little boy, whose great ambition at that moment was to have an interview with the great John Braham, and get the opinion of that eminent musician upon his vocal capabilities. The boy's voice, mind you, had already been pronounced by several competent judges to be a contralto of the finest quality. You, Mr. Braham, listened to the lad's singing, and then, turning to the father, said, "Although your son possesses a remarkably fine voice, you had better put him on the high road to break stones, rather than bring him up to the musical profession.' That was what you said to the boy who hung upon your words as upon those of an oracle, prepared to gather hope or despair from your every syllable. That boy, five minutes before, was full of hope and confidence, your words, Mr. Braham, filled him with despair. He cried bitterly on the way home, and for weeks afterwards was painfully depressed. All his spirit seemed to have deserted him, and every effort of his friends to console him seemed unavailing. The father, believing firmly in the judgement of John Braham, reluctantly placed the boy in a chemist's shop; and it was a wonder that what musical talent he possessed was not crushed out of him by the drudgery he there endured. Mr. Braham, *I was that boy!*"

The tenor, I must candidly say, was much affected by my story. I could see that. Assuming, however, the coldest tone at his command, he said:

> "I remember the circumstance, Mr. Russell, and regret that it left so deep an impression on your mind as to induce you to recall it now. That however, is no concern of mine. Good morning. I cannot accept your offer."

Russell gallantly confessed misgivings as to how his readers would take the story of one who was no longer alive to give his side of the story, but he said that he felt its publication excusable as showing the danger of a too hasty verdict in judging the capabilities of the young. He claimed to feel "a strong resentment against the class of professional men, who . . . unhesitatingly condemn the efforts of younger aspirants to fame, without taking the trouble to properly judge their merits."

As usual, we must have vast reservations as to how much of all this was true. Doubt is cast, for instance, by a passage in the autobiography of actor Lewis Melville (*Not All the Truth*), who, in 1906, called on Russell's son William Clark Russell at the latter's home in Bath. Clark Russell, said Melville, "told me that life with him had begun very early, and that his memory went back a long way. When in the street with his father, Henry Russell, the composer of the song, 'Cheer! Boys, Cheer!,' they saw a tottering old man, the sight of whom delighted his father. The old man joined them, and they walked together for some way. It was John Braham, the famous tenor. . . ." Since William Clark Russell was not born until 1845, that meeting must have occurred in Britain many years after the Boston encounter. Equally, it was long before Russell put his name to his probably imaginary, caustic comments in his autobiography. Moreover, newspaper reports prove that relations between the two cannot have been as acrimonious as Russell later suggested.

Russell arrived back in Boston in February 1841 while Braham was already in residence and preparing a farewell concert for Wednesday, 17 February 1841. Russell's own first concert was at the Masonic Temple on Thursday, 18 February 1841, with "The Gambler's Wife" now under its definitive title. On Saturday, 20 February, the two were then billed, together with Mrs. Franklin and the local Euterpian Minstrels, for a concert given by the Gillingham-born pianist Aaron Upjohn Hayter (1799–1873), once organist of Salisbury Cathedral, at the Melodeon. It concluded with Braham and Russell singing together the well-tested duet "*All'idea di quel metallo*" for the Count and Figaro in Act 1 of Rossini's *Barber of Seville*. It is not quite the picture of antagonism created by Russell's memoirs!

Following John Braham's departure for the South, Russell continued with a concert at the Melodeon the following Wednesday, 24 February. This included at least three further new songs: "The Old Water Mill" and "The Old Night Lamp" with words by Eliza Cook, and also "Nature's Fine Old Gentleman," which was a quite different song from "The Fine Old English Gentleman." Russell's "Farewell Concert" followed at the Melodeon on Saturday, 27 February, though the following evening he also gave a "Grand Sacred Concert" for the Boston Musical Institute that, besides items by Haydn and M. P. King, included extended selections from *The Sceptic*.

The following month, on Tuesday, 23 March 1841, Russell gave his first New York concert for almost a year at the City Hotel, with "The Maniac," "The Old Sexton," and "The Gambler's Wife" on the bill. The crowded hall confirmed his continuing popularity. He had evidently done some wooing behind the scenes, because *The New York Herald* was now altogether more temperate than when it had mocked his misfortunes with Signor Gambati and Mrs. Hardwick. It analyzed his forthright style and made interesting comparisons with New York's current favorite, the Scottish-born ballad singer William R. Dempster, with whom Russell had appeared in New York some years earlier:

> Russell is well known throughout the country, as a vocalist of varied talents—sometimes in hard-cider minstrelsy, sometimes in soft. He has generally been popular, except when he tried coon-skin music, and then he failed, not for want of talent, but of hearers. His style is difficult to classify. It is neither modern nor ancient. He has a more lofty and ambitious taste than Dempster, but wants his delicacy, simplicity and beauty. He is more of the modern than the ancient wandering minstrel—a character in this age that is more pugilistic than poetic.

At the Stuyvesant Institute, on Friday, 26 March, Russell introduced "We Were Boys Together," with words by George P. Morris. Then, on 25 March, ahead of a further Stuyvesant Institute appearance on Tuesday, 30 March, the formerly critical *New York Herald* confirmed its *volte face*: "Russell is rapidly approaching the culminating point in his musical career. He has originated a new school, full of pathos, sensibility, fire, and genius—a rare combination of the poetry of thought and the poetry of sound. He is an original, and, on another occasion, we shall sketch more at length his rise and progress, which are novel and interesting. For the present, go and hear him."

Russell's power to win some people over, just as much as to antagonize others, was seldom better demonstrated than here. The editor of *The New York Herald*, James Gordon Bennett, had now—somehow—been transformed into the friend that Russell calls him in his memoirs. Perhaps it came about partly through Russell's support for the Whig party in the previous year's election. At all events, the relationship was clearly now a close one. At his concert on 30 March 1841 Russell introduced another new song, "The Old School House," with words by Park Benjamin, which in its published form bore a dedication to Mrs. James Gordon Bennett.

The biographical sketch that Bennett had promised, summarizing Russell's American career, duly appeared ahead of his next concert, at the City Hotel on Friday, 2 April. It told of "a bold and original genius, struggling against ignorance and opposition," and continued:

> About five years ago, he was engaged in his art at Rochester and the west, at the rate of some $8 per week—now he clears his $1500 per week. His taste and passion for music hurried him into the hazardous experiment of attempting a new career. Casting aside the modern effeminate taste, he boldly seized the old style, in the old spirit, united with the delicacy and finish of the present age. His songs are so many dramas—full of incident, passion, character, and pathos, the elements of each beautifully arranged together, and set to natural and well conceived music. Poets write his songs, but Russell gives the poets the ideas, and then sets the words afterwards to his own music. —*The New York Herald*

The City Hotel concert on 2 April went ahead, despite a violent storm that prevented many from attending. Russell then announced a concert for the Stuyvesant Institute on Tuesday, 6 April 1841. However, circumstance caused it to be postponed; the circumstance was the death of President Harrison, from pleurisy, in the early hours of Monday, 5 April.

The ninth US president and, at sixty-eight, the oldest before Ronald Reagan, William Henry Harrison was destined to be the first president to die in office, and the one who served for the shortest time—precisely one month. His election to the presidency, in November 1840, had started a four-month interim period during which—national hero rather than

Figure 9.2. "The Old School House" sheet music cover. *Source:* Courtesy the Lester Levy Sheet Music Collection, The Sheridan Libraries, Johns Hopkins University.

politician—he had struggled to form the first presidential administration ever for the Whig party. Then, on a cold day and without wearing a coat, he had been required to ride on horseback (rather than in a carriage) to deliver his election address. At two hours long, it was supposedly the longest ever. Afterwards, he had to stand for several hours receiving guests, and even after taking office he was expected to receive guests from morning to bedtime and perhaps entertain them to dinner. The whole process put an intolerable strain on an ageing man, and the chill he caught turned into pneumonia.

The New York *Evening Post* suggested "that no animal placed by a philosopher in an exhausted receiver for the purpose of experiment, was ever more deliberately put to death than General Harrison. A kind and harmless old man was decoyed from the retirement and the quiet which had become habitual and necessary to him, and killed by the endless public ceremonies in which he was made to take part by the perplexities of office, and the visits of office seekers."

As John Tyler assumed the office of president and matters began to stabilize, Russell restaged his postponed concert on Thursday, 8 April—not at the Stuyvesant Institute but at the Rutgers' Institute. At a further concert at the City Hotel the next evening, he introduced another new song: "The Chieftain's Daughter," with words by George P. Morris. The daughter in question was, of course, Pocahontas, and the song's lyric centered on her relationship with Captain Smith, leader of the first colony in Virginia. Russell also paid tribute to the late president, with a "Requiem on the Death of General Harrison," again with words by Morris:

> Green be the willow bough
> Above the swelling mound,
> Where sleeps the hero now
> In consecrated ground;
> His monument his fame endears—
> His epitaph—a nation's tears.

The occasion was, however, by no means wholly a somber one. As a change from Rossini's "Largo al factotum," Russell ended the concert with a comic Italian song, of undivulged parentage, "O, conocete gia meglio di me," supposedly "describing a person entering a Café, and addressing a deaf waiter, who brings every dish but the one asked for." Russell sang it again at the first two of three further solo concerts the next week: at the Stuyvesant Institute on Tuesday, 13 April; at Rutgers' Institute on

Figure 9.3. "The Chieftain's Daughter" sheet music cover. *Source:* Author's collection.

Thursday, 15 April; and in the Lecture Room of the Society Library on Friday, 16 April. At the second he also introduced a Sacred Song, "The Pilgrim's Address to the Deity," with words by Henry John Sharpe, and at the third a new ballad "The Family Bible" with words by George P. Morris. The Harrison Requiem was included at all three.

That Saturday, *The New York Herald* published a fascinating survey of leading singers currently in New York, culminating in a piece on Russell that completed the paper's astonishing conversion from pouring scorn to heaping adulation:

> This vocalist is unique. We scarcely know how to class him. His voice is a pure, deep, rich *baritone*, and judging from his exhibitions, comprehends one octave and seven notes. It ranges from G to F, but he does not go higher, at his concerts, than to E natural. His middle and lower notes are unusually deep. . . . Russell has a great genius for musical composition, and has struck out an entirely new path for himself. He pays poets to compose his songs, and sets and sings them to his own music, like the ancient minstrels. He is particularly famous for his distinct enunciation, and the dramatic effect he gives to the simplest airs with his own accompaniment. He is also the author and originator of the extraordinary popular musical movement which preceded and produced the election of the late lamented Gen[eral] Harrison. . . .

The series of solo appearances in New York, Russell's most intensive, continued the following Tuesday, 20 April 1841, with a concert in the Lecture Room of the Society Library. On Friday, 23 April, and Monday, 26 April, he appeared there in two concerts in support of William R. Dempster, at the second of which Russell introduced "Old King Time." The two then performed at Ellen Lewis's concert at the City Hotel on Tuesday, 27 April, and at Dempster's final two concerts at the Rutgers' Institute on Wednesday, 28 April, and at the Stuyvesant Institute on Friday, 30 April.

Interestingly, in his solo concerts of Scottish ballads, Dempster included "My Heart's in the Highlands"—sometimes attributing it to Henry Phillips, sometimes billing it as arranged by Russell, sometimes simply as by Russell. Interestingly, too, just as Russell's "Old King Time" was announced for the concert on 26 April, so was a new song by Dempster. This was "Oh! This Love," described as "written for Mr. Dempster by G. P. Morris." The song was announced again, with precisely the same wording, for Dempster's farewell concert on 30 April. Yet no song of that title by Dempster seems to have been published, whereas there are published settings of Morris's words by both Joseph P. Knight and Henry Russell. Russell's setting appeared late in 1841, and with the billing "Sung with

Figure 9.4. "Old King Time!" sheet music cover. *Source:* Courtesy the Lester Levy Sheet Music Collection, The Sheridan Libraries, Johns Hopkins University.

rapturous applause by Mrs. Sutton and Mr. Dempster." Did Dempster really drop a setting of his own in favor of one by Russell? And Mrs. Sutton?

Meanwhile, the death of President Harrison was not the only tragedy that loomed over Russell's time in New York in March and April 1841. Over the last months, the British performers touring the United States had included the Irish actor Tyrone Power (1795–1841). A celebrated interpreter of Sheridan's *Pizarro*, he was father of concert pianist Harold Power, grandfather of actor Tyrone Power (1869–1931), and great-grandfather of Tyrone Power (1913–58) of *Mask of Zorro* fame. According to a tale he later told at his concerts, Russell dined with Power at the Astor Hotel in the company of Charles Kean, George P. Morris, and Nathaniel Parker Willis (1806–67) on 10 March 1841, the day before Power was due to leave for England on the SS President.

In his memoirs, Russell claims that he actually lunched with Power on board the President; but, either way, he reckons to have gone on board to see Power off. He reports that after the departure call was heard: "I shook hands with dear Power, and wished him God speed from the bottom of my heart, jumped on to a tug that accompanied us, and, with three loud hurrahs, we started back for New York. The *President* was never again heard of from that day. The *British Queen* and the *Halifax* mail steamers encountered the same hurricane, and weathered the storm; but although a search expedition was organized by the British and Portuguese Governments, it was fruitless." The story would prove useful once Russell hit Ireland.

Despite intimation in New York's *Evening Post*, in March 1841, that "Mr. Russell contemplates a visit to Europe," Henry continued with engagements elsewhere after leaving New York. Philadelphia enjoyed him in two concerts at the Musical Fund Hall on Saturday, 15 May, and Wednesday, 19 May, at the second of which Russell performed his "Requiem on the Death of General Harrison." Then, in July, we hear of concerts in Cincinnati and "in the far west, singing popular songs to crowded audiences, and pocketing money and laurels in great abundance."

We should perhaps also allocate to this time another tour of which Russell writes in his memoirs:

> During a visit to Halifax, Nova Scotia, I made the acquaintance of that remarkable man, Judge Thomas Chandler Haliburton, of Nova Scotia, alias Sam Slick, who entertained me at his fine residence at Windsor. In 1842, Sam Slick visited England as an Attaché to the American Legation, and in the next year introduced the results of his observation on English Society in his amusing work, "The Attaché, or Sam Slick in England." . . . I met also Sir John Harvey, then Governor of the Colony. At Fredericstown, hard by, I gave a fairly successful concert, and then, crossing the Bay of Fundy, pitched my tent at Eastport,

Maine. Eastport I shall never forget. It was the scene of some of the drollest incidents in my experience. I had not really intended staying at this quaint little town, but sheer fatigue compelled a few days' halt. Borrowing a piano (a matter of no little difficulty) I issued my bills, and prepared the following programme:-

> EASTPORT, SEPTEMBER 18TH, 18—
> PART I.
> Largo Al Factotum ROSSINI
> Woodman, Spare that Tree RUSSELL
> The Soldier's Tear A. LEE Our Native Soil RUSSELL
> A Life on the Ocean Wave RUSSELL
> Meet Me by Moonlight WADE
> The Maniac RUSSELL
> Wind of the Winter Night RUSSELL
> A Fine old English Gentleman
> (Melody supposed to have been written by MARTIN LUTHER)
> PART II.
> Overture (Fidelio) BEETHOVEN
> Laughing Song RUSSELL
> Vera Viso (Somnambula) [sic!] BELLINI
> The Gambler's Wife RUSSELL
> I'm Afloat RUSSELL
> The Old Arm Chair RUSSELL
> The Ivy Green RUSSELL
> Ecce mi a Voi [sic] RUSSELL
> Red, White, and Blue RUSSELL
> Admission, 1 dollar. Back seats, 50 cents. To commence at 6.30.

Russell goes on to tell various stories connected with his appearance in Eastport, stressing that "I have not the smallest intention or desire to ridicule in any way the warm-hearted Americans, from whom I have received such whole-hearted hospitality, . . . only to illustrate the innate drollery of the primitive people with whom I mixed." He tells of one local who sought to obtain tickets at half price on the basis that he and his wife each took up only half the space of a fat man. The same local went on to ask if Martin Luther would indeed be singing that evening, since his name was on the bill, and ended up by revealing that he taught psalmody.

Russell continues the account of his travels thus:

> The concert proved to be a very fair success, considering the size of the town. The day following, I left Eastport for Portland. And oh! that journey! it was the worst I ever performed in the States. The scenery was indescribably lovely, but the roads were bad in an equally indescribable degree. Only those familiar with road travelling in the States nearly sixty years ago can imagine what we endured. The roads were invariably of the sort known as "Corduroy," which were formed by laying rough trees, side by side, and filling in the crevices with mud.
>
> Ever and anon the wheels of one's conveyance would sink into the interstices, and it was a work of time to extricate them. It happened so on my journey to Portland. We had travelled some distance over what the natives of that part were pleased to call a road, when a sudden lurch of the coach awakened me from a drowsy slumber. A moment after I heard the hoarse voice of the driver shouting "Hold hard there—we're in a frizzle fix, and no mistake, we're stuck! Get out, boys, we're in a rut, and I guess it'll take a heap of time to clear us."
>
> Out we men all jumped on to what we thought was terra firma, only to find ourselves sinking to our knees in a black expanse of mud. By a great and united effort—for it was a case of all hands to the pumps—we managed by the assistance of long wooden rails at last to prize [sic] up the sunken wheels and set our vehicle once more in motion. Three miles further on we secured a much-needed change of horses, and at the same time the roads perceptibly improved. My joy on eventually reaching the hotel at Portland is one of the things that can only be imagined.
>
> After wandering long distances, I arrived at Schenectady, a small town inhabited by a number of the early Dutch and German settlers. We travelled, as usual, in a half broken-down, lumbering coach. There was no accommodation for outside passengers; it held three in front, three in the middle, and three at the back. Four out of the nine passengers spoke but little English. They were, however, very talkative, and, at every

> lurch of the coach, the words, "*Der Teufel*!!!" were uttered in loud screeches. . . .

Russell tells at length of his experiences with the "Knickerbockers" (i.e., the Dutch) after one of them struck up a conversation with him approaching Sprechers-basin (a portion of the Erie Canal), on the way to Utica.

Altogether, there would seem to be sufficient clues here to be able to date the trip through Halifax, Nova Scotia, by way of Fredericton, New Brunswick, to Eastport, Maine. Yet, as usual, the attempt founders on the unreliability and contradictions of Russell's details. Certainly lawyer, judge, and writer Thomas Chandler Haliburton (1796–1865), whose Sam Slick writings became hugely popular, lived in his birthplace of Windsor, Nova Scotia, into the 1850s. However, the fact that soldier and politician John Harvey (1778–1852) was Governor of New Brunswick from 1837 to 1841 seems to date it no later than the latter year. Equally, since "Our Native Song" (for which "Our Native Soil" is an obvious misprint) was not performed until 1840, the concert cannot have been earlier than that year.

The implication, therefore, is that the concert could only have taken place in September 1840 or 1841. Yet that reckons without the inclusion of "Red, White and Blue," provocatively attributed to Russell himself. This is, in fact, the song otherwise known as "Columbia, the Gem of the Ocean" or "Britannia, the Pride of the Ocean," and is generally agreed to date from 1843. More particularly, it is generally agreed that Henry Russell had nothing whatsoever to do with its composition, though, in later years, it certainly appeared in print in Britain with Russell's name attached as composer.

Altogether, we have to dismiss that Eastport concert bill as yet another fabrication. Had it been from September 1840, it would surely have included Whig songs. As for September 1841, Russell had by then returned to Britain. After some five years as an entertainer in America, it was a natural progression to try his luck in his own country, and it was also only natural that Russell—and perhaps more particularly since his wife, with her two young children, had ventured back to Blighty—should feel homesick. Of course, Russell never mentions his wife and family in his memoirs, and he, inevitably, gives a more colorful account of the circumstances behind his decision to return home:

> I was strolling one day, aimlessly, along the Broadway, when

> I heard a hand-organ, perhaps a trifle more tuneful than the general run of hurdy-gurdies. Attracted by the instrument, I drew near to listen. The organ was grinding out an air from "Norma," when suddenly I started—the tune was changed, and the familiar notes of one of my own songs, "The Ivy Green," greeted my ears. At its conclusion came two more Italian airs, and then the musical round terminated with another of my compositions, "Oh, Woodman, Spare that Tree." Two of my songs out of a series of eighty! This was paying me an indirect compliment indeed, for, of course, only the best liked and most popular melodies find their way to the organs.
>
> I went up to the proprietor of the organ, an Italian, and addressed him in his own language.
>
> "Da che parte venite voi?" (Where do you come from?)
>
> "Da Parma, signor."
>
> "Chi ha fato il vostro organo?" (Where was your organ made?)
>
> "A Birmingham, signor."
>
> The man's answer set me thinking deeply; the organ had come from England, therefore my compositions were, by this time, tolerably well known there. Probably my airs were as popular in London, Liverpool, and Birmingham as they were in Boston, Philadelphia, and New York, and so there was a good chance for success for me in my native land.
>
> And so, the simple event of having listened to an organ, and conversed with its owner in the streets of New York, proved a turning point in my career—another illustration of the truth that there are no such things as "accidents," and no such things as "little things."
>
> There is, I think, an innate love of country that is born with every Englishman. The mere thought of again seeing my native land set my heart beating and my blood tingling with pleasure and anticipation; and so, ere many weeks had passed, I had bade farewell to America, the land of generous, hospitable people, the land that had been a home to me for many a year, and as I stood upon the deck of the vessel that was bearing me homeward, and gazed at those shores that were vanishing for ever from my sight, my heart felt sad within me and tears of affection and gratitude filled my eyes.

There may, of course, have been a tittle of truth in all this; but it cannot have been the whole story. Deeper insight into the reasons was provided in a paragraph in *The New York Herald* on 3 August 1841. It displayed once more the paper's intimacy with the man it had once been so happy to ridicule:

> The distinguished and original "son of song," took his passage yesterday in the packet ship Europe, for Liverpool. Soft breezes to him! Russell goes to England for the purpose of exhibiting his talents and powers in that country—also to receive a legacy, left to his lady by distant relatives recently dead. Both matters are pleasant pieces of business, and we wish Harry Russell luck, here, there, or elsewhere.

Harry?

10

Home Again

No doubt in need of rest and adjustment, on returning home, after six years' absence, Russell seems to have lain low for several months. Of his ultimate return to the concert platform, he writes:

> I . . . decided to continue in England the entertainments that I had given with success in America. This class of entertainment was then practically a new idea in England, my only predecessors having been [Samuel] Foote, [Charles] Dibden [*recte* Dibdin], and the elder [Charles] Mathews. I opened at the old Hanover Square Rooms, and crowded houses testified to the success of my experiment. "The Gambler's Wife," "The Ship on Fire," and "The Maniac" were the talk, or, rather, the songs of the town. "Cheer! Boys, Cheer!" "The Ivy Green," and "A Life on the Ocean Wave" were to be heard on every barrel organ and hurdy-gurdy in the city, and were whistled and sung by young and old alike, in fact I felt I had made a great hit, and success followed on success.

Typically, Russell (or his amanuensis grandson) gets ahead of himself here, since "Cheer! Boys, Cheer!" was not composed until 1850. Moreover, before he gave his entertainment at the Hanover Square Rooms, he tried it out in the less prestigious surroundings of piano manufacturer Charles Kirkman's premises, at 3 Soho Square. The press announcement of the concert on 23 February 1842 is worth reproducing in full, for presenting to Britain the individual style of entertainment that Russell had developed in America:

> CONCERT.—Mr. H RUSSELL, from America (Author of "Woodman, spare that Tree," and other popular songs and ballads) has the honour to announce that he purposes giving, unaided, a VOCAL ENTERTAINMENT, consisting of several American melodies, which will take place, by the kind permission of Mr. Kirkman, at No 3, Soho-square, next door to the Bazaar, on Wednesday, the 23d of February, 1842, at half past 8 precisely. Mr. H Russell will sing, among others, the following descriptive songs:- "The Maniac"; "Wind of the Winter Night, whence comest thou?" written by Chas Mackay, Esq.; "Woodman, spare that Tree," written by G P Morris, Esq.; "The Ivy Green," written by Charles Dickens, Esq.; "The Old Arm Chair," written by Miss Eliza Cook; "The Ship on Fire," written by Charles Mackay, Esq.; "The Song of a Stormy Night," written by Charles Mackay, Esq.; "The Old Bell," &c. Further particulars will be duly announced. Tickets 5s each. No money will be taken at the door.

It is worth noting, from the reference to Russell as author of "Woodman, Spare That Tree," that George P. Morris's ballad had indeed already won popularity in Britain. Russell's London publisher from the early 1830s, George Walker, had issued it in 1840, and several other publishers followed. It had appeared in print with a guitar accompaniment, and even with piano variations by Carl Czerny. Regarding the reference to the Soho Bazaar at 4–6 Soho Square, this had opened in 1816 as an adaptation of a former warehouse, and it existed until the premises were taken over by publishers A & C Black in 1889.

As for "Mr. H Russell, from America," that may seem misleading, but it was, of course, literally true and, more to the point, was a reasonable representation of the entertainment offered. Perhaps more so, though, it is clear that there was commercial advantage for Russell in presenting himself as being American. On this occasion, at least, the London press was not wholly deceived, since *The Morning Post* specifically recalled Russell's earlier appearances in juvenile operas at the Surrey Theatre:

> These boy-and-girl performances were very successful at the time, as much on account of their musical merit as of their novelty, and amongst the *corps opératique*, young Russell was particularly distinguished for precocious talent. . . . The

> promises put forth by the boy have been realised by the man, and both he and his friends may congratulate themselves upon their fulfilment in the instance of yesterday evening's concert. The voice of Mr. Russell is a bass of much power, richly and roundly toned, and of considerable compass. Moreover, it is capable of great energy of expression, and is altogether free from that monotonous tameness which too frequently spoils the best efforts of many of our native singers.

The report goes on to comment on various songs, among them "Woodman, Spare That Tree," "the extraordinary sale of which in both England and America is only to be accounted for by the happy combination of sense with sound abounding throughout the composition." There is comment, too, on what may have been the very first performance of another of Russell's outstanding successes: "The Ship on Fire." This was a dramatic *scena* after the fashion of "Wind of the Winter Night" and "The Maniac," with a long piano introduction that Stephens rightly describes as "a pianistic tour de force, full of crashing octaves depicting fire, and rolling minor 6ths illustrating the wind and the choppy sea." The ensuing vocal contribution builds up pity with its picture of a woman on board ship with her young child, portraying alternate calm and tempest before the dramatic cry of "Fire!" and the eventual rescue.

Trite it may seem nowadays; but it is easy to sense its effect on audiences who were dependent on live performance, who had seen and heard nothing quite like it before, and for whom fire on board ship was all too real a threat. On just such things did Henry Russell's unique appeal rest. In later American concert announcements he expounded in greater detail his credo for this and similar compositions:

> The attempted expression in Music of a rapid succession of different emotions hope, fear, despair and joy, forms the principal characteristics of what I will venture to designate, "the descriptive school of song composing." Melodies adapted to songs although very beautiful in themselves and often well suited to the general tenor of the words, yet do not usually change with the changing phases of the story in its progress.
>
> In many of my compositions however, and in this among the rest, I have attempted to make the expression both of the principal melody and of the accompaniments go strictly

Figure 10.1. "The Ship on Fire!" sheet music cover. *Source:* Author's collection.

along with the varying idea expressed by the words. It has been my object as far as possible, to adapt expressive music to the feelings and emotions excited by the occurrences of comparatively every day life, and it is obvious that no better

> theme for such an attempt could be chosen than is furnished by the Ship on Fire.
>
> It is a tale of frequent, too frequent occurrence at sea, and yet simple as it is how many vicissitudes, how many perils of the physical and emotions of the moral world does it comprehend. The fate and prosperous breeze at first, the hopes of those who feel its favoring influence, the husband and the youthful bride wrapt in anticipation of a blissful future indulging in dreams of coming happiness, planning out new prospects, happy in themselves and in each other, and then the alarm, the progress of the tempest, the alternating sense of hope and fear of the hapless beings exposed to its fury, the change from one danger to another more fearful and more imminent, and finally the deliverance.

Russell's account of this composition's origin was that it arose from a meeting with Tyrone Power just a few hours (of course) before the latter's ill-fated departure from New York on board the *President*:

> [The idea of] the song called "The Ship on Fire," . . . with some of the words, had, singularly enough, been suggested to him by poor Power a few hours before he embarked on his last fatal voyage in the unfortunate steamer *President*! The incident took place while they dined together at New York; and Power, describing the idea he had formed in his mind, said, "just imagine my case now; I going home full of joy to meet my wife and family, and the ship to be destroyed by fire!" "But it will be too sad, and won't be well received," was the observation in reply. "Oh! you can have them all saved in a boat," was the answer of him, who, alas! was not to find that safety in the dreadful emergency, which, by so singular a coincidence he imagined. The words of the second verse of the song were those said to be given by Power himself. They begin:-
>
> "It is passed; the fierce whirlwind careered on its way,
> And the ship like an arrow divided the spray:
> Her sail glimmered white in the beams of the moon,
> And the wind up aloft seemed to whistle a tune.
> There was joy in the ship as she furrowed the foam.
> For fond hearts within her were dreaming of home," &c

To return to the 23 February 1842 concert, the *Times* review is worth quoting in order to give a further idea of the novelty that a solo entertainment represented for a London audience:

> The company was very numerous, and amongst them were several of the most eminent musicians. The entertainment was of a novel character in this country, inasmuch as it consisted entirely of songs sung by Mr. H Russell himself, unsupported by the talent of any vocalist. The accompaniment was on a remarkably fine-toned pianoforte, made in the manufactory of the gentleman on whose premises the concert took place. It is great praise to Mr. H Russell to say that he got through this very difficult task with complete success. Though he sang many songs, there was no monotony either of manner or execution, and the company were in no hurry for the termination of his efforts. He possesses an extraordinarily fine voice, and, in addition to a perfect knowledge of music and its effects, he has a clear enunciation, and articulates so distinctly that the poetry of the songs is heard concurrently with the melody of the air. This is a great desideratum in English singers, but is one without which all songs are little better than the warbling of a tune. This gentleman is admirably adapted to become a good dramatic singer, and is just the person to attract and please a theatrical audience.

The Morning Chronicle was even more flattering:

> Mr. Russell is not only possessed of vocal attainments of a very high order, but is decidedly a man of genius. His voice, taken in the aggregate of its qualities, is one which (strong as the expression may seem) we have never heard excelled. In *compass* it may be called, we think, a *baritone*; but in power, volume, and that peculiar character more easily felt than described which the French call *timbre*, it is a *bass*. It is a bass, too, without the ponderosity generally belonging to voices of that register, being as light and flexible as most tenors, and sweet and mellow as well as loud and powerful. To these physical gifts, Mr. Russell adds those of feeling and intelligence. He sings with intense earnestness and great expression, and, in one most important

particular, we have no hesitation in saying that he is unrivalled by any English singer, Braham alone excepted—this is, the clearness, variety, and force of his musical declamation. . . . It is evident that the management of his voice and utterance has been acquired in the Italian school of singing; and his own good sense has shown him, that, while distinct articulation of language does not necessarily detract from the beauty of vocal sound, indistinct utterance deprives vocal sound of its greatest charm, its power of heightening and enforcing the expression of sentiment and passion.

Russell followed up this successful debut with two further concerts at the Hanover Square Rooms. For at least the first, on the evening of Tuesday, 8 March, he varied the diet of songs of his own composition by including Mendelssohn's recitative and aria "Santo Padre." *The Musical World* noted among "a room full of company . . . a very large majority of the fair sex; by which circumstance we are led to infer that Mr. H. Russell is a favourite with the ladies at least." The weekly was, though, reluctant to accept the notion of a solo recital, noting "the tale of *toujours perdrix*" ("too much of the same thing") and suggesting that "if he had attempted less, [he] might have effected more." Of his third solo concert—in the "morning" (afternoon in today's parlance) of Friday, 11 March—*The Times* reported a success as great as previously. It noted now that "Mr. H Russell's voice combines the tenor, the barytone, and the bass, is exceedingly clear and powerful, and his enunciation is perfect." It also felt that, "If sung with an orchestral accompaniment, some of [the songs] would be improved." Meanwhile, the previous evening—Thursday, 10 March—Russell had also made an appearance on a program alongside other performers. At the St. James's Theatre, King Street, he was among "fifty distinguished Artistes . . . under the immediate patronage of their Royal Highnesses the Duke and Duchess of Cambridge and other Noble Families . . . at Miss Alicia Nunn's First Concert since her return from Italy."

His appeal was soon increasing the interest of London music publishers in his output. Before the end of March, publishers Cramer, Addison and Beale of Regent Street, and Jefferys and Nelson of Soho Square were jointly announcing the availability of songs old and new. They included "The Ivy Green," "The Old Arm Chair," "The Maniac," "The Gambler's Wife," "The Old Watermill," "My Mother's Portrait," "Song for a Stormy Night' (alias "Our Way Across the Mountains, Ho!"), and "Let's Be Gay."

"The publication of these excellent songs forms a new era in English music," they boldly declared.

On 31 March Russell further varied his venues with a concert at the London Tavern in the City of London. The *Times* announcement lists "The Gambler's Wife" among new songs (new to London at least), and the paper's review also reported a new ballad entitled "My Mother's Portrait," with words by Leigh Cliffe. According to *The Morning Post*, the room "was completely filled with a most respectable company." Further concerts at the same venue followed on 18 April and 2 May.

In addition, John Blewitt's Grand Morning Concert, in the Great Concert Room of the Music Hall, Store Street, on 3 May showcased Russell on a bill with some of the most distinguished British singers of the day, some of whom he would have encountered in America. They included soprano Elizabeth Rainforth (1814–77), mezzo-soprano Elizabeth Poole (1820–1906), contralto Priscilla Horton (1818–95), basses Theodore Victor Giubilei and Adam Leffler (1808–57), bass-baritone Henry Phillips, and entertainer-at-the-piano John Orlando Parry (1810–79), as well as eminent solo instrumentalists. Jonathan Blewitt (1782–1853) was, among other musical occupations, the composer of comic songs such as "Why Don't the Men Propose?," "John Nott, Why Not?," and "Trouble Your Heads with Your Own Ideas" (aka "Trouble Yourself with Your Own Affairs"), which Russell at various times sang in America and Britain—if not always to everyone's satisfaction. In Norwich, in September 1847, a critic with narrow vision panned Russell's performance of "Why Don't the Men Propose?," describing it as "an imitation of the inimitable John Parry,—and fell very short of that vocalist's performance."

The Musical World picked up on current rumor by declaring of three of the singers at that May 1842 concert that "We understand Miss Poole, Mr. H Russell, and Mr. Giubilei, are to strengthen the opera corps next season, and that *Semiramide* is to be one of the earliest productions." It may well be that at this time Russell was seriously considering such an option for the future. He must certainly have been seeking still to gauge the potential for a career in England. That he had to test his appeal on the provincial circuit we can confirm from his appearance in England's second city, Birmingham, at an orchestral concert at the Town Hall on Thursday, 5 May 1842. He was then just one of a group of vocal and instrumental performers, ranking no higher than third among the former. Top-billed was high-ranked soprano Adelaide Kemble (1814–79), younger daughter of actor Charles Kemble (1775–1854) and sister of actress Fanny Kemble

(1809–93). Also billed ahead of Russell was the aforementioned soprano Elizabeth Rainforth.

The concert promoter was violinist Henry Hayward, whose contributions included a Paganini Concerto as well as a set of Variations of his own. Other featured instrumentalists included flautist "Mr. Carte" and pianist "Mr. Hatton." The former, whose contributions included Variations on the Huntsmen's Chorus from Weber's *Der Freischütz*, was Richard Carte (c. 1808–91), later a partner in the instrument firm of Rudall, Carte, and father of Gilbert and Sullivan impresario Richard D'Oyly Carte. The latter, who ended the first half of this Birmingham concert by singing Rossini's "Largo al factotum," was John Liptrot Hatton (1808–86), operatic composer, a future entertainer at the piano, and composer of "Simon the Cellarer" and a setting of Henry Longfellow's "The Wreck of the Hesperus."

The newspaper announcement of the event is noteworthy as much for the quaintness of the housekeeping arrangements as for the program content; "Carriages to set down and take up with horses' heads towards the Old Wharf" was one instruction. The published program began with Beethoven's "Grand Symphony in C" (presumably no. 1), and found room only for two numbers by Russell: the *scena* "The Maniac" in Part 1, and the ballad "My Mother's Portrait" in Part 2. *The Birmingham and General Advertiser* reported that the concert "was attended by one of the most crowded and fashionable audiences which we have witnessed in Birmingham on any similar occasion," and that "the encores during the evening were numerous, and protracted the entertainment to a late hour." The reviewer declared that "Mr. Russell's performance called forth repeated plaudits," but made no secret of the fact that "the great attraction of the evening was Miss Adelaide Kemble." It was the lady's first appearance in Birmingham after resuscitating her career with a long spell in Italy. Within a year, however, she had married and abandoned singing. Russell, of course, would return to Birmingham a great deal in future years.

On the following evening, 6 May 1842, several of the same artists—Kemble, Rainforth, Russell, Hatton—reassembled for a concert in Manchester. Supporting them now was harpist Elias Parish Alvars (1808–49). The evening's first vocal item was the duet "Il pallor, funesto, orrendo" from Donizetti's *Lucia di Lammermoor*, sung by Rainforth and Russell. The final one was the trio "L'usato ardir" from Rossini's *Semiramide*, with Russell in support of Kemble and Rainforth. In between, Russell got to perform "The Maniac" and "A Life on the Ocean Wave." The *Manchester Guardian* critic rather expended his superlatives on Miss

Kemble, whose first song he declared created a sensation "such as has not been witnessed in that room since the departure of Malibran." His view of Russell was decidedly less fulsome: "Mr. Russell's descriptive ballads were well received, although we deem them a style of performance which will certainly be short-lived. He has a good voice—his pronunciation is rather broad; perhaps a *leetle* American. The short step between the sublime and the ridiculous makes some hesitate on which side to place this "school" of singing; it really seems a little over-drawn and we should hope to hear no more of it here." Well, one can see his point, and one must admire his boldness in expressing it! As for his final comments, they provide an interesting comment on the behavior of audiences over 160 years ago:

> We cannot conclude even this brief and hasty notice without expressing the hope, that in future the stewards will do something effectual towards putting down the very annoying practice of parties in the room talking so loud as to disturb those who go to hear the music; and even, in some recent instances, those who go to perform it. On Friday evening, the talking in some of the front benches was so loud as to disturb and disconcert performers in the orchestra, who were desirous only to give due effect to the pieces assigned to them.

If the *Guardian* reviewer had reservations about Russell's style, though, they were nothing compared with those expressed by *The Musical World* when the journal attended his next solo London concert at the Hanover Square Rooms on Thursday, 26 May. As in America, it would seem that loftier minds were slow to understand Russell's appeal. The reviewer acknowledged that the performance "was listened to with marked attention, and greeted with loud applause," and that "Mr. H Russell has a fine clear manly baritone voice, . . . a bold and impassioned style, correct intonation, and absence of extraneous ornament." However, there followed suggestions for improvement that, as so often, say more about the reviewer than the performer: "we wish he would choose pleasanter subjects for his ballads than the ravings of men driven mad, and the horrors of the crew of a ship on fire; and surely he might select something from the works of standard composers. . . ."

Russell again played a supporting role at a further concert at the Hanover Square Rooms on 1 June. Conducted by Julius Benedict (1804–85), it featured as prime attraction the German virtuoso pianist Sigismond Thalberg (1812–71), playing his own fantasias on *Lucrezia Borgia*, *Don*

Giovanni, and *Semiramide*, and his Andante in D flat, op. 32. Russell's position as a supporting attraction is exemplified by the fact that *The Times* gave his name only passing mention. It reserved individual comment for his fellow singers: Elizabeth Rainforth again, William Balfe and his wife, Lina Roser (1806–88), and the new bass Willoughby Weiss (1820–67), later the composer of "The Village Blacksmith."

The indebtedness Russell felt to piano manufacturer Charles Kirkman, promoter of his first London concert in February 1842, was further demonstrated when another son, born on 21 June 1842 at the Russell family home at 5 Allsop Place, Marylebone, was baptized Charles Kirkman Russell. The Russell household now included three children, Isabella being aged six, and Henry Lloyd almost five. The length of the age gap between the latter and Charles Kirkman in those days of primitive birth control and high infant mortality suggests that one or more children might have been lost—or otherwise that Isabella had lingered long, post the Gambati incident, back in England. The newcomer's birth was registered on 25 July 1842, and on 2 August both he and elder brother Henry Lloyd were baptized at St. Mary's Church, Marylebone Road, London. Isabella, as we know, had been baptized in Rochester.

To what extent Russell appeared in the provinces during 1842 is unclear, although seems that, from the summer onward, he did a fair amount of traveling. During July, for instance, he was touring Kent towns. Though close to the place of his birth, he spurned any suggestion of "local boy made good," persisting with the designation "from America." Indeed, reporting on his appearance at the Rochester Theatre on Tuesday, 26 July, *The Rochester, Chatham and Strood Gazette* commented particularly that "Mr. Russell is a stranger amongst us." His reception was sufficient to determine a return visit ten days later, having the previous evening been no less enthusiastically received at the County Assembly Room, Maidstone. *The Musical World* printed a report from there, declaring that his vocal entertainment "if not so fully attended as might have been anticipated left such an impression on the minds of those who attended as will ensure for Mr. Russell a bumper whenever he returns to us."

The establishment of Russell's reputation in Britain was still being strengthened further with the publication of songs both old and new. The firm of Cramer, Addison and Beale of Regent Street brought out several, including "The Ship on Fire," "The Poor Man's Friend" (dedicated to the wife of Frederick Beale), "The Emigrant's Farewell," and others. Fred C. Leader of Bond Street brought out the likes of "The Patriot's Welcome,"

"The Indian Hunter," and "The Old Clock." Both of these publishers were to be found promoting what seems to have been Russell's next London entertainment, on 19 December 1842:

> MR. HENRY RUSSELL (from America) will give a VOCAL ENTERTAINMENT at the Hanover-square Rooms THIS EVENING, when he will introduce The Indian Hunter, the Maniac, the Founding of the Bell, the Ship on Fire, the Old Arm Chair, the Ivy Green, Let's Be Gay, &c. The new horizontal fonda pianoforte, manufactured by Joseph Kirkman and Son, will be used upon this occasion. Single tickets, 2s. 6d.; reserved seats, 4s.; family tickets to admit four to the reserved, 19s. 6d.; to be had of Cramer, Addison, and Beale, Regent-street; Ollivier, New Bond-street; and at Leader's, 63, New Bond-street.

The concert was a definite success, and in a further highly complimentary review, *The Times* commented:

> The concert was commenced at 8 o'clock, but long before that hour all the best seats were occupied, and by 8 o'clock the great room was filled with a perfect crowd of auditors. The whole, both of the vocal part of the entertainment and the accompaniment on the pianoforte, was performed by Mr. Russell himself, who, for nearly two hours, went through the arduous undertaking of amusing upwards of 1,000 persons by his own unassisted musical talent, and went through it with perfect success; he was rewarded by the loud and repeated applause of those who heard him, and certainly not one voice was heard in dissent from the universal approbation.

Even *The Musical World* now showed signs of being won over to Russell's individual style, declaring that "Mr. Russell is improved in style since we last heard him." Praising his "fine manly organ, and dashing style of accompaniment," it noted particularly "a paraphrase of part of Schiller's ode, made into a stirring song, under the title of 'The founding of the bell.' "

Russell was back at the Hanover Square Rooms on 12 January 1843 with, according to advertisements, "several new compositions . . . , namely 'The Dream of the Reveller,' 'The National Melodies of America,' 'The Young Soldier,' several new Indian and Prairie songs, &c." The second of these was presumably "Our Native Song." As for the first, with words by Charles

Figure 10.2. “The Emigrant’s Farewell” sheet music cover. *Source:* Courtesy the Lester Levy Sheet Music Collection, The Sheridan Libraries, Johns Hopkins University.

Mackay, it was a temperance song, in response to the strong anti-drink lobby that was currently gaining force not only in Britain but elsewhere:

> Around the board the guests were met, the lights above them beaming,
> And in their cups, replenish'd oft, the ruddy wine was streaming;
> Their cheeks were flush'd, their eyes were bright, their hearts with pleasure bounded,
> The song was sung, the toast was given, and loud the revel sounded.
> I drain'd my bumper with the rest, and cried, "Away with sorrow!
> Let us be happy for to-day, what care we for to-morrow?"
> But as I spoke my sight grew dim, and slumber deep came o'er me,
> And, mid the whirl of mingling tongues, this vision pass'd before me.

"The Dream of the Reveller" is another of Russell's more extended compositions, albeit basically a five-verse strophic composition that, as Charles Hamm has commented, "could easily pass for a drinking song from an opera of the 1830s or '40s." There is even a flavour of Sullivan's early comic operas about its sprightly melody. Musically it achieved its effect with variations of tempo, rhythm, and accompaniment between the verses, which work up to a frenzy of manic laughter. The effect of Russell's performance of the piece is well conveyed in a report of a concert in Worcester in April 1846:

> "The dream of the reveller" (the words by Mackay) is the finest thing ever attempted by Mr. Russell. The awful vision that haunts the debauchee, of demons tantalizing the lost drunkard with his favourite boast of "not caring for the morrow," and the fiend's bitter laugh of derision, all seem to pass in reality before the singer, who is lost to everything but the horrid scene before him, and with bated breath and in deep and thrilling tones he produces an effect with his magnificent voice and most expressive countenance, which can hardly be conceived.

An explanation of how the lyric of this major Russell piece came about was given in a letter from Charles Mackay that Russell included in later concert announcements in America:

> My dear Sir:-
>
> In presenting to you the accompanying song, permit to say, that it was written during my evening preambles through the streets of London. You are doubtless aware, sir, that in the principal streets of this great metropolis and in fact many of the country towns of England, gorgeous gin shops glare amongst modest and useful trades, and thrive upon the want, misery and ruin, which they spread around them. The extremes of riches and poverty, of luxurious living and the want of the necessaries of life, are hourly exhibited in more marked contrast here than in any other place in the world. . . .
>
> Much of the poverty I mention doubtless proceeds from intemperance; it has hitherto been the grand bane of the labouring classes; it is a deadly adversary to every thing that is good. It ruins the constitution—destroys the powers of the mind—converts a happy home into a place of misery, and sooner or later is wont to consign its miserable victim to the grave.

If announcements of Russell's subsequent concerts in America are to be believed, he also performed "The Dream of a Reveller" in London on 23 January 1843 before an audience of 3,000 people at a meeting of the National Temperance Society at the Exeter Hall. However, even a particularly long report on that event in *The Morning Herald* makes no mention of any such musical contribution. The piece was published in Britain with a dedication to the Temperance Societies of England, Ireland, and Scotland, and in America with one to "The Temperance Ladys [sic] of the United States." In Britain it received two later sets of words: the first (as "The Vision of the Reveller") by George Soane, the second by Eliza Cook.

Meanwhile Russell appeared on 18 January with sundry other performers at a concert given by flautist Richard Carte at the Bridge Hotel, Southwark, at the southern end of London Bridge. His next solo London concert was at the Hanover Square Rooms on 1 February, again using "the new Fonda Horizontal Piano, containing the Iterant Isochronal action, manufactured by Joseph Kirkman and Son, . . . only five feet eight inches in length." Among numbers seemingly new was "The Newfoundland Dog," based on an incident that had supposedly occurred on his crossing from America to Britain, in which a dog named Carlo had leaped into the ocean to save a child that had fallen overboard. The song—about which more later—had words by Frederick William Naylor Bailey (1808–53), the first editor of *The Illustrated London News*.

Figure 10.3a. "The New Foundland Dog" sheet music cover. *Source:* Author's collection.

That Russell's success in London was being followed across the ocean is clear from an item in *The Brooklyn Eagle*:

> In looking over a file of late London papers, we observe that there is scarcely one which does not unite in rendering [Rus-

Figure 10.3b. "The New Foundland Dog" song sheet. *Source:* Author's collection.

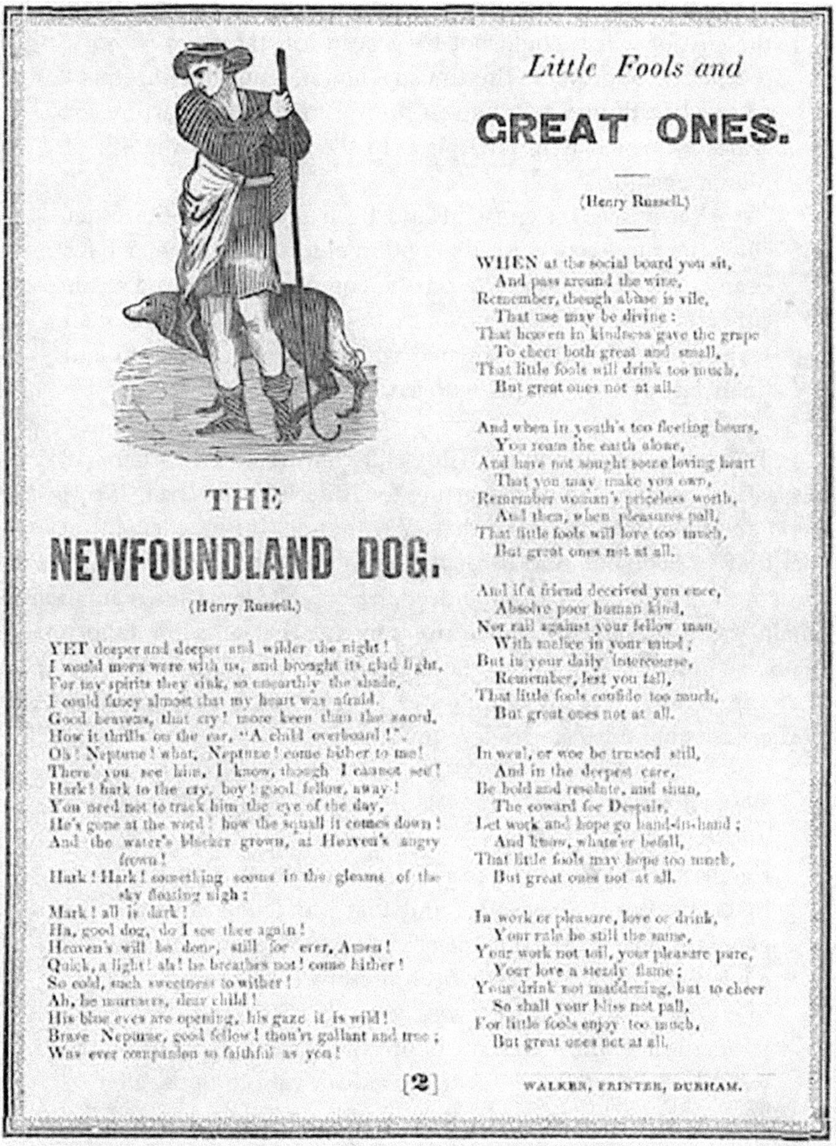

THE

NEWFOUNDLAND DOG.

(Henry Russell.)

YET deeper and deeper and wilder the night!
I would morn were with us, and brought its glad light,
For my spirits they sink, so unearthly the shade,
I could fancy almost that my heart was afraid.
Good heavens, that cry! more keen than the sword,
How it thrills on the ear, "A child overboard!".
Oh! Neptune! what, Neptune! come hither to me!
There' you see him, I know, though I cannot see!
Hark! hark to the cry, boy! good fellow, away!
You need not to track him the eye of the day,
He's gone at the word! how the squall it comes down!
And the water's blacker grown, at Heaven's angry frown!
Hark! Hark! something seems in the gleams of the sky floating nigh:
Mark! all is dark!
Ha, good dog, do I see thee again!
Heaven's will be done, still for ever, Amen!
Quick, a light! ah! he breathes not! come hither!
So cold, such sweetness to wither!
Ah, he murmurs, dear child!
His blue eyes are opening, his gaze it is wild!
Brave Neptune, good fellow! thou'rt gallant and true;
Was ever companion so faithful as you!

[2]

Little Fools and

GREAT ONES.

(Henry Russell.)

WHEN at the social board you sit,
And pass around the wine,
Remember, though abuse is vile,
That use may be divine:
That heaven in kindness gave the grape
To cheer both great and small,
That little fools will drink too much,
But great ones not at all.

And when in youth's too fleeting hours,
You roam the earth alone,
And have not sought some loving heart
That you may make you own,
Remember woman's priceless worth,
And then, when pleasures pall,
That little fools will love too much,
But great ones not at all.

And if a friend deceived you once,
Absolve poor human kind,
Nor rail against your fellow man,
With malice in your mind;
But in your daily intercourse,
Remember, lest you fall,
That little fools confide too much,
But great ones not at all.

In weal, or woe be trusted still,
And in the deepest care,
Be bold and resolute, and shun,
The coward for Despair,
Let work and hope go hand-in-hand;
And know, whate'er befall,
That little fools may hope too much,
But great ones not at all.

In work or pleasure, love or drink,
Your rule be still the same,
Your work not toil, your pleasure pure,
Your love a steady flame;
Your drink not maddening, but to cheer
So shall your bliss not pall,
For little fools enjoy too much,
But great ones not at all.

WALKER, PRINTER, DURHAM.

sell] that praise which is so justly due to his merits. When he sang in this country his concerts were usually crowded; but it fell far, far short of the immense attendance which most of his musical entertainments in London have received. . . .

> We observe that his brother professors in London "have presented him with a most exquisitely chased silver Vase, the cost of which could not have been less than *two hundred pounds*." In addition to this unusual honor, is an announcement of a public dinner to be given him prior to his departure for America, which is to take place in the steamer of the 4th of March ensuing.
>
> Verily has the grass always been greener on the other side! The success of Russell's London entertainments may have been considerable, and the artistic company he enjoyed at his concerts around Britain may have been distinguished; but it all seems relatively little compared with the popular acclaim and financial rewards he had enjoyed in the New World.

The press had announced Russell's concert of 1 February 1843 as "his last . . . previous to his departure for America." However, *The Musical World* amplified this by saying that "We are told, this gentleman makes a brief tour to Scotland, and through the intermediate provinces, prior to his departure for America." So, indeed, he did. However, his reputation in Britain was as yet insufficient to overcome to the full some inhospitable weather, combined with the appearance of the tour being hastily arranged. After his performance in Leeds on 9 February, for instance, *The Leeds Intelligencer* upbraided its readers thus:

> We had supposed that the celebrity and talent of this accomplished singer and composer would have fully compensated for the brief notice which was given of his intended performance in Leeds; but we regret to find that our fellow townspeople generally have suffered themselves to overlook and miss as rich a musical treat as has lately been presented for their patronage. The concert on Thursday was very thinly attended, but the judicious few who seized the opportunity were highly delighted with the performance. . . . It is, we fear, vain to hope, after so cool a reception, that Mr. Russell will be induced to give an opportunity to the phlegmatic people of Leeds of retrieving their neglect of sterling merit.

As he continued north, Britain was hit by a severe snowstorm on 17 and 18 February that saw drifts of twelve to fourteen feet in some lowlands and valleys. In Scotland he gave his entertainment at the Waterloo Rooms in Edinburgh on 21 and 23 February, and at the Assembly and Queen's Concert Rooms in Glasgow on 22 and 24 February. Of the two cities, Glasgow seems to have proved more welcoming than Edinburgh. For the second Edinburgh concert Russell brought in the young Polish tenor, [Julius] Gustav Brandt, to sing songs by Schubert and Proch, and he also announced that "on account of unavoidable engagements in London, he will be unable to give a Third Vocal Entertainment on Saturday Morning, as originally intended."

Back in London he gave yet another farewell concert at the Hanover Square Rooms on 27 February. *The Musical World* noted that he "concluded with an American story, and a 'nigger song,' evincing much dry humor and pleasing his auditors greatly." Between the two halves of the program, Madame Dulcken gave a recital on the Euphonicon, a type of upright piano recently invented by Cramer, Beale & Co. *The Musical World* was not alone in having reservations about the instrument, which it felt was "totally out of its place in the concert room: the elegance and beauty of its construction, which so admirably adapt it for the drawing-room or boudoir, are entirely lost in the orchestre." It added that Russell "accompanied himself on the 'Euphonicon,' which accords well with the voice, but should be used sideways; as Mr. Russell sat, behind the instrument, it gave the effect of his looking at the audience through a splendidly elaborate gridiron."

The announcement of the concert as Russell's last before departure for America aroused much press comment. However, *The Morning Post*, at least, was not completely taken in by his intentions: "We perceive that Mr. Russell announced this as his farewell concert, but from his great success last evening we should not be surprised to hear some 'more last words' from this popular singer." So indeed they did. What really did prove to be Russell's last performance of this particular London season took place at the Hanover Square Rooms on 2 March, for the benefit of the Institution for Clothing and Educating Poor Jewish Children. Miss Frances Isaacs (making her first appearance in public), Mr. John Parry, jun, 'cellist Haussmann, and the Polish viola player Stanislaus Maciejowski (d. 1868) were also featured—along with, of course, the Fonda piano manufactured by Messrs. Kirkman and Son. Besides being available from concert agents Addison and Beale, tickets were on this occasion available from J. Russell's, 31 King Street, Covent Garden and S. Isaacs's, 131 Regent Street. Henry Russell's brother Israel was a "curiosity dealer" (or, as we might say today, antiques dealer) at 31 King Street.

The concert was evidently put together hurriedly, around Russell's imminent return to the United States. *The Jewish Chronicle* reported:

> The performance was only practicable on the evening preceding his departure for America; and he had to hasten up from profitable provincial engagements, in order to perform his promise. . . . A gratifying close of the proceedings was the subsequent presentation, in a private room, of a neat silver cup, bearing a suitable inscription addressed to Mr. Russell, in acknowledgement of his aid to the charity. To the appropriate address . . . Mr. Russell made a feeling reply, expressive of his pride to be known as a Jew, and to be able to be able to assist the philanthropic objects of his brethren. He assured his kind friends, that wheresoever his lot had been cast, his heart had always yearned towards the institutions of his fathers.

The following day Russell set off for Liverpool, where he joined the *RMS Columbia*. This was one of four ships with which Sir Samuel Cunard (1787–1865) had initiated his British and North American Royal Mail Steam Packet Company service in 1840. The Columbia had sailed on its maiden voyage from Liverpool to Halifax, Nova Scotia, and Boston on 5 January 1841, and it was probably to mark its arrival in America that Russell dedicated to its commander, Captain C. H. E. Judkins, his song "The Ocean, or the Merry Mariners." Compared with the eight or nine weeks of his westward crossing of a decade earlier, the voyage across the Atlantic now took only a couple of weeks. With Russell on board, the *Columbia* left Liverpool at 1:00 p.m. on Saturday, 4 March 1843, and arrived at Halifax, Nova Scotia, at 12:30 p.m. on Saturday, 18 March 1843. Having experienced strong westerly gales and heavy head-swells for the greater part of the passage, the ship had then been detained by fog off Halifax for a whole day. Leaving Halifax within six hours of its arrival there, it reached East Boston at 8:00 a.m. on Monday, 20 March.

While Russell was at sea, *The Musical World* published a review of "The Winds Are Free," a new text for the melody of "I Love, I Love the Free." The paper described it as "a capital ballad—the air vocal and flowing, somewhat in the Shield style, the accompaniment easy, and the *ensemble* easy and effective." Much as he no doubt relished the prospect of renewed acquaintance with the country in which he had first made his name, Russell no doubt reflected on the significant strides he had also made in establishing himself in his native country.

11

American Encore

After his ship arrived in America, Russell did not stay for public appearances in Boston, but continued on to New York. Before the end of the month of his last performance in London, he had made the first of several appearances at Niblo's, spread over the next few weeks, introducing Americans to some of the new songs composed in England. Vide the advertised program for the first concert on 28 March 1843:

> PART I
>
> Song—Some Love to Roam o'er the Dark Sea Foam. Words by Charles Mackay, Esq.
>
> Song—A Life on the Ocean Wave.
>
> Scena—The Dream of the Reveller; or the Three Houses. Sung by Mr. Russel [sic] at the Great Temperance Meeting, held in the long room at Exeter Hall, London, in the presence of over 3000 persons. Words by Charles Mackay, Esq.
>
> Aria Comico—Sono Stanco. Composed by Maestro Generale. [sic]
>
> Song—The Indian Hunter. A Song of the Far West—Words by Eliza Cook.
>
> Newfoundland Dog. Words by F W N Bailey.
>
> Cantata—The Maniac.
>
> PART II
>
> Scena—The Gambler's Wife. Words by Dr Coats.
>
> Song—I'm Afloat, I'm Afloat. Words by Eliza Cook.
>
> Scena—The Ship on Fire. Words by Charles Mackay, Esq.

National American Song—Our Native Song.
Song—The Ivy Green. Written by C Dickens, Esq.
Finale—Let's Be Gay—A Laughing Chorus. From an unpublished Opera.

The Brooklyn Eagle reported of Russell's first concert back in America that it was "crowded to overflowing," with "near two thousand persons present." It suggested that "Mr. Russell is much improved since he left us," and reiterated that "the secret of Mr. Russell's success must be the expression with which he renders his music." The paper also ventured unusually enlightened comments on Russell's appeal:

> Mr. Russell has struck out a new track for himself, and his boldness in freeing himself from the fetters of an established and methodical restraint, has called down the wrath of the harnessed disciples of the old school; but on the other hand, his originality and genius have been rewarded by the honest and enthusiastic admiration of those truer and better judges whose natural taste has not been moulded by artificial rule, or whose feelings are not confined within the bounds of a musical despotism.

Russell's performance of "The Newfoundland Dog" at Niblo's was the subject of another of the anecdotes in his 1895 autobiography:

> As was usual with me, I prefaced my song by telling my audience in simple language the true and somewhat pathetic story of its origin. Crossing the Atlantic Ocean in the packet ship *Montezuma*, commanded by Captain Loder, a young mother was one day toying with her child, a boy three years of age, on the bulwarks of the vessel, when suddenly by some extraordinary effort on the child's part it leaped from its mother's arms and fell overboard. The frantic screams of the poor mother were heard in every part of the ship, and passengers and crew came running anxiously to the spot. Among those attracted by the cries was a steerage passenger, the owner of a magnificent Newfoundland dog, that had scarcely left its master's side. With the wonderful instinct of the animal it

> quickly grasped the meaning of the scene, and leaping on to the bulwarks it sprang into the sea and swam rapidly towards the fast drowning child, and then seizing its frock in his teeth, held the little one's head above the water.
>
> In the meantime, a boat was lowered, into which several men sprang, and rowing quickly to the spot they succeeded in saving both child and dog. The poor mother, in the meantime, had fainted and had been carried into the gentlemen's saloon, and I shall never forget the cry of delight that she uttered on awakening, on seeing her little one safe and sound. This incident so impressed me that I wrote a song in honour of that noble dog and called it "Carlo, the Newfoundland Dog."
>
> At the finish of the song, two men rose in the gallery which surrounded the hall, and one of them, clearing his throat, addressed me as follows: "Good evenin," Mister Russell, this is my friend, Joe Taylor" (introducing his companion, who bowed two or three times.) "Excuse me, sir," he continued, "Was that dog yourn?" "No, it was not," I replied. "Did he save the child?" "He did." "Wall," he exclaimed, with the air of a man who was asking a great favour. "I should like a pup. Could you get us one?"

In relation to the refinement (if such it may be called) of Russell's anecdotes over a period of half a century, it is instructive to compare this story with what he reportedly said at a performance in Norwich, England, in September 1847. Confirming the song's origin in an incident on Russell's "first voyage to England," the report continued: "When singing the song at Boston, a Yankee, (and Mr. Russell remarked, that the Yankees, as his hearers knew, were remarkable for wishing to know every particular about every thing, and about every body,) inquired of him, very earnestly, what colour the dog was, whether brown or white? Mr. Russell informed him, he did not know; 'because," said the Yankee, "I should have liked to have had a pup.'" Take your pick! Both—and other variants—are probably apocryphal!

Meanwhile, for a further Niblo's concert, on Monday, 3 April 1843, the program listed "The General's Last Battle," written in London, and two seemingly new pieces, "The Launch" and "If I Had But a Thousand a Year" (otherwise "Robin Ruff"). The occasion was described as, "if possible, more crowded than the previous one . . . cheering at the last." At another performance at the Lyceum, Brooklyn, the next evening, Russell further endeared himself to his audience by announcing that he would give a concert the following Tuesday evening to aid the finances of the Brooklyn Apprentices' Library. That Russell's songs were now part of a wider song repertory is illustrated by a Brooklyn concert the following evening, when one George A. Hoyt, described as a former pupil of the New York Institution for the Blind, sang "The Ivy Green," "Our Way Across the Mountains, Ho!," "The Ship on Fire," and "I Love the Free."

In New York City itself, Russell's concerts continued at Niblo's on Friday, 7 April, with a program introducing "The Drunkard" and "The Hero and the Philosopher," the latter a new song with words by George P. Morris, "written upon an incident connected with Washington and Franklin." At the same venue on Wednesday, 12 April, he offered "The Genius of Temperance," with words by Henry John Sharpe. Even if these pieces were less than enduring, his popularity was clearly as great as ever, and it provoked no lessening of the jealousy from some of his fellow performers. Witness, for instance, a comment from *The New York Herald*, using information clearly fed by Russell himself:

> Mr. Russell's concert on Wednesday evening, was attended by an extremely crowded audience. Mr. Russell has in fact become quite the rage, and all the fashionable people flock in crowds to his concerts. This is one of the most remarkable phenomena of the times. The musicians and other vocalists are in paroxysms of rage. They call Mr. Russell a humbug—a confounded, atrocious, rascally, unprincipled, ignorant, humbug. But all the intelligence, taste, beauty and fashion of New York go in throngs to hear the humbug, and applaud to the skies the exquisite melody, the thrilling pathos, the flashes of sentiment which characterise all Russell's little dramas, as his songs may with perfect propriety be called. Mr. Russell gave a concert last night at the Musical Fund Hall, in Philadelphia, and to-night he sings that thrilling song, "The Dream of the Revellers," [sic] at the great temperance celebration in the Tabernacle. This is astonishing expedition. In this way, Mr. Russell intends to traverse the length and breadth of the Union. He is now clearing money at the rate of $1200 or $1500 a week. In August he returns to England, and will reap another golden harvest there.

Russell was, indeed, fitting in engagements in Philadelphia between those in Brooklyn and New York City. His was a hectic schedule! Having appeared in Philadelphia on Thursday, 13 April, a second concert announced there for Saturday, 15 April, was delayed to the following Monday because of the postponement of the temperance celebration at the New York Tabernacle until the Saturday. The program of this New York event indicates its nature:

> 1—Divine Invocation, by Rev Dr De Witt.
>
> 2—Oration by Professor Greenbank, of England.
>
> 3—Sacred Melody—"The Pilgrim's Address to the Deity"—Written by Henry John Sharpe, of New York, and sung by Mr. Henry Russell.
>
> 4—"The Genius of Universal Temperance"—a National Anthem, written by Henry John Sharpe, of New York. The Music by Henry Russell.
>
> Respectfully dedicated by the Author and Composer to the American Temperance Union.
>
> 5—SCENE—The Dream of the Reveller; or the Three Houses. Sung by Mr. Russell at the Great Temperance Meeting, held in the long room at Exeter Hall, London, in the presence of over 3000 persons. Words by Charles Mackay, Esq. Sung by Mr. Russell.
>
> 6—Recitation—The Rum Maniac. By Prof Greenbank.
>
> 7—SCENA—The Gambler's Wife; Words by Dr Coats [sic] Sung by Mr. Russell.
>
> 8—CANTATA—"The Maniac." By Mr. Russell.
>
> 9—Cantata—"The Drunkard." By Mr. Russell.

Russell never shrank from tying his colors to some mast or other, and the current mast was, clearly, the temperance movement.

As for the *New York Herald* reference to Russell returning to the UK in August, he may well have been scheduled to do so. However, he was hardly likely to give up his US success too readily, even if a final concert at Niblo's on Tuesday, 18 April 1843, was followed by a less successful one at the Lyceum, Brooklyn, the following evening. "Russell's 'vocal entertainment,'" reported *The Brooklyn Eagle*, "was thinly, but fashionably attended last evening—probable cause, the bad weather."

No such problem attended his first concert in Boston on 22 April, at which he introduced to the city "The Newfoundland Dog," "The Dream of the Reveller," "The Ship on Fire," "The Indian Hunter," and "Robin Ruff." "Mr. Russell's concert at the Melodeon on Saturday evening was attended by at least fourteen hundred people," reported *The Boston Post*. "Many were obliged to leave on account of the great crowd. He was very cordially received, and sung with his usual success." As preface to the concert, *The Boston Post* had published the words of Russell's composition "The Pilgrim's Address to the Deity"—a "sacred song" with words by Henry John Sharpe, described as "first introduced by the gifted composer at the grand musical festival in Birmingham with great *éclat*." Quite how he could have done so is, to say the least, "unclear." The Birmingham Festival was a triennial event that had been held in 1840 but not in 1842 when Russell was in England. He had, moreover, already sung the number in New York in April 1841. Henry Russell would, in any case, have been an unlikely participant at the willfully "classical" Festival.

Besides concerts at the Lyceum Hall in Dorchester on Friday, 28 April, and in Roxbury on Thursday, 4 May, Russell gave further concerts at the Melodeon on Tuesday, 25 April (when his program included "The Drunkard" and "The Hero and the Philosopher") and Saturday, 29 April. For all its association with tea, though, Boston seems to have been less than firmly on the temperance bandwagon. Thus, at this Saturday concert, the National Anthem "The Genius of Temperance," which Russell had announced for Niblo's on 12 April and repeated at the Temperance Soirée on 15 April, now became a new National Anthem, pure and simple, of the Movement. Henry John Sharpe's original lines ran:

> In the strength of your might, from each mountain and valley,
> Friends of Temperance, arise! The time is at hand—

In the new National Anthem sung in Boston on 29 April they became:

> In the strength of your might, from each mountain and valley,
> Sons of freedom arise! The time is at hand—

In neither form does the anthem seem to have achieved publication.

On 1 May *The Boston Post* further demonstrated Russell's local popularity by publishing a gentle parody of his songs and concert programs, submitted by one of its readers, in the form of the "Programme of Mr. Snuffle's concert, to be given at the Popodeon on the 15th ultimo." The first half began with a song "Some Love to Meet," continued with a ballad "Old Back Bay," then "The Bull Frog" ("illustrated with a few remarks connected with the incident upon which the song is founded." The first half of the concert concluded with:

> Cantata—"The Maniac."
>
> Some years ago a gentleman of fortune was induced by the solicitation of his friends to enter a fashionable hotel, and imbibe the spirituous compound. The more the unfortunate gentleman poured down, the more he desired, until the landlord was finally obliged to refuse his application for drink, lest he might become what is vulgarly called intoxicated, by the too frequent use of the same. This occurrence gave rise to the accompanying stanzas.
>
> Stay, landlord, stay, and give, I pray,
> Another glass of punch to me,
> For oh, although I am not corned,
> Full well I know I soon shall be.
> He quits the bar—he locks the door—
> Ah! would this day had never dawned—
> I cannot get another glass,
> *Although not corned, although not corned.*

The second part of the parody concert program began with a song "The Old India Rubber Shoe," "sung in Jamaica in the presence of over three thousand black slaves" (shades of claims for his London temperance rally!), and continued with a song "The Dandelion Green" (a parody of "The Ivy Green"), words by Quarles Quickens, Esq.

By May, Russell was reported to be drawing crowded houses at Hartford, Connecticut. Then, on 17 May, he gave a concert at his old stomping ground, the Female Academy in Albany, before traveling briefly back to New York. On Monday, 22 May 1843, he gave a single concert at the Apollo Concert Saloon, Broadway, at which he introduced a new song, "Land, Ho!," with words by George P. Morris. The song's published edition carries a dedication from Russell to his friend Captain C. H. E. Judkins—formerly of the Columbia and now of the Hibernia. A 120-passenger Cunard vessel, the Hibernia had sailed on its maiden voyage from Liverpool to Boston via Halifax, Nova Scotia, on 19 April 1843. The Columbia itself, on which Russell had so recently crossed the Atlantic, was destined to be wrecked on 2 July 1843, shortly after leaving Halifax for Boston—fortunately, with no loss of life. And, strange to say, Russell not aboard.

The press announcement of the New York concert on 22 May declared that Russell was on his way to the South, and that it was "his only opportunity in this city, until immediately preceding his departure for England in the fall." In fact, in June, Russell was in the northeast, the press reporting a vocal entertainment on the evening of Saturday, 24 June 1843, "in a new Hall under the Universalist Church in Saco, Maine. The people were so delighted with Mr. Russell's singing that they immediately resolved to pay him a compliment by naming the room 'Russell Hall.'" At the beginning of July, he was in Nantucket, and when a disastrous fire destroyed the village of Fall River, Massachusetts, on 2 July he offered his services for a concert at nearby New Bedford to aid the sufferers. This was something that he would do again, and again, in his life, to such an extent that he became a target for the grasping "Charitable."

Russell's journey then took him to further concerts at Cabotsville (now Chicopee) and Albany, where other performers in the city at the same time included the legendary Tom Thumb. Later in the month he was at Saratoga, where he gave a final concert on 25 July prior to traveling east. By August, he and Tom Thumb were being greeted warmly in Rochester, where Russell appeared twice in the Concert Hall of the Eagle Tavern. Of the first occasion, for which every seat was occupied, the *Rochester Daily Democrat* reported that "he never sung better," that "many are of the opinion that he has improved, in voice and execution, during his long absence," and that "he sings . . . , probably, as well as any one, during the present century, *will* sing."

Russell now seems to have been darting all over the country. There was evidently a concert in Pittsburgh "early in 1843" when the sixteen-year-old Stephen Foster and his brother Morrison were in the audience. Foster's niece wrote that "His concert must have made a deep impression on Stephen . . . and the fact that Russell was the composer of the songs he sang seems to have inspired Stephen to try great things himself." According to Foster's biographer William W. Austin, what impressed Foster "was not the dialect songs so much as the sentimental ones and the balance of the whole program with its effective variety." He adds that "When Foster began, about five years later, to think of himself as a songwriter, his hope was to supply songs for Russell and his imitators, English and American." Austin is wrong, however, in suggesting that Foster's setting of Charles Mackay's "Good Time Coming" showed indebtedness to hearing Russell sing it in 1843. Russell's setting, like Foster's, dates from 1846.

Even in his absence from the eastern seaboard, Russell's songs were still very much in evidence there, as *The Brooklyn Eagle* indicated when extolling the extent to which music was being cultivated among the public at large and not least in schools:

> Wherever you go you will hear the best of Russell's airs chaunted by striplings, and often with a degree of accuracy, and finish of execution, that would be creditable to adult masters. We have frequently encountered groups of children, which, instead of driving hoops and sliding down cellar cases, (to the imminent peril of their nether garments) had voluntarily resolved themselves into singing parties, and were giving the "Mountain Ho!" and "Brave Old Oak," with all the enthusiasm—if not the excellence—of their author.

In August 1843, Russell was amusing the citizens of Buffalo, with General Tom Thumb again in the city at the same time. By the end of August, the supportive *New York Herald* reported that he was resting at the Bath House, Rockaway. (Was this the home of his friend Henry John Sharpe?) Altogether, the *Herald* could report "a very successful summer tour through the northern and eastern States." At a time when the US was still recovering from recession, and many artistic enterprises were foundering, Henry Russell was one performer the public unashamedly considered worth patronage.

Now, in September, came the previously foreshadowed return visit to New York, and with it came the news that Russell had canceled his planned return to England: "in fact, he is announced to sing at the Birmingham Musical Festival; but the very flattering inducements made to him to visit New Orleans during the winter months, will delay his departure for Europe until early in the ensuing spring." He wooed New York afresh with concerts at the Apollo Saloon on 7, 11, 14, 19 and 21 September 1843, and with new songs that included "The Rising Sun" to words by Henry John Sharpe and "Life in the West" with words by George P. Morris.

In the announcement of the concert of 7 September it is striking that, instead of the locally supplied piano used previously, he now introduced "the newly invented Fonda Horizontal Piano, containing the Iterant Itochronal action, manufactured by Joseph Kirkman and Son, of London, and used by Mr. Russell with much success at his concerts at the Hanover Square Rooms." He was certainly doing his bit for the Kirkman piano! No less significant at the concert on 14 September was "his attempt to give the tent scene from Shakespeare's play of *Richard the Third*, through the medium of song." He declared:

> It is my object to unite, with the pleasing science of music, a taste for the productions of those ancient and illustrious authors, whose works have formed a partial standard of the English language. It is my desire to rivet the attention of the mind, as well as to attract the ear, particularly of the junior portion of my audience—and if I succeed in my intention, and meet with the approbation of the public, the full measure of my ambition will be fulfilled, in offering to their notice "an Intellectual Vocal Entertainment."

The idea served to draw the public, and Russell developed it on 19 September by adding to the program Cato's Soliloquy on the Immortality of the Soul, by John Addison. The *Herald*, naturally, approved:

> The Concert of this gentleman last night was, we believe, the best attended of the series, for great numbers were unable to get within the doors of the Apollo room, capacious as it is. The idea of adapting dramatic pieces to music was a novel one, and it has become exceedingly popular. Indeed, it proves to be the most impressive mode of giving those fine passages of which Mr. Russell has made choice, and never, we venture to say, were they given with such thrilling effect. Hamlet's soliloquy—"To be or not to be," and some beautiful extracts from Milton, will soon be given in the same way, if we are rightly informed, at the Society Library.

Russell introduced Hamlet's Soliloquy at the Apollo Saloon on 21 September. Then, while William Vincent Wallace moved in to the Apollo as pianist on Monday, 25 September, Russell began a week-long series of concerts at the Library Concert Room. According to his faithful *Herald* mouthpiece, his attempt was "to render the production of Shak[e]speare, Milton, Byron, Wolfe, and others of the old masters." He announced "The Tent Scene" from *Richard III* for Monday, Cardinal Wolsey's Farewell Address to Cromwell (Shakespeare) for Tuesday, Marc Antony's Oration over the Body of Caesar for Wednesday, Rev. Chas Wolfe's Monody on the Death of Sir John Wolfe for Thursday, both the Wolfe and *Richard III* pieces for Friday, and the Cardinal Wolsey Farewell for Saturday. There is no better indication of Russell's phenomenal success in America in 1843 than that, after five solo concerts at the Apollo, he could do these six further nightly performances at the Library. Interestingly, among the songs Russell announced during the week was "The Orphan Ballad Singers," with words by Letitia Elizabeth Landon, which had originally been published in London in 1834.

There were further, final concerts the following week: at Rutger's Institute on 3 October, at the Brooklyn Lyceum on 5 October, and at the Stuyvesant Institute on 6 October. *The Brooklyn Eagle* reported that the Brooklyn Lyceum concert was well attended, but that it produced an objection from at least one attendee to "the unwarrantable intrusion of a parcel of urchins—better calculated to figure in a menagerie or a puppet-show than in such a place. . . . Mr. Russell extended an invitation to the children, who were attending the Tea Party in the rooms below, to hear him sing; and that it was very generally accepted both by young and old."

The following week Russell was in Philadelphia, at the Musical Fund Hall on Thursday, 12 October, with the Tent Scene from *Richard III* on the program, then, continuing south, he made concert appearances in Washington and, in November, in Richmond and Norfolk, Virginia. By the beginning of December, he was in Charleston, and on 14 December 1843 in Savannah. At the latter—according to the *Herald*, which so faithfully logged his movements—"his powerful voice, his original style of song, and his winning manner, aided alone by one of Chickering's pianos, were drawing crowded houses." Over the Christmas period, he gave concerts in Macon, Georgia, after which he was reported in Columbus, Georgia, "and making money very fast."

Russell's subsequent advance on New Orleans was equally eagerly monitored by that city's leading mouthpiece, *The Daily Picayune*. The paper reported his appearance in Mobile, Alabama, on 3 January, when, "in spite of counter operatic attraction[s] at the Corinthian, his hall at the Waverley was numerously attended." New Orleans was clearly a magnet for performers at the time; the actors Henry Placide and James Wallack were already in the city, as well as the opera troupe of Edward and Ann Seguin, and two violin virtuosi of world renown were on their way.

On 5 January 1844, the *Picayune* reported that Russell had arrived from Mobile on his first visit to New Orleans. It devoted over three column inches to a description of the Washington Battalion Armory, where, with banners and weapons of the Battalion companies arranged around the walls, he was due to give his concerts. Alas, the visit of Russell and his fellow artists to New Orleans coincided with disastrous weather, to the extent that, on 12 January, the *Picayune* felt moved "to make an apology to our friends and others, whose 'first appearance' in New Orleans has been within the last ten days." It craved indulgence "until the sun *does* shine, and the streets *do* dry, to show what New Orleans *is* when she has a 'fair shake.'"

For New Orleans, Russell put aside the Shakespeare and other settings recently introduced to New York in favor of his most popular songs. Of his first two concerts, on Monday, 8 January, and Wednesday, 10 January, the *Picayune* reported that "Russell has been received by large audiences with every mark of favor, and even this most abominable weather, that has been prevailing ever since his arrival, has not prevented the people from flocking in crowds to hear him. A large number of ladies graced the Armory on Monday evening, and the singer is evidently established in New Orleans already as a fashionable favorite."

Alas, bad weather caused the cancellation of the concert on Thursday, and Russell announced his performance on Saturday, 13 January, as his last. It also featured a change of piano. For his previous concerts Russell had used a Meyers piano, as "preferred by [Vincent] Wallace, [Jeanne] Castellan, and many of the popular musicians of the day," and obtainable at the music store of Charles Horst in St. Charles Street. For the Saturday concert, he was induced to replace it with one "from the manufactory of Lemuel Gilbert, of Boston, and furnished by the agent here, S Allen, 49 Royal street."

The change in instrument seemed also to bring a change in the weather. "After a week or more suffering from the rain, we awoke yesterday morning to find the weather clear, cool and agreeable," reported the *Picayune*. Russell in turn was moved to announce that "in consequence of the late inclemency of the weather, and the utter impossibility of families being able to attend his late concerts, [he] purposes giving, at their suggestion, one more Concert, on Monday evening next, January 15th."

Alas the rain returned, the concert was canceled, and Russell temporarily gave up the uneven struggle, promising to return to New Orleans after concerts already arranged for Mobile. So, indeed, he did, appearing further in New Orleans on Thursday, 25 January, and Monday, 29 January.

By the time of his return visit, not only was the Seguin opera troupe in New Orleans, but so were both virtuoso violinists. Henri Vieuxtemps had been in Charleston at the same time as Russell but had reached New Orleans later. His first concert there was announced for Monday, 15 January—evidently, like Russell's, postponed because of the weather—and his last on Saturday, 26 January. Bull's visit was more fleeting, for he was not due to perform until Wednesday, 17 January, gave his last on Tuesday, 23 January, and by 29 January was performing in Mobile en route to Havana.

These dates of Bull's concerts are important in relation to the reliability, or otherwise, of another story in Russell's memoirs:

> Still pursuing my travels, without much in the way of incident, I proceeded to St Louis, and then by boat down the Mississippi to New Orleans—a magnificent city even in those days. My entertainment, given at the Armoury Hall, seemed to afford great pleasure to a large audience. I found I was not the only travelling entertainer then in New Orleans. Ole Bull, the Norwegian violinist, was there, giving a series of violin recitals. I went to one, taking with me a friend, a cotton planter, whose ideas about music were, to say the least, crude. I had promised him a great treat, and when Ole Bull advanced to the front of the stage, I could see that my friend was all anticipation to see what he irreverently called "the fiddler." Ole Bull played the "Carnival of Venice," with variations. Readers will please imagine one of those pieces in which so many variations are introduced that the original melody is almost entirely lost in fireworks and pyrotechnics of instrumental art.
>
> The poor man—Ole Bull, I mean—was working hard and perspiring freely. When he was nearly through, I turned to my friend and said, with great gusto, "There, isn't he wonderful?" "Waal, he may be all that, but he's a d—long time tuning. Tell me, when is he going to play?" I did not think it advisable to wait for any more tuning. . . .
>
> During the following week I paid a professional visit to Ole Bull, and, I am pleased to say, I had a charming interview

with the great and amiable violinist. He was seated at a table, strewn with music on every side. On my entering the room, he immediately rose, shook me warmly by the hand, and cordially expressed himself in kindly terms, evidently gratified by my visit.

"I have heard a great deal of you, Mr. Russell—I am glad to see you; pray sit down. You have been some considerable time in this country; how do you like it?"

"Very much," I replied, "but I fear the reception accorded to you has not been worthy of your great talent."

"I regret to say that is so," he replied. "I have encountered, since I have been here, nothing but jealousy and rivalry, with but little sympathy from those I most expected it from."

"You must not lose sight of the fact," I responded, "that, until the beginning of this century, musical culture was a thing practically unknown outside such towns as New York, Philadelphia, and Boston. It is only now beginning to take an interest in things musical, therefore do not be downhearted. I need hardly say that those people who know anything whatever of music are charmed with your exquisite playing. Tell me, sir," I continued, "how do you like New Orleans?"

"Not a great deal. The people here prefer the nigger's violin to mine. I have travelled from New York to play to people who do not understand me."

"Yes," I exclaimed, "the generality of the nation are young in scientific music; their idea of fine music consists of simple song. My dear Mr. Bull, you must have patience."

"Sir," he exclaimed, "you are very kind, but I have tried. I commenced to establish a small conservatoire, as a part of the Musical Academy of New York—but it failed. I then offered a prize of one thousand dollars for the best original grand opera by an American composer, and that failed. What more could I do? I know what I *shall* do—leave this country as soon as I can, and return to Europe, where I am appreciated."

I got up from my chair, thanked Ole Bull for his reception, shook him warmly by the hand, and left the great master. It was a deplorable fact that all Ole Bull had said was true. Music, both vocal and instrumental, was in a very crude state. Public concerts and oratorios scarcely paid their expenses. The cultivation of music for the masses was looked upon, with the

> exception of sacred music, with distrust and prejudice. The minds of the majority of the people were unable to appreciate the value of music, which was so able to elevate and improve the affections of a whole nation.

Perhaps Russell did attend Bull's final concert on 23 January; but, once more, a meeting that evidently meant much to Russell appears to have been—alas!—unrecorded by biographers of the other party. Certainly, as we have seen, Russell did not journey to New Orleans down the Mississippi. It was, in fact, on his return journey from New Orleans that he voyaged on the river, traveling northward and giving concerts as he went. During March he was at Nashville, and by the end of that month he was singing to full houses in St. Louis. His final concert there, on 3 April, coincided with the arrival of the actor William Charles Macready, later the object of the Astor Place riots. By 11 April, Russell was giving the first of several concerts in Louisville, Kentucky, "drawing crowded houses," according to *The New York Herald*. In early May he was performing at Chillicothe and elsewhere in Ohio, and by the end of May and early June he was at Cincinnati, where the papers reported that he was soon to leave for Europe. On 17 June he was in Pittsburgh, and on 3 July he was in Columbus, Ohio, on his way back to New York City.

Russell finally reached New York City on 14 July, whereupon the *Herald* summarized the success of his grand tour of the previous few months: "He has been absent from this city nine months, and has given upwards of two hundred concerts, and averaged from sixty to six hundred dollars, according to the place where they were given. Allowing the very moderate profit of fifty dollars on each concert, Mr. Russell has made nearly $10,000 during the last nine months. And well he deserves a fortune. Success attend him!" The *Herald* also reported that Russell "leaves this country on the 17th in the Great Western, to fill an engagement at the Birmingham musical festival. He returns again in the fall, we understand, and will spend three or four months in this country." The alleged Birmingham engagement is, again, wholly questionable, and certainly Russell was not to sail in the Great Western, but on the Montezuma, which left for Liverpool on 17 July 1844.

Potentially more reliable was the following report: "He will give a few concerts in Liverpool and London, and after spending a month or two of the hot season with his family, who are now at Boulogne, a beautiful place on the coast of France, he will return to the United States by the Great

Western in October." This press mention of Boulogne-sur Mer may well be the very first to indicate Russell's association with the resort. Following the opening, in 1843, of the South-Eastern Railway line from London to Folkestone, connecting with the steamboat service to Boulogne, it was to become an increasingly popular retreat for the more affluent British. Russell was to spend a large part of his life there over the next forty years.

As for his family, whom he had evidently not seen during his many months on tour, it had increased further, during his journey up the Mississippi, by the birth of a third son (and fourth child) at the Carlton House Hotel, New York City, on 24 February 1844. The boy was christened William Clark Russell, maybe taking his first names from the American explorer William Clark (1770–1838), who with Meriwether Lewis (1774–1809) had conducted the Lewis-Clark expedition across to the Pacific coast of America in 1804–5, following the Louisiana Purchase.

12

British Concert Touring

Following Russell's return from his second stay in America, London heard him first in concert at the Hanover Square Rooms on the evening of 5 September 1844. *The Times* reported that, "Notwithstanding the lateness of the season, and the consequent emptiness of the town, a very large audience was assembled." As before, "Messrs Kirkman and Son's newly-invented Fonda Pianoforte" was prominently promoted, and *The Musical World* declared it "one of the most beautiful and generally effective instruments we have heard for a long time." As for Russell, the journal reported that "Four songs were encored, and everything he did was loudly applauded." The program mixed old favorites with others that were new to London, notably "The Main Truck, or a Leap for Life." This was a nautical ballad with words by George P. Morris, coming with the promise (typical of Russell's entertainments) that "the incident upon which this song is founded will be hereafter presented to the public."

A second concert followed at the Hanover Square Rooms on 17 September. "Mr. Russell's [. . .] 'Nigger' songs were honoured with the loudest demonstrations of approval," reported *The Musical World*. "His imitations of the Niggers were highly humorous, and his anecdotes quaint and amusing." The program listed two titles designed to satisfy British curiosity about the American Negro: "The Boatman of the Ohio" and "The South Carolina Plantation Song of the Negro." These were evidently both arrangements of Negro melodies, though their published editions give little indication of the fact. Addison and Hodson's edition of the first gives every indication of it being original, with the words attributed to Charles Mackay, and the music described as "Composed by Henry Russell." "The

South Carolina Plantation Song" (otherwise "The Tenasee [sic] Plantation Song") carries on its front cover the statement "The Music and Words Composed and Arranged by Henry Russell."

During the last week of September 1844, Russell and the Kirkman Fonda piano again shared top billing in an unlikely venue. For a concert in Boulogne-sur-Mer, the manufacturer had diligently shipped the instrument across the Channel. Russell's next London concert followed at the Hanover Square Rooms on 3 October. "He sang," reported *The Musical World*, "in addition to his most popular compositions, a capital extravaganza called 'The Spider and the Fly,' and a new song (with some admirable verses by Charles Mackay, Esq.), called 'Tubal-Cain,' the former with much humour, the latter with considerable energy." The latter song was about the son of Lamech and Zillah, the "forger of every cutting instrument of iron and brass" of the Book of Genesis, and *The Musical World* clearly took to it in a big way. It published Mackay's verses one week and reviewed the Charles Jefferys publication of the song the next.

In his memoirs, Russell recalls beginning his British career with a tour with other artists. It was actually during the autumn of 1844 that this took place: "I had been in England but a few weeks, when I received the offer of an engagement from Beal[e], the impresario. It was for a tour of six months. Among the members of the company were the great artists Piatti, Lablache (*fils*), and Dohler. The terms offered me were not munificent, but they were sufficiently satisfactory for me to close with the offer." Mancunian [Thomas] Frederick Beale [sic] (1804–63) has already been mentioned as a partner in the Regent Street music firm of Cramer, Addison and Beale, a London publisher of Russell's songs, in 1842. Later, Beale would be one of the founders of the London's St. James's Hall concerts. We have seen that Russell was on sufficiently intimate terms with him to dedicate to Mrs. Frederick Beale the published edition of "The Poor Man's Friend." Of the artists mentioned for the 1844 British tour, Alfredo Piatti (1822–1901) was a celebrated cellist, Lablache *fils*, the operatic baritone Frederic Lablache (c. 1815–87), son of the famous Luigi Lablache (1794–1858), and "Dohler" was the pianist Theodor von Döhler (1814–56).

Along with those artists were Russell's former "pupil," soprano Mary Steele (by now professor of singing at the Royal Academy of Music), violinist Camillo Sivori (1815–94), and Frederic Lablache's contralto wife, the former Fanny Wyndham (c. 1821–77). Before Russell joined the party, they had played such places as Tunbridge Wells, Dover, Brighton, Worthing,

Figure 12.1. “The Spider and the Fly” sheet music cover. *Source:* Author’s collection.

Chichester, Southampton, and Blackheath, as well as going further afield to Bristol, Exeter, and Bath. With Russell added, the group represented a rare combination of talent, as boasted in the advertisement for their appearance in Birmingham on 21 October 1844:

> UNPRECEDENTED
> COMBINATION OF TALENT
>
> — ————————————————————
>
> A GRAND EVENING CONCERT of VOCAL and INSTRUMENTAL MUSIC will be given at the *TOWN HALL, BIRMINGHAM,* On MONDAY, October 21, 1844, To commence at Eight o'clock precisely, when the following celebrated Artistes will appear:-
>
> VOCALISTS.
> MISS STEELE,
> MADAME F. LABLACHE,
> SIGNOR F. LABLACHE,
> AND THE CELEBRATED
> MR. H. RUSSELL.
> INSTRUMENTAL PERFORMERS.
> GRAND PIANO-FORTE,
> The Celebrated M. DOHLER.
> VIOLIN,
> SIGNOR CAMILLO SIVORI.
> VIOLONCELLO,
> SIGNOR PIATTI.
> The BAND will comprise the most Eminent Performers
>
> LEADER—MR. WILLY, (Of the Philharmonic and Ancient Concerts).
>
> PRINCIPAL SECOND VIOLIN—Mr. H. SHARGOOL.
>
> — ————————————————————
>
> Reserved Seats—Side Gallery, 4s. Entrance in Paradise-street, the Plan of which can be seen at Mr. TOLKIEN's Music Warehouse, New-street; or at Mr. HARRISON's, Colmore-row.
>
> Great Gallery Ticket, 2s.6d.
>
> Floor Ticket, 2s. The whole of this portion of the Hall will on this occasion be thrown open.
>
> To be had at all the Music Shops and Booksellers.
>
> Doors open at Seven o'clock.

Perhaps there was too much talent. It certainly proved so for the correspondent of *The Birmingham Advertiser*. He reported that the concert "was very respectably but not numerously attended; and the performances generally speaking went off rather flatly." He considered that "the instrumental was very superior to the vocal part of the entertainments," and that Russell "did not appear to give so much satisfaction as when he was here before." He then went on wearily to make his grievance clear: "The very great length of the performance was the cause, (and not unjustly), of general complaint; it being past twelve before it was concluded, long before which time, we saw many bright eyes, which (notwithstanding the harmony of sweet sounds) were fast closing from downright weariness, in consequence of the protracted length of the entertainment." Past midnight! Over four hours!

The party moved on to Derby (22 October) and Leeds (23 October). With flautist Richard Carte further added to the roster, they visited Newcastle-upon-Tyne (25 October), Carlisle (afternoon and evening concerts on 26 October) and Lancaster and Preston (afternoon and evening of 28 October). Carte then dropped out, before a further crowded concert in Manchester on Tuesday, 29 October, on which *The Manchester Guardian* reported:

> Mr. H Russell, an American basso, gave a cantata, descriptive of the sufferings of the sane prisoner of a lunatic asylum, driven mad, and which was full of a peculiar wild beauty and power, not easily described. He also sang a rover's song, "I'm afloat" (also composed by himself), with much spirit and vigour; and, on being encored, gave instead, a song (also his own, we imagine), "Our native sun," one strain of which, in slow time, has for a running accompaniment on the piano, the national air of "Yankee Doodle." It was well sung and much applauded.

"Our Native Sun" was, of course, "Our Native Song," Russell's announcement presumably misheard. Russell's insistence on departing from the songs in the book of words on sale at the door did not meet with the *Guardian* critic's approval. At least the running time had been cut sufficiently for the concert to end a few minutes before ten o'clock.

Following concerts at the Theatre Royal, Williamson Square, Liverpool, on 31 October and 1 November, the party crossed the sea to Ireland. A concert for Dublin's Anacreontic Society at the Music Hall in Lower Abbey Street on 4 November was followed by two the following day: at the Rotundo at 2:00 p.m. and the Theatre Royal in the evening. The review of the latter in *The Freeman's Journal* provides clear evidence that Russell was beginning to achieve in the United Kingdom a following similar to that in the United States. After referring to "Mr. H Russell, an American singer of the first order, who has gained all at once for himself a rage of popularity," the review continued:

> We have said that Mr. Russell has become an extraordinary favourite, and no wonder that he should. It is not alone his fine, sweet, full and manly voice, and the masterly character of his accompaniment, that captivate the audience, but his manner, full of soul and genuine humour, does still more to win the hearts of those who hear him. His name appeared on the bills last night for only two songs, yet strange enough he sung at least nine or ten of them, comic and pathetic; for at the end of each the *encore* was so overwhelming that it must needs be obeyed, and each time he sang, with admirable taste, a new piece, each, as the old story says, "finer than all that went before it," or at least so thought the audience, for the *encores* were becoming more boisterous as he advanced. He introduces the peculiarity, too, of prefacing his song with a good anecdote, and related some *nigger* stories with capital effect.

Russell's imaginative story that Tyrone Power had suggested the content of "The Ship on Fire," a few hours before embarking on his fatal last voyage from New York in *The President,* was received with particularly heartfelt applause. It was, of course, a surefire way of appealing to the hearts and minds of an Irish audience, still moved by the tragic loss of their celebrated fellow countryman. Altogether, the reception in Dublin seems to have been as overwhelming as that to which Henry Russell had become so familiar on the western side of the Atlantic.

The group now crossed over to Scotland. If Russell's welcome in Edinburgh in February 1843 had been restrained, it may have been no warmer now, judging by the *Edinburgh Evening Courant*'s comment that "The vocal performances were . . . extremely pleasing; but the instrumental music was the great attraction." Again, Glasgow seems to have been the more receptive—to the extent that Russell additionally gave a couple of solo concerts. Indeed, his time as a member of the concert party seems to have ended here and to have actually lasted no more than three weeks, rather than the six months suggested in his memoirs.

Further solo appearances in Leeds, on 20 and 22 November, revealed that Russell had still to learn how to persuade Yorkshire folk to part with their hard-earned cash. Tenor John Templeton (1802–86) was a rival attraction, offering gallery seats at 6d while Russell charged 1s. There was no doubt where the Yorkshireman's preferences lay. *The Musical World* reported that Russell's first engagement "was unsatisfactory, on account of Templeton's visit on the following evening, with an unusual attraction for Leeds, viz a sixpenny gallery. By adopting the same system, in self defence, Henry Russell was rewarded with a bumper for his farewell night."

Altogether, one senses that Russell had a lot to learn about the nature of audiences in different cities. In Newcastle-upon-Tyne, on 28 November, it was again his departures from the program that upset a local critic: "The liberty which he took with the programme, however, in omitting some of his best songs, including the beautiful descriptive one, of 'Woodman, spare that tree' which constituted, we do not hesitate to say, its chief attraction, was any thing but satisfactory, and the more so, as no explanation or apology was offered. When a programme is published, the public are naturally led to expect it will be completed, and pay their money accordingly." Yet there can be no doubting the overall progress that Russell made on this tour in establishing his popularity in Britain. His arrival back in London in December 1844 was noticed by *The Musical World* thus: "MR. HENRY RUSSELL has returned to town crammed with laurels, and his pockets crammed full of bank notes, the result of an almost unprecedentedly brilliant tour in Ireland, Scotland, and the North of England. Mr. Russell has made up his mind to remain at home—finding, no doubt, that his own countrymen can appreciate his peculiar talent even as warmly as the Yankees."

Family considerations doubtless reinforced Russell's decision not to make a further return to America, where, after all, the success of his 1843–44 tour can hardly have left him feeling played out. The autumn 1844 tour had also made up his mind to concentrate on solo engagements: "The tour proved a success, and to it I ascribe the commencement of my good fortune in my native land. On the termination of the tour I was offered an engagement on better terms, but I declined it, as, after all, I preferred independence. . . ."

For his next solo appearances in London, he sought to develop his entertainment by incorporating the passages by Shakespeare and others that had already featured on his American programs: "It is Mr. Russell's intention to introduce the novel experiment of endeavouring to convey through the medium of song a few passages from the brilliant conceptions of Shakespeare. The first selection will be the Tenth [*recte* Tent!] Scene from *Richard the Third*." That first of his concerts at the Hanover Square Rooms on 20 January 1845 was followed on 6 February by a second, at which he included Cato's Soliloquy on the Immortality of the Soul. Further Negro songs—notably "Going over the Mountains"—were also on the programs.

Meanwhile, concert agent and publisher Frederick C. Leader engaged Russell to give concerts at eight of the Literary and Scientific Institutions dotted in and around London, taking him to Greenwich on 29 January and Croydon on 31 January. Much of his subsequent career would be spent performing at places such as the London Mechanics' Institution in Chancery Lane, the Marylebone Literary and Scientific Institution in Portman Square, and the Western Scientific and Literary Institution in Leicester Square. Such were the meeting places in which more intellectual people congregated, in days long before radio or television.

On 3 February 1845, Russell was also among a host of artists at the eighth annual concert of Bond Street concert agent and "monster concerts" promotor, [F.] William Allcroft (1811–58) at Covent Garden Theatre, singing "The Ship on Fire" and "The Maniac." Other performers on that occasion included Charles and Hamilton Braham (sons of John Braham), W. H. Seguin (1814–50; younger brother of Edward), Lablache *fils*, Mary Steele, and the Distins with their silver Sax horns. There were further occasions, too, when Russell shared the bill with other performers, as on a return to the Institution, Greenwich, on 17 February, when the pianist Brinley Richards (1819–65) likewise performed "upon Mr. Kirkman's fonda pianoforte." However, by contrast with previous appearances on a concert bill dominated by others, he was now without question a prime single attraction.

Indeed, another demonstration of his surging popularity is presented by his involvement with the Jews' and General Literary and Scientific Institution at the newly built Sussex Hall (named for the late Duke of Sussex) at 52 Leadenhall Street. The Institute's opening ceremony took place on Monday, 20 January 1845. After a few lectures in the opening days, the first miscellaneous concert was given on Monday, 27 January in aid of the

Institution's Library. *The Jewish Chronicle* acknowledged that Russell "was the great feature of the evening," and that "his last song, which gained a double encore, was concluded amidst a torrent of applause." The Institution readily recognized in Russell the most immediate route to raising funds for its library. A solo concert was announced for Saturday, 8 February, and one with other performers on Monday, 17 March.

The *Jewish Chronicle* report on the first of these provided instructive comments on Russell's songs and singing:

> To touch the heart is his aim, and he succeeds, even though in these appeals he exhibits a dearth of invention, having but one burthen to nearly all his songs—one subject standing in the foreground of all his pictures, namely, a child placed in a position of imminent danger; but Mr. Russell is also superior to his composers immeasurably in another respect—in feeling. Not a word he utters but seems to fall from the heart—not a letter that is not distinctly articulated, whether in fear or joy, doubt or despair. Who can hear "The Gambler's Wife" thus sung without feeling, during the tolling of the fleeting hours, their own sympathies aroused for the deserted and dying parent and her offspring? or mark the progress of the "Ship on Fire" without anxiety as to the result? It is to the possession of these simple means of causing the heart to leap or fall at will that he owes his good fortune. He never makes an attempt to astonish the public by mere feats of execution, or sacrifices his song for the sake of a roulade, or sings English as if it were some unknown or unintelligible tongue. The profession are startled at the result of his performances, and at their own limited success when they are thrown in competition with him, but they have their remedy. Let them study his style, and wonder not . . .

Russell was now in ready demand wherever he could go in the British Isles. Nowhere does he seem to have been more so than in Ireland, and he made the journey between London and Dublin via Liverpool with some frequency. March 1845 saw him once more crossing the Irish Sea to perform at Dublin's Music Hall, enterprisingly run by Robert J. Mackintosh, who was also co-leader of the Dublin Philharmonic Society's concerts. This time Russell shared the bill with guitarist and concertina player Giulio

Regondi (c. 1822–72), together with two Sapio pupils: Amelia, the sister of William Balfe, and a Miss Morgan. On 18 March, he supported a troupe of "Ioway Indians" in "war dances, their picturesque feats of archery," etc., under the management of his "old friend" Catlin!

Leaving others to purvey his songs to the Dubliners, he returned to London, and the Hanover Square Rooms, in April 1845 for a series of three concerts, whose adverts readily demonstrate the raised profile he now enjoyed:

> HENRY RUSSELL (from America) will shortly give three VOCAL ENTERTAINMENTS, at the Queen's Concert Rooms, Hanover-square. He will introduce for the first time several of his new compositions, comprising the "Drunkard," the "Slave Ship," "Cato's Soliloquy," the "Gambler's Last Stake," the "Deserted," "Our Sailors and our Ships," the "General's Last Battle," the "Felon," and the song of the "Shirt" from *Punch*. In presenting the above compositions to the public, Mr. Russell's object is, as far as possible, to adapt expressive music to the feelings and emotions excited by the occurrences of everyday life, and it is obvious that no better themes for such an attempt could be chosen than the "Slave Ship," "the Drunkard," &c. It is Mr. Russell's desire to unite with the pleasing science of music subjects likely to enlist the feelings of the benevolent, and should he be so far successful as to awaken the sympathies of those capable of ameliorating the sufferings on board the Slave Ship, or induce the Gambler to forego his last stake, the measure of his ambition will be fulfilled. Tickets, 2s; reserved seats, 3s. Kirkman and Son's Fonda pianoforte will be used on each occasion.

Russell was soon back in Liverpool, giving concerts at the Concert Hall, Lord Nelson Street, on 2, 5, and 7 June. Of the first, *The Liverpool Mercury* reported that, "although this spacious building is capable of holding upwards of 2000 persons, more were desirous of admission than could be accommodated." Appreciative concert promoters presented him with a handsome, richly chased silver snuff-box bearing the following inscription: "*Presented to Henry Russell, Esq., by the Concert Committee of the Northern Mechanics' Institution, in testimony of their high appreciation of his talents as a vocalist, and in acknowledgement of the lively interest he has always taken in forwarding their object—the elevation and amusement of the working classes.*"

Returning promptly to London, Russell was out at Gravesend on 9 June, for those who fancied a pleasure cruise down the Thames to hear him. Then, after performing at the Institution in Portman Square on Thursday, 26 June, he set off yet again for Ireland, where he opened—this time at Dublin's Rotundo—on 30 June, supported again by the Misses Balfe and Morgan and by various military bands. His reception was so great that he could continue giving concerts at the Rotundo, and later—after its reopening and redecoration—at the Music Hall, up to 21 July. His success earned him "a superb silver tea service" from the grateful promoter Mackintosh. Russell also made appearances at the Assembly Room in nearby Kingstown, just recently linked with Dublin by train.

From Dublin he returned again to London for what was announced as his last vocal entertainment of the season. It was in aid of the family of the recently deceased poet Thomas Hood (1799–1845), whose "Song of the Shirt" Russell had turned into a popular part of his concerts since its airing at the Hanover Square Rooms on 10 April. Fixed originally for the same venue for 23 July, Russell's benefit concert for Hood was postponed, at the last minute, to 30 July—perhaps because of a delay in getting back from Dublin.

Following that last solo concert of the season, Russell appeared also for five nights in August in a relatively subsidiary role as just one of the attractions in a miscellaneous season at the Princess's Theatre. Doubtless he was happy enough to accept a lower-key engagement as a respite from touring. In any case, the popularity of his songs was then being consolidated by the launch of an extensive series of cheap three-penny sheet music editions published by G[eorge] H[enry] Davidson (1801–75) under the banner of the "Musical Treasury, or Music for the Millions." It covered not only the favorites, but also Russell's lesser songs, sometimes with new words. Russell's versions of the "Indian songs" "Lucy Long" and "Old Tare River" were coupled in one of the early numbers.

In September 1845, Russell was in Scotland, holding his own at the Assembly Rooms, Glasgow, on 8 September against the rival attraction of ballerina Marie Taglioni (1804–84) at the Theatre Royal. Further concerts in Glasgow on 15 and 19 September framed appearances in Greenock and Ayr. Then he crossed the sea again to Ireland, giving two concerts in Belfast before traveling to Dublin for a further extended series of entertainments at the Music Hall, beginning on 2 October. His supporting artistes now were Susan (i.e., Susannah) Pyne (1821–86) and her thirteen-year-old sister, Louisa Pyne (1832–1904). Both pupils of Sir George Smart, they sang solos and duets by J. P. Knight, Thomas Arne, Thomas Linley, Daniel Auber, and Charles E. Horn.

For concert promoter Mackintosh's benefit, on 13 October, not only Miss Morgan and Miss Balfe but also the Hutchinson family from America were added to the program. The Hutchinsons' appearance in Britain was a significant point in what would be an increasingly substantial flow of American popular entertainers to Britain—welcomed, particularly, in the context of the American flavor that Russell himself was cultivating. Comprising three brothers, Judson, John, and Asa; and sister Abby, singing in close harmony with their own accompaniment of two violins and cello, the Hutchinsons had formed their quartet in 1842 and had soon become enormously popular in America. Like Russell, they were performers who promoted a social conscience, being active especially in the campaigns against slavery and drink.

The Hutchinsons recalled their encounter with Russell in Dublin in October 1845 as follows:

> Henry Russell was in Dublin at this time giving concerts, was having fine houses and giving great satisfaction. We saw a good deal of him, sang and consulted with him. He discouraged us very much by saying he did not think we should be able to make any money in that country, at the same time trying to engage us to sing for him. On one occasion we were at his concert and agreed to sing on the chorus of one of his songs. We were behind a screen, out of sight of the audience, and when we struck into the chorus of the "Boatmen of the Ohio," it seemed as if the house would come down. He rushed in to us, and telling us to sing louder, it was repeated.

Russell's Dublin season ended on 16 October to enable him to fulfil the first of a series of engagements in Liverpool two nights later, and these were followed by a tour of northern England. That he had, even now, not completely perfected the art of persuading Yorkshire folk to part with their money is evident from the *Halifax Guardian*'s report on two concerts there:

Figure 12.2. The Hutchinson Family singers. *Source:* Library of Congress, Prints and Photographs Division, https://lccn.loc.gov/2003654025.

"This celebrated American vocalist has given two concerts in the Odd Fellows' Hall, during the present week. The first was on Tuesday evening, when we were sorry to perceive so small an audience. The room, with so slight a sprinkling of auditors, produced too great an echo, and Mr. Russell requested his patrons to retire into the Lodge Room adjoining, where his peculiar powers were heard to greater advantage. . . . Yesterday evening the attendance was larger. . . ." Meanwhile, the Hutchinsons were following their Dublin appearances with their own tour, though they failed to impress *The Times* when they finally reached London. Their reception was certainly nothing compared with that of the Ethiopian Serenaders, who arrived from America in January 1846. *The Times* reacted to the latter with undisguised enthusiasm:

> [An] Ethiopian serenader presents the effect of an American gentleman dressed in the ordinary evening costume, having his hands and face painted black wearing a wig of a woolly texture, playing one of four instruments, the banjo, the accordion, the tambourine, or a species of osteological castanets called "bones," and singing various specimens of the American negro minstrelsy. They are five in number, two performers on the banjo, one on the accordion, one on the tambourine, and one on the "bones." Sermon, the tauborine [sic] player is the spokesman of the party, announces the successive performances, and diversifies them by a species of "clown in the ring" humour disguised in "nigger" dialect. The performances consist of solo songs, always accompanied with a general chorus, glees, and instrumental performances, in which all join. The songs, with the exception of one or two, the tunes of which are European, have been frequently heard before.

Thus was the minstrel show, with its blacked-up performers, introduced to Britain. The Ethiopian Serenaders appeared in April 1846 at a Drury Lane Theatre benefit performance, and in December at Arundel Castle before Queen Victoria and Prince Albert, who "laughed heartily" at the song "Old Dan Tucker." They were followed by a multitude of other troupes who took the genre around provincial Britain. Of these, the New Orleans Serenaders used a testimonial that Henry Russell himself wrote to them. It is of interest not least for the distinction that Russell clearly drew between sympathetically evoking Negro characteristics and mimicking them:

> GENTLEMEN,
>
> Although personally opposed to any imitation of the Negro Character, yet from the very great talent evinced in your personification of the Negroes of the United States, and the excellent harmonies of your arrangements of many of the Melodies you sing, it affords me great pleasure in recommending you to the notice of the Musical Public.
>
> I am, Gentlemen, yours truly,
>
> HENRY RUSSELL.
>
> To the New Orleans Serenaders.

The impact of the Serenaders, and the widespread interest they aroused, was clearly reflected in the way that Henry Russell expanded the use of anecdotes and minstrel songs in his own entertainments. For his London concerts at Miss Kelly's Theatre in Dean Street, Soho, in early 1846, he prominently advertised his compositions as "interspersed with anecdotes illustrative of Negro life and character." *The London Journal* testified that these "were told in so quaint a style as to elicit loud laughter." We get something of the flavor of these stories from an account of a Russell performance in Norwich the following year:

> He repeated many amusing anecdotes of the negroes; and illustrated their method of pumping up their laughs—their curious chuckle, and their "yha, yha, yha," with their method of singing,—which is not done without an effort, and is a forcible aspiration of the breath. An account of two negroes, one of whom was performing "Norval," and the other "Richard the Third" at Baltimore; and who interspersed the dialogue with interlocutions and expostulations with the spectators, convulsed the audience with laughter: as did his account of a negro, "John," a waiter at an hotel, at New York, whom he wanted

> to call him one morning at four o'clock, as he wished to go by the early boat. The negro did not understand calling him at "four o'clock, disturbing de whole house;" after he [Russell] got to his room, John went to his door twice, at one interval of ten minutes, and another of an hour; to ask if it "was four o'clock tomorrow morning" that he was to be called. A third time John came to the door, "Massa, Massa," "Well! What *do* you want!"—"If you ring him bell, Massa at half-past three," responded John, "I'll hab you called at four."
>
> Mr. Russell noted the fondness of the negroes for music; and said most of the melodies sung by them had their origin in England. He had arranged the music of "Lucy Long," "Old Dan Tucker," "Buffalo Gals," "The Boatmen of the Ohio," and "Ober the Mountain," from melodies he heard the negroes sing; they, in their turn, having originally obtained these melodies from white men. He related, as the effect of music on negroes,—an anecdote of two "darkies" who were "boots" at an hotel. One had been at a concert, and he cleaned his boots to an allegro movement, and the tune of "Lucy Long;" whilst his fellow-boots, brushed more slowly and leisurely in the andante style, to the air of "So gently o'er me stealing:" he having been at the "teatre," where he heard the "Slambular" [*Sonnambula*].

Running parallel with Russell's evocation of American Blacks was his role as a musical counterpart of Charles Dickens, highlighting social evils. This was readily apparent in the *London Journal* coverage of his opening engagement at Miss Kelly's Theatre on Monday, 2 February 1846—incidentally, with the suggestion that years of touring might have done his voice no favors. The report makes special reference to "The Gambler's Wife":

> The vocalist who can fix the attention of an audience for two hours, in a succession of songs, without fatigue, and can strongly excite their sympathies, must be no ordinary artist. Mr. Henry Russell has infinite tact in the selection of his subjects—they are calculated to harrow the feelings of his hearers. The striking of the clock hour after hour, whilst the starving mother and child are waiting for the arrival of the gambler, is one of the remarkable illustrations of Mr. Russell's artistical skill—the

> simple sound conveys at once to the senses the whole story. It is, however, a singular fact that he has little or no voice, except two or three notes in his lower register. He has, as a compensation, the most rare gift of an accomplished singer, that of expression, and thus does he achieve his triumphs. Last night he was encored in nearly all his songs, substituting the second time comic ditties, in which he is comparatively weak and inefficient.

A tiny theatre, with just the one entrance, Miss Kelly's Theatre seems to have been badly suited to meet the demand to hear Russell. Opened in 1840 by Fanny Kelly (1790–1882), niece of Irish tenor Michael Kelly (1762–1826), behind her home at 73 Dean Street, it held little more than 200 people. We catch a delightful whiff of the improvisational nature of things there from the *Times* notice of the 1842 reopening, when Chartist petitioners, seeking social reform, delayed an actress on her way to the theatre. "The doors, or rather door of the theatre," reported *The Times*, "was opened at half-past 6 o'clock, and the performance was announced to begin at 7, but fortune would not have it so, and the rise of the curtain was delayed until 8, the audience being meanwhile gratified with a tune every quarter of an hour, and the interesting spectacle of a gentleman in corduroys cleaning and preparing the foot-lamps."

As for Russell's appearances in February 1846, the *London Journal* reviewer was moved to complain that "The entrances might be better managed; there was much confusion and disappointment, and it required all the tact of the officials to preserve good humour." When a second concert was arranged at the venue for 10 February, special arrangements were made to accommodate everyone comfortably. Nowadays we take numbered seats and ushers and usherettes for granted, but they were a novelty in 1846:

> Mr. Russell begs to observe to the many persons that were unable to gain admission at his last concert that the arrangements upon this occasion will be of a superior order. The box-office of the theatre, 73 Dean-street, will be open on Saturday, Monday, and Tuesday next, from 2 until 4 o'clock, when places may be secured from the box sheet; tickets will be given with numbers corresponding with the seats taken; there will be competent

> persons stationed at the entrances of the boxes and stalls on the evening of the performance for the purpose of conducting parties to the seats secured.

Alas, even those arrangements were insufficient, and other improvements were necessary for the concerts that he continued to give at Miss Kelly's Theatre on Monday evenings until April: "Mr. Russell has much pleasure in announcing that the inconvenience formerly existing in reaching places reserved in the dress circle and private boxes will not in future be experienced by parties frequenting this part of the house, Miss Kelly having been induced to make a new entrance exclusively for their accommodation, and which will be opened for the first time on Monday evening next, Feb. 23. . . ." Even in those days, incidentally, popular success evidently brought commercial spinoffs. Thus, in May 1846, *The Musical World* was graced by an advertisement headed "Dr Stolzberg's Voice Lozenge, and Henry Russell's Vocal Entertainments." It quoted Russell's letter of 6 January 1845 to the proprietors: "I have tried Dr Stolzberg's Voice Lozenges for a period of three months, and have derived from them the greatest benefit. At my entertainments I frequently (from encores) sing twenty songs and descriptive pieces of music, and it affords me much pleasure to bear testimony to their great efficacy, and I would strongly recommend them all those who wish to sing with clearness and strength of voice to use them."

Russell's schedule was such that his voice would certainly have needed all the help it could get. In April 1846 he was again in Dublin, announcing that he had to end his engagement there on 14 April in order to appear in Sheffield on 16 April. Two days after that, he was back in London. At Sussex Hall, he sufficiently enthused a packed audience at another concert for the Library Fund of the Jews' and General Literary and Scientific Institution that he was immediately engaged for a further packed-out concert ten days later. Then in May he was back yet again in Dublin, as well as visiting Cork. In Ireland, indeed, he was evidently still an especial favorite. He was back in Dublin not only in September 1846, but in February 1847, again in May and June 1847 (when he shared the bill with the New Orleans Ethiopian Serenaders at the Music Hall, Dublin), and yet again in October 1847.

These were months when the Irish potato famine was beginning to be felt deeply. The repercussions of the crop failure, beginning in 1845, would last until 1850, and the resultant famine would kill thousands and lead many more to emigrate. Russell writes in his memoirs of one particular Irish tour in these years:

> During my provincial wanderings, I crossed over to Ireland. It was in the year of the famine, and the memory of that visit calls forth many very painful associations. In every part of the country I visited I found the peasants, and the lower classes generally, in such abject misery and privation that my heart bled for these unfortunate fellow-creatures; and when I saw men, and women, and children, actually dying on the roadside, I felt that it was my duty to give my mite to these helpless, starving creatures. I consulted with my dear friend, Guiness, of Stillorgan, who entered heart and soul into my project. Very shortly afterwards our plans were matured, and bills were widely circulated announcing that
>
> HENRY RUSSELL
>
> Will give his entertainment at the Rotunda, Dublin, on Monday, and Tuesday next, for the exclusive benefit of the evicted tenants, whose wives and children are starving on the roadside. The programme will consist of Mr. Russell's compositions, "The Maniac," "The Ship on Fire," "Man the Lifeboat," "The Old Arm Chair," "Many Troubles Have I Seen," "Cheer, Boys, Cheer," "I'm Afloat," "A Life on the Ocean Wave," "There's a Good Time Coming," and Mr. Russell's new composition:—"Who Fears to Speak of '98."
>
> To commence at 8 p.m.
>
> Reserved seats 5s., 3s., 2s., and 1s.
>
> The full receipts will be handed to Mr. Guiness, of Stillorgan, who will expend it on the relief to the destitute.
>
> An enormous success awaited me. The Rotunda was filled to suffocation both nights, and hundreds were turned away

> from the doors, and the receipts for the two nights amounted to no less a sum than £473.
>
> This success encouraged me to proceed. I gave the same entertainment at Cork (2 nights), Waterford (2 nights), Limerick (2 nights), Wexford, Dublin (another 3 nights), Drogheda (2 nights), Newry (1 night), Belfast (4 nights), Dundalk (1 night), Londonderry, Antrim; in fact I gave this same entertainment, and for the same purpose in every city and town throughout Ireland. In ten months, the sum I had forwarded to Guiness, from time to time, amounted to no less a total than £6,976 11s. The money was distributed right well to those who were in the direst necessity, and many a poor family received enough to give them a fresh start in life in the New World.
>
> It was hard to believe that those strong men and hopeful women, who, with cheerful-looking faces were starting with their little ones for the New World, with gratitude in their hearts, and a strong hope in the future, were those same poor creatures whom I had seen sitting by the roadside in the most pitiful attitudes of despair, with hunger, starvation, and death staring them in the face. And many a time have the tears come to my eyes, as I thanked God that he had chosen me as the instrument of the Divine mercy.
>
> There still remains one little incident that occurred to me during my stay among the grateful warm-hearted Irish. Before I left the country, a subscription was started with the object of presenting me with a gift. I have in my time received many a presentation, but never did one have the power to touch my heart, as did that given me by the poor Irish peasantry. No one was allowed to give a larger sum than one penny, yet still the large amount of £80 was raised, with which was purchased a silver salver, and a tea and coffee set. Think of that! No less than nineteen thousand two hundred poor people subscribed their mite in order to give me a present which I shall value till the last day of my life.

Typically, it is difficult to tie these details to a specific date. For one thing, Russell did not compose "Cheer! Boys, Cheer!" until 1850; for another, his concerts from July 1845 onward were at the Music Hall rather than the Rotundo (billed as the Rotunda, with an "a," only from 1847); and, for a third thing, his Dublin concerts were customarily promoted by Mr. Mackintosh. What we can say is that "Guiness" would have been Arthur Lee Guinness, grandson of the founder of the Guinness brewing organization and owner of Stillorgan House, Dublin, from 1840. As for the silver salver and tea and coffee set, was this perhaps the tea service we know he received in Dublin in July 1845? Or did he have a collection of such items? One wonders what became of them all. Most likely, this tale of Irish touring was an amalgam of experiences from Russell's many rapturously received visits during the famine years.

13

Russell v Smith

Long before the days of radio and the cinema, let alone television and video, the early Victorians had to rely for their entertainment on evenings at home around the piano or on such live performances as they could find in their neighborhood. Almost anyone who presumed to present himself as an entertainer could be sure of an audience. Henry Russell's success undoubtedly encouraged others to try their luck with similar one-man shows. "Mr. Russell has now been some years before the public," commented *The London Journal* in February 1846, "and, although his style is somewhat peculiar, it has yet found favour, so much so that a host of imitators has started up to share his success."

Imitators there certainly were, totally inefficient ones to the mildly pleasant, and one or two not bad at all, an issue that Russell addressed in his memoirs with a story about Charles Dickens:

> I was walking to and fro on the stage of the Lyceum Theatre, when the stage door-keeper came towards me. "Mr. Charles Dickens wishes to see you, sir." "Ask him to come in," I replied. "How are you, Mr. Russell?" said Dickens, when he had been shewn up. I thanked him, and told him I was very well, but rather worried. "Worried, what about?" "Well, the fact is, Dickens, I have been much annoyed. A fellow of the name of Smith has been singing my songs, and although I have written to him, telling him he is welcome to sing them, but that he at least acknowledge them—he has not taken any notice of this, and so I am rather annoyed." "Don't be," replied Dickens, in

> his quaint way, taking my arm. "You may rest assured, my dear fellow, that there never was a successful man yet who hadn't a Smith upon his back." Dickens's mind had no doubt reverted to Albert Smith, who was then copying his (Dickens') style.

As usual, there are difficulties with the story—most particularly that Russell did not begin his appearances at the Lyceum Theatre until some years after the Smith nuisance arose. Moreover, there was no real comparison between the acknowledged adaptations of Dickens made by the skilled Albert Smith (1816–60) and the blatant piracy practiced on Russell by Henry Smith, who seemingly sought to copy to the last letter without any acknowledgement.

In Britain, at least, the Henry Smith saga seems to have begun in late February 1845 with the following announcement:

> MR. HENRY SMITH (from America) begs to announce that his FIRST VOCAL ENTERTAINMENT in London will take place at Crosby Hall, on Wednesday evening next, March 3, when he will have the honour of singing—The Maniac, Newfoundland Dog, Dream of the Reveller, Old Arm Chair, Ship on Fire, I'm Afloat, &c. Tickets 2s., reserved seats 3s. To be had at the music shops: of Mr. Pearson, bookseller, corner of Great St Helen's, Bishopsgate-street; and at Crosby-hall. To commence at 8 o'clock precisely.

This was the clearest form of plagiarism—a concert of Henry Russell's songs, advertised without any acknowledgement of Russell, and in a form that copied Russell's announcements right down to the words "from America." There was even a rival piano manufacturer (Zeitter and Co.) in support. Perhaps most unashamedly, Smith managed to promote his activities through the subterfuge of a supposed "review" of this concert in *The Times*. Careless readers may not have noticed that the following was prefaced by the word "Advertisement": "A vocal entertainment was given on Wednesday last, at Crosby-hall, by Mr. Henry Smith, a baritone, from America. He sang twelve compositions, and was encored no less than nine times. Mr. Smith possesses a fine voice, good taste, and his pianoforte accompaniment is remarkably good. The most striking features of the performance were the "Old Arm-chair," the "Newfoundland Dog," the "Ship on Fire," the "Gambler's Wife, &c.". . . ."

But Henry Smith did not stop there. Very soon, he was taking his entertainment around the country, following closely in Russell's footsteps—often, quite literally so. As a correspondent of *The Musical World* later saw it, "whenever [Russell] advertizes a concert, he [Smith] does the same in the immediate neighbourhood, and at lower prices, singing the same songs, and narrating the same anecdotes."

Smith's was no idle use of another's copyright material, but something very much more calculated. This is how a correspondent of *The Musical World* saw it when Smith appeared at the Holywell Music Room in Oxford on 20 October 1845:

> Why this gentleman should follow so closely on the path of Mr. Henry Russell is a mystery which time will unravel. He sings the same songs, prefaces them with the same remarks, speaks of the music in connection with the words (to which he gives their due credit), without for a moment alluding to whom he is indebted for that music. There is something very strange in this. Mr. Smith is a servile imitator of Mr. Russell, without possessing that gentleman's taste in execution and ready method of accompaniment.

In March 1846 the same publication further reinforced, and expanded upon, the calculated nature of Smith's imitation of Russell: "Mr. Smith will give the names of the writers of all the songs, he says, except those of Mr. Russell. Again, in the introductory matter, anecdotes, &c, Mr. Smith gives it as if it was his own. If an anecdote told twelve years ago by Mr. Russell is introduced, it is given as an anecdote told to Mr. Smith by the party communicating it." That same article also gave possible clues as to Henry Smith's background: "Some half a dozen years ago Henry Smith, who was then a chorus singer at Covent Garden Theatre, having heard of Russell's success, went to America, learnt Russell's entertainment, and forthwith commenced giving it, *by implication*, as his own; and after Russell's return to England, and giving his concerts with the greatest success, Mr. Smith comes back also and doubles the original in the same way." The name of Henry Smith was, of course, an extremely common one, and it occurs in two other connections in the Russell story—even if only obliquely. First, Russell's song "I Love, I Love the Free," introduced in Boston in January 1840, carries a dedication to one Henry B. Smith. Second, Henry B. Smith—again—was curiously also the name of an individual who during the 1840s became highly celebrated as "the Razor-Strop Man." This latter was apparently an Englishman, who at one time drank himself into poverty before signing the pledge and starting to sell razor strops on a street corner in New York.

What distinguished this second Henry B. Smith was not the quality of his razor strops, but the attraction of his rhetoric, his doggerel verses, and his repartee, which ensured that he soon collected a crowd around him and ultimately achieved plentiful sales of razor strops. It also led to his celebrity preceding him through the main cities of the United States—sometimes where Russell happened to be. On the evening of 13 April 1843, when Russell gave a concert in Philadelphia, the same city was also hosting a "grand temperance concert and lecture." Its attractions included the Razor-Strop Man, who "will have his Still, and perform some curious experiments, by extracting Alcohol from Wine, &c." Then, in January 1844, the Razor-Strop Man's arrival in New Orleans was no less eagerly anticipated and remarked upon than Russell's. However, it can speedily be said that neither of these two Henry B. Smiths was the Henry Smith who would shadow Russell in Britain from 1845.

The state of copyright protection in Britain in the 1840s offered little that Russell could effectively do to counter the threat that Henry Smith represented. By comparison with France, which, as early as 1851, set up its Société des Auteurs, Compositeurs et Éditeurs de Musique (SACEM) for the purpose of collecting performance fees with legal and administrative backing, it would not be until over fifty years later that Britain followed suit. Such copyright legislation as existed in Britain in the 1840s lay in the 1842 Copyright Act (5th and 6th Victoria, chapter 45), which was in practice severely limited. For one thing, as far as performance was concerned, it was limited to dramatic works, its notable legacy being the single "copyright performance" that took place, most famously, in the case of *The Pirates of Penzance* in 1879. Most significantly, the Act failed to provide any sort of punishment for those who chose to contravene the Act, leaving authors and composers to seek redress through the Civil Courts by an application for an injunction and damages. This could have little effect if the transgressor was a man of straw with no means of paying.

In 1845, when Henry Smith appeared on the London scene, even this legislation was not only relatively new but also unchallenged. It must therefore have taxed Henry Russell's legal advisers to know how to meet it. Early in 1846 things evidently came to a head. While Russell was performing at Miss Kelly's Theatre in Dean Street, Soho, in February 1846,

Smith was putting on his own copycat show at Caldwell's Rooms in the very same street. The first public indication of imminent action seems to have been in an advertisement in *The Times* for one of Russell's concerts, at the beginning of March 1846:

> In answer to the numerous inquiries that have been addressed to Mr. Russell relative to the proceedings he has been advised to adopt, in order to restrain the unauthorized public singing of his compositions, Mr. Russell informs the public that he would be extremely unwilling to limit the courtesy under which the right of representation in musical compositions is generally conceded, the only instance in which he has interfered being that in which an individual has had the effrontery to construct an entertainment wholly of Mr. Russell's compositions; appropriating alike his songs and his anecdotes with which he accompanies the delivery, without even mentioning his name as the composer, or having his consent. . . .

The facts were pretty blatant, and Russell and his advisers doubtless hoped for a swift resolution; but, in fact, the saga of Russell v. Smith was destined to drag on for several years. Perhaps the first manifestation of the legal action that was being taken came to light after the announcement of an engagement of Henry Smith at the Victoria Rooms in Southampton in March 1846. The outcome was reported in the *Hampshire Advertiser*:

> It having been announced by advertisements and bills, in the usual way, that "Mr. Henry Smith, *from* America," would give his vocal entertainment on the evenings of Monday and Tuesday last, a tolerable audience assembled on the first of those evenings, but were informed by Mr. [Phillip] Klitz, the lessee of the rooms, that no money could be taken at the doors till the arrival of Mr. Smith. They, therefore, took their seats and waited with some impatience the *denouement*. . . . Mr. Klitz received a legal notice from Mr. Russell's solicitors, that if they permitted Mr. Smith to give his entertainment, as announced, they should proceed against him. Mr. Klitz, therefore, applied to the party who had taken the rooms for the entertainment for a guarantee, but was refused. He therefore waited the arrival of Mr. Smith, who did not go to the rooms till a quarter to

> eight o'clock, on Monday evening, told him of the notice, and produced a guarantee to hold him, Mr. Klitz, harmless, in case of proceedings, for Mr. Smith to sign. Mr. Smith declined, acknowledging that Mr. Klitz was acting perfectly right, and promising to accompany Mr. Klitz into the room, and address the company. He also said that he was not sorry for the interruption—it would put £50 into his pocket—as he should return to London, appeal to the public on the hardship of the case, get a party in his favour, and make a good thing of it. Mr. Klitz walked into the room, expecting Mr. Smith to follow him, when lo! on turning round, the vocalist had disappeared, *vulgo* bolted. Mr. Klitz then explained his position to the audience, and they fully coincided with him in the course he had taken, and requested him to alleviate their disappointment by playing a few pieces on the piano. Mr. Klitz good-humouredly consented, the audience were delighted, and, upon the motion of a gentleman present, passed a unanimous vote of thanks to him.

Disappointed audiences were less easily pacified in those days! Yet, as the above report went on, Smith succeeded in turning even this situation into one where he could be perceived as being the injured party. The following day he issued a circular, saying that he considered it necessary to explain his non-appearance. He claimed that Mr. Klitz had informed him "that he could not allow him to proceed with his entertainment, (notwithstanding the expenses Mr. Smith had already incurred) in consequence of his having received a threatening letter from the solicitor of a Mr. Henry Russell; of course, Mr. Smith had no alternative." Note the reference to "*a* Mr. Henry Russell." Smith was not giving in easily!

Neither was Russell. Further details of Russell's solicitors' legal maneuvers emerged when proceedings against Henry Smith came before the Vice-Chancellor's Court in London on Wednesday, 22 April 1846. Evidently as a step to establishing clear legal ownership, Charles Mackay had on 19 January 1846 assigned to Henry Russell his rights as lyricist of "Little Fools and Great Ones," "Some Love to Roam," "The Ship on Fire," "The Dream of the Reveller," "The Sea King's Burial," "The Maniac," "The Gambler's Wife," "Man the Life-boat," "I'm Afloat," and other songs. Then, on 1 April 1846, Russell had an injunction served on Smith to restrain him from "violating, pirating, publicly performing, singing or reciting the words or music" of those songs, which it was claimed Smith "had performed and sung in public on several occasions without his authority, and imitated the manner and style of singing of the plaintiff."

The Vice-Chancellor's Court duly granted the injunction on 3 April 1846. *Lloyd's Illustrated Paper* of 5 April 1846 reported "In the Vice-Chancellor's Court yesterday (Saturday) Henry Russell, the well-known American vocalist, obtained an injunction to restrain Henry Smith from publicly singing 'The Maniac' and the 'Ship on Fire,' they being his, Mr. Russell's own composition."

However, later that month, the court heard an application by Smith for the dissolution of the injunction, for which he petitioned on various grounds. First, he swore that none of the songs was original, "I'm Afloat" being an adaptation of a song called "Beautiful Rhine," "Man the Life-boat' being set to the air of a waltz by Strauss, "The Maniac" being an adaptation of Auber, and "The Ship on Fire" containing eight consecutive bars from "When Morning first Dawns" from Rooke's *Amilie*. Second, he claimed that the charge of imitation was untrue and that he had, several times, in 1839, in company with Russell, sung the said songs in Philadelphia and elsewhere in America. Third, the injunction having been served on 1 April, it had been considered a practical joke. Fourth, the injunction should by law have been served by 8:00 p.m., whereas it was not served until half past eight. Finally, the songs were not dramatic or musical compositions under the 1842 Act, and had been performed at places that could not be called theatrical.

If the claim that the music was not original was designed to confuse matters, it undoubtedly succeeded. "The Ship on Fire" may well have contained eight consecutive bars of "When Morning first Dawns," and certainly "I'm Afloat" has two bars of its melody (at the words "And I warrant we'll soon leave") that were identical with part of the 1830s song "My Beautiful Rhine." But what of the remainder of those compositions? Smith seems not to have been required to substantiate his claim at all, leaving the judge to decide whether and where in Auber's vast output and Strauss's numerous waltzes might be material Russell had adapted for "The Maniac" and "Man the Life-boat." The verdict was the practical one that the injunction be dissolved as to those two pieces and that Russell should be at liberty to bring such action as he might be advised on the remainder.

If there were any thoughts that Smith might, even now, be deterred from continuing with his piracy, they were soon enough dispelled. A concert promotor from Sheffield, whose bargain-basement terms Russell had refused, took a huge advertisement in the *Sheffield Independent* (18 April) lauding Smith, and damning Russell for causing him, by his injunction, to cancel an Easter engagement. He didn't say that Smith was welcome to appear at his venue—as long as he didn't sing any of Henry Russell's songs!

In one instance of many, after Russell had performed at the Music Hall, Dublin in April and May 1846, Smith duly arrived, at the end of May, to perform Russell's songs at the Portobello Gardens and to sweep up what cash and notoriety was left. The upshot of this persistence was that Russell brought a further action, in respect of "The Ship on Fire" and seven other songs (not including "The Sea-King's Burial"). This time, the action was specifically concerned with the claim that they were dramatic works and that Crosby Hall was a place of dramatic representation. This brought the parties back into Court on 22 November 1846, when Smith's legal team sought to dissolve the injunction of 1 April *in toto*. Their grounds were that the new action had been brought over Smith's right to perform the pieces at places of dramatic entertainment, whereas the Court order of April 1846 was to try the right to perform generally. On 1 December 1846, judgment was given that this subsequent action of Russell was indeed "in flat contradiction of the order of the Court and the injunction should therefore be dissolved." Costs of £113 were awarded against Russell.

Smith responded as any normal man would. He gloated. Ignoring the technicality on which the injunction had been dissolved, he prefaced press advertisements of his future concerts with the announcement that "Mr. Henry Smith (from America) begs to inform his numerous friends, patrons, and the public, that the injunction obtained by Mr. Henry Russell, to restrain him from singing certain songs published and sold by Mr. R, as his compositions, was wholly dissolved, with costs, on the 1st of Dec., by his Honour the Vice-Chancellor of England." Note again the words "published and sold by Mr. R as his compositions!"

Russell and his advisers were left to consider their options. The next stage was the hearing, at London's Guildhall on 13 May 1847, of Russell's action "to vindicate his right to the exclusive performance before the public of his own musical compositions." It was emphasized that "The action was not brought for any vindictive purpose, but simply to try the plaintiff's right." Russell therefore sought only 40s. damages, though he was entitled under the Act of Parliament to recover the full amount of the injury he had suffered.

The action was now, seemingly, concerned exclusively with "The Ship on Fire"—evidently considered the most dramatic of Russell's compositions—in which, it was said, "the author had expressed in the most graphic manner all the incidents and turns of fortune which were likely to arise in such a scene." The action further carried the charge that Smith "had become a servile imitator of Mr. Russell, had dogged his steps, and imitated his entertainments, without any acknowledgement whatever," citing, specifically, a performance by Smith on 22 December 1845 at Crosby Hall, which, presumably, could most readily be argued as being a place of dramatic entertainment.

Curiously it was stated in the action that "The Ship on Fire" (by now "purchased from him by Cramer & Beale") was composed in July 1842, though Russell had already performed it in February that year. Russell's team was, this time, well prepared to dispute the defense provided previously by Smith. They argued most particularly that resemblances in one or two bars were to be found in the works of the most original of authors and composers. There was also a powerful team of witnesses. Frederick Beale, of Cramer, Beale and Co., maintained that "The Ship on Fire" was a song of dramatic and descriptive character, consisting of eleven pages, and beginning with recitative. Mr. Sowell, manager at Cramer and Co., testified that he had seen Russell writing "The Ship on Fire," that he had no other music before him, and that he seemed to be working from his own head.

Composer Henry West (who had provided piano accompaniments for some of Henry Russell's minstrel song arrangements) said he had heard Smith perform "The Ship on Fire," and that it was the same as Russell's, note for note. Russell's piece had a part of the diatonic major scale, the same as Rooke's *Amilie*; but the harmony in Russell's song was original, and the time signature and key were different. A Mr. Le Jeune testified that Crosby Hall had a musical license, a platform for performers, and an elocution class that performed dramatic pieces every quarter. Charles Purday averred that he had heard Clara Seton sing at Crosby Hall and recite from Shakespeare's *The Tempest* there. Sir Henry Bishop testified that "The Ship on Fire" was an original song—"as original as songs are in general in these modern days." He declared that Beethoven was an original composer, but he could find passages in Beethoven similar to passages in previous composers. "The Heavens Are Telling" (from Haydn's *The Creation*) resembled "The Lass of Richmond Hill" but was still original. A verdict was given for Russell, with award of the 40s. damages claimed. However, after an edict had been issued by the Queen's Bench banning anyone from singing the song, on 26 May 1847, Smith's lawyers sought to set this aside on the grounds that "The Ship on Fire" was a single song and not a dramatic piece or entertainment under the Act, and that Crosby Hall was not a place of dramatic entertainment. The Court reserved judgement. With further legal representations in February 1848, a final judgment was destined to wait for almost a year.

Meanwhile Russell sought to consolidate his position in respect of the proprietors of halls where Smith was carrying out his brazen piracy. On 11 December 1847, the Court of Common Pleas at the Guildhall heard an action for infringement of Russell's copyright in respect of "The Ship on Fire" against William Briant, proprietor of the Horns Tavern Assembly Rooms, Kennington Common. There was also a second similar count in respect of "The Gambler's Wife." It was stated that Smith had presented his entertainment at the Horns Tavern Assembly Rooms the previous February, issuing a program announcing the two items. Moreover, the Assembly Rooms were capable of accommodating from 1,000 to 3,000 persons, and had a raised movable stage adapted to performances of a dramatic character. Evidently, Briant was not readily swayed by the threats of Russell's lawyers, and on the evenings of performances he had sold some of the tickets and taken part of the money, thus (according to the prosecution) making him a person who "caused or procured such representations." Russell sought a penalty of 40s. for each infringement of his rights.

For the prosecution, one William Last testified that Russell had publicly performed both works, and that, through its words and music, "The Gambler's Wife" represented a dramatic performance. Henry West testified that he had heard Russell and Smith perform both songs, and the music and words were the same. A witness named King said that he had seen various theatrical performances at the Horns Tavern Assembly Rooms, such as the Ethiopian Serenaders and the Bosjesman Indians. Mr. Fox Cooper, manager of the Strand Theatre, had tried to take the Horns Rooms for theatrical performances and had seen the Bayadères perform there.

The defense case was that a musical (as opposed to dramatic) performance was not covered by the Act and that the works in question were not covered because only the music (and not the words) was Russell's. It was further contended to the jury that the defendant had nothing to do with the actual performance. It emerged that, ahead of the performance, Russell's lawyers had sent Briant a warning of action, but that Smith had threatened Briant with action if the engagement was cancelled. The most extraordinary testimony of all was that of Smith himself. Having stated that he sang the songs without gesture or dramatic action, that he had no music before him, and that he did not sing Russell's music, he went on to claim that he had made the song "The Ship on Fire" his own. In cross-examination he stated that the words were in substance the same as those of Russell's composition, but the music was essentially different. He did not have a copy of his own music. He played from memory.

Russell's Counsel suggested that it would have been more creditable if the defendant, Briant, had not called as witness "Mr. Smith, the pirate," who sang what he was pleased to call "his own music." "Though he had none of his own," Counsel continued, "he sat down voluntarily, and his thoughts voluntarily fell into harmonious numbers, and he happened to hit on the same music and the same words as the plaintiff's songs." The jury needed only a short deliberation before deciding for Russell on both counts, with damages of 40s. on each. Then, on 17 January 1848, Briant's lawyers applied for a new trial on the grounds of misdirection and that the verdict was against evidence. They maintained that neither were the pieces dramatic in character nor the place one of dramatic entertainment, and that the proprietor of the premises was not a person who caused the pieces to be performed within the terms of the Act. The Court granted a rule *nisi* for a nonsuit. As late as 1854, Charles Sloman cited Russell vs. Briant in a published "Caution to Vocal Pirates" in *The Era*.

On 30 May 1848, however, Lord Denman finally delivered the judgment of the Court of Queen's Bench at Westminster in respect of Russell v. Smith. Smith, it seems, was hoisted on his own petard:

> The Court . . . was of the opinion that . . . "The Ship on Fire" was a dramatic musical composition, and that, on the occasion in question, Crosby-hall was a place of dramatic entertainment. Bills had been published inviting the public to the performance, in which the composition in question was described as a "descriptive *scena*" and was joined with another described as a "descriptive *cantata*." The piece was performed on a stage, and the singing was accompanied by music on the pianoforte. It described a storm at sea, the burning of the ship, and the escape of the passengers in boats, &c. It was calculated to move terror and pity, and to excite sympathy in the auditory. It was also described, by all the witnesses for the plaintiff, as a dramatic song. . . . The absence of scenery and dresses made no difference; and though Crosby-hall at other times might have been used for other purposes, on the occasion in question it became, for the time, a place of dramatic entertainment. . . .

Even so, the saga took yet another new slant when, to avoid the financial penalties, Smith sought protection under the Insolvency Act. Action thus switched to the Insolvent Debtor's Court, where, on 14 July 1848, Smith applied for appointment of a day to consider the granting of a final order, claiming that since the recent judgment he had not sung "The Ship on Fire" at any public place of entertainment. He had sung it at Evans's and the Cider Cellars (two song-and-supper clubs in London's Strand), but he was advised that they were not public places, within the meaning of the Act. He incidentally provided information that contradicted his evidence of two years earlier, stating now that he had begun his entertainments in America in 1842, singing many songs besides Russell's and without objections.

Russell's lawyer complained that the "insolvent had wickedly and vexatiously put the opposing creditor to vast expense" and stated afresh that "if the insolvent had not continuously withheld the name of Mr. Russell from the songs announced in his bills, there would have been no objection to his making use of them." Moreover, the judge, Commissioner Law, on examining one of Smith's programs, noted that six out of eight songs announced were Russell's compositions. Unable to resolve the matter under the law as it stood, he issued a warning that

> the litigation which had been going on for two years must be stopped at last, and therefore the parties must communicate before the next meeting, on which occasion, if not further advised, he should, both parties being silent, adjourn the case *sine die*. . . . The law of the case had been settled by the superior Court, but as regarded fair dealing between one man and another he thought it was a discreditable business. It was one man living on the talents of another, which he had no right to invade—a sort of robbery, borrowing without leave. . . .

This stern warning by the judge was probably as strong a vindication of his position as Russell was to achieve. At a further hearing in the Insolvent Debtors' Court on 4 August 1848 it was reported that Smith had made an offer to pay £1 a week off damages and costs. However, on 3 November, Russell's Counsel reported that Smith had refused to accept an injunction restraining him from performing Russell's compositions and had made no payment whatsoever. For Smith, it was stated that he was willing to consent to the injunction, but that it was impossible for him to pay the costs. The presiding Commissioner therefore adjourned the final order of protection from insolvency *sine die*.

Behind the whole Henry Smith saga lie various obvious questions, some of which can readily enough be answered, others much less so. It's easy enough to see that Smith should see the success of Russell's songs as a recipe for making a living. But why he should have done so in such a calculated fashion—effectively ignoring Russell's existence—must remain a mystery. As for how he managed to keep going for so long, in the face of such public opposition, it's clear enough that demand for entertainment of any sort was such that virtually anyone who dared could be assured of an audience. Smith may not, by far, have secured the packed houses that enabled Russell to make a fortune; but he could apparently (in spite of lawyers' costs and lavish advertising) secure sufficient ticket sales to cover his costs and make a living.

What is intriguing is that his actions seem not to have made him an outcast with other artists. He could, for instance, advertise a "Grand Concert" at London's Exeter Hall on 10 January 1848 with an "extraordinary combination of talent" that included many artists with associations with Russell. Among those announced were singers Anna Thillon, Elizabeth Poole, Signor and Madame Fanny Lablache and Henry Phillips, pianist Louise Dulcken, harpist Frederick Chatterton, and trumpeter John Distin and his four sons on sax horns and sax tubas. Was their appearance pro-Smith, anti-Russell, or simple economic reality?

But it is fairly easy to assess just what standard of performer Smith really was. With demand for live entertainment so great, pretty much anything went, and "criticisms" could be exceedingly bland or simple advertising. Perhaps one of the most eloquent comments on Smith's capabilities appeared in *The Musical World* in February 1848. The paper published a somewhat fanciful piece telling of how "Myriads of blue, white, and pink *billets* are circulating through the veins of Paris, in which celebrities perfectly unknown invite the innocent public to their *soirées* and *matinées musicales*." It then named various British performers, whose enthusiasm, it evidently considered, exceeded their talent, and who it suggested might benefit from the procedure. Among them was Henry Smith.

Even now, matters between Smith and Russell were not at an end; after the court hearing of November 1848, legalities dragged on for half-a-dozen years. The whole case had clearly cost Russell a great deal of time, trouble, and money, and it probably availed him little. But there was clearly a little bit of "revenge" in the affair. Russell had no objections to such fine professional artists as George Buckland, Harry Lee Carter, Daniel Saunders, Henri Drayton, and William Woodin—or a host of minor gentlemen "by permission of"—singing his songs, while Smith—who, admittedly, purveyed a full-scale impersonation program—languished in Whitecross jail for unpaid fines of £4. When he came back on the scene, he advertised "Henry Russell's popular songs" in large letters, in a fashion bent to his own ("the rival of HENRY RUSSELL"), seeming, advantage. The most lasting legacy of the case, in the end, was its status as a British legal precedent as to what constituted a dramatic work and a public place of entertainment. As we shall see in later chapters, it was of immediate value to various other solo performers. More particularly, it continued to be invoked from time to time over three-quarters of a century.

As an example, in 1894, Russell v. Smith was cited to determine what constituted a dramatic work in such as the case of Fuller v. the Blackpool Winter Gardens and Pavilion Company (Limited) and William Holland. In this case, music-hall singer Katie Lawrence (Mrs. George Fuller) sued for damages for what she considered unauthorized use of the song "Daisy Bell" ("A Bicycle Made for Two"). She claimed dramatic rights, citing the fact that the sheet music showed her dressed in male bicycling gear. The issue of what constituted a public place of dramatic entertainment was likewise decided, with reference to Russell v. Smith, in 1911, when a filmed version of the play *The Still Alarm* was claimed to infringe dramatic copyright. Even as late as 1926, Russell v. Smith served as precedent, when publishers Harms and Chappell sued for infringement of their copyright when the song "That Certain Feeling," from the musical *Tip-Toes,* was performed by the resident dance orchestra at London's Embassy Club.

So who *was* this pesky Smith fellow? Well, he was, actually, respectably musically related. His brother was the internationally admired operatic bass and entertainer Robert Farquharson. We reprint here the little piece about the poor relation taken from his brother's article in the book *Victorian Vocalists:*

> As for Henry Smith, Henry the foolish plagiarist who, I am delighted to be able to at last affirm, is our Mr. Farquharson's brother, he kept on going. Twenty years after his first controversial appearance as an entertainer in London (5 March 1845), with his blatant pirating of Henry Russell's material; his first long Concert (37 items) at Exeter Hall in 1847 (which

> brought a column of ridicule in *The Musical World*); and after the eight months spent in jail (1851) which he earned by his dubious Russelling activities, Henry Smith was still on the road, trouping his entertainment, with or without his 20,000 sq ft of diorama, with or without "oxy-hydrogen-lime-light dissolving views," and with "free gifts" to encourage an audience. And fighting. Top venues, of course, didn't hire him, but those who couldn't get or couldn't afford Russell, did, and Smith supplied them with snarky scornful paragraphs for their local papers. He was rewarded with notices such as "wretched burlesques of the originals . . . miserable and spiritless imitations" (*West Kent Guardian*) and Gravesend reported "the company [was] about eighty. At the second entertainment the audience was still less."

In 1865, Smith was still advertising himself as available to the Concert Rooms, Corn Exchanges, and Mechanics Institutes of the country with *A Voyage to and Wandering in America* and, as ever, with or without his diorama. He has "a fair voice and sings several popular songs in a pleasing style, accompanying himself on the pianoforte . . . ," the provincial press noted. I see Mr. Smith "of panorama notoriety" in March 1865, touring through Leigh and Oldham with Mr. Fred Clifton and the Rockaway Negro Troupe, doing his panorama with Mr. McFarland's eternal "America" in 1866, and still doing his Russell rip-off in Manchester in 1867. I'm sure it is he, tripping around with the Phantascope of *Faust* in 1869, and with a panorama of the (Franco-Prussian) War in 1870, and as bass singer with Poole and Young's "Paris" "from the Egyptian Hall" in 1872. In 1875, he is still with Poole and Young, this time with their "gigantic diorama of the Overland Route: India! Via Malta, Gibraltar, and Suez Canal." He is pianist and lecturer, and apparently bass singer as well.

The whole history of Henry Smith has never, perhaps understandably, been written. Was he "a chorus singer at Covent Garden" as one tale relates? We know, now, that he was listed as an eighteen-year-old "merchant" in the 1841 census, and probably the Henry Smith who appeared at Dr. Johnson's Music Hall in the 1840s. How do we know? In November 1846 at the Manor Rooms, Stoke Newington, and at the Horns Tavern Assembly Rooms, a concert was given by Mr. J. B. Smith of 16 Sidmouth Street, Regent Square. The vocalists included—apart from the regular Miss Thornton and Messrs Sporle and Genge—Miss Farquharson Smith, Mr. Farquharson Smith, and Mr. Henry Smith (from America). And John

Parry! Well, Sidmouth Street did it. I got him at last: Henry was born on 2 July 1823, at Castle Street, Shoreditch. On his birth registration, even though from a different address, father John is listed as a "feather manufacturer." Just like Robert's father. Got him! And when you know what you are looking for: Henry Smith ex-of 16 Sidmouth Street, vocalist, is up for bankruptcy in 1848. Anyway, Henry the Pilferer wed a Fanny [Sarah née White] from Bristol in 1851, had daughters Caroline [Farquharson] (b. Bristol, 1852) and [Sarah] Agnes (b. Derby, 1854) and a son Henry (b. London, 1857), and he is there in the 1861 and 1871 ("musician") Bloomsbury census . . . before we lose him again. Perhaps, just as well.

14

"The Emigrant's Progress"

During the 1840s, as Henry Russell moved through his early thirties, his personal circumstances changed significantly. To complement his home in Boulogne-sur-Mer, his success as an entertainer brought him sufficient wealth to acquire an elegant London home at 14 Park Place Villas, close to Paddington Green. Before the building of Paddington Station, in the early 1850s, this was a select suburban area—the terminus of George Shillibear's first omnibus service from the City of London in 1829. Russell recalled, many years later in his memoirs, how, when Queen Victoria came to the throne in 1837, Paddington "was a little village on the outskirts of London, surrounded by green fields and meadows. Here and there a few houses had been built where City gentlemen resided, but, saving these, the only dwellings for miles were pretty cottages by the roadside with flowers in the front. Edgware-road . . . was a country lane leading, as the name indicates, straight to Edgware."

It was at 14 Park Place Villas that, just before midnight on 22 December 1845, the Russell family was blessed with the birth of a second daughter to join the three sons. On 3 June 1846, at St. Mary's Church, Paddington Green, the newcomer was baptized Fanny Marcella Russell. Between those two dates, however, Russell's second son, Charles Kirkman Russell, had died on 14 March 1846, aged three years eight months, of whooping cough and consumption, at 163 Friar Street, Reading, where he had evidently been confined.

Within a period of thirteen months, from November 1847, moreover, Russell lost not only his mother, Sarah Russell, who died in London on 20 November 1847, but also his two sisters—the siblings nearest in age to himself. Elizabeth, who died in December 1848, had married Isaac Levy in 1837, and their son Matthias Levy (1839–1918) would become the first historian of the Western Synagogue in Saint Alban's Place, St James's. The eldest Russell brother, Israel, was a leading member of the congregation there, as indeed was their father, and Henry too would attend services when commitments permitted. As for Anne, the youngest of the family, she had married Asher Solomon only in February 1847. Within ten months she was dead—apparently in childbirth, though her death evidently gave rise to mischievous rumors. These prompted an open letter to Asher Solomon placed by Israel Russell, as an advertisement, in the *Jewish Chronicle*, exonerating Solomon from any criticism for the death.

Henry Russell increased his own family shortly afterward with the birth of another son. On 8 June 1849, at 28 rue de Constantine, Boulogne-sur-Mer, Isabella Russell gave birth to John Henry Sharp[e] Russell. Russell, himself, had engagements that week in the London suburbs, but his wife was not alone. The birth was registered the same day by her brother-in-law Thomas Holmes Forrest, from which we may reasonably infer that her sister Emma was in attendance too. The addition of another Henry to join the existing Henry Lloyd Russell, by then aged eleven, may seem strange. However, the name apparently derived not from Henry Russell himself but from the Henry John Sharpe who had supported Russell in the Trumpeter's Lip incident. Russell had set Sharpe's lyrics on several occasions, and Sharpe's copy of *L'Amico dei Cantanti*—with a personal dedication from Russell—is now in the British Library. The newest member of the Russell household, who became known as Jack, was duly baptized at St Mary's Church, Paddington, on 3 November 1849. Henry and Isabella's family was finally completed with the birth of daughter, Emma—evidently named for Isabella's sister—in Boulogne-sur-Mer in 1854.

On the professional front, Russell's schedule continued to be a hectic one. In London he had played to crowded houses at the recently remodeled Sadler's Wells Theatre in Islington, in June 1846. Then, after isolated concerts at various other London venues, he appeared for the first time at the Strand Theatre for a whole week from 3 to 8 August 1846, combining his last night there with an appearance across the river at Emma Albertazzi's benefit concert in the Surrey Theatre. He was back at the Strand Theatre for a further week from 24 to 29 August. Though he also played a fortnight at the Lyceum Theatre in November 1846, the Strand Theatre was to be the venue for his London seasons until 1848. He was there for four weeks from February 1847, a further fortnight in April

Figure 14.1. Chelmsford Races concert program. *Source:* Author's collection.

CHELMSFORD RACES.

UNDER THE PATRONAGE OF

W. P. HONYWOOD, ESQ.
H. C. COAPE, ESQ. } STEWARDS OF THE RACES.

THE RACE COMMITTEE,
&c. &c. &c.

MR. HENRY RUSSELL,

Composer of the Popular Songs "Woodman Spare that Tree," "The Ivy Green," "I'm Afloat," "The Maniac," "Ship on Fire," "Old Arm Chair," "Gambler's Wife," &c. &c.
HAS BEEN ENGAGED TO GIVE HIS

POPULAR VOCAL ENTERTAINMENT,

INTERSPERSED WITH

Anecdotes of Negro Life & Character,

On TUESDAY EVENING, the 11th of AUGUST 1846,

AT THE SHIRE-HALL, CHELMSFORD.

AMONG THE SONGS WILL BE INCLUDED,

I'M AFLOAT. THE SLAVE SHIP. THE SHIP ON FIRE.
THE PAUPER'S DRIVE. THE BOATMEN OF THE OHIO. THE MANIAC.
THE GAMBLER'S WIFE. THE NEWFOUNDLAND DOG

HOOD'S SONG OF THE SHIRT.

LITTLE FOOLS AND GREAT ONES. I'M GOIN' OBER DE MOUNTAIN.
&c. &c.

Mr. H. RUSSELL will accompany himself on Kirkman and Sons, Fonda Piano-Forte.

MR. CARTE

Will, in the course of the Evening, perform a **SOLO ON THE FLUTE,** introducing Popular Airs.
Front Seats (which will be reserved on Application) 4s.; *Back Seats*, 2s.
Tickets may be had at the Office of Messrs. Meggy and Chalk, and of the Booksellers.
Doors open at Half-past Seven. To commence at Eight.
Books of the Words, 6d. each.

1847, and a week in July 1848. Housing around 800 people, the theatre was in something of an interregnum before a return to legitimate drama.

The press advertisements for Russell's season at the Strand Theatre starting on 22 February 1847 sought to emphasize his position as a man of the people by announcing measures to control the behavior of cloakroom attendants seeking tips:

> Mr. Russell wishes to impress upon those visiting the stalls and boxes, that he has engaged competent persons to attend to their comforts, and he earnestly requests that no kind of gratuity may be given to them. Knowing how much it is a source of complaint that visitors to places of public amusement are subjected to the annoyance of having their bonnets, cloaks, &c., all but forcibly taken from them as a pretext for unauthorised exactions, and the consequent vexacious delay, to

Figure 14.2. Concert bill for Henry Russell at the Theater Royal, Plymouth, Feb. 1847. *Source:* Author's collection.

> ladies particularly, on leaving, Mr. Russell adopts the plan of paying his attendants, that those who honour him with their company may be enabled to consult their own convenience in such matters, and he trusts that the public will second this effort to put an end to the system of giving gratuities in theatres.

All this time, of course, London engagements were interspersed with extended tours around Britain. There is even a suggestion that he appeared in Paris sometime in 1847. This appears in a Norwich newspaper report in September 1847 that reported some of the anecdotes Russell had told there. This particular one concerned the song "Woodman, Spare That Tree!": "In Paris, where he sang the same song on his first visit, about seven months ago, on coming to the same line ['Oh let that old oak stand!'], an old Frenchman, got up, amidst all the audience, and stretching out his hands, said—'Mr. Russell, *did* the tree remain?' Russell: 'It did Sir.'—Frenchman:—'Thank God! What a happy nation you must be.'" The story is, of course, a mere variation on the celebrated one that Russell tells (without reference to Paris) in his autobiography, and which is elsewhere linked, by him, to Boulogne-sur-mer. However, as reported in Norwich in 1847, it provides further testimony that Russell was considered at his entertainments as being American.

Norwich was just one of the many, many ports of call in Russell's travels around Britain in those years. Besides higher-profile seasons in places such as Liverpool and Dublin, there were one-night stands in local community halls the length and breadth of Britain. "We know of no corner in merry England where his principal songs are not already established favourites," declared *The Times*. It may have been his appearance in Uttoxeter, in Staffordshire, in January 1847, that generated another of his favorite anecdotes. This concerned the song "The Gambler's Wife," which told in graphic language of a wretched young wife who, through the long hours of the night, hopelessly awaited her gambler husband's return:

> At Uttoxeter, a few months back, Mr. Russell sang the song of "The Gambler's Wife." As he proceeded with it, a lady among the audience appeared greatly agitated; at length he enunciated the words:-
>
> > And I could starve and bless him—but, my child, for you,—
> > Oh fiend! Oh fiend!—hush!—the clock strikes two.

> Scarcely had he uttered the words, when the lady, overcome by her feelings, started up, and exclaimed, "Wouldn't I have fetched him home."

These anecdotes were, of course, flexible, to the extent that his memoirs give the location as Newcastle-upon-Tyne. Be that as it may, the story illustrates Russell's ability to get through to his audiences on the social issues of the day.

The extent of Russell's travels around Britain may be demonstrated specifically by his movements during the summer and autumn of 1847. In July his program included Lowestoft, Dover, Gosport, Guildford, Canterbury, Salisbury, Ramsgate, Margate, Southampton, Exeter, and Ryde. During August, he visited Plymouth, Truro, Chertsey, Farnham, Winchester, Salisbury, Portsmouth, Chichester, Arundel, Worthing, St. Leonards, and Hastings. In September he was in Norwich, Yarmouth, Ipswich, Windsor, Reading, Newbury, Taunton, Liverpool, Northampton, Coventry, Leamington, and Stratford-upon-Avon. During October 1847 he entertained Liverpool, Warwick, Wolverhampton, Shrewsbury, Wellington, St Helens, Ipswich, Derby, Nottingham, Chesterfield, Huddersfield, Halifax, Manchester, Blackburn, Carlisle, and Preston, besides going on to Dublin. In November he was in Barnsley, Birmingham, Wakefield, Hull, York, Darlington, Stockton, Durham, Newcastle, Glasgow, Paisley, Greenock, et al.

On top of all that, Russell furthered his image as a representative of the working man ("the people's singer") with regular appearances at the Saturday Evening Concerts for the Working Classes at the Concert Hall in Liverpool. These culminated in an appearance, on 18 December, that was presided over by the recently elected mayor. Between the two parts of Russell's entertainment there were speeches on behalf of the concert committee and by the mayor himself. Speaking for the committee, a Mr. Rathbone referred to initial fears that their gatherings might be "bringing people together for evil," and that Russell was "the first to break the ice and come amongst us, . . . with a moral courage for which we owe him grateful thanks." In the second half, Russell invited the audience to join him in the chorus of his recent song "There's a Good Time Coming, Boys," and the evening closed with three cheers for the mayor, three cheers for Mr. Rathbone, and three cheers for Henry Russell.

One can only guess at the effect on Russell's constitution of not only the constant traveling but also the need to repeat the same songs, time after time, as well as the same patter and jokes. Even for some of his audiences, this could become a little too much, witness this report from Preston in October 1847:

> Notwithstanding the frequency of Mr. Russell's visits to this town, and the absence of any vocal novelties, the pit and gallery were densely crowded and the boxes were filled. Of the performance we need say out little. All Mr. Russell's peculiarities remain unchanged. The same mixture of pathos and melodramatic extravagance characterizes his singing. It might perhaps be as well if Mr. Russell would make a little change in his prefaces, anecdotes and jokes; as he has retailed his present stock verbatim so very frequently in Preston, that the majority of his audience could narrate them almost as well as himself.

One thing we do not know is the sort of administrative backup that Russell had for this constant touring. The uniform penny post and telegraph existed, but not yet the telephone, so that one imagines there must have been some advance guard to book halls, to get bills printed and distributed, and newspaper notices placed. Then there were proceeds to be collected, accounts to be settled, and so on. Russell made use of concert agents both in London and locally, but there must have been much else to be done on a tour of largely one-night stands to ensure that all went well, as well as the arrangement of Russell's travels from town to town. Clearly, the manufacturer Kirkman would be happy to be responsible for the Fonda piano, and it need not necessarily be assumed that this involved moving and tuning the same instrument from town to town. The announcement of Russell's concerts in Halifax in November 1845 came with the statement that "The PIANO-FORTE will be one of Messrs Kirkman and Sons' 'PATENT FONDA GRANDS,' with Six and Half Octaves, and will be for sale after the Concert." The Kirkmans would undoubtedly have been only too happy to deliver a new piano to every venue with the assurance of a sale afterward!

At the beginning of 1848, Russell was in the Potteries, giving a series of performances from 3 to 7 January at Hanley on Monday and Friday, Longton on Tuesday, Stoke on Wednesday, and Burslem on Thursday. The concerts were "attended by overflowing companies—and in several instances almost as large audiences were collected outside, anxious to catch a flying strain from the delightful melodies of this eminently popular vocalist." The Staffordshire potters were then suffering hard times. At the suggestion of local concert promoter George Simpson, Russell announced at his final appearance of the week that "if he should have an evening at liberty in the coming week—and he hoped it would be the case—he would feel much pleasure in giving a concert in the New Covered Market, Hanley, on that evening, and handing over the gross receipts for the relief of the poor unemployed Potters."

In the event, the concert for the distressed of Hanley and Sheldon finally took place on Thursday, 27 January 1848, between a series of appearances at halls around London. Despite bad weather, it attracted some fifteen hundred people and raised what was then doubtless a welcome sum of £50 after incidental expenses. "There's a Good Time Coming, Boys," with extra verses and the audience participating in the chorus, was a highlight of the evening.

Those Potteries appearances in January 1848 were clearly the inspiration for another of the anecdotes in Russell's memoirs, though, as usual, the details seem only to approximate ascertainable facts:

> I remember on one occasion being invited to the little town of Hanley, in Staffordshire, to give an entertainment in aid of the potters, who were at the time in much distress and destitution. In the course of the evening, thinking it would be appropriate, I sang my song, "There's a Good Time Coming, Boys." I was right, the success of the song was perfectly overwhelming, and then to crown all a man rose in the gallery, and excitedly shouted, "Muster Russell, can you fix the toime?"
>
> Another time I was giving an entertainment at the same place and for the same object, and the success attendant upon my first appearance had induced many to come and hear me. The result was that not more than one half the people could crowd into the small hall where I was singing. Mr. Hancock, a banker, seeing the difficulty I was in, came forward and suggested that I should continue the entertainment at the Market Hall, a huge building eminently suitable, no doubt, for the purposes for which it was built, that is to say for the selling and buying of meat, but not quite an ideal place in which to hold a musical performance.
>
> On the left side of the hall hung sharp gleaming steel hooks, used by the butchers for hanging carcasses on. The necessary platform for myself and my piano was formed in a

> rough and ready fashion by arranging a lot of butchers' chopping blocks. On this temporary structure I was installed. All went well for some time. I gave several songs, which were warmly applauded, but when singing "The Maniac," and coming to the words "I see her dancing in the hall," I happened to look up, and felt considerable surprise to see an elderly female of respectable appearance performing a most fantastic dance, and cutting the most grotesque capers. At the same moment I heard a man's voice shout, "Shut oop, Muster Russell, ere's a old gal caught on t'ooks." And so I "shut oop" till the unhappy lady was liberated.
>
> The day following this performance, I was walking along the streets of Hanley, when at a street corner I came across a group of boys. One of them, noticing my approach, suddenly sang out, "Hullo, muster, 'ere comes 'I see her dancing on the wall,' " by which I suppose he meant "I see her dancing in the hall." Such is fame!

The songs announced ahead of those Potteries concerts show his repertory constantly moving on, comprising as they did "The Wife's Dream," "The Felon's Last Night," "The Wants of the People," "The True Men of Old," "The Song of the Lash," "The Song of the Scaffold," "The Discovery of America," "The Drunkard's Wife," "The Demon Ship," "The Idiot Boy," "The Gin Fiend," "The Gambler's Wife," "The Maniac," etc. The lyricist of "The Wife's Dream" was "I.R."—evidently Russell's own wife, Isabella—and its published edition was dedicated to Russell's Hanley concert promoter, George Simpson.

Alongside the new songs the old favorites endured. However, their continuing popularity seems to have left at least one earlier lyricist with a feeling of resentment. "The notice in Sharpe's Magazine . . . puts matters right with regard to Russell," wrote George P. Morris, in response to this appreciation of Morris's poetry that proprietor George Virtue published in the February 1848 issue of *Sharpe's London Magazine*:

> In every part of the United States, his ballads and songs are deservedly held in high estimation; and by none so zealously as the ladies, who appear, one and all, lavish in their praises of their favourite bard. Many of his stirring compositions have found their way to this country; and though well known and

> appreciated, have had their parentage generally attributed to the talented individual who has been mainly instrumental in introducing them to English ears. Every one who has attended Russell's entertainments must have heard "Woodman, spare that tree" and "Land Ho!" and probably gone away with the idea that the vocalist was their author; or, it may be, read in the criticisms of the daily journals words to that effect. *Palmam qui meruit ferat* [Credit where credit's due] is a fair axiom all the world over; and it is but justice to a clever and amiable man to inform the public to whose muse they are indebted for the delight they have experienced.

Virtue made his point by quoting from Morris's "Land Ho!," which he described as "a sea song . . . written with all the spontaneous heartiness and warmth of feeling for which the lyrics of Dibdin were so justly celebrated." "It breathes of the sea," he adds, "and the words dance along as merrily as the tossing and rolling waves themselves."

Russell's season at London's Strand Theatre, during the week beginning 24 July 1848, produced a curious burst of multilingual advertising. For some reason *The Times* published announcements one after another in English, German, and French. These offered the German reader "Die letzte Nacht eines gefangenen Verbrechers" von Victor Hugo, "Die Welt ist in Bewegung, nehmt euch im Acht," "Der Handwerker," and so on. The French reader was spared translation of the titles, being offered "Soirées de Mons Russell" with " 'The Last Night of a Condemned Felon' sur les motifs de Victor Hugo," and so on.

If the reason for the multilingual adverts is unclear, their content again demonstrates the constantly evolving nature of Russell's programs. That particular season, in July 1848, seems to have brought out quite a number of new songs. Not all achieved publication, but "The World is on the Move, Look Out," with words by dramatist and critic E. L. Blanchard (1820–89), is one that did. Another new song later that same year was "Time is a Blessing," subtitled "An Appeal from the Counter," whose lyric was again attributed to "I.R."—evidently Russell's wife, Isabella. It was written for a concert on 27 December 1848 at the recently opened Whittington Club in the Strand, given on behalf of the Early Closing Association, which campaigned to give shopkeepers one afternoon off each week. Another concert, at the Whittington Club, two days later, was again for a charitable cause: the Commercial Travellers' Schools, "the design of which

Figure 14.3. Concert bill for Henry Russell at the Theater Royal, Bath, April 1849.
Source: Author's collection.

is to clothe, maintain, and educate the destitute orphans of deceased and the children of necessitous commercial travellers of every denomination."

During 1849, Russell continued to divide his time between London and the provinces, and there is evidence that he looked to cross the Atlantic once more. When he undertook a tour of the West Country in July 1849—including appearances at the Theatres Royal in Bristol on 16 and 20 July and Plymouth on 26 July—his concerts were described as the "last appearance of Henry Russell previous to his departure for America." There's no evidence, though, that he actually did cross the Atlantic again. Yet the description "farewell visit" was bandied around again, for instance, in announcements for concerts in Leeds in November 1849. For his 1850 appearances at the Lyceum Theatre in Holy Week (when costumed performances were banned from theatres), he likewise advertised "five farewell vocal entertainments," after which Londoners could also catch a further two "farewell performances" at the Marylebone Theatre "at the earnest solicitation of many families."

A *Musical World* review of the last night of the crowded Lyceum season gives no help with determining just what "farewell" was intended to signify. Indeed, the review concentrated on the continuity of Russell's entertainment, in particular his performance of one song that—Dickens-like—concentrated on the problem of poverty:

> On Saturday night, Mr. Russell addressed the following apology to the audience for his frequent repetitions of a particular song—"The Song of the Shirt":—"Ladies and gentlemen, I owe some apology for continuing to bring this composition so constantly before your notice, but I desire that my songs should have a wider aim than a mere momentary gratification. I use music as a medium for bringing this unfortunate class constantly to public notice, hoping thereby to ameliorate, to some extent, their present horrible position." . . . The entertainment wound up with "There's a Good Time Coming"—the audience, under the direction of Mr. Russell, joining in full and *ad libitum* chorus . . .

That *Musical World* review also stressed Russell's introduction of "nigger" melodies and anecdotes. Indeed, press advertisements for that 1850 Lyceum season seem to have included a particular emphasis on Negro life, slavery, and emancipation, which, with hindsight, indicated Russell's plans for something new for the future:

Figure 14.4. Concert bill for Henry Russell at the Lyceum Theater, 1850. *Source:* Author's collection.

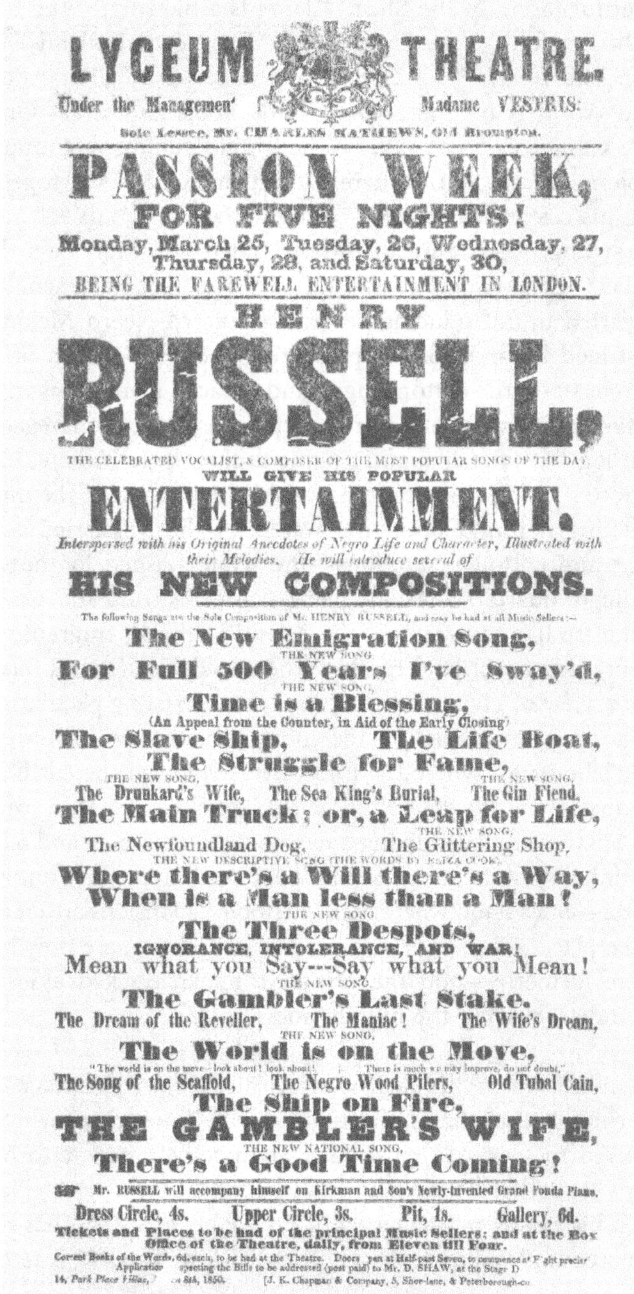

> All his latest and earliest compositions will be introduced during the course of the entertainments:—Hood's popular and beautiful "Song of the Shirt," "Time is a blessing," "The Song of the Scaffold," "The Slave Ship," "The Newfoundland Dog," "The Life Boat," "The Dream of the Reveller," "I'm Afloat," "The World is on the Move," "Little Fools and Great Ones," "The Gambler's Last Stake," "The Three Despots—Ignorance, Intolerance, and War," "There's Room enough for All," together with his celebrated scenas—"The Maniac," "For full 500 years I've swung," "The Ship on Fire," "When is a Man Less than a Man?" "The Gambler's Wife," &c. The Entertainment will be varied by introducing several soi-disant Negro Melodies, illustrated by anecdotes representing the peculiarities of the negroes upon the cotton, sugar, and tobacco plantations in the south-western states of America. After sunset, they congregate in their log-huts, dancing and singing to their beautiful melodies. A more striking scene cannot possibly be imagined. The moon reflecting her rays upon the waters of the Mississippi—the sugar and cotton plantations—the white-washed log-huts of the negro quarters—the long level fields of sugar cane, waving to and fro like the waves of the Atlantic—the air fragrant with odours, can never be forgotten. The anecdotes are thus related with a view of giving a description of the existing peculiarities of the negroes, depleting the most attractive proportions of their labour; for where the forest overshadowed the earth and afforded shelter to the wild beast, corn fields, orchards, towns, and villages are daily giving a new face to the scene, and tell of the industry and enterprise of a people stimulated by untiring efforts—cities stand where hamlets stood—mansions are erected in the place of log-huts, and magnificent streets are now built where formerly stood the primitive forest, tracked alone by the Indian chasing the buffalo and the deer.

For some months, from the early summer of 1850, we lose track of Russell as a performer. Rather than indicating a trip to America, of which though often referred to seems to have been mythology, it seems to have been during this time that he gave up his London home at Park Place Villas and settled his family permanently in Boulogne-sur-Mer. That resort had become increasingly a home for the British during the 1840s, to the extent that by 1852 the subjects of Victoria represented some 5,000 of 31,000 permanent residents of the town, with the British contingent swelling to 15,000 in summer. Russell, then, seems to have used this time to do detailed work on a new entertainment that was to renew his impact on the public. He wrote thus of its background:

> For many years both Mackay and I worked in unison on the subject of emigration. "A Good Time Coming, Boys," "To the West," and others of our joint emigration songs had a beneficial effect on the public. They impressed on many a poor family the absurdity of clinging to a country, if that country refused them and their children bread. Hundreds, nay thousands, followed the good advice, and set out to seek their fortunes in the New World. A novel idea on the subject struck me. If simple song could do so much for the emigration scheme, how much more could be done by adding to the arts of music and poetry the art of painting, and thus illustrating to my audiences every step the emigrant takes from leaving the old country to his final settlement in the new.
>
> Mackay was charmed with the idea, and at once proposed that the entertainment should be called, "THE FAR WEST, or THE EMIGRANT'S PROGRESS FROM THE OLD WORLD TO THE NEW." We were not long in producing the words and songs, but then came the difficult part—the descriptive painting—who could we get to do it? Among my friends, I numbered several celebrated artists, and to them I applied for help. I consulted George Cattermole and David Roberts. Said the former to me, "You know Stanfield, do you not, Russell?"
>
> "Yes," I replied. "Well."
>
> "Then take my advice, and see him, he is our greatest marine painter, and besides which he is the prince of good fellows. If he cannot help you himself, he can no doubt introduce you to someone who can." Heartily thanking Cattermole for his friendly advice, I sought an interview with Stanfield. Clarkson Stanfield was a man who had risen to a very high position in his art, unaided save by his own perseverance and skill. He had commenced life as a common sailor, and to the last day of his life the bluff, honest, manly nature of the seaman formed his chief characteristic.

He received me warmly, and entered with gratifying interest into my project. "And now," said he, "my dear Russell, explain to me exactly what your ideas are." "Well," said I, "briefly, this is what I propose. The first scene consists of a view of a large emigrant ship leaving the dock at Liverpool. Upon the shores are grouped thousands of figures, the friends and relations of the outward bound emigrants, to whom they are waving their last farewells. The anchor is at the bows, and the ship is under way, the pilot is taking leave of the captain, a supposed shout goes up from those on board, "Ho! for the New World," and as the ship is leaving, a song "Farewell, a Last Farewell' is sung. The next scene depicts the ship in full sail crossing the Atlantic, and here the song is sung, "Far, Far, upon the Sea."

"Then comes the arrival at Sandy Hook and the landing of emigrants at New York. Again the scenes change rapidly to the North River, the arrival at Albany and at Buffalo, then the scene showing the emigrants taking ship up the Lakes Erie and Superior, and the arrival at Chicago. From Chicago the travellers start for the wilds of the Far West, where they purchase land at half-a-dollar an acre. Then come the scenes showing life in the Far West, and the gradual building up of the emigrants' home, the felling of the grand trees, the building of the log hut, and the cultivation of the fruitful soil. And then comes the great, the crowning scene of all. The emigrant, who left his own country poor indeed, is now the possessor of a magnificent farm; he has toiled, he has slaved, and he has saved, with one great object in view, and that is to gather around him the dear ones he has left in the old country. At last, after about three years, the long looked-for moment arrives—the money for the passage is sent, and the mothers, wives, sweethearts, and children are on their way. Then, while the song is sung, "Long parted have we been . . . ," the scene changes for the last time, and shows the happy meeting of the settlers in that land where every child is a blessing, and where "the humblest may gather the fruit of the soil.' "

"Bravo!" cried Stanfield, "I like your idea, my dear Russell, immensely, and it is a real sorrow to me that my time, which is so fully occupied, will not allow me to give you any real help to further what I hope and believe will be a most suc-

> cessful entertainment. I know, by-the-by, of an artist—a clever fellow, who, I am sure, would be good enough to follow out your ideas; and, if you like, I will give you an introduction to him—his name is Mills, and I am sure he is capable of giving you every satisfaction." Needless to say, I gladly accepted Stanfield's offer. . . .
>
> A few days later, I called on Mills, with whom I speedily came to terms, and, after a very short delay, necessary for hiring a room and buying the necessary appliances, including a huge quantity of canvas for the work, which we had agreed should be in the form of a panorama—Mills set to work. The work was commenced in a very satisfactory manner, and I was constantly with Mills, suggesting alterations, improvements, additions, and the thousand and one things that crop up in the course of time. . . . In due time the work was completed, and Stanfield accompanied me to see it, and give his judgement on the painting. This he did in a favourable manner, and then he spent some time in giving a few final touches. Shortly afterwards, I produced "THE FAR WEST, OR THE EMIGRANT'S PROGRESS FROM THE OLD WORLD TO THE NEW" to a crowded audience, and the entertainment became the most popular of its day.

Russell tells us he had met marine and landscape artist William Clarkson Stanfield (1793–1867) during the 1830s, when Edward Bulwer took him to Gore House, Kensington, home of Irish-born socialite Marguerite, Countess of Blessington (1789–1849). She was the author of *Conversations with Lord Byron* (1834), which were serialized in the *New Monthly Magazine*, which Bulwer edited, and in 1836 she had moved to Gore House as mistress of the Comte d'Orsay (1801–52). Russell records that it was also there that he met novelist and future prime minister Benjamin Disraeli (1804–81) and statesman and historian Thomas Macaulay (1800–59), novelist Harrison Ainsworth (1805–82), Dickens illustrator George Cattermole (1800–68), and David Roberts (1796–1864), famed for his Egyptian drawings. Well, maybe.

Russell returned to performing with his new entertainment in 1851, trying it out first in Richmond, Surrey: "HENRY RUSSELL (from America) will give his VOCAL and PICTORIAL ENTERTAINMENT, entitled the FAR WEST, or the Emigrant's Progress, at the Theatre Royal, Richmond, on Monday, April 7, and during the week. Morning performance, entitled Negro Life in Freedom and in Slavery, on Tuesday, April 8. Tickets to be had of Mr. Wall. Henry Russell will give his entertainment at the Theatre Royal, Olympic, on Monday, April 14, and during the week."

As will be apparent, Russell actually tried out two entertainments—*The Far West, or The Emigrant's Progress*, and *Negro Life in Freedom and in Slavery*—separately in Richmond and, then, together at the Olympic Theatre the following week. The latter week was Holy Week, when Russell was able to occupy theatres that were closed to costumed entertainment (and closed altogether on Good Friday). The *Illustrated London News* review conveys the nature of the new entertainment in greater detail:

> Among the Lenten Entertainments, that of Mr. Russell, at the Olympic Theatre, claims pre-eminence. In his fertile brain, he has conceived an entirely new kind of entertainment, not only highly suggestive in itself, but capable of being carried out to important issues. He has blended the picturesque and poetic in intimate unison; and shewn how each may be made mutually to assist the other, through the medium of music.
>
> Mr. Russell presents the public with two dioramas in one evening. The first represents, under the title of "The Far West," the emigrant's progress from the Old World to the New. While the scenes succeed each other, Mr. Russell first describes, and then illustrates them, by singing or chanting a poem written by Dr Mackay. The chief recommendation of the scenes themselves is their reality. Mr. Russell himself is their warrant that they are "transcripts from nature."
>
> Some of the poetry by Dr Mackay is exceedingly beautiful. The first piece, entitled "The Parting Tear," is touching; the second, called "Cheer, boys, cheer!" is thrilling; and the third, named "Far, far upon the sea," is telling. But having arrived at New York, the poet parts with the Old World altogether, and sends forth a joyous spirit, delighting in the present, and full of hope for the future. Aloud he singeth, like Chanticleer ushering in a new morrow:-
>
> To the west, to the west, to the land of the free,
> Where mighty Missouri rolls down to the sea,
> Where a man is a man, if he's willing to toil,
> And the humblest may gather the fruits of the soil.

> Arrived at Niagara the poet's soul is awakened, and thus, in tones of inspiration, he gives voice to her impulses. . . . The painting of the Falls of Niagara is very effective. It is followed by pictures of the emigrant's settlement in the western states, of the backwoods, of the inundation, of the rolling prairie, of the sleigh in the winter season, and of the emigrant's domestic happiness increased by the receipt of letters from dear Old England.
>
> The second diorama represents "Negro Life in Freedom and Slavery." The poetry illustrative of the scenes is written by Mr. Angus B[ethune] Reach (1821–1856) ["a member of the London press"]. Both begin with descriptions of a Negro village in the interior of Africa, where
>
> The plumed and painted savage may boast that he is free.
>
> Next, we have the slave battle, and the chase of the slave-ship; soon followed by a slave sale in Havannah [Havana], slave labour in the sugar and rice plantations, and the fugitive slave pursued by bloodhounds and riflemen. Other scenes, such as the forest on fire, the Mississippi, the planter's house, the Negro village, and the Negro-dancing festival (of which we give an Illustration), conclude the exhibition . . .

For both entertainments a booklet was published, containing the song texts, details of the scenes, and a substantial text on the subject—presumably more detailed than what Russell actually spoke. For *The Emigrant's Progress*, the thirty-two-page booklet even gave such detailed information as the provisions that would-be emigrants should take with them: "A party of four persons should provision themselves as follows:- 16 or 18 pecks of potatoes, in a barrel with a cork in it; 40 lbs good beef, well salted in brine; 16lbs. of butter; 3 lbs. of coffee; 3 or 4 dozen old bottled beer; . . ." and so on. The booklet listed fourteen scenes, including eleven after landing in America, viz. New York; The North River; The Genesee Aqueduct; The Rapids in the Niagara; The Falls of Niagara; The Settlement; The Backwoods; The Inundation; The Rolling Prairies; The Sleigh; and Letters from Home.

The format provided Russell with the opportunity to slip in new songs, which he duly did over the six or seven years that he would continue to perform *The Far West*, with great success, in London and the provinces. The standout song was without any doubt "Cheer! Boys, Cheer!" This "anthem of optimism"—a description Russell attributed to *The Daily Telegraph*—was designed as a declaration of patriotic fervor by

Figure 14.5. "The Slave Sale" sheet music cover. *Source:* Author's collection.

emigrants leaving their native land for America; but fate was to decree that, in Russell's own words, it "infused hope and courage in the breasts of our soldiers when they listened to its inspiring strains while embarking

Figure 14.6. "Cheer Boys, Cheer!" sheet music cover. *Source:* Author's collection.

for the Crimean War." That War followed in 1854, and the song's morale-boosting content made it the best known of Russell's songs in Britain for the rest of the nineteenth century. Charles Hamm has described the typically elaborate piano introduction as resembling several of Bellini's marches, though the melody scarcely takes off in the way that one of Bellini's might. Moreover, though its main melodic phrase is appropriately direct for a patriotic chant, it is above all the words (and the timing in relation to the Crimean War) that was to determine the song's durability.

15

To Law Again

Following his week at the Olympic Theatre in April 1851, Russell resumed touring with his new scenic entertainment, into which the old favorite songs were inevitably thrown in. He began by taking it to such London outposts as Woolwich, Kennington, and Peckham, and then went increasingly further afield. The need to transport the panoramic effects inevitably brought extra problems. At the end of January 1852, he was at the Concert Hall in Liverpool. However, his planned opening at the Music Hall, Dublin, was hit by the weather: "Owing to the steamer which contained his Panorama being obliged from stress of weather to put into Plymouth, he was compelled to postpone his opening night from Monday till Wednesday, on which evening the attendance was full and fashionable."

Even without any contribution from the elements, Russell's use of the panorama meant that his entertainment did not always achieve the ultimate in professionalism:

> Mr. Russell's delivery of "The Maniac" always worked a spell upon his listeners; yet once, in singing this song, a drunken fellow who was at work on top of the panorama missed his footing, fell on the stage, and rolled unharmed to the footlights, amid a scene of dismay and merriment no singing could control. The manipulation of the panorama, too, was sometimes troublesome. On more than one occasion Mr. Russell has stood with his back to the scene (as was his custom), pointing out to an attentive audience the solemn and splendid effect of the Falls of Niagara, when, had he looked at the picture he was

> describing, he would have observed it to represent the interior of a log-hut or negroes dancing in a plantation.

By September 1852, Russell and his entertainment were back at the Lyceum Theatre, London, for a whole three weeks, with more and more of the old favorites included:

> HENRY RUSSELL (TO-NIGHT, Lyceum Theatre). Composer of "Woodman, Spare that Tree," "I'm Afloat," "The Maniac," &c., will give his AMERICAN ENTERTAINMENT, entitled "The Far West, or the Emigrant's Progress from the Old World to the New," and "Negro Life in Freedom and in Slavery," every night during the week, at the above theatre. Whilst the painting is passing, portraying some of the principal cities, the rivers, forests, and prairies of the north, south, and western portions of America, Mr. Russell will describe the country, relate anecdotes and his adventures, and will sing the following new songs, his latest compositions:- "The parting tear"; "Cheer boys, cheer, no more of idle sorrow"; "To the west, to the west, to the land of the free"; "Gaily goes the ship when the wind blows fair"; "The Falls of Niagara"; "The African Village"; "The Chase"; "Come who Bids?" and on each evening Mr. Russell will sing one or two from his favourite compositions:- "Life on the Ocean Wave"; "The Gambler's Wife"; "The Ivy Green"; "The Maniac"; "The Newfoundland Dog"; &c. Tickets and places to be had at the box-office, from 11 to 4 each day. Doors open at half-past 7, to commence at 8. Dress boxes 2s 6d., upper ditto 1s. 6d., pit 1s., gallery 6d.; private boxes £1 1s. and 10s.

With his new entertainment established, Russell sought to vary it further with an extension of the emigration idea. Thus, his five nights at Liverpool's Concert Hall, Lord Nelson Street, from 21 to 25 February 1853 were advertised as "GRAND PRIZE NIGHTS!!" We are today accustomed to opportunities to win free holidays (i.e., return passages); but in those days the passages were one-way:

> Each person, on entering the hall on any of the above evenings, will receive a Ticket which will entitle him or her to a chance of obtaining

A FREE PASSAGE TO AUSTRALIA,

in Messrs Gibbs, Bright, and Co.'s Eagle Line of Packet-ship FALCON, 1730 tons burthen, or other first-class vessel, to sail in April next for Port Phillip. A Free Ticket will be drawn for on each evening; and as the Tickets have been secured at the Merchants, and are now in the possession of Mr. John Calderwood, the Secretary at the Concert-hall, the Prize will, each evening, be handed over to the winner, in the presence of the audience.

The DRAWING will take place each evening after MR. RUSSELL has concluded his Entertainment. Duplicates of every Ticket issued will be placed in a basket, and a person from the audience will be selected to draw the numbers. In order to save time, the holder of the duplicate of the SEVENTH Ticket drawn will be the winner, and a Ticket for a Passage to Australia will be handed to him. Of course, this Ticket is transferable, and may afterwards be used by the winner, given away, or sold.

To prevent confusion, the audience on each evening will be limited, and the doors of the Concert-hall will be closed precisely at Nine o'clock.

Remember!

A TRANSFERABLE TICKET,

Entitling the holder to

A FREE PASSAGE TO AUSTRALIA,

will be given as a

PRIZE EACH NIGHT!

One might wonder whether even more time might have been saved by declaring the first ticket drawn the winner. One might also wonder at the relevance of a ticket to Australia for an entertainment focused on America. However, Australia was then very much in vogue. It was as recently as 1851 that gold discoveries in both Australia and California were made public, prompting gold rushes on two continents. Henry Russell's cousin, George, had set off for Australia and New Zealand after marrying somewhat belatedly in 1850, and his two children were born in Sydney and Auckland.

The offer of free passages clearly helped sell admission tickets, and it undeniably produced satisfied customers. Russell tells of entering a news vendor's shop many years later and being recognized by the woman sitting behind the counter:

> The woman then rose from her seat and, clasping her hands, burst into tears. It appeared that many years previously the good lady and her husband were living in the direst poverty at Liverpool. Attending one of Mr. Russell's entertainments, the man obtained one of the free passes and kits and, in company with his wife, emigrated to Australia. Here they entered upon a small business, in which they were so prosperous that they ultimately returned in a comfortable position to spend their remaining days in England. This is but one of many similar cases that might be recorded and, as a token of their gratitude for what had been done for their fellows in this direction, the working men of Liverpool raised a subscription for the painting of Mr. Russell's portrait . . .

When Russell gave his entertainment at London's Strand Theatre the following month, March 1853, it was, instead, a free passage to America that was on offer. There were, indeed, continuing factors to stimulate interest in both America and Australia. The former included the appearance of Harriet Beecher Stowe's *Uncle Tom's Cabin, or Life Among the Lowly*. Published from 5 June 1851, in weekly installments, in the abolitionist *Washington National Era*, it then appeared in 1852 in book form and became an instant bestseller in America and elsewhere. Not only the anti-slavery cause but also the story's appeal and, perhaps more particularly, the popularity it aroused, made it ideal for Russell's purposes, and Charles Sheard's cheap *Musical Bouquet* series brought out several Russell compositions specifically on the subject. Besides the *Uncle Tom's Cabin Quadrilles*, there was the set of songs "Eva's Farewell," "Eliza, the Slave Mother," "Poor Uncle Tom," and "Little Topsy's Song," all with words by Eliza Cook.

Figure 15.1. "Eva's Farewell" sheet music cover. *Source:* Author's collection.

In September 1853, Russell was once more back at London's Lyceum Theatre for what was announced as "a FINAL and FAREWELL SERIES of his ENTERTAINMENT entitled 'The Far West; or the Progress of the

Emigrant.' " *The Illustrated London News* was still able to report that "The house has been crowded to overflowing night after night. We are pleased to see that, notwithstanding the multiplicity of candidates for public favour, Mr. Russell retains his popularity unimpaired. . . ." He was able to extend his Lyceum season to a full four weeks, drawing in the crowds to the very end:

> On the occasion of the last performance of Mr. Henry Russell's entertainment at the Lyceum Theatre, on Saturday night, he came forward after the conclusion of the first part, and informed the house, which was crowded to excess in every part, even to the passages and lobbies, that it was his intention, although it had not been publicly announced, to make them a little present, as some acknowledgment for the great patronage bestowed on him, which should, at the choice of the audience, be either one free passage to Australia or three free passages to America. The verdict having been given in favour of the latter, the prizes were awarded to the full satisfaction of the audience, at the close of the performance, to three working men occupying seats in the pit and gallery, one of whom, a carpenter, is at present at work at the new Crystal Palace at Sydenham.

Even after all these years, this season produced from *The Times* one of the best contemporary descriptions of the nature and appeal of Russell's performances:

> Few of the various "givers of entertainments" have attained a more solid popularity than Mr. Henry Russell. His songs, perhaps, are not greatly sought by the musical connoisseur, but he is especially the songster of the masses, differing from other popular favourites that he not only makes his audiences laugh, but also makes them cry. The fact that his most celebrated songs have found their way to the whistling street boy and the barrel organ, so that there is hardly a soul in London who is not acquainted with "Cheer! boys, cheer!" and "A life on the ocean wave" proves his ability in the composition of "taking" tunes, but it is to his peculiar application of this faculty that he owes a great deal of his celebrity. Seizing on subjects that are most prominent in the minds of the multitude, he illustrates them

by his music, and the audience are not so much applauding a musical artist as a popular orator, who thinks and speaks in song. Emigration is *par excellence* the theme of the day, and there are few families that are not more or less interested in its vicissitudes. Mr. Russell, therefore, has made himself essentially the minstrel of emigration, and there is scarcely a sentiment connected with the topic which does not receive illustration at his hands. The emigrant's lingering fondness for his mother country, his sanguine hopes, the excitement of first crossing the Atlantic, the joy consequent on the receipt of letters from home—have each their characteristic songs, and, though these may not greatly appeal to the *blasé* man of fashion, they have a strong practical interest for thousands of persons all over the kingdom. As a singer, Mr. Russell is exactly what is wanted for the purpose. He can give a song effectively and eloquently, and, what in his particular case is all important, his words are always intelligible. . . .

To appreciate the impression which Mr. Russell makes on his public, it is necessary to be present at the end of the first part of his entertainment, which is illustrative of emigration only. Starting with the "Cheer boys, cheer!" which has signalized the emigrant's departure from his native land, he has conveyed him to New York, taken him into the "Far West," and, after a rough mishap or two, has comfortably settled him down in his new country, and now proposes to sing "Cheer! boys, cheer!" once again, requesting his audience to join in as chorus. The auditors are but too glad to answer the summons, and, at the wave of Mr. Russell's hand, the hearty peal that bursts forth from boxes, pit, and gallery produces the most singular effect possible. It is hard to say whether it is ludicrous or affecting.

The pictures with which Mr. Russell illustrates his "Emigrant's progress" and his "Negro life" are rather sources of information than works of art; but there is one talent which, besides that of singing, he possesses to an eminent degree; he is an excellent storyteller. His tales of nigger eccentricity, though not always of the newest, produce roars of laughter, and yet they are told without any unpleasant straining after effect. Edifying, also, is it to hear him come forward now and then as a moral counseller, and point out to his congregation

> the road of virtue and happiness. His remarks in this spirit do not throw much new light on ethical science, but there is about them a homely truth and a fitness to English notions of right and wrong, which secure for them the hearty assent of an unsophisticated multitude.

It's just possible that the twenty-four nights at the Lyceum Theatre really were intended as a "farewell and final series" in London. Certainly, they were followed during October and November by similar "farewell" evenings at Windsor, Reading, and onward through Worcester, Bradford, Sheffield, and elsewhere. However, Henry Russell was not yet *quite* ready to retire. In late August 1854, he was back in London with *The Emigrant's Progress* and *Negro Life* once more, declaring that his appearance at the Lyceum Theatre was "in accordance with the expressed wish of many friends . . . previously to withdrawing his Entertainment." "To Lyceum in evening," recorded his sometime collaborator E. L. Blanchard in his diary on the first night. "Henry Russell as of yore."

That this was a full thirty-night season, from 28 August to 30 September, proved that Russell was still heavily in demand. What is more, he introduced a substantial body of new songs, among them "The Icebergs" and "The Canadian Sleigh Song." He was in London yet again in December 1854 at the Victoria Theatre, and then in March 1856 at the Surrey Theatre. On the latter occasion, one may note, he was accompanying himself not on a Kirkman piano but on "Collard and Collard's magnificent Bi-chord Pianoforte, made expressly for him by that eminent firm."

Yet, for all his return appearances to satisfy a loyal clientele, Russell's hold on the public was, inevitably, beginning to fade as newer performers came onto the scene. One solo performer of particular relevance who briefly came onto the scene in the 1850s was a certain Harry Lee Carter (1824–62). Late of the Seventh Fusiliers, he had begun in army theatricals before becoming Secretary at London's Her Majesty's Theatre. There, he had been responsible for an ambitious series of Grand National Concerts in the autumn of 1850, with William Balfe as conductor. It was, as Benjamin Lumley reported, an enterprise that "seemed destined to achieve great things. . . . Yet never was failure more signal."

It was evidently that same Harry Lee Carter—with names transposed—who then teamed up with writer Alfred Crowquill (Alfred Henry Forrester, 1804–72) for an entertainment in June 1852 entitled "Carter Lee's Sketches and Crowquill's Scratches." According to *The Times*, this "enables

Mr. Carter Lee to play upon the flute (very skilfully), the concertina (tolerably), the violin (enough for a joke), and the piano (sufficiently well to accompany himself). Mr. Carter Lee also sings comic songs. . . . The next year, having reverted to his original styling, Lee Carter announced 'an entirely new panoramic and musical entertainment, entitled *The Two Lands of Gold; or, The Australian and Californian Directory for 1853*.' "

This entertainment was advertised as being profusely illustrated, with vocal music by Henry Russell, sketches by George Catlin, a panorama by C. S. James, and a lecture by Shirley Brooks and Harry Lee Carter. It was first produced on 11 April 1853 at the Royal Marionette Theatre, Adelaide Street, Strand. Russell's song contributions (to Lee Carter's words) included "Pull Away Cheerily!" (The Gold Diggers' Song), "Fresh Blows the Breeze," and "Welcome Home!" The entertainment lasted eight weeks until Carter announced that "in consequence of ill health his medical advisers have recommended the DISCONTINUANCE of his ENTERTAINMENT for a short time."

Among other entertainments that were now taking a bit of the focus away from Henry Russell there was also one much nearer home, for there were other, younger, Russells taking to the concert boards. During October and November 1853, the press announced various engagements of "The Russell Family" in such places as Hammersmith, Kensington, Croydon, and Peckham. None had finer backing than one advertised thus in *The Times*:

> THE RUSSELL FAMILY.—Under the immediate patronage of Sir Anthony de Rothschild, Baron Lionel, M. P., and Baron Meyer de Rothschild. - The RUSSELL FAMILY, nieces of Henry Russell, the celebrated composer, respectfully inform the nobility, gentry, and public they will have the honour of giving their GRAND MUSICAL ENTERTAINMENT, To-morrow, November 10th, 1853, at the Marylebone Institution, 17 Edwards-street, Portman-square. Stalls, 3s.; family tickets for four, 10s. 6d.; reserved seats, 2s.; unreserved 1s; to be had of all the principal music-sellers, and of Miss Russell, 53, Upper Charlotte-street, Fitzroy-square. Commence at 8.

The patronage could hardly have been more prestigious, comprising as it did three brothers from the most influential Jewish banking family in Britain: Baron Lionel de Rothschild (1808–79), Britain's first Jewish MP; Sir Anthony de Rothschild (1810–76); and Baron Meyer de Rothschild

(1818–74). 53 Upper Charlotte Street was at that time Israel Russell's family home, and "the Russell family" performers comprised three of Israel's six daughters, namely twenty-five-year-old Annette, eighteen-year-old Maria, and sixteen-year-old Charlotte. Charlotte's offerings included "Coming through the Rye," her contralto sister Maria sang the Brindisi from *Lucrezia Borgia* and her uncle's "The Old Arm Chair," and Annette was joined in a duet from *Lucia di Lammermoor* by Signor Onorati, who (*The Era* complained) "sang painfully flat nearly all through."

Encumbered or not by Signor Onorati, the three sisters continued their concert-giving, their engagements including one at Sussex Hall on 26 November. Moreover, for performances at the Royal Pavilion, Brighton, in January 1854, they were joined by their nineteen-year-old brother. Though given the first names of Simon Henry, he preferred to be known as George Henry Russell. He had already appeared separately that month at the Theatre Royal, Canterbury, in another entertainment based on the gold discoveries in Australia and California. As announced in *The Era*, "Mr. George Payne has taken . . . for twelve nights for his entertainment, entitled 'A Tour through Australia and California,' in which Mr. George Russell (nephew of the celebrated composer, Henry Russell), will sing the whole of that gentleman's popular songs."

Perhaps not quite the whole of them! The reference was doubtless to the songs "Pull Away Cheerily!" (The Gold Digger's Song), "Fresh Blows the Breeze," and "Welcome Home!," which Henry Russell had composed for Harry Lee Carter's similarly titled entertainment, and which George Payne had now taken over. During 1853, Payne had toured his entertainment around south-east England with a singer billed as George Henry Wilson. Was this, perhaps, already George Henry Russell, seeking to establish himself without trading on his uncle's name?

After George Henry joined up with his three sisters, the four siblings continued together for some months. On 20 February 1854, assisted by tenor George Perren and Signor Pietro Onorati ("a respectable mediocrity of the modern Italian school"), they were at the Hanover Square Rooms, with Julius Benedict as conductor. Their engagements continued at least into April 1854, and Henry Russell evidently contributed further songs for his nieces and nephew to sing. For Maria, he adapted his 1834 collaboration with Letitia Elizabeth Landon, "The Orphan Ballad Singers," and for George Henry he composed "Sir Harold the Hunter," to words by Eliza Cook and dedicated to the Society of Foresters.

Either the novelty of the siblings soon wore off, or their personal commitments took over. Annette was already a wife and mother and, thereafter, disappears from view. Maria, too, gave up performing, and, after her 1857 marriage to merchant Frederick Manasseh Brandon (1832–1900), lived for many years in Brazil, where their children were born. The Brandons retained theatrical connections through their nieces "Florence West" (1862–1912), who married actor Lewis Waller (1860–1915), and Margaret Brandon, who married critic Clement Scott (1841–1904). A granddaughter, Muriel Lemon, would marry Nevill Wyatt (1889–1933), son of actor Frank Wyatt (1852–1926) and theatre manager Violet Melnotte (1855–1935).

Of the nieces of Henry Russell, Charlotte (c. 1837–1901) was to have by far the most significant career, becoming, from 1857, principal soprano at London's Canterbury Music Hall ("The Queen of the Music Halls"), under Charles Morton (1819–1904). In 1862, she married Morton's brother and biographer William Henry Morton, though the marriage didn't last and Charlotte became the partner of George Frederick Jeffreys, son of the lyricist and publisher Charles Jeffreys. During the 1860s she was leading soprano at the Oxford Music Hall. George Henry Russell continued for some time singing the songs of his uncle as well as some of his own, even traveling to America to do so, before, eventually, he took over his father's antique business.

Of all the entertainers who sought to follow in Henry Russell's wake, the most directly imitative—and the most persistent—remained, even in the early 1850s, Henry Smith. In 1851, as Henry Russell was about to take *The Emigrant's Progress* and *Negro Life* outside London, matters once more came to a head in the still ongoing battle between the two. Back from America, Smith announced an entertainment at the National Hall, 242 Holborn, for 21 May 1851. His announcements proclaimed that, "having come to a friendly and amicable arrangement with Mr. Henry Russell, he has full permission to sing his celebrated songs, ballads, descriptive scenas, etc." Russell, though, saw matters differently. It seems that Smith had merely approached Russell's publisher G. H. Davidson, which was not at all the same thing.

Russell took immediate action, forcing Smith to appear once more in the Insolvent Debtors' Court on 28 May. In a move for a protecting order, it was reported that ". . . the insolvent, since his last hearing, had been to America, whence he had recently returned. Having obtained authority from Mr. Davidson, to whom Mr. Russell had transferred the property of the songs in dispute, to sing those compositions, the insolvent was advertised to appear at the National Hall, but was prevented by being arrested at Mr. Russell's suit. . . ." What now proved significant was the second judgment for damages that Russell had taken out in November 1848. On this Smith was taken into custody as a debtor, and he was destined to remain in Whitecross Street Prison for the remainder of 1851. Thereafter, Smith at least tried to do something different, but it did him little good with the critics. When he opened with a new vocal and pictorial entertainment at the St. James's Theatre in November 1852, *The Era* took him to pieces unmercifully:

> Mr. Henry Smith reminds us of one who, seeing the success of another, has set up in his line without the necessary qualifications. He delivers a sort of lecture, something after the style common to public speakers at fairs, and with about as much regard for Lindley Murray as those polite orators usually display. It is painful to listen to him, considering that he has engaged the St James's Theatre for his performance. His text (by which it is scarcely possible that he speaks, so faulty are his sentences) abounds with miserable jokes—as big, unpalateable [sic] force-meat balls sometimes lie in weak soup, and *don't* go down with the fluid. In these disjointed remarks he tells you a great deal about Australia—just what you may have gathered from the papers, and, it may be, something more. This information he is supposed to have received from different friends, whose communications he reads, and their struggles to be funny are tremendous. A little pruning of bad puns and extravagant jokes would render these communications acceptable to many who take an interest in the gold regions of Australia, but their delivery must be improved upon. Interspersed are various characteristic songs, and, to do Mr. Smith justice, he sings much better than he speaks. He possesses a deep and manly voice, and one or two of his vocal contributions had considerable merit about them, particularly that describing the shifts which people have been put to through the scarcity of labour. The piano performances we most unreservedly condemn—they were execrable and unworthy a boarding-school beginner, so far as correctness went. His fault seems to be no want of power of execution, but a want of acquaintance with the music he affects to play.

It should perhaps be explained that Lindley Murray (1745–1826) was the author of textbooks on grammar that were long standard in American and British schools.

For Smith the bubble may have sprung, at last, a leak. When he appeared in the Assembly Rooms, Stamford, Lincolnshire, on 23 December 1853, *The Era* reported that "the attendance was very limited," adding, in case anyone was still unfamiliar with the nature of Smith's entertainment: "The programme showed that Mr. S had freely availed himself of Mr. Henry Russell's compositions." Yet Smith was nothing if not determined. When Henry Russell presented *The Emigrant's Progress* in Woolwich, Deptford, Croydon, and Peckham in the first week of February 1854, Smith was presenting "his new VOCAL and PICTORIAL AUSTRALIAN ENTERTAINMENT" at the Hungerford Hall in the Strand.

Russell was not the only entertainer who felt he was being ripped off. A notice in *The Era* of 2 April 1854 demonstrates that Russell's legal action of the 1840s had established that legal action could most effectively be focused on proprietors of the premises at which songs were being sung without authorization:

> CAUTION TO VOCAL PIRATES.—CHARLES SLOMAN, the only English Improvisatore and Vocalist, at Evans's Grand Hotel, Covent-garden, hereby cautions Vocalists and Proprietors against singing, or permitting to be sung (without his written permission), any of his original Songs, as he has instructed his "Legal Agent" to issue immediate process against all parties so offending. That there may be no doubt as to the law on the subject, Charles Sloman begs to refer proprietors to the case of "Henry Russell versus Bryant," of the Horns Tavern, Kennington.

It was the proprietors of premises who were targeted also by W. S. Woodin, the one-time Russell burlesquer now famous for his "Carpet-Bag and Sketch-Book" entertainment. He inserted this notice in *The Era* of 7 May 1854: "PIRACY!—CAUTION!—WOODIN'S CARPET BAG AND SKETCH BOOK. WHEREAS certain unprincipled Persons are illegally giving an Entertainment under the above tile, all Proprietors of Concert Rooms, Halls, and Secretaries of Public Institutions are hereby cautioned against letting the same for the purpose of representing this spurious Entertainment. And all Persons thus infringing Mr. W S WOODIN'S rights, and thereby imposing upon the Public, will be prosecuted with the utmost rigour of the law."

Such efforts to limit performance were not, of course, in the interests of the publishers of the songs, though it was evidently for different reasons that ill-feeling had arisen between Henry Russell—for whom controversy was never far away—and G. H. Davidson, publisher of *The Musical Treasury*. It was, indeed, one manifestation of this ill-feeling that had led to Henry Smith's detention in a debtor's jail during much of 1851. Another could be found in a notice in the very next column to Woodin's announcement just quoted:

> HENRY RUSSELL'S COMPOSITIONS. Many Vocalists being restrained from singing these songs on account of the Composer's prosecution of Henry Smith, G. H. DAVIDSON, of PETER'S-HILL, LONDON, the Publisher, hereby gives notice that he is the Owner of the Right of Representation of all the Copyrights in his Catalogue, and he is willing to grant Licenses to all respectable Professionals. He also begs to be apprised of any threats or intimidations that may be resorted to by Henry Russell or his Agents in reference thereto. G H Davidson has several Entertainments constructed on these popular songs, the use of which may be had on eligible terms.

Russell and Davidson had worked closely together during the 1840s. Davidson had published cheap editions of over fifty Russell songs in his *Musical Treasury* in 1845–46, and he had then made them available in a collected edition with a portrait and a highly flattering biographical notice that has previously been quoted. Cheap editions of further songs followed during the rest of the 1840s, including original editions of some new songs. However, according to a handout that Davidson subsequently inserted into one of his *Musical Treasury* issues, differences between composer and publisher arose from a deed dated 25 May 1850. This provided that "Henry Russell for a large pecuniary consideration . . . assigned to G H Davidson all and every Copyright in his Compositions not previously assigned to any other Publisher."

It seems that problems arose over just which compositions were covered by this deed—hardly surprising in view of the complicated publication history and reuse of so many Russell song compositions. In the handout just referred to, Davidson went on to quote the following declaration by one William Wills Taylor:

> . . . on the evening of Saturday, April 19th, 1851, I had an Interview with Mr. Henry Russell at the Olympic Theatre, on the Subject of the various Copyrights, claimed as the Property of Others, which he had sold to Mr. G H Davidson; at which Interview Mr. Russell deputed me to offer his then new Songs [from *The Emigrant's Progress* and *Negro Life*] to Mr. Davidson; and that I afterwards communicated to him Mr. Davidson's Reply to the effect, that he had determined to have no further dealings with him, till his Claims on prior transactions were satisfied.

Cut off by Davidson, Russell came to an arrangement for the publication of cheap editions of his works with the major rival to Davidson's *Musical Treasury*: Charles Sheard's *Musical Bouquet*. Cheap editions of the *Emigrant's Progress* and *Negro Life* songs in the *Musical Bouquet* would quickly be among the best-selling editions of any Russell songs in Britain. Sheard's advertisements for the songs came with a disclaimer from Henry Russell: "As I have, long since, ceased to have any connexion with Davidson's Musical Treasury, it is my intention to have all cheap editions of all my future compositions published exclusively in the Musical Bouquet."

Connection or no between the two, Davidson would continue to include Russell's evidently highly marketable songs in *The Musical Treasury*. Whether these were those that had been obtained under preexisting agreements, or taken over by arrangements with other publishers, or even by fitting new words to music to which Davidson already held the rights, it hardly eased the animosity between Russell and Davidson, which would surface in various court cases over the next year or two.

First there was sniping between Webb, the original publisher of the *Emigrant's Progress* songs, and Sheard, who had then published the cheap editions. On 21 March 1854 the Vice-Chancellors' Court heard the case of Sheard v. Webb, in which Sheard sought to restrain Webb's sales of the eight songs "Cheer! Boys, Cheer!," "Land, Land, Land," "The Parting Tear," "Far, Far upon the Sea," "To the West, to the West," "The Chase," "The Negro [or African] Village," and "The Slave, or Come, Who Bids?" It was reported that Russell had composed the songs in 1850 for *The Emigrant's Progress*, and the defendant (Webb) had bought the words and music for 100 guineas and then marketed the songs at 2s each. In view of their success, on 13 September 1852 the plaintiff (Sheard) had

Figure 15.2. “Rouse, Brothers, Rouse” sheet music cover. *Source:* Author’s collection.

paid Webb 65 guineas for the exclusive right to publish the eight songs in his *Musical Bouquet* series. However, notwithstanding this exclusive agreement, Webb had permitted other cheap editions of the songs—evidently, in *The Musical Treasury*. The Vice-Chancellor declared that Sheard had equally breached the agreement by permitting yet another publisher to issue arrangements for flute, and by failing to include in *The Musical Bouquet* references to Webb's pianofortes and harmoniums. He therefore disapproved of the conduct of both defendant and plaintiff and dismissed the motion without awarding costs.

The skirmish with Webb resurfaced in the Court of Common Pleas at London's Guildhall on 2 July 1854, when Russell was called upon to testify:

> Mr. Davison [sic], a publisher of cheap music, publishes the *Musical Treasury*. It appeared that Mr. Russell was present at the making of the agreement between the plaintiff [Sheard] and defendant [Webb], and, having discovered that some of the songs above mentioned had been published in the *Musical Treasury*, called on the defendant, to remonstrate with him for allowing it. Mr. Russell was called for the plaintiff, and his evidence was that the defendant, upon his (Mr. Russell's) remonstrating with him, said that he regretted it very much; he would do his best to recall what had been done; he had unfortunately entered into an agreement with Mr. Davison to allow him to print 5,000 copies in a cheap form, and how was he to get out of it?

Further evidence suggested that Webb and Davidson had connived to undermine the agreement with Sheard, and the Lord Chief Justice consequently declared in favor of the plaintiff. It was further arranged that unsold copies of the songs should be given up to Sheard, that the printing plates should be destroyed, and that Webb should pay Sheard £50.

Within a mere four days of that case, judgment was given on yet another manifestation of the squabble. This time the case was tried in Edinburgh, perhaps to take advantage of differences between English and Scottish law. The case revolved around an edition of the Henry Russell/Eliza Cook song "The Old Arm Chair," which had appeared in Sheard's *Musical Bouquet*. Proceedings were directed not at Sheard himself but at a Glasgow bookseller, Morrison Kyle, for selling the allegedly illegal edition. Though Davidson had clearly instigated the case, the actual plaintiff was the publisher Charles Jefferys, who, in May 1841, had bought the copyright of the words of "The Old Arm Chair" from Eliza Cook in connection not with Russell's setting, but with one by James Hine. Davidson testified to Eliza Cook confirming Jefferys's ownership of the copyright of the words, which Davidson was publishing in the *Musical Treasury* by agreement with Jefferys. The suggestion was that, in publishing the song in his *Musical Bouquet*, Sheard was taking advantage of Eliza Cook's ill health and reclusive lifestyle and thus her reluctance to complain about the infringement of copyright.

Judgment was pronounced, in favor of Jefferys, in Edinburgh on 6 July 1854, and Davidson took great delight in publishing details in the insert already quoted that appeared in his edition of Eliza Cook's "Song of the Day." There was clearly a great deal of money resting on this *Musical Bouquet* edition of "The Old Arm Chair," though, and this was far from the end of even this branch of the Russell/Davidson joust. Morrison Kyle, or whoever pulled his strings, appealed, on the grounds that no deed of assignment of copyright, duly attested by two witnesses, had been produced, and that the 1841 receipt was insufficient conveyance of copyright. The decision was sufficient to ensure the case between Jefferys and Kyle going to court for a third time, on 24 July 1855, when a jury unanimously found for Jefferys, thereby establishing his claim of copyright. Yet even that was not the end of this particular saga, which was destined not just to run and run, but to run all the way. On 27 June 1859, the decision of the First Division of the Court of Session for Scotland finally made it to the House of Lords in London. The old arguments were trotted out, but their Lordships seem to have wasted little time dismissing the Morrison Kyle appeal, with costs.

The squabble between Davidson and Sheard also showed up in commercial channels. In 1854, Davidson published *Davidson's Temperance Melodist*, a collection of temperance songs. Several of its items were settings of new words to existing Russell melodies, as, for instance, "The Temperance Tree" to the music of "The Ivy Green," and "Old King Coal" [sic; the subject being the fireside] to the music of "Tubal Cain," a song published originally by Charles Jefferys. Russell had, obviously, had no involvement whatsoever in this reuse of his music.

That point, indeed, was confirmed with one further piece of competition between Davidson and Sheard. Early in 1856 both publishers brought out a collection of *One Hundred Songs by Henry Russell*. Both were cheap and compact albums, containing just the vocal line of the music and sometimes more than one set of words for each piece. That Sheard's *Musical Bouquet* album was the authorized edition is clear from another letter to Sheard, dated January 1856, and printed inside the volume above Russell's signature. In it, Russell denounced "spurious and imperfect editions of Songs pretending to be mine, and including many which have been most unconscientiously altered and adapted without my consent." He declared that Sheard's was "the only complete and authentic Edition, and the only one which has my sanction."

16

Retirement

By 1856, Russell had moved house from the docks area of Boulogne-sur-Mer, where his youngest son was born in 1849, to an old castle, the Château Lettsom (once the home of the celebrated doctor of that name), at the top of the rue de Maquétra in the Saint-Martin district—high above Boulogne-sur-Mer and its historic Haute-Ville. *The Era* reported an entertainment at the château on 24 July 1856, got up by the "younger branches of his family." It began with a series of conjuring tricks. Then came the farce *Fish out of Water* with a cast including Miss Russell (presumably daughter Isabella) and Mr. H. Russell (presumably Henry Lloyd Russell), after which it concluded with J. Madison Morton's farce *Box and Cox*, with the same Mr. H. Russell as Mrs. Bouncer.

Presumably Henry Russell was present on that evening. But during the holiday month of August 1856, he was touring through Ramsgate (three evenings), Dover, Folkestone, Cheltenham, Tunbridge Wells, Hastings, Battle, Lewes, Brighton (two evenings), Worthing, Chichester, Portsea, Southampton, and the Isle of Wight (Cowes, Newport, and Ryde). Then came Winchester, Romsey, Salisbury, Gloucester, and engagements farther afield continuing into the autumn. However, a visit to Yorkshire and Lancashire, in November and December 1856, was momentarily upset by a collision on the Manchester, Sheffield, and Lincolnshire Railway:

> On Tuesday an accident of a rather serious nature took place on the Barnsley branch of the railway at the junction about a mile from Pennystone [sic]. The 10.25am train from Barnsley to Penistone on arriving at the junction, instead of passing on to

Figure 16.1. Villa Marquérta, Russell's home in Boulogne-sur-Mer. *Source:* Author's collection.

> the main line was in consequence of the points being left open driven into the siding, where there were several loaded coal waggons, into which it ran with great violence, smashing the foremost one to atoms and doing great damage to the others as well as to the engine and carriages. Several of the passengers, as well as the guard and fireman, were severely injured. Amongst the former was Mr. Henry Russell, the celebrated vocalist, who received a contusion on the forehead . . . The damage done to the engine, carriages and waggons is estimated at nearly £1,000.

In spite of newspaper cries of "almost killed," the "damage" to Russell (a bump on the forehead!) was soon repaired; but one could understand if incidents of this type were making traveling increasingly irksome. For his week of appearances at the Free-Trade Hall, Manchester, it was stressed that "Mr. Russell respectfully intimates to the public that this is the farewell representation of his present entertainment." There were other kinds of irritations, too. Following appearances at various halls in London, in January 1857, and before enjoying the usual overflowing attendance in

Birmingham in February, his Yorkshire engagements were hit by a piece of opportunism at the Theatre Royal, Huddersfield, on 17 February:

> For several days previous to last Tuesday the town was posted with large and small bills, announcing that Mr. Henry Russell would give his vocal and musical entertainment on that evening in the theatre. As is usual on this gentleman's visits to the town, crowds flocked to the place of entertainment, and hundreds gained admission long before the time for commencement, no doubt in lively anticipation of enjoying the treat which is generally afforded by Mr. Russell's anecdotes, &c. After waiting for a considerable time, amidst whistling and shouting, and repeated calls for a beginning, the patience of the audience was entirely wearied, and one individual, more courageous than any other, and determined if possible to ascertain the real cause of delay, made his way to the stage, and drew up the front scene, when it was manifest that the announcement was a hoax, as neither Mr. Russell, piano, panorama, nor anything else appertaining to a journey to the "Far West" was visible. A portion of the gallery gods immediately rushed upon the stage, and commenced a crusade against the scenery, &c., several of which were speedily rendered totally unfit for future use; some of the seats were also broken. Mr. Mosley, the lessee, will thereby be a sufferer to some extent, although ignorant that the affair had been announced. About ten minutes prior to the stated commencement of the concert, the scoundrels got clear away with a booty of between £20 and £30, before suspicion was aroused; but it is to be hoped, that ere the practice is ripened, the perpetrators will be lodged in a place of safety, as an example for swindlers, as such proceedings cannot but tend to injure the high reputation attained by gentlemen like Mr. Henry Russell.

It was not only Russell's reputation that was affected, but also his attendances and, thus, his takings elsewhere in Yorkshire. "Our readers will be grieved to learn," *The Era*'s Bradford correspondent declared, "that the Huddersfield hoax has seriously affected the patronage heretofore liberally awarded by our manufacturers to Mr. H Russell's entertainments, very moderate houses only being brought together to listen to the entertainer's own world-known compositions."

Still, Russell was back on the platform in London in 1857 for Holy Week (6–11 April)—this time at the Princess's Theatre. *The Era* once more reported audiences that were "large and enthusiastic," adding that they "seemed to take as much interest in his entertainment as they did in its earliest times, when the subject matter was fresh, and the half-narrative, half-vocal style of the lecturer something uncommon." Russell did, in any case, offer a new twist to his presentation:

> Mr. Russell seldom tells his tale without invigorating it with a special fillip. He, now, introduces to the audience the son of one John Brown, the latter having been originally a slave, for whom Mr. Russell procured freedom. The man in question, at the request of his father, who has become a prosperous tradesman in New York, has sought out Mr. Russell, in the hope of being permitted to serve a benefactor to whom his family have been under such manifest obligations. That Mr. Russell makes excellent use of this pleasant incident we may be sure; while he does not fail to draw a useful and affecting moral from the political humanitarianism involved in it.
>
> That Mr. Russell made excellent use of it we can, indeed, be sure!

The passing of the years was, meanwhile, brought home to Russell, again, with the deaths in quick succession of his father, Moses, on 16 March 1857—at the age of around ninety—and his brother, Samuel, on 10 June 1857. Samuel had stayed behind in Sheerness when the family moved to London and had been active there as a "general dealer" or, more specifically, furniture broker. The father of fourteen children, Samuel died, aged fifty-nine, as a result (according to the death certificate) of "effusion on the brain from a fall" while he was working on board *HMS Colossus*, moored off Sheerness.

Henry Russell's travels around the country were, by now, inevitably less newsworthy than of old, though *The Era* reported "a crowded house" and Russell "as attractive as ever" when presenting *The Far West* in [King's] Lynn in May 1857. In late summer, he made his customary tour of south-coast resorts, including evening performances in Hastings on 1 September,

St. Leonards on 2 September, Lewes on 3 September, and Brighton on 4 September, together with a Brighton matinée the following afternoon. It may have been significant, though, that the St. Leonards engagement was described as attracting merely "a good audience," rather than being full to overflowing. At all events, we soon thereafter lose trace of him. It seems that, after so long threatening to go, Henry Russell had, finally, slipped quietly away from the platform.

The following is the account that ultimately appeared of how his sudden retirement came about:

> It happened, according to a recounting in *The Biograph* of 1881, when Russell was performing at Lancaster. He was in the midst of his celebrated song "The Ship on Fire." Suddenly pausing, he rose from the piano, on which, as was his wont, he was accompanying himself, and evidently in a state of intense agitation he advanced to the footlights. Having gazed for a few seconds amid the dead silence of the audience, upon the large mass of human beings before him, he uttered an indescribable cry, and quickly ran off stage. On reaching his retiring-room, he burst into a flood of tears, weeping like a very child. His agent, Mr. Crozill, came forward and apologised to the spectators of the strange and sad scene, and manifestations of the utmost sympathy were exhibited. The painful truth was that, under the severe strain of a performance, in which single-handed and unaided, he had for so long a period appeared night after night, and extending over from two-and-a-half to three hours at a time, his fine, though somewhat delicately strung nervous temperament had at length completely given way, and cancelling all the engagements upon which he had previously entered, he determined forthwith to abandon the public stage.

Thus, it seems, was Russell's career melodramatic to the end. It seems that constant touring had led to some form of nervous breakdown and finally made him fulfil his threat to quit the concert platform. It is a typical Russell detail that it has proved impossible to verify the Lancaster setting. The last sighting apparent (for now) of the most popular entertainer in Britain, on a stage, is at the Corn Exchange in Maidstone, 21 September 1857. The tale of this breakdown is nowhere told in the press, in the later months of 1857. Odd, you may think, for a man whose bump on the railway head, not so long ago, made national news. Neither, indeed, is a visit to Lancaster recorded.

Henry Russell's departure from the performing circuit seems, for a time, to have gone unnoticed. Subsequent press references to him for a while made no mention of retirement. When Stephen Massett, an American "vocalist, composer, imitator, and elocutionist," appeared at London's Hanover Square Rooms in March 1858, the *Times* declared, "He sings sentimental songs, much in the style of Mr. Henry Russell, without the racy nasal twang for which the vocal exhibitions of that eminent 'lecturer' are distinguished." "Are," not "were."

Even if Russell himself were exhausted, which given his schedule over the last thirty years can have been scarcely surprising, there can be no question of his songs having lost their appeal, and his absence provided renewed opportunity for the imitators who had so notably plagued him. And yes, Henry Smith was still at it. Few of the soi-disant purveyors of Russell's act and songs were of great merit, and some indeed were simple frauds, as instanced by happenings in Ipswich on 5 October 1858:

> Bills had been issued announcing "The renowned Russell's entertainment," with a list of *the* Mr. Henry Russell's well-known songs. A large audience assembled in the expectation of hearing the veritable Henry Russell. To their surprise, however, a grey-haired person appeared and stated that he was not Henry Russell, but his brother, and could amuse them just as well. He then attempted a song and broke down. With the utmost coolness he proceeded to state that, as he could not sing well, he would tell some Negro anecdotes. He began, "The last time I was in New York—" "In where?" said a wag, and then demanded their money back; but the individual replied, "Don't you wish you may get it? I did not deceive you; I never stated that I was *Henry* Russell; laughed outright in the faces of his dupes, and sung, "'Will you walk into my parlour?' said the spider to the fly." The uproar of hisses and yells which followed was deafening, but he stood it out with a courage worthy of a better cause. When he again obtained a hearing he said, *he* did not think they had anything to complain of; he had done his best to amuse them. He declined to dance a hornpipe or

> "Jump Jim Crow," as suggested to him—placed his hand on his breast, bowed, and retired laughing. That drove the audience mad, and they commenced to destroy the seats; but, fortunately, Mr. Ross, a magistrate, who was present, had sent for a strong body of police, and their arrival prevented further damage.

Popular music piracy was very much alive in 1858, if in a much less sophisticated form than today!

Nobody, at that time, seems to have asked the obvious question of where the real Henry Russell was. Still only in his mid-forties, he was, it seems, recovering from his putative nervous breakdown in the seclusion of the family home in Boulogne-sur-Mer. Of his children, Isabella and Henry junior had by 1857 both reached their twenties, while William, Fanny, and Jack ranged in age from thirteen down to eight. Not surprisingly, Henry senior found some difficulty settling to his newly found idleness. "After a life spent so actively," we are told by *The Biograph*, "leisure at first became somewhat monotonous, and as a means of breaking the tedium he betook himself to amateur photography."

When *The Era* did finally acknowledge that he had "quietly retired to a splendid château near Boulogne" it was to report a further amateur performance by Boulogne's English-speaking community, at the municipal theatre on 28 January 1859. Twenty-one-year-old Henry Lloyd Russell appeared in pieces called *Going to the Derby* and *Take That Girl Away*; but what ensured that all tickets were rapidly sold was the announcement that his father would also take part. *The Boulogne Gazette* reported a warm reception to his singing of "The Ship on Fire":

> We have often heard this song from the feeling and fervid lips of Mr. Russell, but we never enjoyed either the exquisite music, the liquid tones, the sparkling notes, as we did on Friday night. Thunders of applause followed the last note, and continued uproariously till Mr. Russell reappeared and kindly gave "Why don't the men propose, mamma?" This was sung with much comic humour and produced roars of laughter, especially one verse that we never heard before, and which might, by censoriousness, be applied to more than one lady in the house. Continued applause at its conclusion brought forward Mr. Russell, who consented to sing "Cheer! Boys, Cheer!" if the

> audience would join in the chorus. We need not add that it was heartily responded to by the gentlemen present, when Mr. Russell retired amid the applause and admiration of the house.

That the performance was a shaft of light in the life of the town is confirmed by the reporter wondering "whether it would be possible to induce Mr. Russell to give to this dull town one night of his amusing series of life, interspersed with his songs; it would be a relief to our dullness."

That reference to Boulogne-sur-Mer being dull was, it should be added, to the town out of season. *The Era* later acknowledged that in summer it "is the head-quarters of gaiety and happiness; everybody seems well to do in the world, and every thing is tinted *couleur de rose.*" This was by way of prelude to an account of how, during the winter of 1861–62, Henry Russell had been moved to step forward once more into the local news, while this time keeping well away from stage performance:

> The distress this winter has been awful. Those who know France, and the habits of the working classes, can alone understand the full measure of their wretchedness *when their soup fails them*. Poor people! They are always contented with little, very little, and work on bravely; but this year the cold has subdued them. It was known that many hard-working families were actually starving. Our countrymen, never laggard in charitable acts, at once, with English promptitude and English energy, went to work to meet the calamity; all were ready to form a relief fund; but how to employ it with the best advantage to the recipients was a serious difficulty. It was solved by a gentleman whose name, like that of the author of *Gil Blas*, will, while Boulogne stands, be engraven on its walls as one of its benefactors. Mr. Henry Russell, the well-known composer and vocalist, commenced the good work by opening, solely at his own expense, a soup kitchen at his house at Maquétra, from whence no applicant, whether French, English, Protestant, Catholic, or Jew, ever departed without immediate and substantial relief. This noble lead was speedily followed by every English resident, whose handsome subscriptions soon enabled Mr. Russell to make his kitchen one of the most useful institutions in the city; so much so that, in a late meeting of the *Conseil Municipal*, the thanks of the *Maire* and *Conseil* were

> unanimously voted to be presented to him. Honour to *the* Mr. Henry Russell! honour to his Profession! honour to England! honour to the *Maire* and the *Conseil*! We *now* know where the coals and cold meat are kept at Boulogne.

Municipal gratitude for Russell's efforts was formally expressed on the closure of his soup kitchen on 23 February:

> The poor of Boulogne, so generously succoured by Mr. Henry Russell and his English friends, presented him with a monster bouquet on Saturday last, on which day the distribution of relief at Maquétra terminated. The bouquet was accompanied with an address couched in the following terms:
>
> Sir.—It is with the deepest gratitude that we, the poor of Boulogne, have the honour to present you this bouquet as a token of our respectful gratitude for your generous efforts in our favour, and we sincerely wish that you may be able for many long years to exercise your ardent charity towards the unfortunate.
>
> The above address was read on the presentation of the bouquet; and at its conclusion was confirmed with well merited applause.

At least it wasn't another piece of silverware!

Russell had by no means severed his links with London. According to one source, he carried on business as a money-lender and money-broker, though one should perhaps treat the statement with as much care as other information from the same publication. At all events, he and his family no doubt often traveled the route between Boulogne-sur-Mer and London, by boat and train—in 1861, for instance, when his elder daughter Isabella was married, in London, to John Davies, a dentist. Russell even performed in London on 29 March 1862, at a concert at Sadler's Wells Theatre for the benefit of William Edward Love (c. 1805–67). Grandfather of dancer Mabel Love (1874–1953), "Love the polyphonist," or ventriloquist (in days long before the introduction of the ventriloquist's dummy), had given his entertainment with éclat on both sides of the Atlantic, and his path had many times crossed Russell's. Now he had fallen on hard times.

Russell apparently also appeared, later, at a benefit concert at the Lyceum Theatre for his actor-producer friend Benjamin Webster (1797–1882). Such, so the story goes, was the nervousness induced by the prospect that he took to his bed for two days beforehand. Even when no longer performing professionally, Russell was still turning out the occasional composition, for which there was, seemingly, no shortage of takers. On 23 May 1862 his "Lord Dundreary Waltz" was first performed by the orchestra at the Theatre Royal, Haymarket, between the second and third acts of the play *Our American Cousin.*

Then, during March 1863, two solo entertainers—Edwin Ransford (1805–76) and Henri Drayton (1823–1872)—each performed songs Russell had composed for them. For the former it was an individual song "Sunny Days Will Come Again," for the latter, a series of songs for an entertainment at the Polygraphic Hall, King William Street, Strand, based on episodes in the recent American Civil War. Drayton, a Philadelphian, sought to entertain by "narrating by means of song, anecdote, piano, and picture, his recent experiences in America." *The Times* notice added that "the serious object of *Federals and Confederates* (as the 'entertainment' is called) is to prove that the Confederates are all right and the Federals are all wrong." It was a stance that was to land Drayton in hot water when he returned to his native America.

Later, Louisa Pyne sang his song "The Two Boats" on an 1876 tour. However, with Russell, one must always exercise care over composing attributions. In 1864, at the Royal Polytechnic Institution in Regent Street, entertainer Robert Coote (1833–88)—son of pianist and composer Charles Coote senior (c. 1808–80) and grandfather of actor Robert Coote (1909–82)—had revived the song "The Little Maid, or The Gay Deceiver" with Russell's name attached. In fact, this was published in 1836 as "written and composed by the author of *Mephistophiles in England*"—supposedly Robert Folkestone Williams. Russell had evidently used it as one of his encore numbers—seemingly with his own variant of the vocal line—and, through performance, adaptation, and general association over the years it had, like others, become firmly attributed to him.

Russell was certainly still highly prized in certain circles. In May 1865, *The Era* seized upon the tenth anniversary of Sir Henry Bishop's death to suggest that "among the more probable inheritors of the honour of knighthood which the death of Sir Henry Bishop left open to members of the Musical Profession, it is likely that Mr. Henry Russell will be the next to be congratulated." It was wishful thinking.

By that time still barely fifty, however, he had finally found Boulogne-sur-Mer somewhat tedious and had returned to London, acquiring a property at 74 Kensington Gardens Square in Bayswater. His return was doubtless much influenced by family matters. His daughter, Isabella, had already made him a grandfather, and his eldest son, Henry Lloyd Russell, had decided to use the dramatic talents displayed in Boulogne-sur-Mer by going into the Church of England ministry. In 1868, he married Katherine Eliza Willsford Hockin in Deal, Kent, and, after the birth of a daughter in 1869, he took up a living at the newly built Annunciation of the Blessed Virgin Mary Church in Chislehurst, Kent, where he was appointed Vicar in 1875. Seven more children were born, and Henry Lloyd Russell would remain at that same church for the rest of his working life of over forty years.

As for the second son, William Clark Russell, he was following in the creative steps of his parents. After being educated privately at Winchester and in Boulogne-sur-Mer, he had joined the British merchant service in 1858 and served an apprenticeship on the sailing vessel *Duncan Dunbar*. He made several voyages to India and Australia, and supposedly, while off the coast of China in 1860, witnessed the capture of the Taku forts by the combined British and French forces. Alas, the conditions he suffered on board ship caused permanent damage to his health, and in due course he retired to earn a living with his pen.

William had taken early steps in song-writing, having three numbers published in London in 1864 and 1865—a ballad "The Rose and the Bud," a song "The Soldier's Farewell," and a serenade, "Where the white moonbeams creep." He had also had aspirations as a dramatist, and he dedicated to his father a tragedy in verse, *Fra Angelo*. Actor and author John Brougham (1810–80) backed his effort to such good effect that actor Walter Montgomery (1817–71) acquired the play and staged it at the Haymarket Theatre on 30 August 1865. *The Era* described it as "a tragedy, which competent judges declare to be singularly beautiful, very dramatic, and perfectly original." However, the packed and expectant audience was disappointed. "To Haymarket; see an extraordinary play in five acts, seven tableaux, called *Fra Diavolo*, written by W C Russell, son of Henry Russell, composer; laughter more than applause," recorded E. L. Blanchard in his diary. The piece too readily showed the young man's inexperience and soon disappeared from view.

For a time, William Clark Russell relied on a career as a journalist, becoming, in 1868, editor of *The Leader*. Then, during the 1870s and 1880s, he was attached for many years to *The Newcastle Daily Chronicle*. At the same time, however, he was honing talents that would turn him into a significant novelist, beginning, in 1867, with the romance *Hunchback's Charge*. He published various novels under the names of "Sydney Mostyn" and "Eliza Rhys Davies," but he achieved renown with *John Holdsworth, Chief Mate*, published under his own name in 1874. It was the first of a succession of seafaring adventure novels, the most successful being *The Wreck of the Grosvenor*, published in 1875 and still in print today. He had evidently inherited his father's love of the drama of the sea.

In Bayswater in 1868, William Clark Russell married Ann Maria Alexandrina Henry, daughter of D. J. Henry of the Institute of Engineers and niece of Sir Thomas Henry, police magistrate. Henry and Isabella Russell had three children marry within a twelve-month period in 1868–69: following Henry Lloyd Russell and William Clark Russell, their second daughter—now calling herself Frances Marcella rather than Fanny Marcella as baptized—married Charles William Frederic Cooper, only son of William Cooper of Woodville Hall, Forest Hill, at St. Stephen's Church, Bayswater, on 7 January 1869. Only the youngest of Henry Russell's children, "Jack," and his final daughter, Emma, now remained unmarried.

Jack was, indeed, to remain a bachelor for many years, and in his early adult years he became heavily involved with South African mining. The discovery in 1866–67 of the "Eureka" diamond, exhibited at the Paris Exhibition of 1867, had prompted intense speculative interest in South Africa's Northern Cape, increased by the finding of the "Star of South Africa" diamond in 1869. The further discovery of diamonds in 1869 and early 1870 on the "Vooruitzigt" farm (owned by a Boer named Beer) and also on "Du Toit's Pan" farm brought a flood of prospectors. With the discovery of yet a further deposit at the Bultfontein mine, the London Bond Street jewelry merchant Edwin William Streeter (1833–1923) financed an exploratory expedition, led by Thomas William Tobin, Secretary of the Royal Polytechnic Institution. The expedition reached South Africa in June 1871 and was there when a further major find was made at what was first known as "Old De Beer's New Rush" or "Colesberg Kopje." This later became known as the Kimberley mine, when the township that had sprung up nearby was, in 1873, named Kimberley after the Earl of Kimberley, British Secretary of State for the Colonies.

In November 1871 a prospectus was issued in London for the South African Diamond Fields Association Limited, which on 10 March 1872 dispatched its first expedition party on board the screw steamer Saxon from Southampton. With money from his father, "Jack" Russell was among the many prospectors who went out in the early 1870s. We read of his presence in Kimberley in the reminiscences of a fellow speculator, Louis Cohen, who tells of Russell's presence in the audience of an amateur performance of Dion Boucicault's play *The Octoroon*. In the course of the play the actors bid at auction for the octoroon girl, Zoe (played by the daughter of the theatre's lessee and musical director, Cox), and when the bidding reaches 25,000 dollars there is a pause as the hammer is poised to fall:

> Suddenly, during this tense stillness, Russell, in the front row, . . . stood up and cried, "Twenty-six thousand dollars." All eyes were turned in the direction of the dress-suited bidder in the stalls. Cox, in cogitative mood, eyed him with his head on one side and eyes closed warningly, exactly as a bull would watch a red dog. Russell, however, who had dined well, returned the savage looks with complacent smiles, until the astounded Cox shouted from his orchestral seat, "Shut up, Russell! What do you mean by making a row in my theatre?" "That's all very well, Cox, old fellow," returned the benevolent Russell, screwing in his cheeks and regarding the conductor pityingly. "But what kind of a chap do you think I'd be to sit here and see your daughter knocked down for the sake of a paltry thousand dollars?"

Jack Russell evidently inherited much of his father's showmanship!

Cohen reproduces the program of a benefit concert at the Lanyon Theatre, Kimberley, on 18 September 1877, when "Jack" Russell sang the ballad "Nancy Lee." Also on that 1877 bill was the Cockney comedian Barney Barnato (1852–97), who had gone out from London around the same time as Russell. Barnato made a huge fortune by buying worked-out diamond mines in the Kimberley area and mining the abandoned blue earth, before being out-maneuvered into merging his interests with those of Cecil John Rhodes to form the De Beers Corporation in 1888. Jack Russell was apparently one of those who made the mistake of selling his interests too soon. He cannot have done badly out of his years in South Africa mining, but family rumor is that he held the Kimberley club record for losing the most money in a single night, and there was apparently nothing of his inheritance left when he died in 1925.

Meanwhile, on 16 November 1869, Henry Russell was moved, by some rumor or other, to write to the editor of *The Era*: "The report of my death having been very extensively circulated, I should esteem it a great kindness if you would permit me to avail myself of the publicity of your columns to inform my many friends in England and America that I am still in the enjoyment of sound health, and that my faculties are still sharp, and my sympathies acute enough to read with concern this ante-dating of my demise." Russell and his wife were at that stage still resident at 74 Kensington Gardens Square; but, by the time of the British census of April 1871, we find them a mile or so further out of London at 17 Westbourne Park Road.

Finally, with the children off their hands, Henry Russell and his wife returned once more to "the seclusion of Boulogne-sur-Mer." The reason later given for this was that "with advancing years . . . the longing for his old love returned." However, there was another reason why Russell preferred his wife to be based in Boulogne-sur-Mer, while he continued to spend part of his time in London. At a time when Henry Russell had four of his six children married and was already a grandfather, he had begun a new relationship, of the familiar mid-life type: one that was about to provide him with a second family.

17

De Lara

The liaison on which Henry Russell now embarked was to produce two further sons, both of whom would achieve celebrity in the musical world. The elder, another Henry Russell (the third son, after Henry Lloyd and John Henry Sharp, to be given the name Henry), would become celebrated, particularly in America, as an operatic impresario. The younger, Landon Ronald, would be the more celebrated in the United Kingdom—knighted for his services to music as conductor, Principal of the Guildhall School of Music, and much else.

The traditional assumption has been that "Landon Ronald" was a professional name. He himself was happy to have people believe that it was simply a shortened version of "Landon Ronald Russell." In fact, "Ronald" is the surname on his birth certificate and the one under which he was brought up. In an age when extramarital relationships were not publicly acknowledged, no matter how obvious, subterfuge was commonplace, especially for someone such as Henry Russell who was a public figure and who had a wife and grown-up children. That the elder son's birth certificate shows the name of "Henry Russell," under which he became known, was due, as much as anything to chance; but, like his younger brother, he was brought up under the surname "Ronald."

It was because Henry Russell himself registered the birth of the elder son that "Russell" was the surname on the birth certificate. This records that, on 29 November 1871, Henry Russell, gentleman, registered the birth of a son, Henry, born on 14 November 1871 at 12 Westbury Road, London. The mother's name is given as "Hannah Russell, formerly Landon," a form that suggests "Landon" as a previous married name rather than a maiden

Figure 17.1a. Landon Ronald with his mother Hannah, c. 1883. *Source:* Author's collection.

Figure 17.1b. Landon Ronald, c. 1910. *Source:* Boston Public Library, Hale Collection, https://ark.digitalcommonwealth.org/ark:/50959/vh53xm77t.

name. In the case of the younger son, it was the mother, using the name of Emma Ronald, who, on 5 July 1873, registered the birth as occurring at 19 Lancaster Road, Kensington, on 7 June 1873. The space for name and surname of father was left blank, and the boy's given names were entered as "Landon Russell," making him officially Landon Russell Ronald.

Despite the different names given for the mother in the two cases, there is no doubt that "Hannah Landon" and "Emma Ronald" were one and the same. The common link in the two births is the name "Landon" that was given as the mother's former surname in the first instance and the child's given name in the second. We know that Henry Russell customarily gave his sons the names of people who influenced him (William Clark, Charles Kirkman, John Henry Sharpe): it may be that—pressed by the registrar to identify the mother of his first child—he on the spur of the moment came up with the name "Landon" from the poet Letitia Elizabeth Landon, who had provided the words for some of his earliest songs. As for "Emma Ronald," one might note that, as a signature, "Ronald" can be virtually indistinguishable from "Russell."

However the names arose, it is clear that "Ronald" was the name under which Henry Russell installed his mistress in what was to be his new family's home. The 1870 edition of the Post Office London Directory shows an entry for a Miss Ronald at 12 Westbury Road, off Harrow Road. She is there, too, in the 1871 and 1872 editions, but in the 1873 and 1874 editions is at 90 Lancaster Road (near Portobello Road). With motherhood her lot, the "Miss Ronald" in the street registers of the early 1870s is then subtly changed to "Mrs. Ronald." That the address shown on Landon Ronald's birth certificate was 19, rather than 90, Lancaster Road, suggests a mishearing on the part of the registrar!

The one genuinely correct part of the different names under which the mother was shown on the two birth certificates was "Hannah," for the young woman was actually Miss Hannah de Lara, daughter of David Laurent de Lara and his wife Sarah, née Crawcour. Born in Amsterdam, David Laurent de Lara was by profession a lithographic printer and illustrator, who, from various dedications around 1850, could boast the title of "illuminating artist to the Queen." The art of illuminating manuscripts was of considerable interest to churchgoing Victorians, and David Laurent de Lara was its leading exponent. He contributed one of the "One Shilling Handbooks on Art" published by the firm of Winsor & Newton, indicating how he "turned the demand into a prosperous business, selling the special materials with ready-made outlines of scriptural texts for colouring." He even advertised courses in illuminating "with employment afterwards if desired." His *magnum opus* was *Elementary Instruction in the Art of Illumination and Missal Printing on Vellum*, first published in 1850 and running eventually to a seventh edition in 1863.

In the press, David Laurent de Lara advertised his "gallery of fine arts" at 3 Torrington Square, between Gower Street and Russell Square, where he lived from the 1850s. In the 1869 and 1870 Post Office London Directories Hannah de Lara, too, is there listed as "artist," along with her father. Though not in the 1871 directory, she is again at Torrington Square in the 1872, 1873, and 1874 editions, despite the simultaneous entries for "Miss Ronald" elsewhere.

Whereas Henry Russell's wife Isabella was a Quaker, and their children were brought up as Christians, the de Laras were resolutely Jewish. Russell may have known them somewhat through their cousins, the family of the future composer Isidore de Lara (1858–1935), who lived in Boulogne-sur-Mer in the 1860s. But David Laurent de Lara was, in any case, a prominent member of London's Jewish community during the period of Henry Russell's great success in the 1840s and 1850s. When, or whether, Henry Russell's wife and first family became aware of his liaison with Hannah de Lara we cannot be sure. Bridget Duckenfield suggests in her *O Lovely Knight* (1991) that it was his children's objection to the registration of the first child of his new liaison as yet another Henry Russell that caused the second child to be registered in the name of "Ronald." So they knew? However, it seems as likely that the registration was simply a consequence of the father registering the first birth and the mother the second. At all events, Henry Russell's preoccupation in London, from the 1870s onward, was obviously with his second "wife" and family.

One way and another, we know far more about this second of Henry Russell's households than we do about the first. In the first place it seems that Hannah de Lara, alias Emma Ronald, took in lodgers at 90 Lancaster Road, among whom in 1874 were a mother and two children, one of them the future artist Aubrey Beardsley (1872–98). Hannah continued to take in lodgers after a move to a more prestigious address at 11 Harley Street, Marylebone. The April 1881 census shows the residents there headed by Emma L. Ronald and her two sons, Henry and Haneton [sic]. "Haneton" is evidently explained by the census official's unfamiliarity with the name "Landon," which the "L" of "Emma L Ronald" presumably, likewise, represents. Also at 11 Harley Street, on that 1881 census night, were Rosie

P. Moore, the daughter of Hannah's eldest sister, plus a housemaid, waiter, children's maid, kitchen maid, and three visitors.

It was evidently not long afterward that the precocious young Landon had his first song composition published by Marriott & Williams of 295 Oxford Street. The song was "The Future," which the sheet music shows as "affectionately dedicated to Mrs. Lock Roe, the words by E. L. R., composed by Landon Ronald, aged 8 years." It is presumably Henry Russell's concubine who was lyricist, adopting the style "E. L. R.' as though emulating the custom of Letitia Elizabeth Landon of signing her creations "L. E. L." The title page has a portrait of the young Landon holding a violin and bow.

Henry Russell clearly enjoyed such times as he had in London with his second family, and he obviously appreciated young Landon's musical prowess. On one occasion he sought an opinion on the youngster's progress from a Harley Street neighbor, the pianist, conductor and teacher Wilhelm Ganz (1833–1914): "One day, Mr. Henry Russell brought his little son to me and said he wished me to hear him play, and give my opinion about his talent. The boy played the "Moonlight Sonata" to me, and when he had finished I played it to him to correct some of his faults. I told his father that he had great gifts, and should continue to study under a great master, and he was quite satisfied with what I said." By this time Henry Russell was into his sixties and, necessarily, largely an absent father. In his absence, the burden of raising the two young sons inevitably fell upon Hannah and members of her family, all of whom seem to have had musical inclinations. Hannah's father, David Laurent de Lara, died in 1876 at the age of seventy, and his grandsons would barely have remembered him. Their impressions probably resembled those of a cousin, who was just two months younger than little Henry and some sixteen months older than Landon. "I have pleasant recollections of my grandfather," she wrote, "for he was gentle and kindly, but my grandmother terrified me. I can see her now, with her corkscrew curls, her long beaky nose, black eyes, and worst of all, her bad temper."

This cousin was the future concert pianist Adelina de Lara, a daughter of Hannah de Lara's immediately older sister Annie. Annie and her daughter Adelina both provided evidence of the strong musical strain in the de Lara family, for Annie de Lara had herself ventured a career as a singer. Adelina boasted as one of her most valued possessions a miniature of her mother, "painted on ivory when she was nine years old. It was shown at the Great Exhibition of 1851, where she sang to Queen Victoria." Annie certainly did sing at the 1851 Exhibition, at which her father was an exhibitor, though it's less clear that she sang to the Queen. The performance was part of the closing ceremony and was seemingly principally a piano recital. But then, according to *The Jewish Chronicle*, Annie "finished her performance by singing very artistically and gracefully three of the difficult *morceaux* from "Il Don Giovanni" in Italian, amidst the cheers and applause of some thousands of eager listeners." According to the paper, she was only eleven years old, though census returns suggest that she would just have reached thirteen.

Annie de Laras's subsequent career included an appearance as a pupil of the eccentric George French Flowers (1811–72) at a well-attended concert at the Hanover-Square Rooms in June 1852. Describing Flowers as "the well-known professor of counterpoint," *The Times* reported that he "has discovered and brought forward some very remarkable voices. That of Miss Annie de Lara, a child of 12 years old, who sang a difficult air by Mozart with singularly precocious talent, is of extraordinary compass, the lower tones being unusually deep and sonorous." Most people found Flowers, rather, a punctilious joke.

Annie de Lara's career never took off. On 14 December 1853 she appeared under the baton of Wilhelm Meyer Lutz in the second half of one of the Wednesday evening concerts at the Exeter Hall, singing first the cabaletta "Per non istar in ozio" from Donizetti's *Maria di Rohan*, and then, in a collection of "music of a light miscellaneous nature," the song "Jealous Little Jack" by Curschmann. She did not excite universal acclaim. *The Era* reported that "The appearance of a quaint-looking young lady, with the manners of a child, and some of the appearances of a woman was a novelty, which amused rather than pleased the audience. She sang an Italian song, but her voice is not pleasing. She was more at home in a semi-comic English song, 'Jealous Little Jack,' to which she gave force by a well assumed dramatic manner."

Undeterred, Annie de Lara announced her "first annual evening concert" at the Hanover-Square Rooms in June 1854. She assembled a bunch of musicians of undoubted eminence, among them vocalist Frank Bodda, harpist Frederick Chatterton, and conductors Meyer Lutz and Wilhelm Ganz. *The Era* reported that "the attendance was large" and that "the performances of the *beneficiaire* were not calculated to invite criticism." That December, Annie further announced "three soirées musicales" at her residence at 14 Torrington Square—the first, on 28 December

1854, in aid of the Crimean Army Fund, to assist those serving in the Crimea. Violinist Viotti Collins was among those announced, as was also that Signor Onorati who had been something of a fixture at the Russell family's concerts.

Annie's second "Annual Evening Concert" at the Hanover Square Rooms included in its impressive list of performers many of the same names as before. However, the general standard of the concert may perhaps be inferred from *The Musical World*. Having referred to a hall "crowded by a full and very fashionable audience," the review continued: "Miss Annie de Lara must indeed be a highly-favoured lady to attract such a distinguished company, since the programme, with one or two exceptions, was meagre and commonplace in the extreme." Still undeterred, Annie de Lara struggled on with her career, her subsequent appearances including an evening concert in May 1856 at the mansion of the Right Honorable Lady Pollock in Guildford Street. There was also another on 21 August 1857 at the Exchange Hall in Grantham in the company of bass singer Hamilton Braham, son of John.

This provincial location was significant because it was the hometown of the man who three months earlier (19 May 1857) had become Annie's husband. According to her daughter Adelina, Annie had "spoiled a brilliant career by running away from home when only sixteen, to marry a solicitor named Laurence." She would actually have been eighteen, going on nineteen, at the time, and, as we have seen, her career may have been altogether a little less than brilliant. Moreover, Joseph Lawrence's 1861 census return suggests that any soliciting he did was as a commission broker. At all events, there were four children of the union, after which, Adelina reported, "he took to drink, treated her badly and finally left her destitute."

Annie then contracted what seems to have been a de facto rather than de jure union. Her new "husband" had himself married in 1857 and had at least three children of that marriage. His name at the time of his marriage was George Matthew Tilbury, but for some reason he changed the family name to "Preston." He was clearly a far more suitable partner for Annie, partly because he had followed David Laurent de Lara's profession of engraver and illuminator, but also because he played several instruments as well as having "a beautiful baritone voice." The result of the union was the daughter Lottie Adelina Preston, born on 23 January 1872 in Carlisle. She inherited her parents' musical bent and was to achieve fame as Adelina de Lara.

Adelina writes in her memoirs of her parents' constant traveling, attempting to make ends meet, but always with a piano, on which she was kept practicing for hours on end:

> At times we were so poor that there was nothing to eat, and when that happened our lives centred upon the postman's knock. Somewhere in a vague land called "Harley Street" it appeared I possessed a rich aunt. In my small mind she became the "fairy godmother" of all fairy tales—for from her, at the height of our hunger, would come a registered envelope, out of which would roll five gold sovereigns. When this happened we all became very excited and hugged each other, and mother would buy a wonderful dinner and we would eat again.

The fairy godmother was, of course, "Emma L. Ronald," and her ability to help out financially was, no doubt, due to the wealth of Henry Russell.

Adelina de Lara goes on to tell of how, in their poverty and with two daughters of Annie's first marriage also to support, her parents were forced to exploit their daughter's exceptional gifts as a pianist. For this, the name of "Adelina de Lara" was deemed far more marketable than "Lottie Preston." Her engagements included recitals at the waxworks gallery in Liverpool run by Mr. and Mrs. Charles Reynolds, whose son Alfred (1884–1969) would later become a composer of comic operas and other theatre music. During 1882, Adelina followed the career of a child prodigy, but then tragedy struck. The winter of 1882–83 was a harsh one, with keen winds and snow, and the strain of going out in all weathers to sell his engravings proved too much for her father, who died in Liverpool of pneumonia, aged forty-five. Adelina, just eleven years old and now the only wage earner, went on playing at the Reynolds gallery. However, worse was to follow. Her mother, inconsolable and refusing to eat, soon died of heart failure, leaving eleven-year-old Adelina alone with Annie's older daughters, Nellie and Pen Lawrence, themselves only twenty and seventeen: "Our thoughts turned to our Harley Street aunt, mother's sister. . . . She wired that owing to neuralgia she could not come. Somehow, she could not have understood our plight, and when later I came to know and love her I realized that. Instead she sent us half a sovereign! It helped—and I still had to play at the Gallery. Perhaps it was as well, as it took my mind off my loneliness." Yet there was even worse still to come:

> Nellie looked after us, but she became more and more silent. It was a terrible responsibility for so young a girl. "You and Pen would be better off without me." I was too young to heed the warning in those words, and to understand the brooding which must have been going on in her mind. All I know is that one day Pen and I returned from the Gallery to find our supper left ready, but no Nellie. On the table we found father's silver watch and my mother's wedding ring. . . . Our worst fears were fulfilled. Nellie had been seen last at about nine-fifteen by two or three people, walking very fast towards the docks, her face noticeably white and stricken. The police also discovered that the day before she had been making enquiries about the outgoing tides. The tide went out that night at nine-thirty—the hour and day exactly a fortnight after my father died. Her death was presumed. There was no doubt she had drowned herself, for everything was done to find her alive or dead. She had left all her belongings behind—even her purse with silver in it on the dressing table.

Remarkably, Pen and Adelina were able to pull their lives together and survive on Adelina's earnings, with Pen effectively acting as her manager. Adelina's career prospered, and during the mid-1880s she appeared in Eastbourne with the Devonshire Park Orchestra under Julian Adams: "[In Eastbourne] we stayed with an aunt and uncle while I fulfilled my engagements at Devonshire Park. For the first time I was really happy, for my cousins Henry and Landon Ronald arrived to hear me play. We went for walks and enjoyed the sea air." This aunt and uncle were perhaps the second De Lara sister, Rachel, and her husband, Henry Lax. He was a musician, and so he may have been engaged with the Devonshire Park Orchestra for the summer. Rachel had been a witness at Annie de Lara's 1857 wedding, but did not marry until 1867. She was actually some ten years older than her husband but managed to halve the gap for the purpose of census returns.

Adelina then became increasingly involved with the eldest of the de Lara sisters, Simharia. (There was also a brother, Isaac.) Simharia had married a London lawyer, William Playters Moore, grandson of Sir William John Playters, Bart (1757–1832), of Yelverton, Norfolk, and son of Captain Robert Moore of the First Life Guards. It was their daughter

Rosa, born in November 1868, who was staying with the "Ronald" family in Harley Street on census night in April 1881. The Moore marriage did not last, and the pair were evidently separated long before the husband's death in hospital in Dalston, east London, on 30 November 1882. Of this, Adelina de Lara wrote:

> *One aunt leads to other!* Quite unexpectedly our eldest aunt, who had hitherto ignored us, now asked Pen and me to stay with her in London. She was the widow of a well-to-do barrister whom she had nagged so much in his lifetime that, when he was run over by a tram and killed, it was found he had left all his money to his two sisters, leaving his wife, son and daughter destitute. It was aunt Russell of Harley Street who came to the rescue and put her into a house in Notting Hill, where she lived lavishly by taking paying guests. . . . Auntie, like my Polish grandmother, had a hooked nose, flashing black eyes, and was very tiny. . . . I soon discovered that my aunt had a wonderful sense of humour and she kept me in fits of laughter. Unfortunately, I was not so impressed with her high soprano voice, with which she would render, all out, Tosti's *Good-bye*.

It seems that Henry Russell was keeping not only his own two families, but much of the de Lara family as well!

Meanwhile, after their initial schooling in Marylebone and at All Souls' Grammar School, Henry and Landon Ronald had gone on to further education at the High School in Margate (later Margate College). Perhaps it was deemed convenient for their father to visit them from Boulogne-sur-Mer. In 1884, Landon's talents gained him admission to the Royal College of Music, and the following year Adelina de Lara and her sister, Pen Lawrence, joined the Harley Street household. Money had been raised for Adelina to spend a year in London as a pupil of Fanny Davies, prior to studying in Frankfurt with Clara Schumann:

> To crown my happiness, we were to go as paying guests to aunt Russell! I, who for so long had never had a home or security, was to have both at last. . . . I made great friends with my cousin Landon Ronald and his brother Henry. Landon was then at the Royal College of Music learning to play the piano

and violin under Sir Hubert Parry and Villiers Stanford; but when he was supposed to be practising he spent most of the time using his bow to play with the cat. How cross auntie used to get with him! There were times however when he would work very hard, and I remember the time we stood to win a gold sovereign from my uncle Henry Russell, of whom I was in great awe. We never were allowed to sit in his chair or look at the daily paper before him. . . . Uncle Henry was passionately fond of the Overture to *William Tell* and he promised Landon and me a reward the day we could play it as a duet. How we slaved at it! We laughed and quarrelled and plodded on, planning to put our skill to the test on uncle's birthday. We both knew how critical he was, and when the actual day arrived we were a mass of nerves and excitement and could hardly speak to each other. Landon had a great sense of rhythm even as a boy, and so had I, which was fortunate, for *William Tell* calls for it, working up to a terrific finale.

Uncle sat in his chair, all attention, as we took our places at the piano and off we started. Soon we were playing for dear life in such a rhythmical manner that we were nudging and banging each other's elbows in our excitement and energy. I can imagine our flushed faces and eager eyes as we finished, both wondering if we had won our reward. We did not have to wait long. Uncle's heavy applause told us he was delighted. "Upon my word, never have I seen a sovereign better earned!" Out it came from the sovereign case which looked like a gold watch and hung on his watch chain. How we thanked him, and how pleased we were! Not till many years later did I ponder upon the word "seen," and not "heard."

My aunt used to dress my cousins in black velvet with lace collars and cuffs! They looked like the Princes in the Tower. Later, when they were promoted to Eton suits and top hats, we used to have great fun in the park during the London "season." We would walk in Rotten Row and I would bow to the people in the smartest carriages and my cousins would doff their hats. In return we would receive gracious bows from the ladies who thought we must be children of friends of theirs! We were especially delighted when the carriage of the Prince

> and Princess of Wales with the three Princesses swept past. We would salute them respectfully and as a reward we would receive a most radiant smile and bow from the Princess of Wales.

With Victorian moral standards as they were, Henry Russell's second home in Harley Street was never a matter of public knowledge. An occasional press reference served to inform that he was still alive, but fostered the perception that he was firmly retired to Boulogne-sur-Mer. Thus, a paragraph in *The Era,* in August 1886, repeated one of his favorite anecdotes (about the Newfoundland dog), adding that "by-the-way, [he] is alive and may be seen in excellent health on any day at the Boulogne Casino." The reference was presumably associated with his featuring, that very day, as "Celebrity at Home" in *The Penny Illustrated Paper*, whose representative interviewed him at the Hôtel du Nord in Boulogne-sur-Mer. There Russell reminisced particularly about his return from America to Britain and his subsequent establishment of himself in his homeland through the tour with Piatti, Döhler, and Lablache.

It was only occasionally during the '70s and '80s that Russell's name came before the British public. In 1871, at the Royal Polytechnic in Regent Street, George Buckland presented a revival of Songs and Scenas by Henry Russell, "whose productions," declared *The Times*, "will be remembered when the sorry stuff by which in a measure they have been put out of vogue is forgotten." On 9 April 1879, Russell was seen, in person, among a group of highly distinguished "extras" at a celebrity afternoon performance of his late friend Lord Lytton's comedy *Money* at the Haymarket Theatre for the benefit of E. L. Blanchard. Others with him included J. R. Planché, H. J. Byron, F. C. Burnand, and W. S. Gilbert. This reappearance on the public stage proved that he was also still remembered in America, where the *Chicago Daily Tribune* noted that "The veteran looks hale and hearty."

Later, for a Promenade Concert at the Theatre Royal, Covent Garden, on 6 November 1880, it was announced that "a special selection of Mr. Henry Russell's songs will be given by eminent artistes; and the orchestra will perform an overture, composed on his most favourite and popular melodies." Most significant of all, in hindsight, was the Admiralty authorization in 1882 for the Royal Marines to adopt "A Life on the Ocean Wave" as its regimental quick march. It was this that created perhaps the main means by which Henry Russell's music has survived in British consciousness into the twenty-first century.

A less happy press reference came in connection with his second daughter, Fanny Marcella. She had married civil engineer-turned-journalist

Charles Cooper and produced four children, among them future novelist (and co-author of Henry Russell's memoirs) Henry St. John Cooper (1869–1926). However, in February 1883 the couple found themselves in the divorce court. *The Times* reported thus on Mrs. Cooper's petition for divorce on the grounds of adultery and cruelty:

> Mrs. Cooper was examined, and stated that she was the daughter of Henry Russell, the composer, and was married to the respondent in 1869. There were four children of the marriage. Her husband had a salary of £350 in a merchant's office, and she had a sum of £3,600 settled on her, which produced during the time she cohabited with her husband £200 a year. This interest was during that period received by her husband. In the year 1880 she remonstrated with him on his attentions to a married lady. This she did on several occasions. He answered her by acts of violence. He caught her by the throat and pushed her down to the ground, against which he bumped her head. Early in 1881 she complained to her father, who came to the house and endeavoured to speak quietly on the subject to the respondent, but the latter would not listen to a word from Mr. Russell. There was a French nurse in her service, and she gave that woman notice to leave, but the nurse said she would only obey her master, and the respondent sent the children to Brighton in charge of the nurse, and thus separated them from their mother. This was in February, 1881, and in April of the same year Mrs. Cooper left her husband's house. In August, 1882, she went to Epping to see her children, who were then with her father, and she learnt that the respondent had had a child by the French nurse.

The court received corroboration of the adultery but adjourned pending evidence of cruelty. Eventually the divorce was granted, after which Charles Cooper married a second time on 10 November 1887. Just over a year later, on 18 December 1888, he became the father of another daughter. She would become celebrated as stage and film beauty Gladys Cooper (1888–1971), mother-in-law of actor Robert Morley (1908–92), and grandmother of theatre critic Sheridan Morley (1941–2007).

The fact that any public connection with a certain residence in Harley Street was taboo meant that Clubland was where Russell was officially to be found in London. Henry Chance Newton ("Carados" of *The Referee*) recalled in his garrulous memoirs how Russell "used to join us at some of Henry Irving's dinners and suppers, either at the Garrick Club or in the Beefsteak Room in the Lyceum Theatre roof. There old Henry Russell, vigorous veteran that he was, would play and sing to us in marvellous fashion." In April 1889 he attended a celebratory dinner for the election of actor Edward Terry (1844–1912) as Grand Treasurer of the Masonic body, the Savage Club Lodge, composed chiefly of actors and musicians and some journalists. "Among the guests," reported *The Penny Illustrated Paper*, "was MR. HENRY RUSSELL, the venerable and cheery author of 'Cheer! Boys, Cheer!' who sang as blithely as if he were twenty-six instead of *seventy-six*. Have Masons discovered the elixir of life?"

Russell's own club was the St. George's Club at 4 Hanover Square, a "proprietary and non-political" club, "founded with a view of providing a centre where residents in England, Americans, Colonials, and Anglo-Indians, might meet in social intercourse" and offering forty bedrooms for the use of members. He was there the night of the 1881 census, while Hannah was looking after their two sons in Harley Street, and that was, doubtless, the usual arrangement for his time in London. At the St. George's Club, he was always happy to relate the anecdotes that he had gathered (and embroidered or invented) from his touring life many years ago. He was always keen to keep up with his cronies and, evidently, also to beg tickets for their latest theatrical offerings. When comic actor John Lawrence Toole (1832–1906) opened at the Gaiety Theatre in F. C. Burnand's *Artful Cards* in February 1877, Russell wrote to him on St. George's Club notepaper:

> My dear Toole
>
> I want to see you in "Artful Cards." I know I may ask you to leave my name for a couple of seats for next Saturday. With warmest regards.
>
> Thine ever,
>
> Henry Russell

In private with friends he was also still happy to perform one of his own songs. The actor Squire Bancroft (1841–1926) recalled how he and his wife—the former Marie Wilton (1839–1921)—attended a dinner party given by J. M. Levy, founder of the *Daily Telegraph*, at his home in Grosvenor Street. Henry Russell was also among the guests:

> After dinner the two old friends talked of the days of their youth, and in his enthusiasm our host begged Russell to sing once more "The Ship on Fire." The old man at last consented, on condition that his host should sing a verse of a ballad too. It was delightful. Russell dashed at the piano, and amazed all present by the force of his voice and the earnestness of his accompaniment. Afterwards, when Mr. Levy warbled, in a sweet, soft voice, true of time and tune, the old song, "She Wore a Wreath of Roses," the reader will readily believe that tears trickled down the cheeks of several who had the good fortune to be present.

The artist George Augustus Sala (1828–96), writing in 1893, recalled another such instance from around 1887:

> Some six years ago I was present at a fashionable garden party, given by a friend, in the extensive grounds attached to his dwelling at Hammersmith, and among the company were a few notabilities in art, music, and the drama. One of them was Mr. George Grossmith, and in the course of some entertainments, given under cover in the drawing-room of the house, he was called upon more than once to "oblige." Other "professionals" and several amateurs also took part in the improvised programme, and included in the last-mentioned category—at least, so I thought at the time—was a short, stout, squarely-built gentleman of uncertain age . . . his gay, confident manner, his firm step and upright figure, scarcely corresponded with the years represented by his silvery locks and well-marked and somewhat rugged face, to which were appended a pair of grey Dundreary whiskers and a determined-looking moustache. There was, besides, a brightness and vivacity about his keen grey eyes and a look of animation in his mobile features which belonged to a man who had seen active service rather than to an elderly person. In fact, I set the "amateur" down as being not more than sixty, and I also set him down as a retired major in the army.

Figure 17.2. Henry Russell, c. 1900. *Source:* Author's collection.

Having been prevailed upon to give the company "something," this sturdy gentleman placed himself at the piano with a perfectly self-possessed air, and after addressing a few words to the audience in a clear, incisive, and commanding sort of voice, to remind them, for some reason which I did not then understand, that it was some years since he had last played and sung before a large assembly, and requesting their indulgence, he proceeded to run his fingers over the ivories with all the air of a practised performer, or of one that feels quite at home with the instrument, and after a well-executed prelude of a distinctly descriptive nature, he followed this up by a song which I had a faint recollection of having heard in the days of my extreme youth. It was a song that told a dramatic story, though what it was called and by whom I had one heard it sung, I could not remember.

When it was over, the audience, which was a numerous and for the most part critical one, applauded my typical Major to the echo, not so much for his vocal powers and executive skill, as for the fire and expression imparted to the melody and its running accompaniment upon the piano. It was this that seemed to electrify the hearers more than anything else, and in my own opinion accounted for their extraordinary enthusiasm at the end of the performance. But it was evident that they took also a personal interest in the performer, for, during the recital, I noticed that Mr. George Grossmith, who was standing at the narrow end of the grand piano with both arms resting upon it, appeared lost in admiration of the little man, and taking in greedily his every gesture and movement. So when the crowd had nearly dispersed, I went up to Grossmith, whom I knew well, and asked him who the amateur was.

"Don't you know?" said he, with a look of incredulity in his spectacled eyes. I confessed to complete ignorance, and asked for information. "Why, Henry Russell, of course," was his astonishing answer. "Not *the* Henry Russell?" I said, half-doubtfully; "he has been dead and buried long ago, has he not?" "Oh, no, he hasn't," returned the popular humorist dryly, "he is very much alive, as you have seen and heard to-day, though I believe the old boy is occasionally killed in print."

This wholly unexpected encounter with the original composer of "Cheer! Boys, Cheer!" "The Ship on Fire," and I know not how many songs of the kind besides, was regarded by myself as quite an event; and when I was presently introduced to the veteran in the garden, the pleasure of seeing him again after so many years was vastly increased. But a greater pleasure still awaited me, and this happened when at no distant date he was sitting to me for his portrait.

At that time my studio was in Brighton, where I lived four years from September, 1887, and as my sitter resided in town, he had a rather long way to come. He did not, however, appear to mind the trouble, and as for the fatigue, judging by his robust condition, his activity and energy, he seemed capable of accomplishing twice the distance without in the least feeling it. But, of course, Mr. Russell did not travel from town for posing purposes every day, though he expressed himself quite ready to do so if necessary, saying, "You have only to send me

> a wire in the morning, and I'll be with you in the middle of the day." So, whenever I wanted him, I took him at his word, when, sure enough, he turned up in time for early lunch; after which he sat for a couple of hours; then went for a drive along the Front, and returned to town at the hour usually devoted to his evening repast. This, for a gentleman in his seventy-sixth year, was not so bad; but to a person of Henry Russell's temperament—and one, moreover, who had crossed the Atlantic something like twenty-four times—it was child's play.

Sala adds that he exhibited his portrait of Russell at the Institute of Painters, producing from a writer in *Punch* the comment "Why, bless me! I recollect Henry Russell singing 'The Ship on Fire' at the very first public entertainment I ever was at." There were doubtless many who shared that nostalgic sentiment.

George Grossmith (1847–1912), who features prominently in that Sala recollection, was the principal comedian in all the major Gilbert and Sullivan comic operas. Along with the likes of John Parry (1810–79) and Corney Grain (1844–95), he had first made his name as one of the many solo entertainers at the piano who flourished in the wake of Henry Russell. Even after being recruited by Gilbert and Sullivan, he continued his solo appearances, producing compositions of his own such as "See Me Dance the Polka." He also features in another (and presumably earlier) Henry Russell story, told this time by Margaret Clement Scott, second wife of Clement Scott (1859–1904), principal dramatic critic of the *Daily Telegraph*, and herself related to Russell by marriage, as her uncle was Frederick Manasseh Brandon, who married Maria Russell, one of the musical daughters of Israel Russell:

> Gee-Gee billed himself one afternoon to give imitations of the late John Parry and Henry Russell at the small St. James' Hall, and after giving his version of how Parry did things, he announced that he would now sing a song after the style of the late Henry Russell. . . . Whereupon a lusty voice from the stalls bawled out: "What the devil d'you mean, young man? I was here before you began your antics, and if you mean I'm dead, I'm not, and I'm ready to call you a liar." . . . Henry Russell had been told [by J. M. Levy of the *Daily Telegraph*] to go and report as to Gee-Gee's justifiability in billing himself as an entertainer after the style of John Parry and himself. Only one alternative rested with George

> Grossmith when challenged by the "old vet," as his comrades named him. He begged him to mount the platform and give an account of himself in one of his own songs. But Henry Russell could not be so unkind. When he stepped on to the stage, he only shook hands with Gee-Gee and complimented him on his excellent mimicry of John Parry.

There were indeed many who sought to get Henry Russell to perform again in public, but always without success. Among those thus disappointed was a young Manchester impresario named T. A. Barrett (1863–1928), who would later achieve worldwide success as Leslie Stuart, composer of the musical *Florodora*. Promoting a series of popular concerts in Manchester, Barrett wrote to Russell in December 1885 but received from him the reply, "I cannot again appear before the public. My nerves are gone."

Russell was still not averse to composing the occasional song, though, as in 1886 when Queen Victoria's impending golden jubilee inspired him to a high-profile composition, "Our Empress Queen." The words were by Clement Scott, whose second wife, Margaret Clement Scott, has been quoted above. Alfred Fryer sang the new song at the Christmas dinner of Henry Russell's own St. George's Club on 23 December 1886, and Frank Roth sang it at a further banquet there for the Chancellor of the Exchequer in February 1887.

According to Margaret Clement Scott, she and her husband stayed several weekends with Russell, "a marvellously hale old fellow," in Boulogne-sur-Mer. As the 1887 jubilee approached, Russell evidently felt it worth a little publicity that his collaboration with Scott was being sung not only in Britain but also in Boulogne-sur-Mer. On the notepaper of the St. George's Club he wrote on 8 May 1887 as follows:

> My dear Clement Scott,
>
> Can you do anything with the enclosed? Its [sic] more in Bennett's way than yours, it being musical and news. On the 21st of June, there is to be a grand Jubilee at Boulogne & as you will perceive by the enclosed, they have invited me to lead a chorus of "Our Empress."
>
> Yours as ever,
>
> Vet

After the event, he followed it up with a further letter, this time on the notepaper of the United Club, Boulogne-sur-Mer:

> My dear Clement Scott,
>
> Enclosed is an account of the doings of loyal Boulogne. The streets are a mass of bunting—the display gor-ge-ous, and I must add the French deserve our eternal gratitude. "Our Empress Queen" was performed by 300 musicians—Hats off!—and a tremendous encore.
>
> The words translated into French "*wret-en* by Monsieur *Shott*," music by Monsieur *Rouselle*. Good spelling, eh? There were at least 8,000 people present—and "GORD SHAVE DE QUVEEN" was really grand. Will the (by your aid) description be news for your Friday paper?
>
> Ever thine,
>
> Henry Russell

18

Howley Place

With Henry Russell long in retirement, appearances of his name in the press were increasingly likely to be pendant to those of other members of his family. At London's Marlborough Street Court, in August 1889, for instance, seventeen-year-old George Johnson, of no occupation or fixed abode (and who had lost his left arm and three fingers of his right hand), was charged with stealing a gold watch and chain from Henry Russell, a clerk of the Vicarage, Chislehurst. This Henry Russell was our Henry's grandson, the eldest son of Rev. Henry Lloyd Russell.

Most of these press references to a Henry Russell, though, were to or through one who was associated with a string of London clubs, at 316 Regent Street, and "whose success in organising such institutions," relates Victorian gossip writer Henry George Hibbert, "had earned him the name of King of Clubs Russell." This Henry was our Henry's nephew Charles Henry Russell, a son of Samuel Russell, the brother who had died after an accident on *HMS Colossus* in 1857. The premises at 316 Regent Street, opposite the Polytechnic, had in 1861 served as the Institution of Fine Arts, or Portland Gallery, before becoming the chief offices of the British Nation Life Assurance Association in 1863. Then in 1870, over the name of "C H Russell, Hon Sec" appeared an advert for the Corinthian Club, to be opened at the same address. By June 1872 the premises had become the Regent Club, and by October of that same year they were being advertised as the Civil and Military Club, "established to give the usual club accommodation to officers in the Army and Navy, Civil Service, merchants and private gentlemen."

Under that last name, the premises featured in an intriguing small advertisement in *The Times* on 5 August 1875: "LOST, on Monday last, on board the Alexandra steamboat, from Boulogne to Folkestone, a POCKET-BOOK, containing three £5 notes and some papers. The notes will be given to the finder if the papers are restored to Henry Russell, Civil and United Service Club, 316, Regent-street, W." We cannot be sure whether this was the club secretary himself, or the songwriter using his nephew's club as a convenient dropping-off place for a pocket-book containing what, in view of the double life he was leading, may well have been "sensitive information."

Later still, in March 1880, the name of Henry Russell appeared in a list of theatrical notables on the provisional honorary committee for the Lotos Club. This had been founded at that same 316 Regent Street "for Ladies and Gentlemen connected with, or interested in, the Drama, Music, and the practice of Literature and the Fine Arts generally." It offered public and private rooms, French cuisine, a well-stocked cellar, a "pretty Bijou Theatre," and, not least, periodical concerts and *soirées dansantes.* According to Hibbert, this club had been founded to supply an opportunity for late dancing and drinking, following the closing of the now notorious Argyll Rooms in 1878. However, this venture was evidently no more successful than its predecessors, even after reorganization in August 1882 as the New Lotos Club. In September 1883, Charles Henry Russell found himself in the Court of Bankruptcy, with liabilities of £16,139, secured debts of £33,149, and assets of £7,378—amounts that need to be multiplied by over fifty times to arrive at today's equivalents. Reduced, thereafter, to working as a servant at the Prince of Wales's Club in Coventry Street, Charles Henry Russell died suddenly on 16 October 1893.

Of course, having outlived many of his contemporaries, the veteran Henry Russell's appearances in London all too often involved attending funerals. In May 1884, for instance, he was noted among the mourners at the funeral of the conductor Sir Michael Costa (1808–84), and in January 1889, that of *Times* music critic Francis Hueffer (1845–89). The latter year also brought the death of Russell's major collaborator, Charles Mackay, on 24 December 1889. As for Russell's own family, his own eldest brother, Israel Russell, died on 15 March 1884, aged well into his eighties. A year earlier, Israel's son George Henry, who some time previously had sought to emulate Henry Russell as an entertainer, had died at the age of only forty-seven.

Even closer to our Henry Russell, his eldest daughter, Isabella, wife of the dentist John Davies, died in Brixton on 29 November 1886 after a week's chronic bronchitis, aged fifty-one. The most significant event for

Henry Russell, though, was the death of his wife, Isabella. It occurred in the presence of their son, Rev. Henry Lloyd Russell, at the Granville Hotel, Ramsgate, on 14 November 1887, and was certified as from "dilated right heart vascular, emphysema of lungs and congestion of right lung." Isabella was buried in Ramsgate, as isolated from her husband in death as latterly, it seems, in her life. Now Henry was free to regularize his relationship with Hannah de Lara. Leaving Boulogne-sur-Mer for good, he moved, with Hannah, into a new home at 18 Howley Place, Paddington. On 21 August 1888, a tolerably decent nine months after Isabella's death, Henry and Hannah were married, with the blessing of the Church of England, at St Mary's Church, Paddington. "Emma L. Ronald" was no more.

For the two offspring of the newly recognized union, things were not necessarily so simple. For Henry, the elder, it was relatively straightforward to change his surname from "Ronald," under which he had grown up, to "Russell," which was, anyway, the name on his birth certificate. For the younger, Landon, it was more difficult. He was still in education at the Royal College of Music, where his musical precocity was such that, even at the age of fifteen, he was already making a name for himself. At the age of only seventeen, he stepped straight out from the Royal College of Music to play the piano accompaniment for a mimed play without words, *L'Enfant Prodigue* by Michel Carré *fils* and André Wormser, produced at the Prince of Wales's Theatre on 31 March 1891. The Victorian moral code made it difficult for him suddenly to acquire a father with as high a profile as Henry Russell.

Landon was thus effectively stuck with the name under which he was brought up, and which was, anyway, on his birth certificate. As for being recognized as Henry's son, the problem merely increased with his increasing celebrity. Even as late as December 1896, *The Era* could do no more than refer to "the young conductor and song writer, Mr. Landon Ronald, in whom Mr. Russell takes a deep interest." Not until two years later, over ten years after Henry and Hannah had been married, did that paper openly refer to Landon Ronald as Henry Russell's son.

Even without immediate freedom to acknowledge his youngest son publicly, Henry Russell must have derived great joy from Landon's progress, just as marriage to Hannah must have brought him a welcome sense of ease. He was now able to live openly in what was an intensely musical household. Not least, he and Hannah were free to entertain and be entertained in London, as Mrs. Clement Scott, for one, recalled: "When well over seventy, and he had again taken up his abode in London, he used to roll up in his carriage to see us, eat a hearty meal, brag that he smoked twenty-five cigars a day, that his hand was as firm as a rock and that he'd never had a day's illness in his life." George Augustus Sala, too, recalled visits to Howley Place, arising from the friendship forged by the portrait sittings in Brighton in 1887:

> I shall not easily forget those amusing sittings, or the many pleasant evenings I have since passed at my subject's pretty home in Maida Vale, where I hope still to be received for several years to come, in spite of my host's present fourscore-and-odd years. It is there that I often find the veteran busily engaged in composing—not tuneful melodies, but miniature chests of drawers, which he manufactures neatly with his own hands, assisted, of course, by various implements of carpentry, and these he gives away to young friends and to charities and bazaars.
>
> It was there also that the veteran once gave me a practical illustration of the origin of some of his negro melodies. Not a few were, he said, founded upon old hymns or Christmas carols, and, in order to show me his meaning, he played over the "Old Hundredth" in the ordinary slow way, and then repeated it in much quicker time, till at last it developed into no less a ditty than "Lubly Rosa, Sambo come; don't ye hear the banjo—tum, tum, tum?"

This final observation, referring to the song "The Coal Black Rose" (1829), provides an interesting addendum to the passage from Henry Russell's memoirs quoted earlier, in which "The Old Hundredth" was the source of both "Old Dan Tucker" and "Goin' ober de Mountain"!

Going into the 1890s, Henry Russell's own songs were still not completely forgotten. On Thursday, 8 October 1891, Sir Augustus Harris included a Henry Russell night in another season of Promenade Concerts at Covent Garden Theatre. In a lengthy homage headed "A Veteran Composer" (and not, as Russell's memoirs claim, "An Octogenarian Composer"), *The Daily Telegraph* reported:

> Covent-garden Theatre was crowded last evening. Indeed, judging by results, the promise of a "Henry Russell Night" proved the most potent attraction that Sir Augustus Harris has held

Figure 18.1. Ally Sloper meets Henry Russell. *Source:* Author's collection.

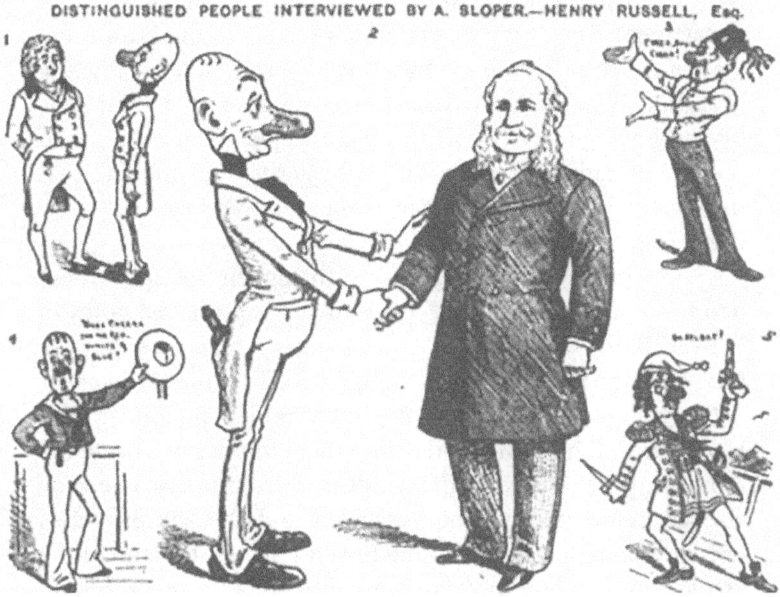

out to patrons this season. The first part of the programme was, as usual, miscellaneous; the second part was ushered in by a *pot pourri* overture, arranged by Signor [Alessandro] Romili, introducing the themes of many of the Russell songs. Then came a vocal selection which fairly represented the composer in his different moods. "The Maniac," given by Signor Abramoff, was followed by "Woodman, Spare that Tree" and "The Ivy Green," sung respectively by Miss Kate Flynn and Mr. C E Ellison. The familiar strains of these numbers fell as pleasantly as ever upon the ears of the audience, though it must be confessed that rather scant justice was done to them by the singers. The tender simplicity, indeed, of most of the songs seemed to have taken the artists by surprise. Mr. Kelson Trueman came nearest the mark, perhaps, in "Sunshine and Rain," but either the vocalists as a body had never acquired the art of singing straightforward melodies with effect, or their voices played them strange and unaccountable tricks. The throng of listeners, however, had not come to be critical; and if they

> had the brightness and vigour of the children's choruses might well have been held to atone for the shortcomings in the solo department. The swinging emigrant's song, "To the West"; that sea-spray ditty, "A Life on the Ocean Wave"; and, finally, the immortal "Cheer, Boys, Cheer," were all sung in capital style by the boys and girls in their picturesque naval attire, who seemed to gather strength and enthusiasm from the fact that the kindly face of the veteran composer was beaming upon them from a private box.
>
> On more than one occasion during the selection there had been cries for "Russell," but scarcely had the last notes of "Cheer, Boys, Cheer!" died away than the huge opera-house rang with the name of the evening's hero. The "boys" *did* cheer with a will; indeed, their applause grew louder and louder until Henry Russell himself stood before them in the place occupied a moment previously by the conductor. Even then some time elapsed before the clamour subsided and the handkerchiefs ceased waving in honour of the firmly-knit, white-haired little gentleman who had proved the mighty power of song in days gone by. At last there was silence, and Henry Russell spoke. In clear and penetrating tones, he thanked one and all for the reception they had accorded to his "early works," some of which, he proudly informed them, were composed no less than sixty years ago. Then, with all his old dramatic instinct burning strongly within him, he both impressed and amused his hearers with the anecdote of the Hanley potter related above. Many years had rolled by since Henry Russell last faced an audience, but he spoke as freely and firmly as if he were at the zenith of his public career. Three more loud and spontaneous cheers followed him as he left the platform, retiring once more to the quiet restfulness of an honoured old age. Truly a remarkable occasion, and one not unworthy of a remarkable man!

Like much popular music before and since, Henry Russell's songs clearly lost something with the passage of time and without the individual impact of their original performer. Again, as with so much popular music before and since, those present were well satisfied with a happy recall of earlier days. It was perhaps the climax of Henry Russell's old age.

Yet, as was seemingly always the case with Henry Russell, the occasion did not give unalloyed pleasure to everyone. One observer expressed disappointment at Augustus Harris having been the one to get Henry Russell back before the public:

> Ascertaining that the only Henry could be seen at the St. George's Club, Hanover Square, an appointment was made, and he and I met for the first time. A proposition was made that Mr. Russell should appear at an entertainment to be given in the Great St James's Hall, and that his old songs should be revived, and a speech be given by him on the occasion. He was delighted with the proposition, but said he had made an unalterable resolve never to face the good British public again. All my truly eloquent arguments went overboard, and the old man simply reiterated his resolve with increasing emphasis. He would be glad to aid me in every way to get the evening up, but he never would appear again.

Perhaps the fact of his having agreed to take Landon Ronald on as rehearsal pianist for his Italian Opera season, at Covent Garden Theatre, had something to do with Sir Augustus Harris's success.

Admiration between Harris and Russell was certainly mutual. In July, Russell wrote to the editor of *The Era* suggesting "the efforts of Sir Augustus Harris to establish in this country an opera worthy of the name, and in accordance with the best traditions of its history" deserved "some sort of public recognition." For the purpose he was donating ten guineas to start an "Operatic Testimonial Fund." His lead was taken up, with the idea of a portrait of Sir Augustus being placed in the Covent Garden Opera House. In the event, it was at Drury Lane that the portrait was unveiled, in May 1894.

The October 1891 Promenade Concert raises afresh the question of precisely when Henry Russell was born. As we have noted at length, reference works up to that time seem to have given his year of birth as 1813 or 1814. However, that *Daily Telegraph* review of the Promenade Concert stated that "he stands upon the very threshold of his eightieth year," while the *Pall Mall Gazette* referred to him as "a veteran of eighty summers" and a report elsewhere referred to him already as "an octogenarian." It seems to have been around this time that his quoted age jumped a year or two.

If he had indeed been born in 1812, we might have expected his eightieth birthday on 24 December 1892 to generate some press recognition. Yet there appears to have been none. By contrast, the following year *The Era* began what became an almost annual acknowledgement of the anniversary: "We wish very many happy returns of the day to Mr. Henry Russell, who will complete his eighty-first year to-morrow (Sunday)." By December 1894 his age had seemingly jumped yet again:

> Mr. Henry Russell celebrated his eighty-third birthday on Christmas Eve, and the event was well remembered by his many friends, from whom he received a large number of letters, cards, and telegrams, together with a few more substantial tokens, one of these being a handsome scarf-pin with the veteran's initials in diamonds placed over a bar of music. Mr. Henry Irving wired, "Love and greeting, old friend. Reciprocate with all my heart returns of this day, and God bless you always." Sir Augustus Harris sent a box of choice cigars, and among others who did not forget their old friend were Mr. J L Toole, Mr. Lionel Brough, Mr. Edward Terry, Mr. W Kuhe, Mr. W Ganz, Mdlle Olitzka, Mr. Clement Scott, and Sir Edward Lawson. In the evening the veteran was serenaded by a surprise military band, under Warwick Williams's conductorship. And, greatly to his astonishment (for the band was concealed in his house), they played a selection from his popular melodies in a most soul-stirring manner. Several musical friends called to pay their respects to the composer of "Cheer! Boys, Cheer!" and Miss Esther Palliser, who was among them, sang a number of songs, three of which were by Mr. Landon Ronald. Mr. Richard Green, of Covent-garden, was also heard in the Prologue to *Pagliacci* and in Ronald's "Love in Absence;" Miss Cecile Elieson contributed some fine violin solos; and that promising young baritone Mr. Henry Russell gave with much spirit and vocal power his father's latest composition, "The Struggle for Fame."

Even if Landon could still not be acknowledged as Henry Russell's son, young Henry could. During 1895, in a Jewish ceremony, he married Hannah Da Costa Andrade, of Portuguese descent, known as Nina, and a year or so older than himself. When their first child, a son, was born the following year, he was named Henry Tosti Russell, in tribute to young

Henry's singing-teacher friend, Sir Francesco Paolo Tosti (1846–1916). A second son, born on 23 March 1900, was named Sheridan William Robin Russell.

Young Henry Russell for a time followed a medical training, while also seeking recognition as a baritone singer. Since 1891 he had been taking lessons from a Swedish singing teacher named Hugo Beyer. In 1895–96, though, relations between the two became strained when Beyer discovered that young Henry was himself taking singing pupils. Worse still, young Henry sought the opinion of other singing teachers (perhaps Tosti was one of them), who laughed in his face at the idea that his voice had ever been large enough for a singing career. Matters came to a head when young Henry told friends that Beyer was a fraud, that he encouraged pupils who had no hope of a singing career, and even that he was an impostor—the brother of the real Hugo Beyer.

It was all too reminiscent of the arguments into which his father had entered half a century or so earlier. When Beyer sued, the case came before the Queen's Bench Division in February 1897. As young Henry fairly summarized in his memoirs:

> Much of the plaintiff's evidence proved to be mere tea-table tittle-tattle, and the witnesses were neither serious nor convincing. A verdict was returned in my favour—gratifying in all but one respect, which was that it proved that I would never make a singer, and, moreover, that never at any time had I been justified in the expectation. . . . But it is often from disillusionment that life takes its permanent colour. During the trial I had announced that I was a singing teacher in a "pathological" sense, and this after having studied for some time the art of breathing and the physiology of the throat. The Press, though it made sport of the trial itself, gave this fact wide publicity; and when I ceased to receive vocal instruction and began to give it, I found that I had achieved a reputation without effort, and my pupils multiplied rapidly.

In this passage, at least, young Henry Russell's memoirs proved more reliable than those of his father, which had appeared in 1895. Much of the material in Henry's *Cheer! Boys, Cheer!* was a regurgitation of the anecdotes that he had, for years, been telling visitors to Boulogne-sur-Mer, to the habitués of the smoking-room at the St. George's Club, and to visitors to Howley

Place. Since many of them stemmed from concert appearances, made up to sixty years earlier, it is only to be expected that they had become not a little embroidered along the way. However, as we have so often noted, the *Who's Who* entry of his novelist grandson, Henry St. John Cooper, indicates that it was he—Gladys Cooper's half-brother—who put the memoirs together. Perhaps the vigor of Russell's storytelling had misled his grandson, as it had others, into believing that he had been present at certain events, and he no longer cared to disillusion them.

On 19 September 1895, what was still Henry Russell's best-known song in Britain was recalled by a drama called *Cheer, Boys, Cheer*, produced—once again by Sir Augustus Harris—at Drury Lane Theatre. It starred Henry Neville, Fanny Brough, and Lionel Rignold and commemorated not Russell's song itself, but the war to which soldiers had marched with it on their lips. "Mr. Henry Russell . . . will doubtless be seen among the audience at Drury-lane upon the first night," predicted *The Era*. Sir Augustus Harris suggested that Henry Russell should prepare a hundred of his songs in an album to be presented as a souvenir to each member of the audience on the hundredth night, but "he found that he had not a single right to any of his own compositions. Publishers threatened all sorts of legal penalties, and so the happy idea had to be abandoned."

The Era later reported that the Glasgow Society of Musicians had approached Russell with a view to a banquet in his honor about the date of his eighty-third [sic] birthday on Christmas Eve 1895. Alas, Henry Russell could no longer maintain his untruthful boast of never having had a day's sickness. However, by February 1896, *The Era* could report:

> Mr. Henry Russell's many friends and admirers will hear with pleasure that the veteran composer of "Cheer! Boys, Cheer!" is slowly yet surely recovering from a serious illness which, for the past month, has caused those near and dear to him considerable anxiety and not a little alarm. A large number of Mr. Russell's personal friends have called or sent to make inquiries concerning the progress of the invalid, and it was only during the past week that he was able to see one or two visitors, the first being Sir Augustus Harris, who wished to satisfy himself that his old friend was in a fair way towards complete recovery, as now appears to be the case.

He was certainly sufficiently back to his normal self for the birthday celebration on Christmas Eve 1896:

Figure 18.2. Three scenes from the Drury Lane stage production of *Cheer Boys, Cheer*. *Source:* Author's collection.

Mr. Henry Russell completed his eighty-fifth [sic] year on Christmas Eve, and his birthday was not forgotten by his many friends and admirers, from whom the old composer received a large number of letters and telegrams of heartiest

> congratulation. Prominent among the senders were Sir Henry Irving, Sir Edward Lawson, Mr. W Kuhe, Mr. W Ganz, Miss Esther Palliser, Mr. Richard Green, Mr. Alderman Green, and Mr. Charles Copland. . . . Among several acceptable birthday gifts, was a large portrait in crayons of the young conductor and song writer Mr. Landon Ronald, in whom Mr. Russell takes a deep interest. This drawing was from the pencil of Mr. Walter Goodman, and was greatly admired on Thursday by the many callers at Howley-place . . .

It was still not considered appropriate to acknowledge the relationship with Landon Ronald. Readers might have been forgiven for wondering, though, why Henry Russell's interest in the young man was such that he should welcome a large portrait of the latter as a birthday present! After touring America as accompanist to Adelina Patti, Landon had that year made his début as opera conductor at Covent Garden.

To visitors to Howley Place, Russell could still display remarkable vigor, as when the editor of *The Strand Musical Magazine*, Emile Hatzfeld, visited him for a feature:

> To pay a visit to Mr. Russell after a hard day's work is as refreshing, invigorating, and, I might almost add, appetising, as a breath of Margate air would be in a Fleet Street newspaper office. With animal spirits that few men of thirty can boast of; with a fund of humour and anecdote that would astonish many an acknowledged wit; and with an abundance of manly sentiment that causes his big heart ever to sympathise with the distressed; it is easy to imagine how this exceptional man inspired his audiences with feelings of wonderment and veneration. . . .
>
> If anybody asks Mr. Russell his age to-day, he replies, "I am just turned thirty-two," and verily, as I looked myself up and down, I felt old and bent by the side of that dapper little man of upright bearing and ruddy complexion. His home life is typical of the man, being surrounded by nought but affection, cheerfulness, and good-will. He has but two foes to combat with: the runaway urchin who rings his bell and the cats that spoil his garden! I have seen him pursue the former and threaten the miscreant with a policeman, but should the

> child begin to cry, it was given a sixpence and warned not to repeat the offence. I have seen him take careful aim with an air-gun at "pussy" who was making love amongst his choice flowers, when, should he discover that it had a pretty cat, he would call to the servant to give it some milk.
>
> Mr. Russell has a hobby that has practically become second nature, namely, carpentering. In his charming villa residence at Maida Hill, one of the prettiest rooms in the house is kept exclusively for him, and it is there he will be found during the day, not surrounded, as might be expected, by portraits of musicians or souvenirs of past triumphs, but by large planks of wood, by divers pots of paint and every imaginable tool. He turns out miniature chests of drawers, exquisitely finished, bearing his autograph, and sends them to charity bazaars.
>
> Musically, he keeps with the times, as far as the fixed tastes and opinions of sixty years' duration will allow him. Wagner he manages to swallow, and he can digest "Tannhäuser" and "Lohengrin," but the "Ring" or "Tristan" are liable to case him severe dyspepsia—even though taken in small doses . . .

Later that year, on 14 June 1897, Russell was present when Sir Henry Irving unveiled Chavalliaud's marble statue of the actress Sarah Siddons at Paddington Green. At the end of the ceremony Irving took Russell by the arm, while Ellen Terry walked with Hannah. Amid the cheers of those present, the strains of "Cheer! Boys, Cheer!" passed around the Green. A few weeks later still, on 4 August 1897, Landon Ronald married Mimi Ettlinger, a singer whom he had met during studies at the Conservatoire in Frankfurt. The relationship came about, most particularly, through the fact that Landon's cousins, Adelina de Lara and Pen Lawrence, had been living with the Ettlinger family, in Frankfurt, at the time when Adelina was studying with Clara Schumann, and Pen was working as a teacher. Landon's marriage to Mimi took place at the West London Synagogue, using the formal name "Landon Ronald Russell," as was now his custom. A son, Vernon Emile, was born in 1899.

During 1895, Landon had been musical director for the musical comedy *Dandy Dick Whittington* at the Avenue Theatre, and in 1898 he took the same role for *Little Miss Nobody* at the Lyric Theatre, an engagement that also required him to compose some additional numbers. It was in that year's note on Henry Russell's birthday that *The Era* finally acknowledged the relationship between him and Landon Ronald, though the mathematics of Henry Russell's age were again haywire: "Henry Russell, the veteran composer, entered his eighty-sixth year on Saturday last. Mr. Russell . . . is as hale and hearty as ever, and is very proud of his two clever sons, Clarke Russell, the novelist, and "Landon Ronald," the composer, much of whose music is to be heard in *Little Miss Nobody* . . ." The message was reinforced just over three months later, in April 1899, when T. P. O'Connor's magazine *M.A.P.* marked the production of *L'Amour Mouillé* at the Lyric Theatre: "It will surprise many folks, no doubt, to learn that Mr. Henry Russell, the veteran composer of "Cheer, Boys, Cheer" and so many other popular songs, is not only alive and enjoying the best of health, but is also keenly participating in the musical success of his son, Mr. Landon Ronald, who is making rapid strides in his profession."

Neither of these features conveyed any impression of continuing activity on Henry Russell's part, and indeed old age may finally have been catching up with him. He lived on through most of 1899 and 1900, but seemingly without press coverage. Then—with just a few weeks to go to the end of the nineteenth century, of which he had been one of the most noted popular entertainers—he died, at Howley Place, in the first few minutes of 7 December 1900. It was in time for that same day's morning newspapers to publish lengthy obituaries. The death certificate showed the cause of death as "senile decay."

The funeral took place on Monday, 10 December 1900. The cortège left Howley Place, Maida Vale, shortly after 10:00 a.m. and arrived at Kensal Green Cemetery some half an hour later. Russell's eldest son, Rev. Henry Lloyd Russell, Vicar of the Church of the Annunciation, officiated. The second son, William Clark Russell, now confined to a wheelchair by arthritis at his home in Bath, was absent. The principal mourners were thus the two youngest sons, Henry Russell and Landon Ronald. In addition, press reports named grandsons Henry and Charles Russell (presumably sons of Henry Lloyd Russell and William Clark Russell, respectively), John Lloyd Davies (son of the late Isabella, whose widower, John Davies, was apparently also there), and Henry St. John Cooper. Others present included John Spencer Curwen (1847–1916) of the J. Curwen & Sons publishing firm, photographic artist Horatio Nelson King (1830–1905), John Hammond, John T. Borman, and Thomas Catling. About 100 people followed the oak coffin, with brass furniture, to the grave in new ground, behind the chapel, opposite the catacombs. An impressive stone monument in the form of an old armchair now marks the grave.

Henry Russell's widow, Hannah, stayed away from the ceremony but sent a wreath, a pillow of chrysanthemums with two bars of music blazoned upon it in purple heather, and the inscription "Farewell, my England; farewell for ever more," the refrain from "Cheer, Boys, Cheer." There were also wreaths from Sir Edward Lawson ("In memory of a very, very old friendship"), Clement Scott, Johnny Toole ("With affectionate remembrance"), Sir Henry Irving (a handsome wreath of violets, with the inscription "In loving remembrance, from Henry Irving"), and the orchestras of the Lyric and Prince of Wales Theatres, where Landon Ronald had served as musical director.

Quite why Hannah was absent is unclear. It may have had something to do with antagonism between Henry Russell's two families, or it may simply have been due to the service being Christian rather than Jewish. Perhaps it was simply that funerals were customarily all-male affairs in those days. The second possibility certainly upset *The Jewish Chronicle*:

> To the great surprise and disappointment of his Jewish friends and connections, Mr. Russell was buried on Monday at Kensal Green Cemetery with Christian rites. This remarkable arrangement may perhaps be explained by the fact that his children by his first wife were brought up in the Christian faith, and that one of them, the Rev Henry Lloyd Russell, is a clergyman of the Church of England. The Rev Mr. Russell officiated on Monday, and he would not have been able to do so if his father had been buried in a Jewish cemetery.

Reverend Henry Lloyd Russell lived on for many more years, dying at Eltham on 1 August 1923 at the age of eighty-five. Of the other two sons of Henry Russell's first marriage, William Clark Russell remained an invalid in Bath until his death on 8 November 1911, aged sixty-seven. From his nautical adventure novels, once so popular, *The Wreck of the Grosvenor* and *The Yarn of Old Harbour Town* have remained in print and retain their devotees. The youngest son of the first marriage, John Henry Sharp Russell, died in his mid-seventies, in South Africa, in 1925, the fortune he made from gold speculation gone.

Among the grandsons from the first marriage, William Clark Russell's son Herbert William Henry Russell (1869–1944), a nautical novelist like his father, distinguished himself more particularly as Reuter's War Correspondent during the Gallipoli Campaign and on the Western Front between June 1915 and November 1918, earning himself decoration as a Chevalier of the Légion d'Honneur and, in 1920, the knighthood that his grandfather never achieved. A passion for the sea also gripped grandson Henry St. John Cooper (1869–1926), who has been so much mentioned for his collaboration on Russell's memoirs. He made a reputation as a writer of serial stories, both humorous and serious, was an excellent artist and designer, had an extensive knowledge of fine art, and was a bulldog breeder. He also constructed several large-size models of ancient Spanish galleons and English ships of the Elizabethan and Stuart periods, correct to the minutest detail, in the workshop of his Tudor house at Sunbury-on-Thames.

Occasionally, in the years after Henry Russell's death, some other person by the name of Russell emerged into the public eye claiming kinship and, usually, direct descent. In 1903, for instance, one Leonora Russell made her début at London's Bechstein Hall. She had made an especial reputation in Buenos Aires and—latterly as Madame Leonora de Mello—continued in the public eye for some thirty years. This lady was actually Florence Leonora Russell and the granddaughter of the George Russell who had emigrated to Australia, after his marriage in 1850. Less clear is the precise relationship of a Margaret Russell, who, in 1955, was stated to be writing music for the Folies Bergère in Paris, and who was described as a great-granddaughter of Henry Russell.

Henry Russell's widow, Hannah de Lara, lived on for a further twenty-one years until 15 March 1922, when she died of a heart attack at the age of seventy-seven. As Henry Russell's widow, she had remained as willing a hostess as she had been as his wife. So, at least, is the recollection of her niece, Adelina de Lara:

> She was such a character, and had a fine sense of humour. She remained Early Victorian to the last; she always wore black, with white stockings and elastic-sided boots which were specially made for her, very expensive, and I thought very hideous. She wore bonnets with "bugles" (little black jet pendants) and, trying them on me, would say I looked beautiful in them! She hated modern fashions and, when she got angry, she called me "my darling" with the accent on *darling*. My aunt numbered among her friends such artists as Melba, Calvé and Duse. I met Lopokova, the Russian dancer, there very often. I shall never forget the day when at a tea party one of the guests ventured to

> smoke. Aunt Russell's face was a study in indignation. "Ladies! This has never happened before—smoking in *my* presence—I cannot allow it!" The offender, who was famous, hastily apologized and put out her cigarette, looking like a small child.

Landon was devoted to his mother, who always insisted upon treating him as a small boy: "My *darling*, don't rumple the antimacassar." Adelina de Lara herself was to live into the 1960s, performing on television and LP recordings and noted as one of the last pupils of Robert Schumann's widow, Clara.

Of the two sons of Hannah de Lara and Henry Russell, Landon Ronald enjoyed much the greater fame in Britain. Conductor, accompanist, and composer of ballads such as "O Lovely Night!" (1901) and "Down in the Forest" (1906), he conducted major orchestras both in Britain and on

Figure 18.3. Henry Russell, opera promoter. *Source:* Boston Public Library, Hale Collection, https://ark.digitalcommonwealth.org/ark:/50959/vh53xm59w.

the continent. He was a close friend and associate of Edward Elgar, who dedicated his *Falstaff* to him. Landon Ronald was a pioneer and stalwart of the recording industry, acting for many years as official accompanist to The Gramophone Company. He was also noted as an educator and editor, being Principal of the Guildhall School of Music from 1910 until his death on 14 August 1938, at the age of sixty-five. He was knighted in 1922.

In America, by contrast, it was Landon's elder brother Henry Russell who enjoyed the high profile, after graduating from singing teacher to impresario. In 1904, as a friend of Caruso, he brokered an arrangement with the San Carlo Opera Company in Naples for an Italian opera company to mount an autumn season at Covent Garden that included *Manon Lescaut* supervised by its composer, Puccini, and *Carmen* with Caruso as Don José. The following year he staged a further season of Italian operas and plays at London's Waldorf Theatre, which in turn led to him organizing an American opera tour for the Shubert brothers, Lee (c. 1873–1953), Sam (c. 1876–1905), and Jacob (1879–1963). Between 1905 and 1908, this took Henry Russell the length and breadth of a United States, which (with the development of the West Coast) was now much larger than that toured by his father over sixty years earlier. It led, in turn, to his appointment as manager of the newly built Boston Opera House, which he ran from 1909 to 1914. In that latter year, he promoted opera in Paris, and in 1924 he organized an opera company in Australia, led by Nellie Melba. Like his younger brother, he too died at the age of sixty-five—in London on 11 October 1937.

Neither brother's first marriage lasted. Henry's was over relatively soon, and after various relationships he married a second time, in 1919. Landon's wife, Mimi, severely depressive, died of self-inflicted poisoning in 1932, permitting him to marry his mistress, who had nursed both Ronald and his first wife. Of the brothers' children, it was Henry's younger son, Sheridan (1900–91), who most notably carried on the musical line. He began as a "cellist, a pupil of W H Squire, and toured Britain (with Clara Butt), as well as Europe and the USA." However, he left his biggest mark as an almoner, or social worker, at the National Hospital for Neurology and Neurosurgery in Queen Square, London. He hit on the idea of borrowing pictures from his artist friends and loaning them to hospitals to improve the surroundings in which he saw patients. With funding from the Nuffield Foundation, he set up a registered charity called Paintings in Hospitals, which has survived into the twenty-first century and mounts exhibitions at the Sheridan Russell Gallery at 16 Crawford Street in London's West End.

If the work of Henry Russell's youngest son and youngest grandson thus survives today, there is all too little left of Henry Russell's own output. Tied so closely to his own performances in an era when there was no sound recording, recognition of even his most successful songs largely died with those who recalled his performances of the mid-nineteenth century. Though their intent and effect had similarities to the work of Charles Dickens, they almost entirely lacked Dickens's enduring popular impact. In Britain, indeed, even "Cheer! Boys, Cheer!," his most enduring song at the time of his death, is now forgotten. Only "A Life on the Ocean Wave" has retained a tenuous link, either as a constituent of seaside singsongs, school assemblies, or, more particularly, as the regimental quick march of the Royal Marines. The bicentenary of the Battle of Trafalgar, in 2005, at least caused it to be recalled afresh as one of Britain's sea-faring classics.

In America, "Woodman, Spare That Tree" does still retain a tenuous hold on public consciousness, though primarily through George P. Morris's words. The verses were an early favorite of Rebecca of Sunnybrook Farm in Kate Douglas Wiggin's novel, published in 1903. More recent memory of the song, though, has primarily been through the satirical adaptation by Irving Berlin and Vincent Bryan, performed in *The Ziegfeld Follies* in 1911 by comedian Bert Williams (1874–1922) and committed to record by Phil Harris in a classic version in his southern drawl.

Apt, perhaps, is a comparison—adverse though it may be—with the output of Stephen Foster. The latter was some thirteen years Russell's junior, but was directly influenced by the older man, and was close to him in terms of date of output. Foster's "Oh! Susanna," for instance, dates from 1848, "Camptown Races" from 1850, "Jeanie with the Light Brown Hair" from 1854, and "Beautiful Dreamer" from 1864. It is easy to draw stylistic parallels between the two composers. Yet Foster's best songs have a gentle, wistful melodic charm and heart-on-sleeve manner that is missing from the songs of Henry Russell, which achieved their effect through the force of their singer-composer's personality.

Perhaps even more telling is a comparison with Russell's immediate contemporary J. P. Knight. The latter's "She Wore a Wreath of Roses" and "Rock'd in the Cradle of the Deep" have survived more strongly than Russell's songs, even though Knight failed miserably in his attempt to emulate Russell as a performer. Ultimately Russell's songs were too closely tied not only to their creator but also to the sentiments and social circumstances of their time, lacking the timelessness that has enabled Foster's, and to a much lesser extent Knight's, to endure. It is not without significance that it is "A Life on the Ocean Wave," which does have something of that timelessness, and a rollicking tune to boot, that has proved the exception to most of the above strictures.

America, of course, takes a more enlightened view of its popular musical heritage than Britain. Thus, Russell's name at least has retained an honored place in the history of American popular song. In his major history of the genre, Charles Hamm has declared Russell "the most important writer of songs in America before Stephen Foster." In 1977 Nonesuch Records recognized the fact by putting out an LP of Russell's songs, performed by the baritone Clifford Jackson accompanied by pianist William Bolcom. It incorporated spoken introductions taken from Russell's memoirs—delivered, alas, by Jackson in a spurious Irish accent. The ten numbers on the LP comprise "Wind of the Winter's Night" (1835), "Woodman, Spare That Tree" (1837), "The Ivy Green" (1837), "The Maniac" (1838), "A Life on the Ocean Wave" (1838), "The Old Arm Chair" (1840), "The Ship on Fire" (1842), "The Dream of the Reveller" (1843), and "Cheer! Boys, Cheer!" (1850), together with Russell's adaptation of Henry Phillips's "My Heart's in the Highlands."

Such is no more than they or their composer deserve. Henry Russell made a hugely significant contribution to popular culture over a period

Figure 18.4. Handwritten score for "Cheer Boys, Cheer" and Henry Russell's signature, 1895. *Source:* Author's collection.

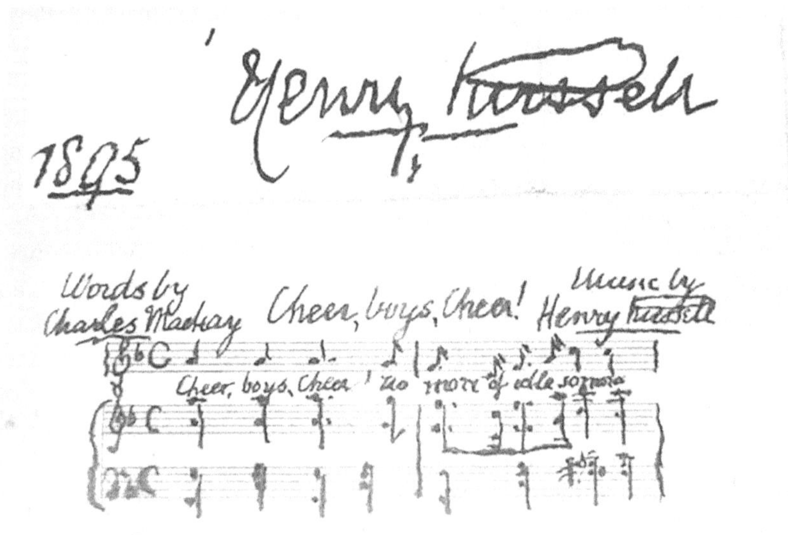

of twenty years in the mid-nineteenth century. Aptly, indeed, has he been described as "sort of the Elton John of his era: an Englishman who set other people's lyrics to music . . . and sang histrionically to his own piano accompaniment." It is to be hoped that, in recording Russell's career far more accurately than he himself was inclined to do, this volume will bring due awareness of one of the great popular music performers of the nineteenth century.

Appendix A

Performing Engagements

This list, built up largely from press announcements and reports, is very far from complete, but it indicates the diversity and extent of Russell's travels. It has not been a straightforward list to compile, as nineteenth-century newspapers often differed on the day, week, venue, et al. of a performance. Henry rarely canceled an appearance, however, through anything but force majeure; he only occasionally double-booked; and, unlikely as it may seem, he did appear, on occasion, in two different towns in one day.

1828

Mar 4 intermittently until Nov 13 Surrey Theatre: from Mar 4 singing "The Pilgrim of Love" and "The Horn of Chase" and other songs; from Mar 28 Lucas in *Die Nachtigall und der Rabe* (Weigl); Apr 12 *The Talisman;* from June 26 Walter in *The Swiss Family* (Weigl); July 26 Benefit; from Sep 16 Artabanes in *Artaxerxes* (Arne); Nov 3 *The Young Queen on Her Travels*; Nov 13 Master Burke's farewell benefit Dec 4 Mr. Rayner's Benefit

1829

Feb 3 Surrey Theatre

1833

May 27 Argyll Rooms, London
July 8 Argyll Rooms, London

1834

June 23 Argyll Rooms, London

1835

Apr 7 Music Hall, Store Street, London

1836

Jan 7 First Presbyterian Church, Rochester

June 14 Rochester

Oct 6, 11 Sacred Music Society, New York; 15 Concert Hall, 406 Broadway; 20 Young Ladies' Academy, Albany; 27 Musical Fund Hall, Philadelphia; 31 City Hotel, New York

Nov 4 Young Ladies' Academy, Albany; 9 Musical Fund Hall, Philadelphia

1837

Jan 24 American Hotel, Buffalo

Feb 28 Young Ladies' Academy, Albany

Mar 9 Masonic Temple, Boston; 12 Parson's Concert Room, Georgia

Apr 12 City Hall, New York; 17 City Hotel, New York; 20 Sacred Music Society, New York; 19, 24, 25 Lyceum, Brooklyn

May 11, 16 Masonic Hall, Philadelphia

June 5 Masonic Hall, Philadelphia

July 4 Young Ladies' Academy, Albany; [Troy; Utica; Rochester; Syracuse]

Aug 4 Musical Hall, Buffalo; 11 Cleveland; n.d. Detroit; 28 Rochester

Sep 8 Female Academy, Albany; 12 Academy, Albany; 19 City Hotel, New York; 21 Niblo's, New York; 22 Lyceum, Brooklyn; 26 City Hotel, New York; 27 Lyceum, Brooklyn; 28 City Hotel, New York

Oct n.d. Hempsted, New York; 13, 21, 27 Masonic Temple, Boston

Nov 20 and/or 27 Brinley Hall, Worcester, Massachusetts; 30 Second Presbyterian Church, Albany

Dec 9, 16 Masonic Hall, Philadelphia 30 Masonic Hall, Philadelphia

1838

Jan 4, 10 City Hotel, New York City; 25 City Hotel, Alexandria, DC; 29 Carusi's Saloon, Washington

Feb 5 (or 2, 9) Terpsichore Hall, Richmond, Virginia; the South; 21, 26 Fayolle's Room, King Street, Charleston

Mar 5 Masonic Hall, Augusta; 5, 12 Parsons' Concert Rooms, Augusta; 30 Female Academy, Albany

Apr 6 City Hotel, New York; 22, 28, 29 Masonic Temple, Boston (Boston Musical Institution) including *The Sceptic* on 22 and 29); 26 Musical Fund Hall, Philadelphia

May 6 Masonic Temple, Boston (*The Sceptic*)

June 11 Young Ladies' Academy, Albany

Oct 8, 15, 17, 25 City Hotel, New York

Nov 1 Young Ladies' Academy, Albany; 12, 15 Musical Fund Hall, Philadelphia

Dec Boston (*The Sceptic*) (?) 15 Temple, Boston; 28 Musical Fund Hall, Philadelphia

1839

Jan 3 Chapel of Female Seminary, Albany; 11, 18 Musical Fund Hall, Philadelphia

Feb 8, 13 City Hotel, New York; 18 Stuyvesant Institute, New York; 21 City Hotel, New York; 25 Sacred Music Society, New York

Mar 1 Apollo Saloon, New York; 4 Lyceum, Brooklyn; 5 Chatham Street Chapel, New York; 12 Female Seminary, Albany; Troy House, Troy; 18 Female Academy, Albany

May 28 American Hotel, Buffalo; 31 Webster's Concert Hall, Cleveland

Aug 9 Rochester

Oct 9, 10 Masonic Hall, Philadelphia; 14, 16, 18 City Hotel, New York; 23 Music Fund Hall, Philadelphia; 24 Stuyvesant Institute, New York; 26 Lyceum, Brooklyn; 31 City Hotel, New York

Nov 1 Lyceum, Brooklyn; 4 Apollo Saloon, New York; 6 Lyceum, Brooklyn; 11, 13, 15, 20, 22 Museum, Philadelphia; 26 Odeon Assembly Building, Philadelphia

Dec 9, 11, 13, 18, 20 Niblo's Saloon, New York; 25 City Hotel, New York; 26 Lyceum, Brooklyn

1840

Jan 18, 22 Melodeon, Boston; 25 Masonic Temple, Boston

Feb 1, 2, 4, 9, 16, 23, 29 Masonic Temple, Boston (*The Sceptic* on 2, 9, 16, 23); 8, 15, 19, 22, 26 Melodeon, Boston

Mar 1 Masonic Temple, Boston; Brooklyn; 12 Niblo's, New York; 31 Masonic Hall, New York

Apr 6, 9 Knickerbocker Hall, Albany; n.d. Troy

May 8, 13 National Hotel, Rochester; 15 Court House, Rochester

June 9 Eagle Assembly Room, Rochester

Aug 8 Washington Hall, Louisville; [Nashville (Southern Whig Convention), Lexington]

Sep 1, 2 Frankfort, Kentucky

Oct 10 Rochester House, Rochester; 31 Masonic Hall, Boston

Nov 5, 11, 14 Melodeon, Boston; 17 Town Hall, Roxbury

1841

Feb 2 Hotel, St. John; 12 City Hall, Portland; 18, 20, 24, 27 Masonic Temple/Melodeon, Boston; 28 Musical Institute, Boston

Mar 23 City Hotel, New York; 26 (?), 30 Stuyvesant Institute, New York

Apr 2, 9, 27 City Hotel, New York; 6, 13, 30 Stuyvesant Institute, New York; 8, 15, 28 Rutger's Institute, New York; 12 Brooklyn; 16, 20, 23, 26 Society Library, New York

May 12, 15, 19, 22 Musical Fund Hall, Philadelphia

June 4 Carusi's Saloon Washington; 10 Assembly Rooms, Fayette Street, Baltimore; 15 Concert Hall, Pittsburgh; 24 McCandle's Store, Cincinnati

July 3 Apollo Garden, Louisville; 13 Mechanics Institute, Cincinnati

1842

Feb 23 Kirkman's, no. 3 Soho Square, London

Mar 8 Hanover Square Rooms, London; 10 St. James's Theatre, King Street, London; 11 Hanover Square Rooms, London; 16 London Tavern (London Orphan Asylum); 31 Great Concert Room, London Tavern

Apr 18 Great Concert Room, London Tavern; 26 Music Hall, Sheffield

May 2 Great Concert Room, London Tavern; 3 Great Concert Room, Store Street, London; 5 Town Hall, Birmingham; 6 Manchester; 9 Town Hall, Reading; 23 Town Hall, Reading; 26 Hanover Square Rooms, London

June 1 Hanover Square Rooms, London; 16 University Hospital Dinner, London Tavern 21, 22 Yorkshire Amateur Music Meeting at Music Hall, Sheffield

July 5 Mansion House, Newbury; 6 Town Hall, Reading; 18 Newburgh Rooms, Brighton; 19 Guildhall, Rochester; 20 Assembly Rooms, Canterbury; 21 Royal Pier Hotel, Herne Bay; 22 Hale's Library, Margate; 23 Temperance Hall, Ramsgate; 25 Apollonian Hall, Dover; 26 July Theatre, Rochester

Aug 4 County Assembly Room, Maidstone; 5 Theatre, Rochester 13 Gravesend and Milton Lecture Rooms; 15, 17 Assembly Rooms Wolverhampton

Sep Literary Institute, Essex "fourth concert"

Nov 22, 25 Assembly Rooms, Queen Street, Wolverhampton; 29 and Dec 2 Royal Assembly Rooms, Great George Street, Liverpool; 14 Mechanics Institute, Liverpool; 15 Town Hall, Reading

Dec 14 Mechanics Institution, Liverpool; 15 Town Hall, Oxford; 19 Hanover Square Rooms, London

1843

Jan 2, 3, 6, 7 Royal Assembly Rooms, Great George Street, Liverpool; n.d. Canterbury Music Club; 12 Hanover Square Rooms, London; 18 Bridge Hotel, London Bridge; 23 (?) Exeter Hall, London; 30 Theatre, Rochester, Kent

Feb 1 Hanover Square Rooms, London; 3, 4 Royal Music Hall, Leamington; 8, 9, 16 Athenaeum Room, Derby; 9 Music Hall, Leeds; 13, 15 Philosophical Hall, Huddersfield; 14 Music Hall, Sheffield; 21, 23 Waterloo Rooms, Edinburgh; 22, 24 Assembly and Queen's Concert Rooms, Glasgow; 27 Hanover Square Rooms, London; 28 Dee's Royal Hotel, Birmingham

Mar 2 Hanover Square Rooms, London; 28 Niblo's, New York

Apr 3, 7 Niblo's, New York; 4, 11 Lyceum, Brooklyn; 12 Niblo's, New York; 13 Musical Fund Hall, Philadelphia; 14 Tabernacle, New York; 17 Musical Fund Hall, Philadelphia; 18 Niblo's, New York; 19 Lyceum, Brooklyn; 22, 25 Melodeon, Boston; 28 Lyceum Hall, Dorchester; 29 Melodeon, Boston

May 4 Town Hall, Roxbury; 9 Gilman's Saloon, Hartford, Connecticut; 17 Female Academy, Albany; 22 Apollo Saloon, New York; 29 Musical Fund Hall, Locust Street, Philadelphia

June 5 Musical Fund Hall, Philadelphia; 6 Baltimore; 10, 13, 16, 19 Melodeon, Boston; 23 Portland, Maine; 24 Saco, Maine; n.d. Bangor, Maine

July n.d. Nantucket; n.d. New Haven; 17 New Bedford; 18 Cabotsville (now Chicopee); 19 Albany; 22 Saratoga; 25 US Hotel, Saratoga; "a very successful tour of the Eastern provinces"

Aug The east, incl. Pittsburgh; 8, 11 Concert Hall, Rochester; 15, 17 American Hotel, Buffalo

Sep 7, 11, 14, 19, 21 Apollo Concert Saloon, New York; 25 to 30 NY Society Library Concert Room, New York

Oct 3 Rutgers' Institute, New York; 5 Lyceum, Brooklyn; 6 Stuyvesant Institute, New York; 12 Musical Fund Hall, Philadelphia; 17, 19, 21 Calvert Hall, Baltimore; 23, 26 Carusi's Saloon, Washington; 25 Lyceum, Alexandria

Nov 3 Lyceum Hall, DC; 6 Carusi's Saloon, Washington; Richmond; Norfolk; 24, 27 Temperance Hall, Charleston;

Dec 2 postponed to 4 Charleston; 3 Mobile; 14 Savannah; Columbus; St. Charles Theatre, New Orleans; 20 Central Hotel, Macon

1844

Jan 3 Waverley; 5 Mobile; 8, 10, 13, Armory, New Orleans; 18 Mobile; 25, 29 Washington Battalion Hall Armory, New Orleans

Feb Northwards up Mississippi 7 Mississippi; 9 Natchez; 17 Southron's Hall, Vicksburg 28 Memphis

Mar 9, 13, 15 Masonic Hall, Nashville; 19 Upper Room, Presbyterian Church, Nashville; 30 St. Louis

Apr 3 St. Louis; 11, 13, 16 W. C. Peters's Apollo Rooms, Louisville 18, 20 Amateur Musical Hall, Cincinnati

May 24 Apollo Saloon, Louisville; Chillicothe; 27, 29, 30 Amateur Musical Hall, Cincinnati

June 1 Amateur Musical Hall, Cincinnati; 17, 20 Pittsburgh; 25 Court House, Wheeling

July 3 Columbus

Sep 5, 17 Hanover Square Rooms, London; Boulogne-sur-Mer

Oct 3 Hanover Square Rooms, London; 10 Western Institution, Leicester Square, London; 21 Town Hall, Birmingham; 22 Athenaeum Room, Derby; 23 Music Hall, Leeds; 24 Assembly Rooms, York; 25 Theatre Royal, Newcastle-upon-Tyne; 26 Crown and Mitre Hotel, Carlisle (mat and eve); 28 (mat) Music Hall, Lancaster; (eve) Theatre Royal, Preston; 29 Exchange Rooms, Manchester; 30, Town Hall, Macclesfield; 31 Theatre Royal, Liverpool

Nov 1 Theatre Royal, Liverpool; 4 Music Hall, Dublin; 5 (afternoon) Rotundo, Dublin; 5 (eve) Theatre Royal, Dublin; 8 (afternoon), 8 (eve), 9 Music Hall, Edinburgh; 11, 12 Assembly Rooms, Glasgow; 13 Assembly Rooms, Greenock; 14 City Hall, Glasgow; 16 Liverpool; 20, 22 Music Hall, Leeds; 18, 19, 21 Philosophical Hall, Huddersfield; 25 Music Hall, Lancaster; 28 Theatre Royal, Newcastle-upon-Tyne; 29 Theatre Royal, Durham

Dec 2, 5 Music Hall, Sheffield; 4 Large Room, Royal Hotel, Halifax; 6 Hull and Sculcoates Public Rooms; 11, 12 Exchange Rooms, Nottingham

1845

Jan 9 Large Public Hall, Reading; 20 Hanover Square Rooms, London; 22 Crosby Hall, London; 27 Sussex Hall, London; 28 Mermaid, Hackney; 29 Lecture Hall, Greenwich; 31 Literary and Scientific Institution, Croydon

Feb 3 Covent Garden Theatre, London; 4 County Assembly Rooms, Maidstone; 6 Hanover Square Rooms, London; 7 Crosby Hall, London; 8 Sussex Hall, London; 11 County Assembly Room, Maidstone; 18 London Mechanics Institution, Chancery Lane 15, 22 Mechanics Institution, Liverpool; 17 Institution, Greenwich; 20 New Public Rooms, Reading; 24 Music Hall, Wolverhampton; 25 (?) Princess's Theatre; 25 Music Hall, Nelson Street, Newcastle; 27 Theatre, Durham; 28 and Mar 1 Coffee House, Carlisle

Mar 3 to 11 Music Hall, Dublin; (engagements canceled); 17 Sussex Hall, London; 19 Marylebone Literary and Scientific Institution; 18 Music Hall, Dublin; 24, 25 Assembly Rooms, Above Hill, Lincoln; 26, 28 Public Rooms, Kingston Square, Hull

Apr 7, 8, 9, 12 Princess's Theatre, Oxford Street, London; 10 Hanover Square Rooms, London; 14 British School, Shelton; 15, 16 George Hotel, Burslem; 17 Institution Lecture Hall, Newcastle; 18 Town Hall, Longton; 19 Concert Hall, Liverpool; 21 Athenaeum Room, Derby; 22 Marylebone Literary and Scientific Institution; 24 Hanover Square Rooms, London 23 Music Room, Holywell, Oxford; 26 Concert Hall, Lord Nelson Street, Liverpool; 28 (mat and eve) Town Hall, Brighton; 30 Theatre, Rochester

May 1 New Hall, Reading; 2 Literary Institute, Greenhithe; 5, 7 Victoria Concert Hall, Canterbury; 6, 8 Apollonian, Hall, Dover; 9 Literary Institution, Fitzroy Square, London; 10 London Mechanics' Institution, Chancery Lane; 2, 14 Theatre, Sheffield; 13 Court House, Rotherham; 17 Red Lion Hotel, Sheffield; 20 Music Saloon, Wakefield; 21 Exchange Rooms, Bradford; 23 Western Literary and Scientific Institution, Leicester Square, London; 26 Royal British Institution, City Road, London; 27 Literary Institution, Fitzroy-square, London; 28 Literary Institution, Greenwich; 29 Marylebone Literary and Scientific Institution

June 2, 5, 7 Concert Hall, Liverpool; 9 Literary Institution, Harmer Street, Gravesend; 10 Literary and Scientific Institution, Fitzroy Square, London; 11 Marylebone Literary and Scientific Institution; 12 King's Arms, Kensington; 13 Western Literary and Scientific Institution, Leicester Square, London; 15 Institution, Croydon; 16 Assembly Rooms, Hackney; 17 Southwark Literary Institution; 26 Marylebone Literary and Scientific Institution; 30 to July 4 Rotundo, Dublin

July 2, 5 Assembly Rooms, Kingstown; 7 to 12 Rotundo, Dublin; 14 to 17, 21 Music Hall, Dublin; 30 Hanover Square Rooms, London

Aug 6 to 13 Princess's Theatre, Oxford Street; 12 Shire Hall, Chelmsford; 27 Literary Institution, Gravesend

Sep 8, 15 Assembly Rooms, Ingram Street, Glasgow; 9, 12, 20, 24 Waterloo Rooms, Edinburgh; 16 Assembly Rooms, Cathcart Street, Greenock; 17 Ayr; 19 Assembly Rooms, Glasgow; 20 School House, Ardrossan; 23 Thistle Hall, Dundee; 27 City Hall, Glasgow; 28 Dunfermline; 29, 30 Music Hall, Belfast

Oct 2 to 16 Music Hall, Dublin; 18, 23, 25 Concert Hall, Liverpool; 19 (?) Warrington; 20, 22 Athenaeum, Manchester; 21 Theatre Royal, Preston 24, 25 Music Hall, Newcastle; 27 Coffee House, Assembly Rooms, Carlisle; 28 New Music Hall, Nelson Street, Newcastle 29 Theatre, Durham 31 Theatre, Wolverhampton

Nov 4 Odd Fellow's Hall, Barnsley; 6 De Grey Rooms, York (mat and eve); 11 Town Hall, Stockton-on-Tees; 17, 20 Music Hall, Leeds; 18, 21 Odd Fellows' Hall, Royal Hotel, Halifax; 24 Philosophical Hall, Huddersfield

Dec 1, 2 Music Hall, Gateshead; 5, 7 Assembly Rooms, Glasgow; 8 Marylebone Literary and Scientific Institution; 11 Eastern Institution, Commercial-road, London; 12 Western Scientific and Literary Institution, Leicester Square, London 15 Town Hall, Hanley; 16, 17 George Hotel, Burslem; 18 Union Town Hall, Longton; 19 New Town Hall, Hanley

1846

Jan 5, 7 Assembly Rooms, Ingram Street, Glasgow; 6 Assembly Rooms, Greenock; 10, 17 City Hall, Glasgow; 19 Waterloo Rooms, Edinburgh; 20 Red Lion Inn, Falkirk; 21 Alloa; 24 (mat) Assembly Rooms, Glasgow; 31 Waterloo Rooms, Edinburgh

Feb 2 Miss Kelly's Theatre, London; 4 Lecture Hall, Greenwich; 5 Literary Institution, Croydon; 6 Kensington Theatre, London; 9 Covent Garden Theatre, London; 10 Miss Kelly's Theatre, London; 11 Lecture Hall, Greenwich; 12 Harmonic Hall, Woolwich; 13 Kensington Theatre; 16, 23 Miss Kelly's Theatre, London; 18 New Public Rooms, Reading; 19 King's Arms, Kensington; 28 Mechanics Institution, Manchester

Mar 2 Miss Kelly's Theatre, London; 6 Marylebone Literary and Scientific Institution; 9, 16, 23, 30 Miss Kelly's Theatre, London; 12 Western Literary and Scientific Institution, London; 13 Theatre, Preston; 14 Mechanics Institute, Manchester; 19 Town Hall, Birmingham; 20 Music Hall, Shrewsbury; 21 Concert Room, Wellington; 26, 27 Concert Hall, Lord Nelson Street, Liverpool; 30 Covent Garden Theatre, London 31 and April 2 Concert Hall, Lord Nelson Street, Liverpool

Apr 6 Miss Kelly's Theatre, London; 6 to 9, 11 Covent Garden Theatre, London; 8, 12 Western Literary and Scientific Institution, Leicester

Square, London; 13, 14 Music Hall, Dublin; 16, 17 Sheffield; 18 Sussex Hall, London; 20 Music Hall, Kingston Square, Hull; 23 Odd Fellows Literary Soc., Town Hall, Birmingham; 24 Natural History Society, Worcester; 27 Corn Exchange, Maidstone; 28 Sussex Hall, London

May 4, 5 Royal Victoria Archery Rooms, Southampton; 7 Theatre Royal, Canterbury; 8 Theatre Royal, Dover; 11, 12, 14 Music Hall, Dublin; 15, 20 Theatre Royal, Belfast; 18, 19, 21 Music Hall, Dublin; 25 Cork

June 8, 11 Sadler's Wells Theatre, London [Maidstone, Rochester, Tunbridge Wells]; 24 Hanover Square Rooms, London; 29 Zoological Gardens, Birkenhead

July 1, 3 Zoological Gardens, Birkenhead; 6 New Hall, Leicester; 21 Rochester; 21 Dover; 31 Kensington Theatre

Aug 1 City of London Theatre; 3 to 8 Strand Theatre, London; 8 Surrey Theatre, Southwark; 10 New Public Hall, Reading; 11 Shire Hall, Chelmsford; 12, 14 Theatre Royal, Bristol; 13 Theatre Royal, Gloucester; 15 City of London Theatre; 17 Lecture Hall, Greenwich; 19 Croydon; 20 Richmond; 21 Kensington Theatre; 22 Theatre Royal, Bath; 24 to 29 Strand Theatre, London; 31 Literary Institution, Borough Road

Sep 1 Southwark Literary Institution; Crown Inn, Gosport; 2 Theatre Royal, Portsmouth; 3 Theatre, Landport; 4 Theatre Royal, Winchester; 9 Northampton; 15 Mechanics Institution, Nottingham; 15, 16 Dee's Hotel, Birmingham; 18 St. Mary's Hall, Coventry; 21 (1 week) Theatre Royal, Church Street; Liverpool; 28, 30 Music Hall, Dublin 29 Mayoralty Rooms, Drogheda

Oct 2, 3 Theatre, Preston; 5, 6 Music Hall, Sheffield; 8 Music Saloon, Wakefield; 9 Beverley; 12 Lecture Hall, Goodramgate, York; 13 Town Hall, Scarborough; 15, 19, 21 Music Hall, Leeds; 20 Commercial Hall, Wigan; 24 Mechanics' Institute, Manchester; 27 Theatre Royal, Blackburn; 28 Lecture Hall, Goodramgate, York; 31 Mechanics Institute Manchester

Nov 3 Theatre, Durham; 4, 9 Music Hall, Newcastle; 10 Golden Lion Hotel, South Shields; 13 Theatre, Durham; 16 to 28 Lyceum Theatre; 18, 21 Sussex Hall, London; 20 Southwark Literary Institution; 25 Marylebone Institution 30 (mat and eve) George Hotel, Northampton

Dec 2 Theatre Royal, Worcester; 4 Theatre, Wolverhampton; 7, 12 City Hall, Glasgow; 8, 11 Waterloo Rooms, Edinburgh; 10 Red Lion Inn, Falkirk; 14 Assembly Rooms, Greenock; 15 Exchange Rooms, Paisley; 18 Assembly Rooms, Ingram Street, Glasgow; 21, 22, 26 Concert Hall, Lord Nelson Street, Liverpool; 23, 24 Town Hall, Birmingham 28 New Town Hall, Hanley; 29 George Hotel, Burslem; 30 New Town Hall, Burslem; 31 Wheatsheaf Hotel, Stoke

1847

Jan 1 New Town Hall, Hanley; 2, 9 Mechanics Institution; Manchester; 4 (mat and eve) Music Hall, Leamington; 11 Star Hotel, Stafford; 12 Red Lion Hotel, Uttoxeter; 14 Town Hall, Congleton; 15 Town Hall, Tunstall; 20 Assembly Rooms, Salisbury; 25 New National School, Cheadle; 26 Athenaeum Rooms/Theatre Royal, Derby; 27 Mechanics Hall, Nottingham; 28 New Hall, Leicester 29 Theatre Royal, Blackburn

Feb 1 to 5 Music Hall, Dublin; 8 Lyceum Theatre, London; 9 Lyceum Theatre; 10 Mechanics Institute Reading; 11 (mat and eve) Assembly Rooms, Cheltenham; 12 Theatre, Gloucester; 15, 19 Royal Subscription Rooms, Exeter; 16, 18 Theatre Royal, Plymouth; 22 to March 20, 16 (mat) Strand Theatre, London

Mar 22, 26 Concert Hall, Lord Nelson Street, Liverpool; 30 Haymarket Theatre, London; 30 London Tavern; 31 Literary Institution, Chertsey

Apr 3 Free Trade Hall, Manchester; 5 to 17 Strand Theatre 12 (mat) Strand Theatre; 19, 21 Theatre Royal, Brighton; 26, 28 Theatre Royal, Bristol; 27 Theatre Royal, Bath; 29 (mat and eve) Assembly Rooms, Cheltenham

May 3 Theatre Royal, Windsor; 6 Star Hotel, Oxford; 10, 12 Theatre Royal, Sheffield; 11 Philosophical Hall, Huddersfield; 13 Bradford Theatre; 17 Theatre, Coventry; 19 Music Hall, Leeds; 20 Music Hall, Hull; 21 de Grey Rooms/Lecture Hall, Goodramgate, York; 24, 25 Theatre Royal, Preston; 26 Music Hall, Lord Nelson Street, Liverpool; 27; Chester Theatre; 29 Music Hall, Lord Nelson Street, Liverpool; 31 to June 5 Music Hall, Dublin

June 7 Music Hall, Liverpool; 11 Theatre Royal, Southampton; n.d. Town Hall, Devonport; 9 Theatre, Winchester; 10 Theatre, Portsmouth; 17, 18 Theatre Royal, Blackburn; 21, 22 Theatre Royal, Ipswich; 24 Concert Room, Bury St. Edmunds; 25 Town Hall, Thetford; 28, 30 Swan Inn, St. Peter's, Norwich; 29 Corn Exchange, Yarmouth

July 2 Town Hall, Lowestoft; 14 Theatre Royal, Canterbury; 15 Theatre Royal, Dover; 16 Apollonian Hall, Ramsgate; n.d. Gosport; 19 Public Hall, Guildford; 20 Theatre, Salisbury; 21 Theatre Royal, Southampton; 22 Ryde; n.d. Canterbury; n.d. Royal Hotel, Margate; 27 Assembly Rooms, Taunton; 28, 29 Theatre Royal, Exeter

Aug 4 Theatre Royal, Plymouth; 13 Assembly-Room, Truro; [n.d. Chertsey; n.d. Farnham; n.d. Theatre Royal, Winchester]; 19 Theatre, Salisbury; n.d. Portsmouth; 24 Assembly Rooms, Chichester; [Arundel; Worthing]; 28 (mat) Assembly Rooms, St. Leonards; 28 (eve) Swan Hotel, Hastings

Sep n.d. Paris (two concerts); 6, 8 Theatre Royal, Norwich; 7 Corn Exchange, Yarmouth; 9, 10 Theatre, Ipswich; [Colchester, Sudbury]; 21 Theatre, Windsor; 22 New Hall, London Street, Reading; 23 Newbury; 24 Assembly Rooms, Taunton; 25 Concert Hall, Liverpool; 27 George Hotel (mat) and Theatre (eve), Northampton; 28 Theatre Royal, Coventry; 29 Royal Music Hall, Leamington; 30 Stratford-on-Avon

Oct 2 Concert Hall, Liverpool; 3 (?) Warwick; 4 Theatre, Wolverhampton; 5 Theatre Royal, Shrewsbury; Wellington; St. Helens; 7, 9 Concert Hall, Lord Nelson Street, Liverpool 9, 10 Theatre, Ipswich; 11 (mat, eve) Athenaeum Rooms, Derby; 12 Mechanics' Hall, Nottingham; 13 Theatre Royal, Chesterfield; 14 (?) Huddersfield; 15 Odd-fellows Hall, Halifax; 16 Concert Hall, Manchester; 18, 19, 21 Music Hall, Dublin; 20 Mayoralty Rooms, Drogheda; 23 Concert Hall, Liverpool/Mechanics Institution, Manchester; 25 Theatre Royal, Blackburn; 26 Theatre Royal, Preston; 27 Whitehall Assembly Rooms, Kendal; 28 (mat and eve) Coffee House Hotel, Carlisle; 29 Lancaster

Nov 1 Odd Fellows' Hall, Barnsley; 3 Town Hall, Birmingham; 5 Music Saloon, Wakefield; 8 Theatre Royal, Hull; 9 Lecture Hall, Goodramgate, York; 10 Assembly Rooms, Darlington; 11 Assembly Rooms, Stockton; 12 Theatre, Durham; 15, 17 Music Hall, Nelson Street, Newcastle-upon-Tyne; 20 Lecture Room, Newcastle-on-Tyne; 22, 27 City Hall, Glasgow; 25 Exchange Rooms, Paisley; 29 Assembly Rooms, Greenock; 30 George Hotel, Kilmarnock

Dec 8 Guild Hall, Cupar; 9 Thistle Hall, Dundee; 10 City Hall, Perth; 21 Theatre, Preston; 18, 20, 23 Concert Hall, Lord Nelson Street, Liverpool

1848

Jan 3 Town Hall, Hanley; 4 Town Hall, Longton; 5 Stoke-on-Trent; 6 George Hotel, Burslem; 7 Town Hall, Hanley; 11 Red Lion, Uttoxeter; 12 Assembly Rooms, Green Man and Black's Head Royal Hotel, Ashbourne; 18 Lecture Hall, Greenwich; 20 Theatre Royal, Windsor; 24 Rosemary Branch, Peckham; 25 Eastern Institution, Commercial Road, London; 27 Covered Market, Hanley; 31 Mechanics' Institution, Walworth

Feb 1 Albion Hall, Hammersmith; 2 Mechanics' Institution, Westminster; 3 Mechanics' Institution, Chancery Lane, London; 4 Institution, Borough Road, London; 7 Reading; 8 Maidenhead; 9 Uxbridge; 10 Western Literary and Scientific Institution, Leicester Square, London; 11 Crosby Hall, London; 12 Temperance Hall, Westminster; 14 Eastern

Institution, Commercial Road, London; 15 Drury Lane Theatre, London; 16 Institution, Walworth; 17 Woolwich; 18 Theatre, Milton Street, Finsbury; 19 Mechanics' Institution, Manchester; 21 Theatre, Northampton; 22 Assembly Room, Bedford; 23 Highbury Barn Tavern; 24 Mechanics' Institution, Chancery Lane, London 26 Mechanics' Institution, Manchester; 28 Theatre, Wolverhampton

Mar 1 Theatre Royal, Worcester; 6 Sussex Hall, London; 7 Assembly Rooms, Kentish Town; 8 Assembly Rooms, Highgate; 9 Theatre, Milton Street, Finsbury; 10 Marylebone Institution; 11 Concert Hall, Lord Nelson Street, Liverpool 13 Theatre Royal, Chester 15, 18 Concert Hall, Lord Nelson Street, Liverpool; 20, 22 Theatre, Sheffield; 21 Music Hall, Leeds; 25 Mechanics Institution Manchester; 27 Theatre Royal, Leicester; 29 Theatre, Chesterfield; 30 Theatre, Derby; 31 Town Hall, Newark

Apr 3 Theatre, Shrewsbury; 5 City Arms Hotel, Hereford; 7 Town Hall, Newport; 10, 12 Theatre Royal, Bristol; 11 Theatre Royal, Bath; 13 Theatre, Gloucester; 14 Assembly Rooms, Cheltenham; 15, 17 Concert Hall, Lord Nelson Street, Liverpool; 18, 19, 20 Olympic Theatre, London; 19, 20 Sadler's Wells Theatre; 25 Western Literary Institution, Leicester Square; 26 Albion Hall, Hammersmith; 27 Lecture Hall, Institute, Walworth; 28 Mechanics' Hall, Great Smith Street, Westminster

May 4 Assembly Rooms, Gravesend; 5 Lecture Hall, Greenwich; 9 Town Hall, Birmingham; 10 Theatre, Coventry; 11 Mechanics' Institution, Chancery-lane, London; 12, 13 Sadler's Wells Theatre, London; 15 Mechanics' Institution Chelmsford; 16 Theatre Royal, Colchester; 17 Theatre Royal, Ipswich; 18 Theatre Royal, Bury St. Edmunds; 19 Music Hall, Store Street, London and/or Town Hall, Cambridge (eve) 22 Theatre Royal, Norwich; 23 Large Room, Cumbergate Street, Peterborough; 23 Yarmouth, 24 Dereham; 25 Swaffham, 26 Theatre, Lynn; 29 Theatre, Wisbech

June 7 Corn Exchange, Lincoln; 8 Theatre, Gainsboro; 14 Town Hall, Ware; 15 Shire Hall, Hertford; 20 Corn Exchange, Maidstone; 21 Theatre Royal, Canterbury 22 Harveian Literary Institute, Folkestone; 23 Theatre, Dover

July 5 Temperance Hall, Broad Street, Ramsgate; 12 Queen's Rooms, Newport; 14 Assembly Rooms, Chichester; 24 to 29 and 27 (mat) Strand Theatre, London

Aug 7 Town Hall, Brighton; 9 Queens Rooms, Mill-Dam, Portsea; 10 Town Hall, Salisbury; 11 Town Hall, Poole/Royal Hotel, Weymouth; 24, 25 Music Hall, Dublin; 28, 29 Town Hall, Waterford; [Limerick]

Sep 1 Music Hall, Dublin; 7, 8 Concert Hall, Lord Nelson Street, Liverpool; 18 Literary Institution, Deptford; 25 (six nights) Strand Theatre, London

Oct 2 Theatre, Coventry; 4 New Hall, Leicester; 5 Theatre, Derby; 9, 11 Leeds/Philosophical Hall, Huddersfield; 10 Theatre, Stockton-on-Tees; 12 Music Hall, Sheffield; 13 Town Hall, Market Harborough; 15 Town Hall, Holmfirth; 16 Music Hall, Jarratt Street, Hull; 17 Lecture Hall, York; 23, 25 Music Hall, Newcastle

Nov 2, 4 City Hall, Glasgow; 15 City Hall, Perth; 17, 18 Theatre, Dundee; 20 Merchants' Hall, Hutcheson Street, Glasgow; 21 Guild Hall, Montrose; 27 Theatre Royal, Newcastle; 28 Theatre, Durham; 30 Athenaeum Lecture Room, Carlisle

Dec 1 Theatre Royal, York; 4, 6 Concert Hall, Lord Nelson Street, Liverpool; 5 Theatre Royal, Chester; 6 Exeter Hall, London/Lecture Hall, Warrington; 9 Concert Hall, Liverpool; 11, 13 Free Trade Hall, Manchester; 12 Commercial Hall, Wigan; 20 Theatre, Northampton; 21 Theatre Royal, Worcester; 22 Princess's Theatre, London/Assembly Rooms, Smith's Hotel, Dudley; 26 Westminster Literary, Scientific and Mechanics' Institution; 27, 29 Whittington Club, Strand, London

1849

Feb 5 Assembly Rooms, Wandsworth; 6 Institution, Croydon; 7 Epsom; 8 Theatre Royal, Windsor; 9 Uxbridge; 13 Town Hall, Marlborough; 16 Town Hall, Devizes; 19 Town Hall, High Wycombe 26, 28 and March 2 Assembly Rooms, Prince-Street, Bristol

Mar 5 Theatre Royal, Gloucester; 6 Assembly Rooms, Cheltenham; 9 Three Tuns Inn, Pershore; 12 Music Hall, Leamington Spa; 17 Lecture Hall, Scotland Road, Warrington; 19, 21 Corn Exchange, High Street, Birmingham; 23 Theatre Royal, Ainsworth Street, Blackburn; 26, 28, 31 Concert Hall, Lord Nelson Street, Liverpool; 29 Craven Rooms, Woodside; 30 Theatre, Preston

Apr 2, 4 Marylebone Theatre; 3, 5 New Surrey Theatre, London; 9–13 Music Hall, Dublin; 23 Town Hall, Brighton; 26 Beaumont Institution, Mile End; 27 Crosby Hall, London 30 Queen's Rooms, Portsea

May 1 Theatre Royal, Southampton; 2 Theatre, Winchester; 3 Theatre Royal, Salisbury 8 Lecture Hall, Greenwich; 9 Marylebone Theatre; 17 Theatre Royal, Canterbury

June 4 Beaumont Institution, Mile End; 5 Lecture Hall, Tottenham; 6 Manor House Institution, Hackney; 7 Town Hall, Woolwich; 8 Lecture

Hall, Greenwich; 11 Mechanics' Institution, Chelmsford; 12 Theatre, Colchester; 13 Town Hall, Hadleigh; 14 Theatre, Ipswich; 15 Theatre Bury St. Edmunds; c. 20 Theatre, Lynn; 21 Theatre, Cambridge; 25 Sadler's Wells Theatre, London; 26 Assembly Rooms, Wandsworth; 27, 29, 30 Sadler's Wells Theatre, London

July 3 Theatre Royal, Dover; 16, 20 Theatre Royal, Bristol; 17, 19 Theatre Royal, Bath, 21 Concert Room, Wisbech; 23 Bridgwater; 24, 25 Royal Subscription Rooms, Exeter; 26 Theatre Royal, Plymouth; 27 Devonport

Aug 6 Town Hall, Torrington; 7 Theatre, Barnstaple; 8 Ilfracombe; 13 Freemasons Hall, Essex Arms Inn, Watford; 16 Subscription Rooms, Tiverton; 17 County Hall, Aylesbury; 21 Assembly Rooms, Woburn; 22 Public Hall, Newport Pagnell; 24 Town Hall, Buckingham; 27 Town Hall, Brackley; 28, 30 Theatre, Banbury; 29 Town Hall, Deddington

Sep 4, 8 Lord Nelson Concert Hall, Liverpool; n.d. Douglas, Isle of Man; 17, 19 Princess's Theatre

Oct 1, 2 Music Hall, Dublin; 5 East Grinstead; 8 Theatre Royal, Reading/Theatre Royal, Windsor; 9 Staines; 10 Chertsey; 11 Guildford; 15 New Public Hall, Reading; 16 Mansion House, Newbury; 17 Town Hall, Andover; 18 Town Hall, Romsey; 19 Queen's Concert Rooms, Portsea; 22 Theatre, Coventry 25 Town Hall, Birmingham; 29 New Hall, Leicester; 30

Nov 5 Theatre Royal, Derby; 6 Mechanics Hall, Nottingham; 8 Ellis's Music Hall, Worksop; 9 Mansfield; 11, 12, 17 Concert Hall, Lord Nelson Street, Liverpool; 16 Philosophical Hall, Huddersfield; 19, 21 Music Hall, Leeds; 23 Oddfellows Hall Halifax; 27 Public Room, Selby; 28, 30 Lecture Hall, Goodramgate, York

Dec 3, 5 Music Hall, Newcastle; 20, 21 Theatre Royal, Preston; 26 Sussex Hall, London 27 Mechanic's Institute, Chancery Lane

1850

Jan 7 Theatre Royal, Chester; 8 Wynnstay Arms, Wrexham; 9 Black Lion, Mold; 11 Theatre Royal, Shrewsbury; 14 Festival Concert Room, York; 15 Music Hall, Hull; 16 Music Hall, Newcastle; 17 Athenaeum, Sunderland; 21 Wellington; 22 Theatre Royal, Wolverhampton; 23 Dudley; 24 Stourbridge; 25 Kidderminster; 28 Music Hall, Worcester; 29 Leominster; 30 Theatre, Hereford, 31 Barrett's Hotel, Ross

Feb 1 Borough Court, Monmouth; 5 Theatre, Cardiff; 6 Commercial Rooms, Newport; 7 Goddard Arms Hotel, Swindon; 8 Town Hall, Brecon; 11, 12 Theatre, Swansea; 18 Hammersmith; 19 Richmond Theatre; 20

Woolwich; 21 Bexley; 23 Lecture Hall, Walworth; 28 and 1 Mar Town Hall, Brighton

Mar 8 King's Head Assembly Rooms, Cirencester; 14 Assembly Rooms, Cheltenham; 25 to 28, 30 Lyceum Theatre, London; n.d. Assembly Rooms, Swindon

Apr n.d. Theatre Royal, Windsor

May 13, 15, 16 Marylebone Theatre; 27 Theatre, Winchester; 31 Assembly Rooms, Chichester

June 7 Corn Exchange, Lewes; 17 Theatre, Dover 19 Bull Inn, Cranbrook; n.d. Pavilion Hotel, Folkestone

1851

Apr 7 to 12 Theatre Royal, Richmond; 14 to 17, 19 Olympic Theatre, London; 21, 22 Woolwich Institution; 24, 25 Horns, Kennington; 28, 29 Rosemary Branch, Camberwell

May 5 Town Hall, Brighton 13, 14 Theatre Royal, Southampton; 19, 21, 22, 28, 30, 31 etc. Music Hall, Dublin

June 4, 5, 6, 7, 9, 10, 12, 14, 15, 16, 17, 19, 20, 23, 24 etc. Music Hall, Dublin; 30 Theatre Royal, Cork

July 3, 5, 8 Theatre Royal, Cork; 14, 15, 16, 18, 19 Theatre Royal, Belfast

Aug 4 to 16 Miss Kelly's Theatre, Soho; 25 to 30 Theatre Royal, Birmingham

Sep 1 Theatre Royal, Leamington; 8, 9 Theatre Royal, Coventry; 15 (1 week) Theatre Royal, Manchester; 29 (5 nights) Theatre Royal, Sheffield

Oct 6 to 9 (mat) Theatre Royal, Derby; 13 (five nights) Theatre Royal, Nottingham; 27, 28, 29, 30 Theatre Royal, York

Nov 3 (five nights) City Hall, Glasgow; 24 Theatre Royal, Liverpool (six nights)

Dec 2, 3, 4, 5 Theatre Royal, Chester; 9 Assembly Rooms, Cheltenham

1852

Jan 26 to 31 Concert Hall, Lord Nelson Street, Liverpool

Feb 4 to Mar 4 Music Hall, Abbey Street, Dublin

Mar 8 to 19 Cook Street Theatre, Cork; 22, 24 (mat) 25, 26 Theatre Royal, Limerick

April 25 to 30 Theatre Royal, Leicester

Aug 30 to Sep 18 Lyceum Theatre, London

Oct 4 to 8 Theatre Royal, Sheffield; 11 to 15 Theatre, Leeds; 18 to 23 Hull; 25 to 30 Concert Hall, Lord Nelson Street, Liverpool

Nov 1 Halifax; 2 Philosophical Hall, Huddersfield; 3 Temperance Hall, St. Peter's Square, Stockport; 4, 5, 6 Free Trade Hall, Manchester; 8 Beaumont Institution, Mile End; 9 Rokeby House, Stratford, Essex; 10 Assembly Rooms, Kensington; 11 Stoke Newington; 12 Tottenham; 15 Lecture Hall, Greenwich; 16 Crosby Hall, London; 17 Walworth; 19 Marylebone Institution; 22, 24 Croydon; 23 Beaumont Institution, Mile End; 25 Angel Assembly Rooms, Edmonton

Dec 1 Theatre Royal, Windsor; 2 Sandy's Assembly Room, Henley-on-Thames; 6 Star Hotel, Oxford; 7 Goddard Arms, Swindon; 9 Assembly Rooms, Cheltenham; 10 Music Hall, Worcester; 13 Corn Exchange, Stourbridge; 14 Town Hall Assembly Rooms, Walsall; 15, 17 Town Hall, Birmingham; 16 Theatre, Lichfield; 22 New Music Rooms, Euston Square, London

1853

Jan 17 Dover; 18 Theatre Royal, Rochester; 19 Public Rooms, Sittingbourne; 20 Corn Exchange, Maidstone; 26 Theatre Royal, Canterbury; 27 Guildhall, Deal; 31 to Feb 5 Strand Theatre, London

Feb 14, 15, 18 Town Hall, Hanley; 16 Crown Hotel, Stone; 17 Town Hall, Crewe; 21 to 26 Concert Hall, Lord Nelson Street, Liverpool

Mar 10 to 12 Strand Theatre, London; 18, 19, 20, 21, 22 Concert Hall, Lord Nelson Street, Liverpool; 28, 29 Odd Fellow's Hall, Halifax

Apr 6, 7 Lecture Room, Mechanics Institute, Bradford; 8 Philosophical Hall, Huddersfield; 9 Sobriety Hall, Todmorden, 10, 13 Burnley; 12, 14, 15 Music Hall, Leeds; 13 Music Saloon, Wakefield; 19, 20, 21, 22 23 Concert Hall, Lord Nelson Street, Liverpool 27, 29 Theatre Royal, Preston; 28, 30 Theatre Royal, Blackburn

May 2 Theatre, Bolton; 10, Court House, Burnley; 16 Town Hall, Macclesfield; 17, 18 Concert Hall, Lord Nelson Street, Liverpool; 24 Town Hall, Stalybridge; 30 Corn Exchange, Barnsley; 31 Doncaster

June 1 Assembly Room, Worksop; 2 Corn Exchange, Grantham; 6 Mechanics Hall, Nottingham; 7 New Hall, Leicester; 8 Theatre, Stamford

Aug 22, 23 Town Hall, Brighton; 23 Society's Hall, Portsea; n.d. Theatre Royal, Portsmouth; 25, 26 Victoria Rooms, Southampton

Sep 5 to Oct 1 Lyceum Theatre, London (24 nights)

Oct 10 Theatre Royal, Windsor; 11 Town Hall, Reading; 12 Town Hall, Melksham; 13, 14 Broadmead Rooms, Bristol; 17 Assembly Rooms,

Cheltenham; 18 Music Hall, Worcester; 20 Theatre Royal, Leamington; 21 Theatre Royal, Coventry; 25 Town Hall, Birmingham; 26 Theatre, Wolverhampton; 29 Theatre, Shrewsbury; 30 St. George's Hall, Bradford; 31 Lyceum, Stafford

Nov 1 Town Hall, Burton-on-Trent; 7 St. George's Hall, Bradford; 8 Music Saloon, Wakefield; 10 Selby; 11 Festival Concert Room, York; 14 to 18, Theatre Royal, Humber Street, Hull; 21 to 26 Theatre Royal, Sheffield; 29 Pump Room, Harrogate

Dec 2 Theatre Royal, Durham; 5, 6, 7, 8, 9 Music Hall, Newcastle; 16 City Hall, Glasgow

1854

Jan 23 Eyre Arms, St. John's Wood; 24 Manor Rooms, Hackney; 25 Camberwell Hall, Camberwell; 26 King's Arms, Kensington; 27 Lecture Hall, Tottenham

Feb 1 Lecture Hall, Nelson Street, Woolwich; 2 Deptford; 3 Croydon; 6 Rosemary Branch, Peckham; 7 Athenaeum, Islington; 8 Institution, Poplar; 9, 10 Music Hall, Store Street, London; n.d. New Albion Hall, Dalston; 13 Spread Eagle, Wandsworth; 14, 15 Theatre, Richmond; 16 Albion Hall, Hammersmith; 17 Institution, Poplar; 24 Munn's Rooms, Dartford

Mar 6 Institution, Chelmsford; 7 Three Cups Assembly Rooms, Colchester; 8 Mechanics Lecture Hall, Ipswich; 9 Town Hall, Bury; 13 St. Andrew's Hall, Norwich; 15, 17 Assembly Rooms, Wentworth Street, Peterborough; 16 March, Cambs; 20 Huntingdon; 22 Theatre Royal, Cambridge; n.d. Town Hall, Hitchin

Apr 5 Town Hall, Leighton Buzzard; 6 Assembly Rooms, Bedford; 7 British School Room, Banbury; 4 Town Hall, Longton; Passion Week, Standard Theatre, London; 17, 18 Broadmead Rooms, Bristol; 19 Theatre Royal, Gloucester; 20 Assembly Rooms, Cheltenham; 24 Town Hall, Longton; 25, 27 Town Hall, Hanley; 28 Theatre, Newcastle

May 1 Lyceum, Stafford; 5 Theatre Royal, Shrewsbury; 8 Albion Hotel, Chester; 12 Theatre Royal, Hereford (cancelled); 16 Borough Court, Monmouth (cancelled); 19 Town Hall, Newport

Aug 15 Corn Exchange, Maidstone; 18 Town Hall, Brighton; 21 Queen's Rooms, Portsea; 22 Theatre Royal, Southampton; 23 Assembly Rooms, Salisbury; 24 Theatre Royal, Winchester; 28 to Sep 30 Lyceum Theatre, London

Oct 9 to 14 New Theatre, Bingley Hall, Birmingham; 16 to 21 Corn Exchange, Manchester

Nov 6 to 11 Philharmonic Hall, Fountain Street, Manchester; 13, 14 Temperance Hall, Bolton; 15 Temperance Hall, Stockport; 16 Town Hall, Ashton-under-Lyme; 17 Public Hall, Rochdale; 20 to 24 Theatre Royal, Leeds; 27 New Oddfellows Hall, Grimsby; 28 Corn Exchange, Louth; 29 Assembly Rooms, Boston; 30 Gainsborough

Dec 9 Concert Hall, Lord Nelson Street, Liverpool; 18 to 23 Royal Victoria Theatre, London

1855

Jan 15 Theatre Royal, Gloucester; 16 Assembly Rooms, Cheltenham; 17 Music Hall, Worcester; 18 Temperance Hall, Leicester; 19 Theatre, Loughborough; 22 Mechanics Hall, Nottingham; 25 Whitehead's Lecture Room, Chesterfield; 31 Philosophical Hall, Huddersfield

Feb 1 Music Saloon, Wakefield; 5 Theatre Royal, Blackburn; 7 Theatre Royal, Preston; 8 Music Hall, Lancaster; 9 Whitehall Concert Rooms, Kendal; 12 Victoria Concert Hall, Ulverstone; n.d. Workington; 16 Athenaeum Lecture Hall, Carlisle; 17 Theatre Royal, Preston; 19 Music Hall, Newcastle-upon-Tyne; 21 George Tavern, North Shields; 22 New Town Hall, Durham; n.d. Athenaeum, West Hartlepool; 27 Borough Hall, Stockton-on-Tees

Mar 5 Music Hall, Edinburgh; 6 Courthouse, Stirling; 7 Assembly Rooms Greenock; 9 City Hall, Glasgow; 12 Music Hall, George Street, Edinburgh; 13 Thistle Hall, Dundee; 14 Trades Hall, Arbroath; 15 Guild Hall, Montrose; 16 Theatre Royal, Aberdeen; 19 City Hall, Glasgow; 23 Music Hall, George Street, Edinburgh; 26 Music Hall, Newcastle; 27 Festival Concert Room, York

Apr 2 Temperance Hall, Bolton; 3 Borough Court, Halifax; 16 Town Hall, Hanley 17 Newcastle; 18 Longton; 19 Stone; 20 Uttoxeter; 26 Theatre, Coventry; 27 Royal Music Hall, Leamington; 30 Theatre Royal, Shrewsbury

May 7, 8, 9, 10, 11, 12, 14, 16 Music Hall, Dublin

Aug 20 Hastings; 21 Brighton; 22 Worthing; 23 Portsea/Assembly Rooms, Salisbury; 24 Theatre Royal, Southampton; 27 New Hall, Reading; 28 Star Assembly Rooms, Oxford; 29 Theatre Royal, Northampton; 30 Corn Exchange, Wolverhampton; 31 Royal Hotel, Chester

Sep 3 to 9 Music Hall, Lord Nelson Street, Liverpool; 17 to 28 Corn Exchange, Manchester

Oct 1 Town Hall, Ashton; 2 Gymnasium Hall, Huddersfield; 3, 4, 5 Music Hall, Leeds; 8 to 13 Dee's Royal Hotel, Birmingham; 15, 16,

Mechanic's Hall, Nottingham; 17, 18 Lecture Hall, Derby; 19 Temperance Hall, Leicester; 22 Music Hall, Sheffield (twelve nights) to Nov 2

Nov 7 Guildhall Assembly Rooms, Walsall; 8 Music Hall, Worcester; 9 Assembly Rooms, Cheltenham; 12 Theatre Royal, Gloucester; 13, 14 Broadmead Rooms, Bristol; 20 Theatre Royal, Leeds; 30 Gainsboro

Dec 9 Concert Hall, Lord Nelson Street, Liverpool

1856

Jan 14 King's Arms, Kensington; 15 Eyre Arms, St. John's Wood; 16 Myddleton Hall, Islington; 17 Albion Hall, Dalston; 18 Manor Rooms, Hackney; 21 Beaumont Institution, Stepney; 23 Lecture Hall, Walworth; 24 Camberwell Hall, Camberwell; 25 Assembly Rooms, Wandsworth, 28 Lecture Hall, Greenwich; 29 Lecture Hall, Woolwich; 30 Angel Hotel, Edmonton; 31 Gravesend

Feb 1 Eyre Arms; 6 Literary Institution, Portman Square; 11 Lecture Hall, Chelmsford; 12 Cups Assembly Rooms, Colchester; 13 Corn Exchange, Sudbury; 14 Lecture Hall, Tower Street, Ipswich; 15 Town Hall, Bury St. Edmunds; 18 Lecture Hall, Yarmouth; 19 St. Andrew's Hall, Norwich; 22 Town Hall, Lowestoft

Mar 4 Theatre Royal, Windsor; 6 New Hall, Reading; 7 Town Hall, Newbury; 12 Court Hall, Trowbridge; 12 Cups Assembly Room, Colchester; 10, 11 Theatre Royal, Bath; 14 County Hall, Abingdon; 17 to 20, 22 Surrey Theatre, London; 25 Brighton; 28 Corn Exchange, Maidstone; 31 Theatre Royal, Dover

Apr 3 Town Hall, Bideford; 4 Hall, Canterbury; 5, 6 Union Hall, Torquay; 14 Guild Hall Bodmin; 15 Assembly Rooms, Devizes; 18 Town Hall, Wells; 21 Victoria Hotel, Dorset; 22 George Assembly Rooms, Crewkerne; 23 Town Hall, Yeovil

May 1 Athenaeum, Tiverton; 2 New Music Hall, Barnstaple; 3 Town Hall, Bideford; 5, 6 Union Hall, Torquay; 8 Athenaeum, Tiverton; 14 Guildhall, Bodmin; 15 Assembly Room, Truro; 20 Angel Hotel, Helston; 21 Prince's Assembly Rooms, Penzance

Aug 4, 5, 6 Ramsgate; 7 Apollonian Hall, Dover; 8 Harveian Institute, Folkestone; 9 Assembly Rooms, Cheltenham; 1 Tunbridge Wells; 12 Hastings; 13 Battle; 14 Corn Exchange, Lewes; 15, 16 Town Hall, Brighton; 18 Worthing; 19 Assembly Room, Chichester; 20, 21 St. George's Hall, Portsea; 22 Theatre Royal, Southampton; 25 Town Hall, Cowes; 26 Queen's Rooms, Newport; 27 to 29 Town Hall, Ryde

Sep 2 Theatre Royal, Winchester; 3 Town Hall, Romsey; 4 Assembly Rooms, Salisbury; 8 Theatre Royal, Gloucester; 9 Assembly Rooms, Cheltenham; 10 Music Hall, Worcester; 11 Theatre Royal, Coventry; 12 Lecture Hall, Wardwick, Derby; 15 (12 nights); Theatre Royal, Sheffield

Oct 4 to 1 November Concert Hall, Lord Nelson Street, Liverpool

Nov 2 Theatre, Preston; 10 Theatre, Blackburn; 11 Temperance Hall, Bolton; 13 Philosophical Hall, Huddersfield; 14 Music Saloon, Wakefield; 17 Mechanics Hall, Barnsley; (18 train accident); 21 Public Hall, Baillie Street; Rochdale; 24 to 29 Lord Nelson Street, Liverpool

Dec 2 Music Hall, Chester; 4 Theatre Royal, Wigan; 5 Mechanics Institute, Heywood; 9 to 13 Free Trade Hall, Manchester

1857

Jan n.d. Marylebone Institution; Eyre Arms, St. John's Wood; 21 Lecture Hall, Greenwich; 22 Lecture Hall, Woolwich; 23 Institution, Deptford; 26 Lecture Hall, Carter Street, Walworth; 27 Myddelton Hall, Islington; 28 King's Arms, Kensington; 29 Institution, Portman Square, 30 Eyre's Arms, St. Johns Wood

Feb 2 Spread Eagle Hotel, Wandsworth; 3 Griffin Hotel, Kingston-upon-Thames; 4 Theatre Royal, Windsor; 5 New Hall, Reading; 6 Newbury; 9 Town Hall, Oxford; 10 Town Hall, Banbury; 11 Music Hall, Leamington; 12 Town Hall, Birmingham; 13 Lichfield; 16 Temperance Hall, Leicester; 17 Town Hall, Loughborough; 19 Town Hall, Newark; 24 Music Hall, Leeds; 26 to 28 Mechanics' Institute, Bradford

Mar 14 Salem Chapel, Otley; 16 Festival Concert Room, York 18 Town Hall, Richmond, Yorks; n.d. Mechanics Hall, Nottingham; 24 Town Hall, West Hartlepool; 25 New Town Hall, Durham 27 Theatre Royal, North Shields

Apr 1 Music Hall, Jarratt Street, Hull; 6 to 9, 11 Princess's Theatre, London; 20 Mechanics Institute, Chelmsford; 21 Maldon; 22 Braintree; 23 Cups Assembly Room, Colchester; 27 Town Hall, Bury; 29 St. Andrews Hall, Ipswich

May 4 Theatre Royal, Lynn; 5 Public Hall, Wisbech; 7 Public Institution, Godmanchester; 8 Town Hall, Cambridge; 13 Bedford Rooms, Bedford; 14 Theatre Royal, Northampton; 18 (six nights) Theatre Royal, Bath

Aug 27 Apollonian Hall, Dover

Sep 1 Assembly Rooms, Hastings; 2 Assembly Rooms, St. Leonards; 3 Corn Exchange, Lewes; 4, 5 Town Hall, Brighton; n.d. Worthing; 9, 10 St. George's Hall, Portsea; 11 Theatre Royal, Southampton; 14 Theatre Royal,

Winchester; 16 Public Hall, Guildford; 17 Red Lion Assembly Rooms, Dorking; 21 Corn Exchange, Maidstone

1859

Jan 28 Boulogne-sur-Mer

1862

Mar 29 Sadler's Wells Theatre, London

1866

Oct 22 Albion Hall, London Wall

Appendix B

Chronological List of Compositions

A fully definitive list is impossible in view of variations in title, re-settings of words to the same music, numerous unpublished pieces, and imprecise and inaccurate attributions. Only more important editions are listed here, including London reissues in G. H. Davidson's "Musical Treasury" and Charles Sheard's "Musical Bouquet"—both held in the British Library and other major libraries. Years of origin may in some cases be approximate. In particular, dates of British Library deposit are often substantially after publication, which can more accurately be dated from newspaper announcements and publishers' plate numbers. The absence of a song's lyricist indicates that he or she is unknown or uncredited.

p.n. = plate number.

c. 1828

The Tocsin of War (words J[ohn] M[atthews] F[raser] Dodgson). Published by J. Russell, London (BL, 15 November 1876), as sung by Master Russell, with dedication to Mr. and Mrs. King.

My Broken Lute (words J[ohn] M[atthews] F[raser] Dodgson). Published by A[lfred] Pettet, London (BL, 31 March 1871), as sung by Miss Helme at Vauxhall Gardens, Master McEvoy at the Brighton Concerts, and Master Russell at the Surrey Theatre, with dedication to Miss Mary Solomon.

My Father's to the Battle Gone (words G. Higham). Published by Bedford Musical Repository, London (BL, n.d.), as sung by Master Russell at the Surrey Theatre.

c. 1832

The Azure Eye, "prize ballad" (words A. T. McDouall) (possibly John A. McDouall). Published by William Wybrow, London (BL, 15 January 1875), as composed for Mrs. [Harriet] Waylett, with dedication to Mrs. Dinah Myers; and in Musical Bouquet album *One Hundred Songs by Henry Russell* (1856). Advertised in *The Satirist,* 5 August 1832.

The Old Abbey Walls (words A. T. McDouall). Published in Musical Bouquet album *One Hundred Songs by Henry Russell* (1856).

The Pirate's Bride (words J. Delma). Published by J[ohn] Duncombe, London (p.n. 183; BL, n.d.).

Let Others Rejoice in the Merry Moonlight (Bandit's Song). Published by G[eorge]Walker & Son, London (*Times*, 24 November 1832). Music reused for Come, Brothers, Arouse! (THE BRIDE'S BAND, 1834, words W. Bayle Bernard).

When I Rov'd a Young Highlander (words Lord Byron). Published by G[eorge] Walker & Son, London (*Times*, 24 November 1832; BL, 21 April 1876), as sung by Eliza Inverarity at Theatre Royal, Covent Garden, with dedication to Miss Waring; and by Hewitt & Jaques, New York, with a dedication to Mrs. J. E. Jackson of Philadelphia.

The Lady Leaves the Banquet Hall (words Charles Arnold). Published by G. Walker & Son, London (BL, 21 April 1876), as sung by Madame Vestris, Miss Cawse, and Mrs. Waylett; by Firth & Hall, New York, as sung by Mrs. Franklin; and in Musical Treasury. Music reused for Home of Her Childhood's Days (Eliza Cook), published as Musical Bouquet 467. Advertised in the *Liverpool Mercury*, 30 March 1832.

1833

Come, Maidens, Come! (words Charles Mackay). Published by G. Walker & Son, London (*Times*, 20 February 1833; BL, 13 June 1907), as sung by Madame Stockhausen; and by Firth & Hall, New York, as sung by Mrs. Franklin.

When the Wild Wind Blows, A Song of the Waves (words J R P) [Planché?]. Published by G. Walker & Son, London (BL, n.d.), as sung by Madame Cinti-Damoreau and Miss Evans; and by Firth & Hall, New York. Advertised as "When the Wild Winds Blow" as sung by Malibran in August 1833, and in *The Satirist,* 25 August 1833, as by Russell.

IL MARITO GELOSO, opera. Supposed prize winner, Naples, November 1833.

Some Love to Roam o'er the Dark Sea Foam (words Charles Mackay). Advertised October 1833 by Walker. Published by G. Walker & Son, London (*Morning Post*, 8 April 1835), as sung by Henry Phillips at Theatre Royal, Covent Garden; by Firth & Hall, New York (© 20 May 1836), with dedication to Mrs. Gardiner of Rochester, NY; and as Musical Treasury 32. Music reused for the "original ode" A Sober Spouse for Me! (words George P. Morris), published by Firth & Hall, New York (© 13 January 1844), and for Some Love to Drink in *Davidson's Temperance Melodist* (1854).

The Rhine Glee ("Fill High! Fill High!") (words Charles Mackay) advertised as "the prize glee" May 1833. Published by G. Walker & Son, London, and later by [John] Duncombe and [Frederick] Moon, London.

1834

THE BRIDE'S BAND, opera (words William Bayle Bernard). Supposedly rehearsed London, 1834.

Overture. Announced for Albany, 4 November 1836.

Come, Brothers, Arouse! Announced for Albany, 20 October 1836. Published in New York by Firth & Pond (p.n. 261; © 1837), by James L[ang] Hewitt, and by Hewitt & [Edward] J[ones] Jaques, with dedication to Colonel George P[ope] Morris; in London by T[homas] E[dward] Purday (BL, 4 November 1845) and by G. Walker & Son (BL, 23 March 1846); as Musical Treasury 184 (*Times*, 11 September 1845); and as Musical Bouquet 378. Music from The Bandit's Song (Let Others Rejoice in the Merry Moonlight) (1832).

Let's Be Gay—A Laughing Chorus. Announced for Albany, 30 March 1838. Published by William H. Oakes, Boston (p.n. 46; © 29 October 1841); in London (*Times*, 31 March 1842) by Cramer, Addison & Beale, and (words Charles Jeffreys) by Jefferys & [Sidney] Nelson (BL, 16 March 1843), with dedication to Mr. [George] Dawson, of Sheffield; as Musical Treasury 186 (*Times*, 11 September 1845); and as Musical Bouquet 483.

On the Brave Who Have Fallen No Tear We Bestow, or The Patriot's Welcome (words Jane Anne Porter). Published by Balls and Son, London (*Times*, 22 October 1834); by Hewitt & Jaques, New York (*Boston Musical Gazette*, 22 August 1838); by Frederick C[hristopher] Leader, London (p.n.1; BL, 24 August 1842), with dedication from Jane Anne Porter to Mrs. Alexander Munroe; and as Musical Treasury 177 (*Times*, 18 July 1845). Music reused for Oh, Forge Not a Chain for the Brave (words Eliza Cook), published as Musical Bouquet 450.

When Tempests Fly o'er the Cloudy Sky (words Charles Mackay). Published by Balls and Son, London (*Times*, 22 October 1834). Announced for Albany, 4 November 1836. Words re-set as Our Way Across the Mountains, Ho! (see 1838). Music reused for The Minstrel of the Tyrol (words Jonas B. Phillips), published by James L[ang] Hewitt, New York (© 1838; *Albany Evening Journal*, 5 June 1838), as Musical Treasury 174 (*Times*, 18 July 1845), and as Musical Bouquet 387.

The Orphan Ballad Singers (words Letitia Elizabeth Landon). Published in *Fisher's Drawing Room Scrap Book for 1835* (BL, 1834), with dedication to Mrs. Edward Lytton Bulwer; and by John F[rancis] Nunns, Philadelphia, 1842. Announced for New York, 28 September 1843.

Ivy Bridge (words Letitia Elizabeth Landon). Published in *Fisher's Drawing Room Scrap Book for 1835* (BL, 1834).

Cottage Courtship (words Letitia Elizabeth Landon). Published in *Fisher's Drawing Room Scrap Book for 1835* (BL, 1834).

The Merry Spring (words Charles Mackay). Published by George Shade, London. Sung by Mrs. Waylett in Dublin. Advertised 12 November 1834. Advertised 18235 as sung by Malibran. Published by Firth & Hall, New York, as sung by Miss [Charlotte] Watson, and with dedication to H. B. Williams.

1835

Believe Not the Tales They Have Told Thee of Me, descriptive ballad (words Leigh Cliffe). Published by G[eorge] Luff, London (p.n. 217; BL, May 1835), with dedication to Miss Emma Lloyd; by G. Walker & Son, London; as Musical Treasury 220; and as Musical Bouquet 451. Advertised April 1835.

The Lay of Hope, or I Love to Dwell in the Bosom's Cell (words Leigh Cliffe). Sung by Mary Steele, London, 7 April 1835. Published by G[eorge] Luff, London (p.n. 218; *Morning Post*, 9 April 1835; BL, May 1835), with dedication to Christopher Vickery; by G. Walker & Son, London; by Firth & Hall, New York (p.n. 628); and as Musical Bouquet 433–34.

L'AMICO DEI CANTANTI. Published by G[eorge] Luff, London (p.n. 219; BL 30 August 1860), with dedication to H R H Princess Victoria.

Wind of the Winter Night, Whence Comest Thou? (words Charles Mackay). Announced for Albany, 20 October 1836. Published by G[eorge] Luff, London (listed on BL deposits, May 1835); by William Hall then Firth & Hall, New York (© 26 September 1836), as sung by Mr. [William Francis] Brough and with a dedication to the Rochester Academy of Sacred Music; in London (*Times*, 31 March 1842) by Cramer, Addison & Beale (p.n. 2961; BL, n.d.) and by [Charles] Jefferys and [Sidney] Nelson; and (words George Soane) as Musical Treasury 209–10. Words from *Mackay's Poems* published London 1834 as "To the Wind[s]."

Dear Janet (words Frederick West). Published by G. Walker & Son, London; advertised in the *Morning Herald* 6 March and as "Phillips's beautiful ballad"; 1835 by Firth & Hall, New York, as sung by Mrs. Waylett and Jane Shirreff, and with dedication by Frederick West to William Mansfield King; and as Musical Treasury 344.

Pledge Me in Ruby Wine, or Drink! Drink! Drink! bacchanalian song (words Frederick West). Published by B[enjamin] Williams, London (BL, 18 January 1858), as sung by Henry Phillips, with dedication to Benjamin Lumley.

The Crimson Hue of the Fair Sunset advertised in Ireland by Shade June 1835. "Sung by Miss Mordaunt." Music reused for "I Love the Night."

1836

We Have Been Friends Together (words Mrs. Caroline Norton). Published in *New-York Mirror* (19 November 1836) and by James L[ang] Hewitt, New York. Music reused for God Bless the Widow's Son (words Mrs. Laura H. Sigourney), published by T[homas] E[dward] Purday, London (BL, 23 June 1853); for The Happy Days of Childhood (words George Pendrell), published as Musical Treasury 220; and for Oh, Give Your Heart to Me (words Eliza Cook), published as Musical Bouquet 464.

1837

THE SCEPTIC (Boston, Masonic Temple, 22 April 1838) words published by Kidder & Wright, Boston, 1838.

O, Thou Eternal Being, opening chorus. Announced for Albany, 25 December 1837.

All Praise Him, chorus. Announced for Albany, 30 November 1837.

Behold the Spirit of the Lord. Announced for Boston, 28 February 1841.

Faith in God, air. Cited in *Boston Morning Post*, 1 February 1840.

Hail, All Hail Him, double chorus. Announced for Albany, 30 November 1837.

Hush, Hush, He Comes. Announced for Boston, 22 April 1838.

Look Up to Him, chorus. Cited in *Boston Morning Post*, 1 February 1840.

O God in Mercy, duet. Announced for Boston, 21 October 1837.

O Thou Sceptic, chorus. Announced for Boston, 22 April 1838.

Shout, All Ye Angels, double chorus. Announced for Albany, 30 November 1837.

Supreme and Universal Light. Announced for Boston, 28 February 1841.

'Tis Present to My Thought (The Sceptic's Soliloquy). Announced for Albany, 4 July 1837.

'Twas One Night, One Bitter Cold Night (The Sceptic's Dying Lament) (words Leigh Cliffe). Announced for Albany, 20 October 1836.

The Wreck of the Mexico, descriptive scena (words H[enry] Harrington ?*recte* Hannington, of Boston). Announced for Albany, 28 February 1837.

Woodman! Spare That Tree! (words George P[ope] Morris). Words published *New-York Mirror*, 7 January 1837. As *The Oak*. Announced for Albany, 4 July 1837. Published by Firth & Hall, New York (© 1837), with dedication by George P. Morris to Benjamin M. Brown; in London (with alternative title The Old Oak Tree) by G. Walker & Son, by Duff & Hodgson, by Cramer, Addison & Beale, by Jefferys & Nelson, and by T[homas] E[dward] Purday; as Musical Treasury 48; and as Musical Bouquet 11. Music reused for Traitor, Spare That Flag (words William J[arvis] Wetmore), published by S. T. Gordon, New York, 1861.

I Love the Night (words George P. Morris). Published in *New-York Mirror* (20 May 1837), by Firth & Hall, New York, as sung by Mrs. Bailey, with dedication to Mrs. Josephine Parker; by T[homas] E[dward] Purday, London; as Welcome, Lovely Night, or I Love the Night (words H. Harcourt [or Harcourt Russell]) by Leader & Cock, London (p.n. 286; BL, 20 May 1845); and as Musical Bouquet 10. Music reused from By the Crimson Hue of the Fair Sunset (words Leigh Cliffe), published in 1835; and as Musical Treasury 25.

Washington's Tomb, ode to the memory of Washington (words Mrs. Laura H. Sigourney). "Introducing the 'Marseillaise' Hymn." Announced for Albany, 4 July 1837. Published by James L[ang] Hewitt (© 1837), with dedication to Hon Daniel Webster. Music reused for A. Lament for Wellington (words Eliza Cook), published as Musical Bouquet 373–74.

The Ivy Green (words "Boz" = Charles Dickens). Announced for Boston, 27 October 1837. Published in New York by James L. Hewitt (© 1838) and by Hewitt & Jaques (© 1839), with dedication to Lynde M[inshull] Walter of Boston; in London (*Times*, 31 March 1842) by Cramer, Addison & Beale (p.n. 2957; BL, 6 November 1844) and by

Jefferys & Nelson; as Musical Treasury 21; and as Musical Bouquet 9. Music reused for The Temperance Tree in *Davidson's Temperance Melodist* (1854).

Rockaway, or On Old Long Island's Sea-Girt Shore (words Henry John Sharpe). Announced for Brooklyn September 1837, October for Hempstead, and Philadelphia, 9 December 1837. Published by William H. Oakes (© 13 November 1840), with dedication to Mrs. T[homas] C[olley] Grattan; as Musical Treasury 172 (*Times*, 18 July 1845); and as Musical Bouquet 380. Music reused for Old English Hospitality (words Charles Swain), published by Cramer, Addison & Beale, London (p.n. 2951; BL, 8 April 1842), and in Musical Treasury.

1838

The Corsair Glee, ("Row Onward Row, my brave Corsairs") four-part male chorus (words Henry Russell). Published Boston (© Edward Eldridge 11 May 1838), with a dedication to the gentlemen of the Corsair Boat Club of Boston, Massachusetts.

I've Heard the Forest Birds by Day (words H. S. Vandyke) published in *The Boston Weekly Magazine*, 4 April 1838.

The Maniac, descriptive work [grand scena] (words [in part] "Monk" Lewis). Announced for New York, April 1838. Published by Parker Ditson, Boston, with dedication to Mrs. Claudius Edward Habicht (© 2 May 1840); in London (*Times*, 31 March 1842; words Leigh Cliffe) by Cramer, Addison & Beale (p.n. 2948; BL, 8 April 1842) and by Jefferys & Nelson; as Musical Treasury 169–70 (*Times*, 18 July 1845); and as Musical Bouquet 65–66.

Our Way across the Mountains, Ho! (words Charles Mackay—see When Tempests Fly, 1834). Announced for Albany, 12 June 1838. Published by Parker & Ditson, Boston (© 5 June 1838), with dedication to M[ordecai] M[anuel] Noah of New York (words George Soane); as Musical Treasury 205; and (words Eliza Cook) as Musical Bouquet 473. Music reused for A Song for a Stormy Night (words Charles Mackay), announced for London, 23 February 1842, published in London (*Times*, 31 March 1842) by Cramer, Addison & Beale and by Jefferys & Nelson, and in Musical Treasury.

A Life on the Ocean Wave (words [Samuel J. Arnold &] Epes Sargent). Announced for New York, 8 October 1838. Published by Hewitt & Jaques, New York (© 1838), as sung by Henry Russell and Edward Seguin, with dedication to Joseph B. Green of Columbus, Georgia; by Duff & Hodgson, London; by G. Walker, London; by Cramer, Addison & Beale, London (p.n. 2956; BL, 8 April 1842); by Jefferys & Nelson, London; by T[homas] E[dward] Purday, London; as Musical Treasury 40; and as Musical Bouquet 76.

A Christmas Carol (I Care Not for Spring on his Fickle Wings) (words "Boz" = Charles Dickens). Announced for New York, 15 October 1838. Published by Hewitt & Jaques, New York (© 1838), with dedication to Miss Sarah [Evelin] Upjohn and Mrs. Crittenton of Albany; and as Musical Treasury 195 (1845–46). Music reused for The Greenwood Tree (words Charles Mackay), published by Cramer, Addison & Beale, London (p.n. 2975; BL 17 September 1881); and in Musical Treasury.

We Met in Other Years, Love (words "Ione"). Published by James L[ang] Hewitt & Edward J[ones] Jaques, New York (© 1838), with dedication to Claudius Edward Habicht of Boston; and as Musical Treasury 181 (*Times*, 11 September 1845). Music reused for Think Not that I Forget, Love (words Eliza Cook), published as Musical Bouquet 451.

1839

The Old Year's Gone and the New Year's Come (words "Ione" [Mary Anne Hewitt]). Announced for New York, 13 February 1839.

Charter Oak! Charter Oak Ancient and Fair! (words Mrs. Laura H. Sigourney). Announced for New York, 13 February 1839. Published by Hewitt & Jaques, New York (*Evening Post*, 5 March 1839), with dedication to Dr. John D. Russ of Hartford, Conn. Music reused for Come, Fill the Cup, bacchanalian song (words Henry John Sharpe), published as Musical Treasury 221 (1845–46), and for The Flag of the Free (words Eliza Cook), published as Musical Bouquet 42.

I Love the Man with a Generous Heart. Announced for New York, 5 March 1839.

O, How Shall I Woo Thee? (words Zebulon Barton Stout). Announced for Albany, 12 March 1839.

My Old Wife (words Jonas B[enjamin] Phillips). Announced for Albany, 12 March 1839. Published by Hewitt & Jaques, New York (© 1840), by Firth, Hall & Pond as sung by J. P. Knight and Mr. Russell and dedicated to Mrs. Frederick Backus, as Musical Treasury 171 (*Times*, 18 July 1845), and as Musical Bouquet 69. Music reused for My Own Dear Wife (Leigh Cliffe), published by Cramer, Addison & Beale (p.n. 2950; BL, 8 April 1842), and in Musical Treasury.

The Dying Legacy (words J. M. Church). Published by Hewitt & Jaques, New York (© 1839), and as Musical Treasury 213. Music reused for My Father's Song (words Edward J[oseph] Gill), published by T. E. Purday, London (BL, 21 August 1844).

The Rochester Union Grays, quick step. Announced for Rochester, 9 August 1839. Published by Hewitt & Jaques, New York (© 1839).

The Old Bell (words "W"). Announced for Rochester, 9 August 1839. Published by Hewitt & Jaques, New York (© 1839). Published as a quartet by Firth & Pond n.d. Music reused for The Old Church Bell (words Eliza Cook), published by T[homas] E[dward] Purday, London; as Musical Treasury 222; and as Musical Bouquet 432.

1840

I Love, I Love the Free (words Eliza Cook). Announced for Edward Seguin, Boston, 23 January 1840. Published by William H. Oakes, Boston (© 27 April 1840), with dedication to Henry B Smith; as Musical Treasury 192 (as Song of the Mariners: I Love the Free), and as Musical Bouquet 384. Music reused for The Winds Are Free (words Leigh Cliffe), announced for Glasgow, 22 February 1843; published by Cramer, Addison & Beale, London (p.n. 2960; *Musical World*, February 1843; BL, 11 July 1879) with dedication to Mrs. [Mary Elizabeth] James L[ang] Hewitt, and in Musical Treasury.

The Fisher-Boy Merrily Lives (words Eliza Cook). Announced for Mrs. Ann Seguin, Boston, 25 January 1840. Published by George Reed, and by Oakes & Swan (© 13 March 1840), with dedication to Edward Bertie Ranger; by Cramer, Addison & Beale, London; and as Musical Treasury 173 (*Times*, 18 July 1845).

The Old Arm Chair (words Eliza Cook). Announced for Boston, 25 January 1840. Published by Oakes & Swan, Boston (© 7 February 1840), with dedication to Holton Olmstead; in London (*Times*, 31 March 1842) by Cramer Addison & Beale and by Jefferys & Nelson; as Musical Treasury 505–6; and as Musical Bouquet 382. Music reused for The Spirit and the Stream (words Eliza Cook) as Musical Treasury 217, and for I Love it, My Own Fireside in *Davidson's Temperance Melodist* (1854).

The Mad Girl's Song, descriptive work (words T[homas] C[olley] Grattan). Announced for Boston, 29 February 1840. Published by Oakes & Swan, Boston (© 28 July 1840), and as Musical Bouquet 385–86.

Figure A.1. “The Mad Girl’s Song” sheet music cover. *Source:* Courtesy the Lester Levy Sheet Music Collection, The Sheridan Libraries, Johns Hopkins University.

The Old Sexton or, We Gather Them In (words Park Benjamin). Announced for New York, 31 March 1840. Published by Henry Prentiss (© 19 March 1841), with dedication to William Babcock; by Cramer,

Addison & Beale, London; as Musical Treasury 187 (*Times*, 11 September 1845); and as Musical Bouquet 64.

Our Native Song (words Eliza Cook). Announced for Rochester, 13 May 1840. Published by Hewitt & Jaques, New York (© 1841); by Cramer, Addison & Beale, London; and by Jefferys & Nelson, London (BL, 16 March 1843).

The Old Farm Gate (words Eliza Cook). Words published April 1840. May 1840 in *Cheltenham Chronicle.* Announced for Boston, 31 October 1840. Published by Henry Prentiss, Boston November 1840, William H. Oakes, Boston (© 4 December 1840), with a dedication to Mrs. J. L. Tucker, by Geo Reed, Boston; by G. Walker & Son, London; and as Musical Treasury 219. Music reused for My Mother's Portrait (words Leigh Cliffe), sung London, 31 March 1842; published in London (*Times*, 31 March 1842) by Cramer, Addison & Beale (p.n. 2949; BL 8 April 1842), with dedication to Mrs. J. J. Farley, and by Jefferys & Nelson; as Musical Treasury 720; and (words Eliza Cook) as Musical Bouquet 550. Music also reused for My Old Cottage Home, published by Z[enas] T[rivett] Purday, London (BL, 25 February 1851).

The Old Water Mill, or The Old Mill Stream (words Eliza Cook). Announced for Boston, 24 February 1841. Published by Henry Prentiss, Boston (p.n. 138; © 11 December 1840), with dedication to Mrs. Henry John Sharpe; in London (*Times*, 31 March 1842) by Cramer, Addison & Beale and by Jefferys & Nelson; and as Musical Treasury 191. Music reused for The Old Abbey Clock (words Edward J[oseph] Gill), published by T[homas] E[dward] Purday, London (BL, 21 August 1844).

I'm Afloat! (words Eliza Cook). Announced for Boston, 5 November 1840. Published by William H. Oakes, Boston, (© 1 February 1841), with dedication to Mrs. Leander Starr; by Duff & Hodgson, London (p.n. 838; BL, 20 January 1843), with dedication to Handel Gear; by R. Addison, London; as Musical Treasury 201 (with original words, and also new words by Eliza Cook as The Rover's Song); and as Musical Bouquet 67. Music also reused for I'm a Gent in *G. Vickers' Penny Songster and Reciter* (BL, 1851), and (according to Stephens) for War Song of the Texas Rangers.

The Gambler's Wife, descriptive ballad (words Dr. Reynell Coates). Announced for Boston, 14 November 1840. Published by Joseph F[airfield] Atwill, New York (© 16 June 1841; *New York Herald*, 20 July 1841), with dedication to Dr. Washington; in London (*Times*, 31 March 1842) by Cramer, Addison & Beale (p.n. 2952; BL, 6 January 1843) and by

Jefferys & Nelson; by [John] Duncombe & Moon, London (p.n. 582–83); as Musical Treasury 179–80 (*Times*, 11 September 1845); and as Musical Bouquet 71–72.

1841

The Ocean, or The Merry Mariners. Published by Hewitt & Jaques, New York, as sung by Messrs. Seguin, Giubilei & H Russell, with dedication to Captain Judkins of the Steam Ship *Columbia*; and in Musical Bouquet album *One Hundred Songs by Henry Russell* (1856).

The Old Night Lamp, or The Rushlight (words Eliza Cook). Announced for Boston, 24 February 1841. Published by Henry Prentiss, Boston (© 1841) and as Musical Treasury 204 (1845–46).

Nature's Fine Old Gentleman (words uncredited). Announced for Boston, 24 February 1841. Published by Henry Prentiss, Boston (© 1841), with dedication to memory of Richard Haughton.

We Were Boys Together (words George P. Morris). Announced for New York, 25 March 1841. Published by Firth & Hall, New York (© 15 April 1841), with dedication to John Brower; by G. Walker & Son, London; as Musical Treasury 202; and as Musical Bouquet 485.

The Old School House (words Park Benjamin). Announced for New York, 30 March 1841. Published by William Hall New York (p.n. 3885; © 20 April 1841), with dedication to Mrs. James Gordon Bennett; and as Musical Treasury 382. Music reused for The Village Green (words Leigh Cliffe), published by Cramer, Addison & Beale, London (p.n. 2958; BL, 23 December 1844), and in Musical Treasury.

The Chieftain's Daughter (words George P. Morris). Announced for New York, 9 April 1841. Published by Firth & Hall, New York (© 4 May 1841), as Musical Treasury 211 (1845–46), and as Musical Bouquet 74. Music reused for The Emigrant's Farewell (Leigh Cliffe), published by Cramer, Addison & Beale, London, with dedication to Mrs. B[enjamin] L[awrence] Sowell (p.n. 2945; BL, 23 December 1842); by Firth & Hall, New York (© 14 June 1843); and in Musical Treasury.

Requiem on the Death of General Harrison (words George P. Morris). Announced for New York, 9 April 1841.

All Things Adore Thee, So Do I (The Pilgrim's Address to the Deity) (words Henry John Sharpe). Announced for New York, 15 April 1841. Published by Hewitt & Jaques (© 1841), with a dedication to Right Honorable Lady Falkland; by Walker & Son, London (BL, 22 November

1877), with dedication to Mrs. Robert [Eliza] Rio of Cheltenham; and as Musical Treasury 203 (1845–46).

My Mother's Bible (The Family Bible) (words George P. Morris). Announced for New York, 16 April 1841. Published by Firth & Hall, New York (© 9 August 1841); by Cramer, Addison & Beale, London, with dedication to Mrs. Henry John Sharpe (p.n. 1792; BL, 16 September 1843); by T[homas] E[dward] Purday, London; as Musical Treasury 185 (*Times*, 11 September 1845); and as Musical Bouquet 68.

Old King Time! Announced for New York, 26 April 1841. Published by Joseph F[airfield] Atwill, New York (© 26 June 1841; *New York Herald*, 20 July 1841), with dedication to George P. Morris; by Jefferys & Nelson, London; and (words Eliza Cook) as Musical Treasury 182 (*Times*, 11 September 1845).

Not Married Yet, comic song (words George P. Morris). Published by Joseph F[airfield] Atwill, New York (© 11 May 1841; *New York Herald*, 26 April 1841) and as Musical Treasury 206 (1845–46).

Major McPherson Was a Very Nice Man, comic song. Published by Firth & Hall, New York (© 2 June 1841).

The Mother Who Hath a Child at Sea. Published by Joseph F[airfield] Atwill, New York (© 23 June 1841), with dedication to Henry John Sharpe; and as Musical Treasury 595. Music reused for So Young and So Lovely, published as Musical Treasury 215 (1845–46), and by Oliver Ditson, Boston (p.n. 1595; 1848).

The Soldier and His Bride (words George P. Morris). Published by Firth & Hall, New York (© 21 July 1841); as Musical Treasury 177 (*Times*, 18 July 1845); and as Musical Bouquet 73. Music reused for The Soldier's Wife (words Leigh Cliffe), published by Cramer, Addison & Beale (p.n. 2959; BL 6 November 1844) with dedication to Miss Cowell of Walworth, as Musical Treasury 724, and (words J. V. Blackburn) as Musical Bouquet 506–7.

The Heart That's True (words Eliza Cook). Published by Frederick D[amish] Benteen, Baltimore (p.n. 1339; ©1841), with dedication to C Tiffany. Announced for Baltimore 10 June 1841. Words published in *Baltimore Daily Commercial*, 27 March 1845.

The Drunkard, cantata (words John H[ill] Hewitt). Announced for Baltimore 10 June 1841. Announced for New York, 7 April 1843.

Oh! This Love! (words George P. Morris). Published by Joseph F[airfield] Atwill, New York (© 29 December 1841), as sung by Mrs.

[Emily] Sutton and Mr. [William Richardson] Dempster, with dedication by George P. Morris to Louis A[ntoine] Godey; and as Musical Treasury 183 (*Times*, 11 September 1845).

Will Nobody Marry Me? or Heigh Ho! for a Husband! comic song (words George P. Morris). Published by Joseph F[airfield] Atwill, New York (*New York Herald*, 20 July 1841), with dedication to Judge Robert T. Conrad; as Musical Treasury 193; and in Musical Bouquet album *One Hundred Songs by Henry Russell* (1856).

1842

The Dismissed, comic song (words George P. Morris). Published by Firth & Hall, New York (© 26 January 1842).

The Ship on Fire, descriptive scena (words Charles Mackay). Announced for London, 23 February 1842. Published by Addison, Cramer & Beale, London, with dedication to T. Frith (p.n. 1917; BL, 1 October 1842); by Joseph F[airfield] Atwill, New York; by James L[ang] Hewitt, New York; and as Musical Treasury 717–18.

Father, Turn Once More to Me, duet. Announced for Birmingham, 5 May 1842.

Monody on the Death of Sir John Moore (words Reverend Charles Woolfe). Announced for Rochester, Kent, 5 August 1842.

The Indian Hunter (words Eliza Cook). Announced for London, 19 December 1842. Published by Frederick C[hristopher] Leader, London (p.n.19; BL, 24 August 1842), with dedication to Henry John Sharpe; and by Firth, Hall & Pond, New York (p.n. 668, 1843).

The Old Clock (words Eliza Cook). Published by Frederick C[hristopher] Leader, London (p.n. 20; BL, 21 October 1842), with dedication to Mrs. Wayley [Waylett (?)]; by Firth & Hall, New York, and advertised 1842 by James L[ang] Hewitt, New York.

The Poor Man's Friend (words Eliza Cook). Published by Cramer, Addison & Beale, London (BL, 1 October 1842), with dedication to Mrs. Frederick Beale; and by James L[ang] Hewitt, New York, Firth & Hall, New York, and Oliver Ditson, Boston, with dedication to Mrs. Sophia Ostinelli, of Portland, Maine.

The Founding of the Bell (words Charles Mackay). Sung London, 19 December 1842. Published by Cramer, Addison & Beale, London (p.n. 3180; BL, 16 September 1843); by Oliver Ditson, Boston; and as Musical Treasury 732–33.

The Land of the North. Advertised on publications of Cramer, Addison & Beale, London. Possibly an earlier song with new words.

1843

The Young and the Gay (words Rosalind Davis). Published by Leader & Cock, London (p.n. 149.a; BL, 1 May 1858).

Nature's Gentleman (words Eliza Cook). Published by Leader & Cock, London (p.n. 161; BL, 21 November 1844), with dedication to George Dawson.

The Dream of the Reveller [or, The Three Houses], descriptive work (words Charles Mackay). Announced for Hanover Square Rooms, London, 12 January 1843. Published by James L[ang] Hewitt, New York (© 1843), with dedication to the Temperance Societys [sic] of the United States; by Leader & Cock, London (p.n. 242; BL, 12 November 1844), with dedication to the Temperance Societies of England, Ireland, and Scotland; and as The Vision of the Reveller (words George Soane) as Musical Treasury 199–200.

The Young Soldier. Announced for Hanover Square Rooms, London, 12 January 1843. A song of the same title by Balfe was brought out in 1842.

The General's Last Battle (words Charles Mackay). Announced for Hanover Square Rooms, London, 1 February 1843. Performed at Niblo's Saloon, 31 April 1843.

The Newfoundland Dog, descriptive ballad (words F[rederick] W[illiam] N[aylor] Bailey [*recte* Bayly]). Announced for London, 1 February 1843. Published in New York by James L[ang] Hewitt, and by Firth & Hall (© 1 Dec. 1843); by T[homas] E[dward] Purday, London; and (words Eliza Cook) as Musical Treasury 207 and Musical Bouquet 418.

The Launch. Announced for New York, 3 April 1843.

Robin Ruff, or If I Had But a Thousand a Year (words uncredited). Announced for Niblo's, New York, 3 April 1843. Part words published *New York Daily Herald*, 11 April 1843. Published by James L[ang] Hewitt & Firth, Pond & Co., New York (p.n. 612, © 1 December 1843), with dedication to "my brother, J Russell." Music reused for Health is Wealth (words W. Bartholemew), published in *The Musical Bijou for 1845* by D'Almaine & Co., London (BL, 30 November 1844), and for The Wife's Song (words "A Lady") as Musical Treasury 216.

The Hero and the Philosopher (words George P. Morris). Announced for New York, 7 April 1843.

The Genius of Temperance, national anthem (words Henry John Sharpe). Announced for New York, 12 April 1843. Announced as non-temperance National Anthem for Boston, 29 April 1843.

Land, Ho! (words George P. Morris). Announced for New York, 22 May 1843. Published by Oliver Ditson (© 29 June 1843), with a dedication to Captain C. H. E. Judkins of the steam ship Hibernia; as Musical Treasury 212 (1845–46); and as Musical Bouquet 453.

The First Dear Thing That Ever I Loved (words Reverend A[rthur] C[leveland] Coxe). Published by William H. Oakes, Boston (© 25 December 1843), and as Musical Treasury 197 (1845–46).

The Emigrant's Daughter (words Leigh Cliffe) Published by Firth & Hall. Advertised *New York Tribune*, 16 June 1843

The [The] Rising Sun (words Henry John Sharpe). Cited in *New York Herald*, 6 September 1843. Published by James L[ang] Hewitt, New York (© 1843), with a dedication to Miss Eliza Swain of Philadelphia; as Musical Treasury 194 (1845–46); and in Musical Bouquet album *One Hundred Songs by Henry Russell* (1856).

Life in the West (words George P. Morris). Announced for New York, 11 September 1843. Published by W. C. Peters, Louisville (p.n. 51; © 5 September 1844), with dedication to Miss Anne Mary Bacon; as Musical Treasury 195 (1845–46); and as Musical Bouquet 487.

The Tent Scene, from *Richard III* (words William Shakespeare). Announced for New York, 14 September 1843.

Cato's Soliloquy on the Immortality of the Soul, from *The Tragedy of Cato* (words John Addison). Announced for New York, 19 September 1843. Hanover Square Rooms, 6 February 1845.

Hamlet's Soliloquy, from *Hamlet* (words William Shakespeare). Announced for New York, 21 September 1843.

The Friends We Esteem (words Charles Marshall). Announced for New York, 26 September 1843.

Cardinal Wolsey's Farewell Address to Cromwell (words William Shakespeare). Announced for New York, 26 September 1843.

Our Sailors and Our Ships (words Eliza Cook). Announced for New York, 27 September 1843.

Marc Antony's Oration over the Body of Caesar, from *Julius Caesar* (William Shakespeare). Announced for New York, 27 September 1843.

The Main Truck, or A Leap for Life, nautical ballad (words George P. Morris). Announced for New York, 28 September 1843. Published by W. C. Peters, Louisville (p.n. 96; © 1844 or 24 June 1845), with dedication to Donald MacLeod, of Nashville; as Musical Treasury 305–6; and as Musical Bouquet 521–22.

The Bubbles of the Day, or Share Companies in General. Announced for New York, 30 September 1843.

The Main, the Flowing Main (words Henry John Sharpe). Announced for New York, 6 October 1843. Published by W. C. Peters, Louisville (p.n. 56; © 3 September 1844), with dedication to Hamilton Smith; as Musical Treasury 214 (1845–46); and as Musical Bouquet 468.

'Tis Now the Dead of Night. Announced for Philadelphia, 12 October 1843.

1844

Return to Me Again published by Joseph F[airfield] Atwill, New York. Advertised by them April 1844.

Tubal Cain (words Charles Mackay). Sung London, 3 October 1844. Published by Charles Jefferys, London (*Musical World*, 17 October 1844; BL, 14 July 1845) with dedication to Earl of Zetland; and as Musical Treasury 189–90. Music reused for Old King Coal [sic] in *Davidson's Temperance Melodist* (1854).

Weep Not! (words Charles Jefferys). Published by Jefferys & Co., London; and by Oliver Ditson, Boston (p.n. 1060; 1845–46).

1845

'Tis Eve on the Ocean. Announced for London, 20 January 1845. Published by Cramer, Addison & Beale; in Musical Treasury (as The Emigrant to His Wife—'Tis Eve on the Ocean); by W. H. Oakes, Boston (p.n. 565; post-1849) and by Oliver Ditson, Boston. Sung under original title in 1852.

The [Good Old] Coloured Gentleman [from Old Virginia State]. Announced for London, 6 February 1845.

The Felon. Announced for London, April 1845. Possibly identical with The Last Night of a Condemned Felon/The Felon's Last Night (Victor Hugo), announced for Strand Theatre, London, 9 March 1847.

The Gambler's Last Stake. Announced for London, April 1845. Words from *Hood's Magazine*, March 1844, subtitled "A Scene in Madrid."

The Deserted (words M. Hooper, of Dublin). Announced for London, April 1845, and Rotundo, Dublin 1 July 1845.

The Slave Ship (words Henry Russell). Announced for London, 10 April 1845. Published as Musical Treasury 229–30, and by Oliver Ditson, Boston (p.n. 2275; c. 1851).

The Song of the Shirt, or The Lay of the Emigrant Sempstress (words Mrs. [Frances Ann] George Henry Davidson, after Thomas Hood). Announced for London, April 1845. Published as Musical Treasury 231–32.

Man the Life-Boat (words Mrs. [Louisa Macartney] Crawford). Announced for London, 24 April 1845. Published by R. Addison, London, Firth, Hall & Pond, New York, and as Musical Treasury 337–38 (*Times*, 12 March 1847).

The Bear Hunt. Announced for London, 26 June 1845. Possibly the same as the prairie scene The Wolf Hunt ("Neighbours Assist Me, I've Lost My Child").

Niagara. Announced for London, 26 June 1845. See THE FAR WEST (1851).

The Exile (words Charles Mackay). Announced for Dublin, 2 October 1845. Published as Musical Treasury 175 (*Times*, 18 July 1845), and by Oliver Ditson & S. Brainard, Boston.

I Can't Make Up My Mind. Announced for Dublin, 13 October 1845.

1846

The Feast of the Despots (words Charles Mackay). Cited in *Times*, 3 January 1846; announced for London, 2 February 1846. Published as Musical Bouquet 566–67.

The Pauper's Drive (words T[homas] Noel). Words published 1841. Cited in *Times*, 3 January 1846; announced for London, 2 February 1846. Published as Musical Treasury 78–79.

The Cry of the People (words Charles Mackay). Cited in *Times*, 3 January 1846. Presumably identical with The Wants of the People, announced for Dublin, 1 February 1847, and sung at the Lyceum 9 February 1847.

Little Fools and Great Ones (words Charles Mackay), announced for London, 2 February 1846, and presumably identical with Little Minds and Great Minds, cited in *Times*, 3 January 1846. Published by R. Addison, London, and as Musical Treasury 339 (*Times*, 12 March 1847).

The Sea-King's Burial (words Charles Mackay). Cited in *Times*, 3 January 1846; announced for London, 23 February 1846. Published by R. Addison, London; as Musical Treasury 340 (*Times*, 12 March 1847); and by Oliver Ditson, Boston.

The Three Preachers (words Charles Mackay). Cited in *Times*, 3 January 1846. Words published 10 February 1846 in *The Daily News.*

Hope's Sepulchre (words Anne A[mos] Fremont). Published by Addison & Hodson, London, with dedication to Michael Wilson (BL, 11 May 1848), and as Musical Treasury 233.

The Struggle for Fame (words Charles Mackay). Published by R. Addison, London, and as Musical Treasury 343.

Almighty Spirit (words Eliza Cook). Published as Musical Treasury 242.

Where There's a Will There's a Way (words Eliza Cook). Published as Musical Treasury 228.

A Happy Home Is Mine (words Angus B[ethune] Reach). Published by Cramer, Beale & Co., London (p.n. 3625; BL, 23 July 1884), with dedication to Mrs. T. B. Forrest; in Musical Treasury; and by Oliver Ditson, Boston (p.n. 1114; *c*1846).

The Olden Time and the Present Time. Published by Oliver Ditson, Boston. Published by Cramer, Beale & Co. (BL, 7 December 1876), as sung by Miss [Alicia] Nunn, with dedication to Mrs. Thomas Lamie Murray; and in Musical Treasury.

Mazeppa (words Lord Byron). Announced for London, 3 August 1846.

There's a Good Time Coming, Boys (words Charles Mackay). Announced for London, 3 August 1846. Published by R. Addison, London (p.n. 1377; BL, 11 May 1848), and as Musical Treasury 421–22.

The Idiot Boy. Possibly based on William Wordsworth. Advertised at Newcastle and Manchester October 1846; announced for London, 20 November 1846.

The Wife's Dream (words I[sabella] R[ussell]). Announced for Marylebone, 25 November 1846. Published by R. Addison, London (p.n. 1379; BL, 11 May 1848); as Musical Treasury 423–24; and by Oliver Ditson (p.n. 2286; 1851). Music reused for "The Husband's Dream," published as Musical Treasury 579.

The Prisoner of Chillon (words Lord Byron). Announced for Marylebone, 25 November 1846.

1847

The True Men of Old (words Charles Mackay). Announced for Dublin, 1 February 1847. Published as Musical Bouquet 570–71.

Let the Draught be Water. Announced for Dublin, 5 February 1847.

Serjeant Talfourd's Tragedy of Ion. Announced for Strand Theatre, London, March 1847.

The Emigrant's Dwelling. Announced for Strand Theatre, London, March 1847.

The Demon Ship (words Thomas Hood). Announced for Strand Theatre, London, March 1847.

The Gin Fiend (words Charles Mackay). Announced for Strand Theatre, London, March 1847. Published as Musical Treasury 553–54.

The Ship Becalmed. Announced for Strand Theatre, London, March 1847.

The Discovery of America. Announced for Strand Theatre, London, March 1847.

The Slave Sale (words Angus B[ethune] Reach). Announced for London, March 1847. See NEGRO LIFE (1851).

The Song of the Scaffold. Sung at Liverpool 20 December 1847. Published as Musical Treasury 564.

The Lash (words C. Sears, of Lancaster). Announced for Liverpool 20 December 1847. Published as Musical Bouquet 946.

1848

John Littlejohn (words Charles Mackay). Words from *Town Lyrics*. Announced for London, 26 February 1848. Published as Musical Bouquet 568–69.

The Vision of Mockery. Announced for London, 26 February 1848.

The Floating Straw, a Thought in the Panic, 1847 (words Charles Mackay). Announced for London 26 February 1848. Words, from *Town Lyrics,* published in the *Gloucester Journal*, 19 February 1848.

The Three Mowers, an Anticipation of the Cholera, 1848 (words Charles Mackay). Announced for London, 26 February 1848. Words, from *Town Lyrics,* published in the *Gloucester Journal*, 19 February 1848.

Said I to Myself, Said I (words Charles Mackay). Words, from *Town Lyrics*. Announced for London, 26 February 1848.

The Artisan. Announced for London, 24 July 1848.

Our Father Land. Announced for London, 24 July 1848.

Mean What You Say. Announced for London, 24 July 1848.

The World Is on the Move, Look About! (words Edward Leman Blanchard). Announced for London, 24 July 1848. Published by R. Addison (BL, 8 June 1881), with dedication to Arthur Holmes, of Derby; and as Musical Treasury 513–14 (*Times,* 12 October 1849). Music reused for Take the Pledge in *Davidson's Temperance Melodist* (1854).

Time Is a Blessing (An Appeal from the Counter), Early-Closing Song (words I[sabella] R[ussell]). Announced for London, 27 December 1848. Published by R. Addison, London (BL, 27 February 1849), with dedication to Henry John Sharpe; as Musical Treasury 511–12 (*Times*, 12 October 1849); and by Oliver Ditson, Boston.

1849

There's Room Enough for All, Emigration Song (words Edward Leman Blanchard). Announced for London, 2 April 1849. Published by R. Addison, London (BL, 27 February 1849), with dedication to Robert

D[aniel] Mercer, of Upper Clapton; as Musical Treasury 507–8 (*Times*, 12 October 1849); and by Oliver Ditson, Boston (p.n. 1742; c. 1849).

When Is a Man Less than a Man? (words Charles Mackay). Announced for London, 2 April 1849. Published by R. Addison, London; as Musical Treasury 509–10; and by B[enjamin] Williams, London, with dedication to J[oseph] M[oses] Levy (BL, 7 April 1869).

Strike for Hungary's Cause. Advertised in Liverpool, September.

1850

The Kiss (words Henry Howard Paul). Said to be published by C. Frederick Hupfeld & Son, Philadelphia (1850), and by S. T. Gordon, New York.

The Happy Change [sequel to The Wife's Dream] (words L[ewis] M[ansell] Thornton). Published as Musical Treasury 562.

The Cry from the Courts (words Edward Leman Blanchard). Published as Musical Treasury 563. Music reused for The Slave Auction (words Edward Leman Blanchard), published as Musical Treasury 645 (*Times*, 5 November 1852).

The Poor Man's Funeral (Eliza Cook). Published as Musical Treasury 731.

1851

Gather Ye Nations, Gather! or The Festival of Labour (words Charles Mackay). Printed in *The Illustrated London News*, 22 April 1851; Published as Musical Bouquet 416–17, with a dedication to Richard Cobden; and as Festival Song of the World's Fair (Gather, Ye Nations, Gather!) by F[rederick] D[amish] Benteen, Baltimore (p.n. 2100).

Mazurka and Waltz. Published in *The Illustrated London News*, 12 April 1851.

Trade and Spade (words Charles Mackay) Printed in *The Illustrated London News*, 17 May 1851.

THE FAR WEST, or THE EMIGRANTS' PROGRESS (words Charles Mackay; Theatre Royal, Richmond, 7 April 1851).

The Parting Tear, or Farewell, A Last Farewell. Published by Webb's Royal Music Saloon (BL, 3 May 1852), with a dedication to Mrs. Cowan; and as Musical Bouquet 366.

Farewell, my Country! sung in Dublin 1851.

Cheer! Boys, Cheer! No More of Idle Sorrow. Published by Webb's Royal Music Saloon (BL, 3 May 1852), with a dedication to Henry Cowan; and as Musical Bouquet 361–62.

Far, Far upon the Sea! Published by Webb's Royal Music Saloon (BL, 3 May 1852), with dedication to Reverend Thomas Harvey; by Chappell (p.n. 9247); and as Musical Bouquet 363–64.

To the West! To the West! To the Land of the Free. Published by Webb's Royal Music Saloon (BL, 3 May 1852), with dedication to Mrs. Herbert Ingram; and as Musical Bouquet 365.

Mighty Niagara. Published, with dedication to Miss Sophia Davieson, as Musical Bouquet 441–42. The Falls of Niagara assumed identical. See also Niagara, 1845.

Land! Land! Land! Published by Webb's Royal Music Saloon (1852), and as Musical Bouquet 367.

Long Parted Have We Been, or They're Coming with the Flowers. Published as Musical Bouquet 371–72.

Gaily goes the Ship as the Wind blows fair

NEGRO LIFE IN FREEDOM AND IN SLAVERY (words Angus B[ethune] Reach; Theatre Royal, Richmond, 8 April 1851).

The Negro Village. Published by Webb's Royal Music (1852), and (as The African Village) as Musical Bouquet 369.

The Slave Chase. Published by Webb's Royal Music (1852), and as Musical Bouquet 370.

The Slave Sale, or Come, Who Bids? Published by Webb's Royal Music (1852) and as Musical Bouquet 368. See also 1847.

England's Welcome to All Nations (words Frances Anne Davidson). Published as Musical Treasury 587–88, with dedication to Queen Victoria.

1852

The Emigrant's Progress Quadrilles. Published as Musical Bouquet 375.

Uncle Tom's Cabin Quadrilles (arranged mostly on melodies from *Negro Life*). Published as Musical Bouquet 376.

New American Quadrilles (on Negro melodies). Published as Musical Bouquet 392.

The Emigrant (words J. Coutts). Published by D'Almaine & Co., London (BL, 19 October 1852).

The English Emigrant (words Eliza Cook). Published as Musical Bouquet 400–1, with dedication to Mrs. Henry Jordan.

1853

THE TWO LANDS OF GOLD (words Harry Lee Carter; Royal Marionette Theatre, Strand, 11 April 1853).

Pull Away Cheerily! (The Gold Digger's Song). Published by Webb's Royal Music, and as Musical Bouquet 691–92.

Fresh Blows the Breeze. Published by Webb's Royal Music, and as Musical Bouquet 693–94.

Welcome Home! Published by Webb's Royal Music, and as Musical Bouquet 695–96.

The Return of the Dray advertised August 1853.

UNCLE TOM'S CABIN (words Eliza Cook) advertised May 1853.

Eva's Farewell. Published as Musical Bouquet 404.

Eliza, the Slave Mother. Published as Musical Bouquet 405.

Poor Uncle Tom. Published as Musical Bouquet 406.

Little Topsy's Song. Published as Musical Bouquet 419.

Eugénie Waltz. Published as Musical Bouquet 420.

Imperial Mazurka. Published as Musical Bouquet 420.

The Ballad Singer (words E. W. Tracy). Published as Musical Bouquet 440 (*Times*, 2 February 1854), as sung by Maria Russell.

The First Cannon Shot (words Charles Mackay). Published in *Illustrated London News* (15 October 1853), and as Musical Bouquet 443–44 (*Times*, 2 February 1854).

1854

Sir Harold the Hunter (words Eliza Cook). Published as Musical Bouquet 478–79, as sung by G[eorge] H[enry] Russell, with dedication to Society of Foresters.

Fanny Mavourneen (I Leave Thee for a While, My Love) (words Eliza Cook). Published as Musical Bouquet 481.

Be Not First to Cast the Stone (words Eliza Cook). Published as Musical Bouquet 510.

THE EMIGRANT'S PROGRESS (words Charles Mackay; Lyceum Theatre, London, 28 August 1854).

The Icebergs, descriptive song.

Rouse! Brothers, Rouse! Published as Musical Bouquet 560–61 (*Times*, 20 September 1854).

Sunshine After Rain. Published as Musical Bouquet 562–63 (*Times*, 20 September 1854).

Many Changes Have I Seen. Published as Musical Bouquet 564–65 (*Times*, 20 September 1854).

The Canadian Sleigh Song. Published as Musical Bouquet 597–98 (*Times*, 16 December 1854).

When I Was a Little Child. Published as Musical Bouquet 599–600 (*Times*, 16 December 1854).

The Far West Quadrilles. Published as Musical Bouquet 684.

1855

THE EMIGRANT'S PROGRESS additions/alternatives.

The Lords of the Forest (words Charles Mackay). Published as Musical Bouquet 689–90. Advertised September 1855.

1856

Strike, Men, Strike! (words S[tephen] J[oseph] Meany). Published as Musical Bouquet 898–99, with dedication to Mrs. James Davis.

Sound, Britons, Sound! or The Song of Progress (words Charles Sheard). Published as Musical Bouquet 1165–66, with dedication to Maurice Davies. Advertised November 1856. Sung in *The Far West* 12 February 1857, Birmingham.

1857

THE EMIGRANT'S PROGRESS (Royal Princess's Theatre, London, March 1857).

Ho for the West. Cited by J. A. Stephens as in an undated list also containing the following song.

Up for the Right (words S[tephen] J[oseph] Meany). Published as Musical Bouquet 1182–83, with dedication to Michael James Whitty, Liverpool newspaper editor. Sung in *The Far West* 12 February 1857, Birmingham.

The Souls of the Children. Sung in *The Far West* 12 February 1857, Birmingham.

1860

The Volunteers of England (words "Rosalind"). Published in *The London Illustrated News*, 5 May 1860.

1862

Forward, Onward, Never Despair! (words James Bath). Published by James Bath in *The Standard Vocalist*, March 1862. Published by Boosey &

Sons, London (BL, 14 April 1863), with a dedication to George Hammond Whalley, M P. Advertised January 1862. Performed 11 February 1862.

Lord Dundreary Waltz. Performed Theatre Royal, Haymarket, 12 May 1862, between the acts of *Our American Cousin*. Published by Ransford & Son (p.n. 697; BL, 15 September 1862), with dedication to Mrs. Guillaume Frederic Coster.

1863

Farewell to Freedom (words Henri Drayton). Sung by Henri Drayton, Polygraphic Hall, London, March 1863, in *Federals and Confederates*. Published by Duff & Hodgson, London (p.n. 2572; BL, 19 June 1863).

The Sea Is Before Us (words Henri Drayton). Sung by Henri Drayton, Polygraphic Hall, London, March 1863, in *Federals and Confederates*. Published by Duff & Hodgson, London (p.n. 2573; BL, 19 June 1863).

Sunny Days Will Come Again! (words Edwin Ransford). Words published January 1863. Sung by Edwin Ransford, Kennington, 17 March 1863. Published by Ransford & Son, London (p.n. 717; BL, 3 September 1863). Sung by Henri Drayton in *Federals and Confederates* March 1863.

1865

Mother, Take Me to the Ball Tonight (words John Brougham). Dedicated to Mrs. Phillip Vanderbyl. Published by The Music Library Company, London (BL, 13 June 1865).

Try Again (words "Rosalind"). Published by Hopwood & Crew, London (*Illustrated London News*, 9 December 1865).

1866

The Quiet Little Man (words Charles Mackay). Published by Robert Cocks & Co., London (p.n. 14,552; BL, 30 October 1866); by W. A. Firth, New York; and by Oliver Ditson, Boston as "The Little Quiet Man."

1867

The Two Boats (words "Ada Cambridge" (Mrs. George Frederick Cross)). Published by Robert Cocks & Co., London (p.n. 14,747; BL, 31 May 1867).

1868

The Trysting Tree. Published by Hopwood & Crew in monthly *Bond Street*, no. 4 (*Times*, 2 April 1868).

1870

Hope a Little Longer (words John Bath). Published by Cramer & Co., London (p.n. 10,759; BL, 9 February 1870).

1871

God Bless the Fire Brigade (words George Douglas Phillips). Published D'Alcorn & Co., London.

Guard Our Homes. Published by Weippert & Co., London (BL, 28 February 1871), as sung by Charles Santley, with dedication to Mrs. Robert Charles Croft.

1872

Not Lost! sacred song (words Reverend J. G. Gilmore). Published by Cramer, Wood & Co., London (p.n. 6205; BL, 23 May 1872).

The Good Is Great (words Reverend J. G. Gilmore). Published by Cramer, Wood & Co., London (p.n. 6213; BL, 23 May 1872).

1874

She's from Cork! (words Sydney Mostyn). Published by J. B. Cramer & Co., London (p.n. 6847; BL, 19 May 1874), with dedication to Mrs. George Hale.

1876

The Sea Bird (words Florence Tucker). Published by J. B. Cramer & Co., London (BL, 8 April 1876), as sung by Pattie Laverne.

1886

Our Empress Queen (words Clement Scott). Sung London, 23 December 1886. Published by Weekes & Co. (BL, 1886).

c. 1889

Fifty Years Ago (words Clement Scott). Published by J. B. Cramer & Co., London (p.n. 9764; Bodleian Library, Oxford).

1895

The Cripples' Christmas Carol (words Clement Scott). The Daily Telegraph Christmas Carol for Crippled Children, 1895. Published by Cocks & Co., London (BL, 25 February 1896).

1897

Victoria, Queen of Our Nation (words Clement Scott). Published by Weekes & Co., London (BL, 1897).

Appendix C

Other Songs Attributed to Russell

In James Duff Brown's *Biographical Dictionary of Musicians* (1886):

Birds of Passage; The Blind Girl; Canadian Song; Dance of Death; The Fishman; The Lady of the Lake (Walter Scott); Last Tree of the Forest; The Midnight Watch; Over the Waters; The Patriot's Farewell; The Sea Diver (Henry W. Longfellow); The Signal Gun; The Sky-Lark; Song of the Indian; Song of the Raft; Song of the Silent Night; The Weaver; The Wine Cup; The Wreck of the Hesperus (Henry W. Longfellow)

In Russell's *Cheer, Boys, Cheer!* (1895) [supposedly sung in Dublin in 1840s]:

Many Troubles Have I Seen—Probably Many Changes Have I Seen (1854); Who Fears to Speak of '98

Undated or Alternatively Titled Songs

The Land of St. Patrick (words John Brougham) published William A. Pond, New York

Why Should We Bewail the Dead (Charles Mackay) published Firth & Hall, New York

Published Arrangements of Songs by Others

The Brave Old Oak (words Henry F. Chorley), music by Edward J. Loder. Announced for Albany, 20 October 1836. Published by James L. Hewitt, New York (© 1837), with dedication to Dr. Kelsey of Rochester, NY. Music reused for The Brave Old Chief in *The Log Cabin*, 26 June 1840; for A Song for the Man, or A Song for the Chief (words Epes Sargent), published by Firth & Hall (© 11 July 1844); and for The Reeking Still in *Davidson's Temperance Melodist* (1854).

The Fine Old English Gentleman, old ballad (attributed by Russell to Martin Luther). Announced for Albany, 20 October 1836. Published in *New-York Mirror*, 12 November 1836; in New York by Wm A. Pond, Firth & Hall, and James L. Hewitt, with dedication to the readers of *The New-York Mirror*; and as Musical Bouquet 706. Music reused for A Fine Old Kentucky Gentleman (words "A Gentleman from South Carolina"), published by Firth & Hall, New York, and for The Real Staunch Teetotaler in *Davidson's Temperance Melodist* (1854).

My Heart's in the Highlands (words Robert Burns), music by Henry Phillips. Announced for Albany, 4 November 1836. Published by James L. Hewitt, New York (© 1837), with dedication to Mrs. Lewis Gaylord Clark.

The Friar of Olden Times (I Am a Friar of Orders Grey) (words O'Keefe), music adapted from "The Friar" by William Reeve. Announced for Albany, 11 September 1837. Published by James L[ang] Hewitt, New York (© 1837), and *inter alia* as Musical Bouquet 500.

John Nott, Why Not? comic song (words W. H. Freeman), music by Jonathan Blewitt. Published by James L[ang] Hewitt, New York (*Albany Evening Journal*, 20 June 1838).

Oh, Lonely Is the Forest Shade (words Zebulon Barton Stout), music by N[athan James] Sporle. Announced for Albany, 19 March 1839. Published by Hewitt & Jaques, New York (© 1839).

The "Total" S'iety. Published by Henry Prentiss, Boston (© 11 December 1840). As The Old Total Society, announced for Dublin, 1 February 1847.

Washington and Glory (to the tune of "Yankee Doodle") (H. P. Grattan). Announced for the Melodeon, Boston, 16 June 1843.

The Boatman of the Ohio (words Charles Mackay). Announced for London, 17 September 1844. Published by Addison & Hodson, London (p.n. 1838; BL, 10 December 1844), and as Musical Bouquet 132.

The South Carolina [or Tenasee] Plantation Song (words Henry Russell). Announced for London, 17 September 1844. Published by Addison & Hodson, London (p.n. 1839; BL, 10 December 1844).

The Spider and the Fly (words Mary Botham). Sung London, 3 October 1844. Published by W. C. Peters, Louisville (p.n. 59; © 1844 and 24 June 1845), as Musical Treasury 444, and as Musical Bouquet 702.

All to Astonish the Browns, humorous song, by Jacob Beuler. Announced for Dublin, 3 July 1845. Published as Musical Treasury 456.

The Little Gay Deceiver. Published as Musical Treasury 400 (*Times*, 8 January 1848), in revised form by Hopwood & Crew (p.n. 630; BL, 6 January 1865) as The Little Maid, or The Gay Deceiver, sung by Robert Coote, and (words R. F. Williams) by B. Williams (BL, 15 July 1869).

Wery Pekooliar, or The Lisping Lover, by Jacob Beuler, arranged by Jonathan Blewitt. Published in G. H. Davidson album *One Hundred Songs by Henry Russell* (1856).

Other Published Songs Misattributed to Russell

The Old Night Cap, descriptive ballad (burlesque) (words William By), music by "the composer." Published by Millets Music Saloon, New York (© 1841), with dedication "to admirers of Henry Russell."

Britannia, the Pride of the Ocean, adaptation of David T. Shaw's Columbia, the Gem of the Ocean. Attributed to Russell in William Clark Russell's *Representative Actors* (1875); as Columbia's the Pride of the Ocean in James Duff Brown's *Biographical Dictionary of Musicians* (1886); and as The Red, White and Blue in Russell's *Cheer! Boys, Cheer!* (1895).

Here Stands a Post (words Clement Scott), National Ode to Britannia, music by William Charles Levey (1878). Attributed to Russell in Mrs. Clement Scott's *Old Days in Bohemian London* (1919).

Negro, or Minstrel, Melodies Associated with Russell as Singer or Arranger

Buffalo Gals; Cheer Up, Sam; Dance, Boatman, Dance; Dandy Jim of Caroline; De Merry Shoe-Black; Dearest May; The Fine Old Colour'd Gentleman; I'm a-goin' ober de Mountain; Lucy Long; Lucy Neal; Massa's in de Cold Ground (Stephen C. Foster); My Old Kentucky Home, Good Night! (Stephen C. Foster); Nancy Till; The Negro Wood-Pilers (Pile on the Wood, Boys); Nelly Bly (Stephen C. Foster); Nelly Was a Lady (Stephen C. Foster); Old Dan Tucker; The Old Folks at Home (Stephen C. Foster); The Old Jaw-Bone; Old Tare River; Oh! Susannah (Stephen C. Foster); Ole Bull and Old Dan Tucker; The Original Mississippi [Negro] Song; The Prairie Song of the Far West; Rosa Lee, or Don't Be Foolish,

Joe; Sing, Darkies, Sing; 'Twill Nebber Do to Gib it Up So; Uncle Ned (Stephen C. Foster); Walk Along, John, Come Alon' my Yellow Girls,

Compositions of Isabella Russell

In the Hour of Trial, sacred song. Published by Hale & Co., Cheltenham (*Illustrated London News*, 1865).

Watchful Angels (words Isabella Law). Published by Lamborn, Cock, Addison & Co., London (p.n. 4167; BL, 19 August 1867), with dedication to Miss Julia Smith of Cheltenham.

Sleep, My Darling, cradle song (words Isabella Law). Published by Lamborn, Cock, Addison & Co. (p.n. 4240; BL, 29 January 1868), with dedication to Miss Henrietta Morris.

My Love Is Coming in the Spring (words M C R). Published by E. Hale, Cheltenham (BL, 1870).

Compositions of William Clark Russell

The Rose and the Bud (words W. C. Russell). Published by Ransford & Son, London (p.n. 748; BL, 4 February 1864).

The Soldier's Farewell (words W. C. Russell). Published by Ransford & Son, London (p.n. 782; BL, 1864), with dedication to General Garibaldi.

Where the White Moonbeams Creep, serenade (words W. C. Russell). Published by Ransford & Son, London (p.n. 809; BL, 1865).

The Lover's Appeal (words W. C. Russell). Published by Ransford & Son, London (p.n. 939; BL, 8 July 1869).

Biddy Malone, Irish ballad (words W. C. Russell). Published by Weippert & Co., London (BL, 5 October 1874).

Compositions of George Henry Russell

The Alma Polka-Mazurka. Published by H. White, London (BL, 20 July 1855), with dedication to Miss Isabella Russell.

Military Polka. Published by H. White, London (BL, 20 July 1855), with dedication to Miss Lucy Garcia.

Figure A.2. Cover of New Compositions of Henry and George Henry Russell. *Source:* Author's collection.

The Queen and the Navy for Ever. Published by H. White, London (BL, 1855).

There's Fortune On Before Us, Boys. Published by H. White, London (BL, 20 July 1855), with dedication to George Payne Esq., and as Musical Bouquet 746–47 (*Times*, 21 January 1856).

Freedom or Slavery? Published by Musical Bouquet (*Times*, 21 January 1856).

A Farmer's Wife I'll Be. Published by Oliver Ditson, Boston (p.n. 18,103; 1857).

The Sealers. Published by Oliver Ditson, Boston.

There's Fortune Before Us, Boys. Published by Oliver Ditson, Boston.

We Are Brothers, a masonic song. Published by Oliver Ditson, Boston.

Name Index

www.ingramcontent.com/pod-product-compliance
Lightning Source LLC
LaVergne TN
LVHW021314070826
845179LV00022B/241
* 9 7 9 8 8 5 5 8 0 6 0 0 7 *